AmigaBASIC
Inside and Out

Hannes Rügheimer • Christian Spanik

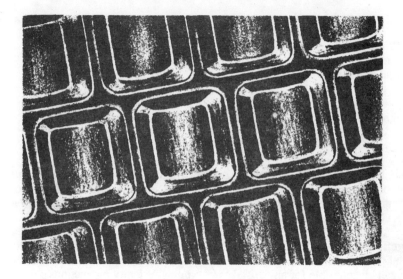

A Data Becker book

Published by

Sixth Printing, 1991
Printed in U.S.A.
Copyright © 1988, 1989, 1990, 1991

Abacus
5370 52nd Street SE
Grand Rapids, MI 49512

Copyright © 1986, 1987, 1988, 1989, 1990, 1991   Data Becker, GmbH
Merowingerstrasse 30
4000 Deusseldorf, Germany

Every effort has been made to ensure complete and accurate information concerning the material presented in this book. However, Abacus Software can neither guarantee nor be held legally responsible for any mistakes in printing or faulty instructions contained in this book. The authors always appreciate receiving notice of any errors or misprints.

Aegis Animator is a trademark of Aegis Development, Inc. Deluxe Music Construction Set, DeluxeVideo and Instant Music are trademarks or registered trademarks of Electronic Arts. AmigaBASIC and MS-DOS are trademarks or registered trademarks of Microsoft Corporation. Amiga 500, Amiga 1000, Amiga 2000 Amiga, Graphicraft, Musicraft, Sidecar and Textcraft are trademarks or registered trademarks of Commodore-Amiga Inc. PC-BASIC is a registered trademark of International Business Machines Corporation. Star Wars is a trademark of Twentieth Century-Fox, Inc.

ISBN   0-916439-87-9

Table of Contents

Introductions

About this book

This AmigaBASIC book was written for the beginner as well as the more advanced programmer. Depending on your level of ability, you have a choice of two introductions (more about this below).

Format

The chapters that follow the introductions were written for all readers. Those who have no computer background at all should read the book carefully, chapter by chapter. Don't skip ahead to later chapters, since the material in each is based on material covered previously. If you know a lot about computers, you'll probably be quite familiar with some of the subjects covered. Still, the advanced programmers should read each chapter in sequence, and not skip anything. This is because many aspects of the Amiga are slightly different from those of other computers.

Checkmarked messages like the following will often appear in the text of the book:

√√   TURN ON YOUR AMIGA AND MONITOR.

These are instructions that you should perform in sequence to produce the desired effect or Amiga operation that we're after.

You'll also find words in *italics* throughout the book. These italicized words appear the first time that the terms are mentioned in the text. Many of the italicized technical terms are defined in the Glossary (Appendix E).

The Appendices

While we're talking about appendices, we'll mention that there's quite a bit of practical information there. In your first attempts at programming, you're bound to make a few mistakes. AmigaBASIC will alert you to these errors with *error messages*. The error messages usually result from typing mistakes or incorrect numbers that you enter. Appendix A lists in alphabetical order the typical BASIC errors that you might come across. We can't foresee all errors, though, since these depend on your program and the internal status of the Amiga—and there are many different types of errors. Appendix A will tell you what could have caused the error, what it means, and what you might do to fix the error.

Once you've finished our book, you'll want to write your own BASIC programs. You'll probably have some questions about a command and its usefulness in your program. Appendix B was included so that you don't have to search the main part of the book for the command. Since we don't use all of the commands and options in our programs, this appendix will be a valuable reference from the start.

Of course, we (the publishers) can make mistakes, too. This book contains some long programs which might have some printing errors, even though the programs were checked quite carefully before going to press. To ensure that the programs are error-free in at least one place in the book, Appendix C is our "error-free" appendix. This expression is often found on diskettes. Each of the longer programs has been included in this Appendix as a program listing which was transferred directly from the Amiga to the computer on which this book was typeset. Since all of these programs were tested, the listings should run without problems. Therefore, if you suspect a command or line to be incorrect, just verify it in Appendix C.

Commodore gave you some sample programs on the Extras diskette. Appendix D gives brief explanations of how they work, what you should look for when running them, and what you can do with them.

Amiga x 3

The text and programs in this book were written for the Amiga 500, Amiga 1000, Amiga 2000 and Amiga 3000. As you may already know, the Amiga has undergone a number of changes since the original model was released (the Amiga 1000). Early in 1987, Commodore began the production of three new machines: The Amiga 500, a self-contained unit with keyboard, computer and disk drive in one housing; and the Amiga 2000 and 3000, an "open system" capable of becoming a PC clone as well as an Amiga. The Amiga 1000 is no longer being manufactured.

We wrote this book to make it as useful as possible to all models of the Amiga. This wasn't very hard to do, since all three Amigas are fully compatible with each other. When necessary, we include remarks that apply to only one particular Amiga model.

Attention:
Amiga 1000
owners

Here's the first remark: If you own an Amiga 1000 with 256K of RAM ("read/write" Random Access Memory) with no memory expansion, you are going to have to be careful with your memory usage. (This doesn't apply to the Amiga 500 or Amiga 2000 owners—you have plenty of free memory). An Amiga 1000 with no memory expansion lacks some of the capabilities available with the other Amigas. Your best bet is to go out and buy a 256K memory expansion as soon as possible, since the majority of the programs in this book are geared toward Amigas with 512K, standard for the 500 and 2000 models. Don't even think about getting a second disk drive or other peripherals before purchasing the memory expansion.

However, you can still learn AmigaBASIC and run most of the programs included in this book, even if you lack 512K of memory.

We are assuming that if you own an Amiga 1000, you are using the Kickstart 1.2 diskette as well as the Workbench 1.3 and Extras 1.3 diskettes. The Amiga 500 and Amiga 2000 don't use Kickstart diskettes; their startup data is built into the computer). If you don't own these diskettes, get them from your dealer as soon as possible. If you cannot purchase them right at the moment, perhaps you can borrow them until you can order them by mail or by phone. If you have an Amiga 500 or Amiga 2000, you have the right diskettes.

About the Extras diskette: Commodore has used various names for the same diskette. The most frequent variations are Extras or Extras 1.2 or Extras 1.3. It's important that we stick to the same diskette names in this book, to avoid confusion. If your Extras diskette is called anything other than Extras, rename your diskette to this name. See Section 3.1 of this book for renaming instructions.

Screen Output

All references to color are based on the original colors of the Workbench. Also, all programs in this book were designed for use with 80-character screen output. That means that if you want the programs to appear correctly on your monitor, your must switch your Amiga 1000 to 80-character output using Preferences.

NOTE:

You may wish to remove the Amiga 500's RAM diskette to free up memory. To remove the RAM diskette from the Amiga 500, do the following:

√√   TURN ON THE AMIGA

√√   INSERT THE WORKBENCH DISKETTE WHEN THE AMIGA ASKS YOU.

√√   AS SOON AS THE BLUE SCREEN APPEARS, PRESS <CTRL><D> (THIS BREAKS YOU OUT OF THE STARTUP SEQUENCE AND ENTERS YOU INTO THE CLI [COMMAND LINE INTERPRETER]).

√√   TYPE LOADWB AND THEN PRESS <RETURN> AT THE 1> PROMPT. (THIS LOADS THE WORKBENCH).

√√   TYPE ENDCLI AND THEN PRESS <RETURN> (THIS DROPS YOU OUT OF THE CLI AND RETURNS CONTROL TO THE WORKBENCH).

Editor's note: We have updated this book to include Workbench 1.2, Workbench 1.3 and Workbench 2.0. The Amiga Workbench is an ever expanding and improving system. Programs are changed and added to the Workbench to upgrade and improve the Amiga operating system. Therefore the programs listed in this book may not appear in the drawers or diskettes listed. If a program does not appear in the drawer mentioned, try looking in other drawers on the Workbench and Extras diskettes for the program. Most explanations will use Workbench 1.3 since this is the most popular operating system for the Amiga.

Choose your introduction

Are you already familiar with the operation of the Amiga? How much experience do you have with computers in general? At this point you should determine what type of reader you are, and determine the level of your abilities.

We've written two different introductory chapters to start you off as quickly as possible. The first introduction is for those of you who haven't had much experience with computers and have just purchased an Amiga. The second introduction is designed for people with a solid experience with computers. Select the introduction with which you'd like to start. If you want to start from Square One, read Introduction 1. Otherwise, skip ahead to Introduction 2.

By the way, the decision you are now making would look something like this in BASIC:

```
IF NOT experienced THEN GOTO Introduction 1
IF experienced THEN GOTO Introduction 2
```

But don't let your Amiga decide this for you. Typing in and running these lines would result in a Syntax error. Why? The answers to this and other questions are revealed in the pages that follow. Once you've read this book you'll have very few questions about AmigaBASIC, and you'll be getting a lot more enjoyment out of your Amiga.

Introduction 1:
The mouse, the windows, and the Workbench

If you chose to read this chapter, you probably aren't very familiar with the Workbench or the Amiga's basic functions. Or perhaps you feel a refresher course wouldn't hurt. Because of this we'll stress the fundamental topics of starting and using the Amiga.

√√   TURN ON YOUR AMIGA AND MONITOR.

Starting up your Amiga: Kickstart

When you turn the power on, the monitor first displays a plain dark-grey screen. This means the Amiga is taking a self-test. Finally, the screen turns white, and a picture of a hand holding a diskette appears on the screen. This is your first encounter with the Amiga's most important feature: symbol or *icon* language. If you own an Amiga 1000, this icon asks you to insert the Kickstart diskette. The Amiga 1000 needs this diskette before it can begin any operation, like some people need coffee to start their day.

Here is one difference between the Amiga 1000 and the Amiga 500 or 2000. The Amiga 500 and 2000 have built-in operating systems, so you won't have to use the Kickstart diskette to get started. If you own a 500 or 2000, skip to the Workbench procedure on the following page.

√√   IF YOU OWN AN AMIGA 1000, INSERT YOUR KICKSTART DISKETTE.

Be sure to insert the diskette in the direction shown by the picture on your screen. The metal cover must be facing forward and the label facing up.

The operating system

The Kickstart diskette contains the Amiga 1000's *operating system*. An operating system is a program that tells the computer how to perform its computer operations. Without an operating system program, even the most advanced computer is useless. The Amiga's operating system tells it how to react to keyboard or mouse inputs, and how to display graphics and text on the screen, for just a few examples. The operating system's information is stored in a special area of memory within the Amiga 1000, and can't be erased while the computer remains turned on. The Amiga 1000 loads its operating system in about 20 seconds. Then the Amiga requests another diskette, again through an icon. This time the icon's diskette label says Workbench.

√√   AFTER THE DISK DRIVE LIGHT GOES OFF, PRESS THE EJECT BUTTON ON THE DISK DRIVE.

The old diskette is partially ejected from the drive.

√√   REMOVE THE KICKSTART DISKETTE.

√√   INSERT THE WORKBENCH DISKETTE INTO THE INTERNAL DRIVE.

**The
Workbench**

The drive will spin and load the Workbench. You'll now see a white line (called the *title bar*) at the top of a blue screen. Under this bar is an icon with the name Workbench. This name refers to the diskette currently in the drive. Whenever a new diskette is inserted in the drive, its icon will appear on the Workbench screen.

√√   START MOVING THE MOUSE AROUND.

When you move the mouse, you'll see that the red arrow on the screen also moves. This arrow is called the *pointer*.

√√   MOVE THE POINTER ONTO THE WORKBENCH DISKETTE ICON.

√√   PRESS THE LEFT BUTTON OF THE MOUSE ONCE.

As you'll see, the icon turns black. Why? The left mouse button activates icons on the Workbench screen. The Amiga changes the icon's color so you know which object is currently active. If you now click the mouse again anywhere outside the icon, its color will change back to white. Normally, only one symbol can be active at any time.

√√   MOVE THE POINTER ONTO THE WORKBENCH DISKETTE ICON.

√√   PRESS THE LEFT MOUSE BUTTON TWICE IN RAPID SUCCESSION.

Pressing the mouse button like this is called *double-clicking*.

The pointer will now turn into a small cloud with two Z's in it. This is called a *wait pointer*. The Amiga is again using pictorial language to tell us that it is right in the middle of some important internal business at the moment, and that you'll have to wait until it's done with the activity. A frame then appears on the screen, and contains four different kinds of icons. Once this is done, you'll see a picture similar to the one on the following page.

The Amiga 500 screen will include an icon representing a RAM diskette (see Section 3.5 for more information). The amount of free memory displayed in the title bar will depend on which Amiga you own, and how much memory is installed.

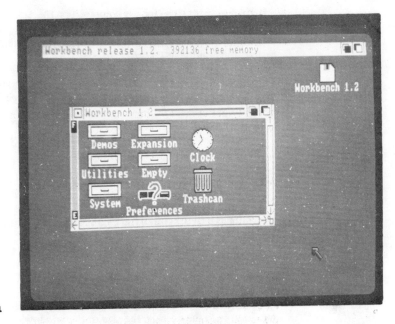

Figure 1:
The
Workbench
window

The frame is called a *window*. Some windows display the contents of diskettes. The window frame, or border, also contains some important elements. Figure 1 shows exactly what the window contains:

Title Bar

Every window has a name, in this case Workbench. If you can't decipher this name, it's not because the Amiga is using some special alphabet, but because the window hasn't been activated. In this case move the pointer into the window and click the left button once. Now the window is selected and the name should be easily readable.

Move the pointer onto this bar and press the left mouse button, and hold it down. You can move the entire window back and forth on the screen. At first only an orange frame proportional to the window moves. This way you can tell where the window will be positioned if you release the mouse button. Only when you release the button is the new window repositioned.

Back/front gadgets

These symbols are the small boxes in the upper right corner of the window. They allow you to choose which window is displayed when several windows are overlapping each other. To try this, select the Clock icon. In case you don't remember how to do this, move the pointer onto the Clock icon, and click the left mouse button twice in rapid succession.

After a few seconds a clock is displayed on the screen. It probably won't display the correct time, but that's irrelevant at the moment. (You can use Preferences to change the time. See your Amiga manual for instructions on using Preferences.)

The clock should cover part of the Workbench window. If it doesn't, move the clock window so that it's "in front".

√√ MOVE THE POINTER ONTO THE RIGHTMOST TWO SYMBOLS IN THE TOP BORDER OF THE WORKBENCH WINDOW AND CLICK ONCE.

The clock disappears behind the window.

Click the symbol on the left. The clock will be in the foreground once more. These two symbols are called the *front gadget* and the *back gadget*.

When you open many windows on the screen all at once, these gadgets let you choose the windows "in front" and "in back" of each other.

Sizing gadget

When you *drag* the *sizing gadget* (in the lower right corner of the window) with the pointer, the size of the window changes. You *drag* by positioning the pointer on the symbol, pressing and holding the mouse button, and then moving the mouse in any direction. Just as when you shift the window's position on the screen, the size of the new window is indicated by an orange frame. The actual size of the window changes only when you release the mouse button.

Scroll bar

The *scroll bar* indicates that a window is not big enough to display all of its contents. In such a case, a blue area appears above or below the scroll bar. These surfaces let you approximate which part of the window is currently visible at the moment. By moving the scroll bar, you can select a particular portion of the window. Instead of shifting the bar, you can also click one of the *scroll arrows* positioned at either end of the bar. This advances the window in the indicated direction, although at slower speed. Windows have horizontal scroll bars as well as vertical scroll bars. Of course, you can also change the size and shape of the window, as we mentioned above.

Disk gauge

The *disk gauge* bar to the left of the window indicates how much memory is used up on a diskette. E stands for empty while F stands for full. The closer the bar to F, the fuller the diskette.

Close gadget

Click the *close gadget* (in the upper left corner of the window) to *close* the window. This will make the window disappear from the screen.

Drawers

The *drawers* are handy places to put your programs. If you double-click on one of the drawers, a new window appears with more programs or subdirectories. You could think of a diskette as a very tall file cabinet with many drawers. If you're a neat person, you can organize programs into drawers by category. You'll be able to view the contents of these drawers whenever you open them. Go ahead and try this with the Workbench drawers:

√√   DOUBLE-CLICK ONE OF THE DRAWERS IN THE **WORKBENCH** WINDOW.

A new window opens which belongs to the drawer you selected. In this new window you may or may not find more icons.

√√   NOW CLOSE THIS WINDOW BY CLICKING THE CLOSE GADGET IN THE UPPERLEFT CORNER.

You can put anything you want into these drawers, even drawers within drawers within drawers. The entire concept was patterned after the structure of a workbench in a workshop. If you put tools into a Workbench drawer, the surface of the desk will be clear for work. Thus the name Workbench.

Trashcan

The *trashcan* lets you dispose of programs you no longer need. Again, this icon is modeled after an everyday object. If a program has been placed in the trashcan, it's not necessarily lost yet. In fact, it will stay in the trashcan until you *empty* the trash (how you do this is explained in a little while). We can open the trashcan like a drawer, and recover everything that you previously threw away.

√√   DOUBLE-CLICK THE TRASHCAN ICON.

The trashcan should be empty.

√√   CLOSE THE **TRASHCAN** WINDOW.

Menus

How can you get rid of files and programs for good? This question brings us to *pulldown menus*. Since this book isn't supposed to be boring (like the rest of those Amiga books), we'll try to provide some variety now.

√√   PRESS THE RIGHT MOUSE BUTTON.

If you haven't pressed the right button before, you'll notice that the following three words are displayed instead of the title bar:

Workbench   Disk   Special

√√   MOVE THE POINTER TO THE WORD Special WHILE HOLDING DOWN THE RIGHT MOUSE BUTTON.

When the pointer reaches this word, `Special`'s corresponding *pulldown menu* appears. Menu sounds like something you'd expect to find in a restaurant. In fact, this computer menu also offers you a choice of items. For example, this menu has the menu items `Cleanup`, `Last Error`, `Redraw`, `Snapshot`, and `Version`. Some of these items may not be very interesting right now, because they are not *active* at the moment.

√√   KEEP THE RIGHT BUTTON DEPRESSED AND DRAG THE POINTER DOWN.

While the cursor is moving down the menu, you'll see the individual items outlined in black as the pointer passes them. However, this only happens with active items. The right mouse button is referred to as the *menu button*, since it is used to control the pulldown menus. The left button is called the *selection button*. If you hear terms like "selection button", "action button" or "activation button" in other books, it will usually refer to the left mouse button. Now on to pulldown menus and what you can do with them.

√√   LEAVE THE `Special` MENU AND CLOSE ALL WINDOWS ON THE SCREEN.

√√   ACTIVATE THE WORKBENCH DISKETTE (CLICK IT ONCE).

√√   SELECT `Open` FROM THE `Workbench` PULLDOWN MENU.

Playing with the windows   Here's another way to do this: Activate the Workbench diskette. Move the pointer onto the word `Workbench` and then, while holding down the right mouse button, onto the word `Open`. When the background of the word `Open` turns black, release the button. You'll see that this does the same thing as a double-click: The `Workbench` window opens. Now you know two methods of opening a diskette icon.

√√   IF THE WORKBENCH DISKETTE ICON ISN'T BLACK ANYMORE, ACTIVATE IT NOW BY CLICKING IT.

√√   SELECT THE `Cleanup` ITEM FROM THE `Special` MENU.

The `Cleanup` function straightens up the icons in a particular window. This is useful when you have dozens of icons scattered around in a window. `Cleanup` will arrange them for you.

We still owe you an explanation: How do you get rid of the "trash" that you don't want anymore?

Before we answer that, an important **Warning**: The files on your Workbench diskette are all very important to the Amiga—none of these files should be thrown away. Therefore, do not select `Empty Trash` at this time.

Backup!

It's always advisable to work with a *backup copy* of the Workbench original. The manuals that came with your Amiga explain how to copy diskettes. You should also make backups of the other diskettes that came with your Amiga. In this book we'll assume that you have made these backup copies.

The final disposal of the files and programs in the trashcan is very simple. When everything you want thrown away is in the trashcan, activate the trashcan icon and select `Empty Trash` from the **Disk** pulldown menu. Once this is done the data is lost forever, and you have an empty trashcan.

This concludes our introduction to the Workbench. The additional functions and capabilities of the Workbench are discussed in detail in the book *AMIGA for Beginners*, available from Abacus.

What you have learned in this introductory chapter should be enough to guide you through our expedition into AmigaBASIC. Nevertheless, it probably won't hurt to read the "expert" introductory chapter as well. Don't worry if you don't understand everything written there—you've already learned the most important things.

Introduction 2:
Workbench—a quick review for advanced readers

If you've chosen to start with this section, you already have some experience with the Amiga. Here we would just like to briefly explain what happens when you start the Amiga, and review the basic functions of the Workbench. If there is anything you don't understand, please refer back to Introduction 1 for clarification.

Once the Amiga is turned on, it executes a self-test. If you own an Amiga 1000, this self-test includes an audio output check (you'll hear a short burst of sound). If you don't hear anything, there could be a bad connection between your Amiga 1000 and your monitor speaker or stereo system.

Kickstart

After this test an Amiga 1000 displays an icon requesting the Kickstart diskette. This diskette contains the Amiga's operating system, also referred to as the *kernel*. The kernel contains various routines that are utilized by the Amiga (for instance, screen output, input and output control, and multitasking management). The contents of the Kickstart diskette are loaded into a 256K region of the Amiga 1000's memory. This region is treated as *ROM* (Read Only Memory) from that point on. The Amiga 500 and Amiga 2000 operating systems are contained in ROM chips, which eliminate the need for the Kickstart diskette.

However, the Amiga 1000 has one advantage: you can upgrade your operating system by simply switching to upgraded Kickstart diskettes. You can't do this with the Amiga 500 and 2000 computers.

Workbench

The Amiga needs the Workbench diskette after the Kickstart (Amiga 1000) or the power-up procedure (Amiga 500 and 2000). Your work area, or *Workbench*, is loaded from this diskette. The Workbench diskette contains the AmigaDOS commands, system programs such as printer output or speech synthesis, and some utilities. Once it is loaded, you are in the Workbench itself, a graphic interface that lets you easily control the Amiga using the mouse and windows.

The pointer is synchronized with the movement of the mouse on a flat surface. The left mouse button is used mainly to activate icons and start programs, while the right mouse button is used for selecting pulldown menus.

Icons

The diskette symbol in the upper right corner of the screen represents either the Workbench diskette or the RAM disk. These symbols are called *icons*. When you move the pointer onto the Workbench diskette icon and click the left mouse button twice, the diskette opens the **Workbench** window. It contains other icons which represent the contents of the Workbench diskette. If you were to click the clock icon, for example, a program would be started which displays a clock.

The drawers (Demos, Utilities, System, Empty) represent subdirectories. You must double-click these drawers individually if you want to view their contents. Drawers may be nested inside of drawers, etc.

There are several symbols in the window borders. If you are not familiar with these symbols, please refer to Figure 1 and its corresponding text in Introduction 1. These symbols are very important for the use of windows and are explained in detail there.

The Menus

You access the pulldown menus with the right mouse button. The right button is also known as the *menu button*. As long as you hold down the button, the titles of the available pulldown menus will be visible at the top of the screen. When you move the pointer onto one of these menu words, its pulldown menu will appear. To select one of the menu choices, move the pointer onto the item and release the mouse button. Only the easily readable items are available to you; the others, called *ghost items*, are not active if they are not readable. The same goes for windows. You can recognize active windows by their easily readable titles.

Workbench

The Open and Close items in the **Workbench** menu allow you to open and close icons or windows. The Duplicate item copies programs and diskettes. Rename allows you to give programs new names. Discard erases programs. Info, opens an information window that will let you view data such as the size, filetype, write protection status, and documentation of a program.

Disk

The Empty Trash command from the **Disk** menu disposes of files in the trashcan, which we will talk about later. Initialize allows you to format diskettes.

Special

Cleanup in the **Special** menu sorts and arranges disordered windows. Last Error displays the operating system's last message. You can recreate the previous screen with Redraw in case you made a mistake. You can fix active icons in their present positions with Snapshot. Version displays the version number of your Workbench.

Trashcan

After this quick rundown of the pulldown menus, we'd like to discuss one more thing: the trashcan. The trashcan is used to discard files that are no longer needed and that you want erased. The trashcan is actually nothing more than a special subdirectory. Only when you have activated it and selected `Empty Trash` are the programs erased. However, you cannot reverse an `Empty Trash` operation. For this reason alone, you should only work with <u>backup copies</u> of your original diskettes.

You can find out how to make backups in the manuals that came with your Amiga. We'll assume that you are already working with backup copies of your original Amiga diskettes.

Object animation

1

1   Making things move:
Object animation

In the following chapters we'll be explaining and programming some of
the Amiga's amazing graphic capabilities. You've probably seen many
of its demonstrations already—and the graphics may be why you
purchased your Amiga in the first place. Believe it or not, you'll be
able to create most of these sophisticated graphic effects with
AmigaBASIC programs.

The following pages are a solid introduction to computer animation in
BASIC. In this first chapter, we'll show you what the Amiga has to
offer in animation (moving graphics). If you enter all of the listed
program examples, by the end of the chapter you'll have a short
program that will create custom animated title graphics. The graphics
can be used to title your videos by hooking up a VCR to the Amiga.
Even if you don't have a VCR, you're still sure to enjoy the results of
your first AmigaBASIC program.

Editor's note: We have updated this book to include Workbench 1.2,
Workbench 1.3 and Workbench 2.0. The Amiga Workbench is an ever
expanding and improving system. Programs are changed and added to
the Workbench to upgrade and improve the Amiga operating system.
Therefore the programs listed in this book may not appear in the
drawers or diskettes listed. If a program does not appear in the drawer
mentioned, try looking in other drawers on the Workbench and Extras
diskettes for the program. Most explanations will use Workbench 1.3
since this is the most popular operating system for the Amiga.

1.1

The Amiga's tutor: the Extras diskette

As a first programming step, we have to "teach" the Amiga what BASIC actually is. You'll want it to be able to respond to statements like GOTO or IF...THEN. You might ask, how can I teach a computer the BASIC language? This is a lot easier for the Amiga than you think. The Amiga simply loads everything it needs from the diskette labeled Extras. You'll need to read this whole book to learn BASIC.

WARNING: Since the owners of single drive systems need to switch diskettes often from this point on, a bit of advice. <u>Eject diskettes from the drive only when the disk drive light is off.</u> Ejecting the diskette prematurely could cause all data on the diskette to be lost. You old computer pros should take special note. Some computers allow you to take out the diskette while the drive is running—the Amiga doesn't, and can be very unforgiving if you try! Remember, the lit disk drive light means "Don't remove the diskette!!"

First things first:

√√   MAKE A BACKUP OF YOUR EXTRAS DISKETTE.

If you don't already know how to make backups, check your manual to see how this is done.

If you own a second disk drive, insert the Extras diskette into the external drive. Otherwise, eject the Workbench diskette and insert the backup of the Extras diskette in the drive.

NOTE: Amiga 1000 owners should use Preferences to set your text width to 80 columns. The programs in this book perform correctly only in 80 column mode.

You will now see the icons for the Workbench and the Extras diskettes on the screen, even if you had to remove the Workbench diskette from the drive. The Amiga has a special area reserved for this data, so that it doesn't forget the Workbench.

√√   OPEN THE EXTRAS DISKETTE

The Extras diskette   Move the pointer onto the Extras diskette icon and press the left mouse button twice (double-clicking). A window appears on the screen containing seven icons: AmigaBASIC, BasicDemos, FD1.3, PCUtil, ReadMe, Tools and Trashcan. The first two are of the most interest to us.

We'll take a moment to discuss the other icons: ReadMe is a document that you can read from the Notepad on the Workbench diskette. It has some notes on the current version of the Extras diskette. The Tools drawer contains some programs which are described in detail in that drawer. The same goes for PCUtil.

We'll discuss the contents of the FD1.2 drawer later. <u>Do not delete this file under any circumstances.</u>

The white square with orange symbols in the foreground is the AmigaBASIC icon. Click it. After a moment AmigaBASIC is loaded, and the following windows are displayed:

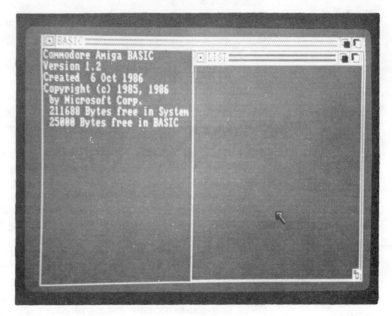

**Figure 2:
Amiga-
BASIC
after loading**

Again, a reminder that you must set your screen mode to 60 characters using Preferences.

1.2

Introducing...
AmigaBASIC

We have finally loaded AmigaBASIC—but what does all that stuff on the screen mean? AmigaBASIC displays two windows. One is named **BASIC**, the other is named **LIST**. (The **LIST** window is active, as you can recognize by its easily readable title). The **BASIC** window contains the following information:

BASIC

```
Commodore Amiga BASIC
Version 1.2
Created 6 Oct 1986
Copyright (c) 1985, 1986
by Microsoft Corp.
220536 Bytes free in System
25000 Bytes free in BASIC
```

Don't worry if some of these items don't coincide exactly with what you see on your monitor—it won't make any difference.

*Version
number*

The version number might be entirely different. Software companies like Microsoft Corp. always give their products version numbers. Software manufacturers keep correcting errors and improving features in software even after it has been released, and thus the versions keep getting updated. This version number is an easy way for you to find out how old or new your product is. Because of the continuous upgrade system, throughout the book we'll point out errors you might have in your earlier AmigaBASIC version.

The first official release of a program is usually Version 1.00. Sometimes you will see pre-releases with version numbers such as 0.99. This means that the programs aren't quite finished yet. When small errors are corrected, Versions 1.01 and 1.02 follow. If more is changed, Version 1.1 is released. To release Version 2.0, the developer usually must make major strong improvements in the software.

During this upgrade process, however, more errors are made, so you won't have to wait too long for Version 2.01—and so on. Some programs have version numbers of 5.21. This doesn't necessarily mean the original was error-ridden, but rather the program was quite successful. Otherwise the software publisher wouldn't have kept putting that much effort into improvements and expansions.

Your AmigaBASIC should be version number 1.2. Version 1.1 went by the wayside, since there were problems adapting it to the Workbench and Kickstart versions. You should <u>not</u> be using AmigaBASIC Version 1.0. If you have no other AmigaBASIC, buy the newest version of the Extras diskette (Extras 1.2).

*Date of
completion*

The next line reads `Created 6 Oct 1986`. This means the developers of AmigaBASIC typed the last line on 10/6/1986. (This date will change in later versions, of course).

*Copyright
notice*

`Copyright (c) 1985,1986 by Microsoft Corp.` Means BASIC was written by Microsoft Corp. Microsoft has created many successful versions of BASIC. The IBM PC, the Apple Macintosh and almost all of the Commodore machines (from the old PET to the Commodore 128) have BASIC implementations from Microsoft. Because writing a BASIC interpreter is a lot of work, the company will copyright it.

*Memory
available*

The last two statements display the memory available in your Amiga. Memory is usually given in *bytes* (see the technical Glossary for the definition of a byte).

The first number indicates the number of free bytes in the Amiga — the amount of memory that can be used by your BASIC files and other programs. Depending on how many windows and diskettes you opened before loading AmigaBASIC, and if there are any programs running in the background, this value can be much lower than the 220536 bytes on an Amiga 1000. A 256K memory expansion in our Amiga 1000, will give us 512K RAM (Random Access Memory) total. The free memory on the Amiga 500 or 2000 can be considerably more. If you loaded AmigaBASIC without doing anything else beforehand, your free system memory should be around 44000 bytes. You should also have about 44000 free bytes displayed in the second line. This number represents the memory available to AmigaBASIC for files and programs. Normally this is 25000 bytes, and 14000 without the expansion. You might wonder why AmigaBASIC uses so little of the available system memory. There are several answers to that question. First, through *multitasking* other programs can run in the background (which uses memory). Also, the color graphics the Amiga can produce require a lot of memory. For example displaying all 4096 colors require as much as 128K per graphic.

1.3   Experimenting with AmigaBASIC

LIST

Take a closer look at the **LIST** window, now. It's not completely empty: in the upper left-hand corner you'll see an orange line. This line is the BASIC cursor, which is presently in the **LIST** window.

Since we are more familiar with the **BASIC** window, let's see if we can make it the active window.

Position the pointer somewhere in the **BASIC** window and click the left mouse button once. The computer acknowledges this displaying an OK on the screen. The window is now active. You can reactivate the **LIST** window by clicking it, too. Up to now the Amiga is acting the way it does in the Workbench— only one window can be open at a time.

Cursors

The first difference is in the number of cursors available. Here you have two of them, the pointer and the BASIC cursor. The cursor shows where the characters you type in at the keyboard will be written. This cursor will be used often in BASIC.

PRINT

We are finally ready to start some experiments with AmigaBASIC. Type this line:

```
print "hello"
```

The line above should look exactly the same on the screen.

NOTE:

The Amiga 1000 has a <BACKSPACE> key, while the Amiga 500 has a "left arrow" (←) key, which does the same thing as <BACKSPACE>. Throughout this book, we'll refer to the <BACKSPACE> key. While we're discussing keys, the Amiga 1000 has a <RETURN> key; the Amiga 500 use a key marked (↵) which does the same as the <RETURN> key. Throughout this book, we'll refer to the <RETURN> key.

What is the purpose of the <RETURN> key? The Amiga doesn't know that you are finished typing until you press that key. Pressing <RETURN> tells the Amiga, "I'm done typing this line, you can process it now." In case you made a typing error you can use the <BACKSPACE> key to erase the characters at the left of the cursor. Press the <RETURN> key once you've entered the line without errors.

The Amiga processes the line, then displays a friendly `hello` on the screen, followed by the familiar OK. You told the Amiga to display anything within quotation marks on the screen. It doesn't matter whether you enter the command in upper or lower case. If you like, you could even enter pRiNt without getting any different results. To tell you it is done with all of its tasks, the Amiga follows up with OK.

It won't be to difficult to figure out what the next statement does:

```
print "how are you?"  ¶
```

Throughout the rest of the book, the symbol ¶ reminds us to press the <RETURN> (↵) key after the statement.

Polite questions deserve polite answers, so enter:

```
Thank you, I'm fine. ¶
```

Error messages

You'll notice right away that it's not this easy to converse with the computer. First you'll hear a beep, then see a requester with the message `undefined subprogram`, followed by an OK gadget. As you might have expected, this is an *error message*. The Amiga is telling us that it cannot understand this sentence, which isn't surprising. "Thank you, I'm fine" might be polite, but it certainly isn't a BASIC command. To let the Amiga know that you acknowledge the error message, you must click the OK gadget once. It will be easier to leave the pointer in this area, since you may encounter a lot of errors in the beginning.

Next you might wonder what the quotation marks are for. Well, try the same command without them:

```
print hello ¶
```

As a response your Amiga will display:

```
0
OK
```

LET

Where did that 0 come from? Well, try the following lines.

```
let hello = 100 ¶
print hello ¶
```

Variables

Now instead of a 0, you get 100 on the screen. Earlier we said that text after PRINT statements must be within quotation marks. In this case, hello is a *numeric variable* instead of text. These are the same variables that always cause headaches in mathematics, mainly because their values are unknown. In BASIC things aren't quite so difficult.

One of the things that BASIC can do is to execute mathematical calculations. To be able to remember the values of such calculations BASIC needs a place to save the results of these calculations. We use variables for this purpose. The LET command assigns a value to variables. Please enter the following.

```
print 7+5 ¶
```

The Amiga will print 12 as a result. If you now enter

```
let hello = 7+5¶
print hello¶
```

the Amiga will print 12 again. This time, though, the result of the calculation was saved in the variable hello. If you don't believe this, feel free to verify it:

```
print hello ¶
```

Again the result is 12. We got a 0 at first because we asked the computer to display the contents of a variable that wasn't defined yet. Since all variables are 0 before they are defined, the Amiga responded with the 0.

In case you are getting tired of typing, here's another tip. The LET command isn't necessary. These two commands

```
let hello = 5¶
hello = 5¶
```

give the same result. Also, the PRINT command can be replaced by a simple question mark (?).

```
print "hello"¶
```

and

```
? "hello"¶
```

do the same thing, and save some typing.

You can combine everything you've learned into this:

```
? "The sum of the numbers 5 and 7 is " 5+7¶
```

Front gadget You may have a slight problem typing this in, since after typing the word is, the cursor reaches the **LIST** window. The cursor will vanish behind this window. However, using the front and back gadgets in the **BASIC** window will remedy this (these are the icons in the upper right-hand corner of the **BASIC** window). As soon as you click the front gadget, the **BASIC** window will become completely visible, which gives you enough room to finish typing:

```
? "The sum of 5 and 7 is " 5+7¶
```

That looks pretty good, doesn't it? You probably noticed that the
BASIC window looks rather cluttered. It can be cleaned up quite easily
with this command:

```
cls ¶
```

CLS

Looks better, don't you think? The CLS command clears the screen
(CLear Screen) and positions the cursor in the upper left-hand corner.
This command is very useful if you are going to do a lot of work and
need an empty screen so that you have room for everything. If you want
to clear the screen just before something is printed, you can do this:

```
cls :? "hello" ¶
```

*Multiple
statements*

Here you've learned something else: You can write more than one
statement in a line if you separate them with a colon.

If you think this is pretty dull stuff, we can do something more
interesting. As a taste of what's ahead we'll show you a program that
produces a few flying balls.

The first step is to name the program:

```
? "Flying balls" ¶
```

Now the title of our program is displayed on the screen, but what
happened to the line we wrote? This is where the **LIST** window
becomes important. Don't worry, you don't always have to retype a
line after you execute it.

1.4

First program: only flying is better

The **LIST** window is partially hidden behind the **BASIC** window. If you click the back gadget (the left gadget of the two) the **LIST** window will come into the foreground once more. Actually, the **BASIC** window is moved into the background. Because of this you'll be able to see two windows at this time. One is the **LIST** window we were looking for, the other is the window for the Extras diskette. The cursor is useless to us for now. Simply click the close gadget in the upper left-hand corner of the **Extras** window.

Entering the program

If you're ready we can write our first program. Activate the **LIST** window by clicking the mouse within it. The BASIC cursor disappears from the **BASIC** window and reappears in the **LIST** window.

√√   TYPE IN THE FOLLOWING LINE

```
? "Flying balls" ¶
```

The Amiga now responds differently than before. Instead of executing the line, it changed the ? to PRINT. The cursor also moved down one line and now waits for you to type more:

```
? "by John Doe" ¶
```

Type your own name if you like. Don't hesitate to take credit for all your hard work (but don't call the family in until you have the program up and running!). The Amiga again responds to the <RETURN> key by changing the ? to PRINT and moving the cursor to the next line.

The **LIST** window differs from the **BASIC** window in other aspects as well. For instance, if you press one of the cursor control keys. (These are the four keys with arrows on them, located to the lower right of the <RETURN> key). The cursor will move in the direction indicated by the arrow. If the cursor doesn't move and the Amiga emits a beep, you've tried to move in a direction which the cursor cannot move at the moment. Using the cursor keys and the <BACKSPACE> key you can edit and correct errors within the windows. The window is known as the *screen editor*, where you can move the cursor freely within the whole window. The **BASIC** window, on the contrary, has a *line editor*, since corrections can only be made within a single line.

NOTE:

Look at the first line of the program below. If your diskette containing AmigaBASIC has any name other than Extras (like Copy of Extras), this program won't work. Rename the disk to Extras from the Workbench (see page 198 of this book for instructions).

√√   ENTER THE FOLLOWING LINES IN THE **LIST** WINDOW:

```
p$ = "Extras:BasicDemos/Ball" ¶
open p$ for input as 1 ¶
object.shape 1,input$(lof(1),1) ¶
close 1 ¶
¶
Start: ¶
for x=2 to 5 ¶
object.shape x,1 ¶
object.x x,320 ¶
object.y x,80 ¶
object.hit x,0,0 ¶
object.ax x, ((x=2 or x=4)+.5)*6 ¶
object.ay x, ((x>3)+.5)*1.5 ¶
next x ¶
¶
for x=2 to 5 ¶
object.on x : object.start x ¶
next x ¶
¶
for x=1 to 3500 : next x ¶
```

Bravo! You've just entered your first program in AmigaBASIC. Now
double check to make sure that everything is entered the way it is
printed here. The Amiga will change the BASIC command words into
uppercase when you press <RETURN> after each line. AmigaBASIC
will leave the words and letters that are not BASIC commands as they
were when you typed them in. If you discover an error you can use the
cursor keys and <BACKSPACE> to correct it.

√√   CLICK ON THE **BASIC** WINDOW AND ENTER:

```
run ¶
```

*The program
in action*

Hopefully you'll see four small balls that fly out from the middle of the
screen. It is possible that the Amiga will sound a protesting beep and
display the error requester in the upper part of the screen. In this case,
there's still an error in the program. Move the pointer into the OK
gadget and click the left mouse button once. Then compare your
program with ours carefully to check for any other typing errors.

That was pretty good, wasn't it?

You may not understand too much of what you typed. That's perfectly
alright — this was just supposed to give you a taste of what's ahead.
You can see how much you can accomplish with a little effort. The
individual commands and functions used will all be explained in
Chapter 2.

Save   As

Now select the save as item from the **Project** menu. To do this press the menu button (the right mouse button) and move the cursor over the word **Project**. Pull the menu down with the pointer until the cursor is on top of the words Save As. Then release the button. A selector will appear in the upper left-hand corner of the screen. Move the pointer into the box below the Save program as: item and click the left mouse button once. Then type:

```
flying balls¶
```

Saving your programs

The box will disappear and the drive will spin for a short time. Wait until the disk drive light is out again. You've now saved the new program on the diskette for future experiments. This is very important: unless you save a BASIC program, it will be lost entirely as soon as you turn the Amiga off. Whether you turn the computer off intentionally or your cat tears the plug out of the wall while pawing at flies makes no difference. The only way you can store the program for future use is to save it on a diskette.

√√   CLICK INTO THE **BASIC** WINDOW AND ENTER THE FOLLOWING:

```
new ¶
```

You'll see that the contents of both windows are erased, and the BASIC cursor is again ready for anything that might come its way.

1.5   Here and there:
BASIC and LIST windows

Our experiments in the **BASIC** window were in *direct mode*. This is when the Amiga processes the commands immediately after you press <RETURN>. In the **LIST** window the Amiga simply remembers the entries until the program is started with the RUN command.

Where are the line numbers?

Maybe you've already seen some BASIC program listings. If so, you probably noticed the line numbers preceding BASIC lines on other computers. Why don't we have any line numbers in AmigaBASIC? The answer is quite simple: Since the Amiga doesn't need them, there are none.

Conventional computers require line numbers for various reasons. One reason is that the computer uses line numbers to distinguish between direct mode and *program mode*. Normally a command preceded by a line number won't be executed right away (program mode). A command without a line number in front of it will be executed immediately (direct mode). The Amiga uses different windows to distinguish between the two modes. This doesn't mean, however, that you're not allowed to use line numbers. If you really want to use them, you can do so. We'll talk about that later.

Starting the video title program

After our previous program it's about time to start something more detailed. Let's work on the video title program. Please enter all the following lines, since at the end of this section they will combine to form a program. As you type these lines in, you'll be learning to use BASIC.

Click in the **LIST** window and type this:

```
?"Video Title Program"¶
?"by Hannes Ruegheimer"¶
```

These are the first two lines of our program. By now you should be familiar with everything these two lines do. They will tell the Amiga to print the name of the program, and your name on the screen (don't forget to substitute your name for Hannes).

RUN

If you'd like to see if the program works you use the RUN command. However, you can't use this command in the **LIST** window, since the Amiga would ignore it there. The RUN command must be entered in direct mode. Click in the **BASIC** window and type:

```
run¶
```

LIST

If you have entered everything correctly, the **LIST** window will disappear and the text will be printed in the **BASIC** window. Beneath the text the Amiga will print OK. Therefore, the output of a BASIC program is displayed in the **BASIC** window. There are several ways to bring the listing back to the foreground. One of them is to type:

list¶

The **LIST** window will return to the foreground.

Menus in BASIC

For those who aren't all that fond of typing, the Amiga has some shortcuts you can use. AmigaBASIC also has the pulldown menus which you'll remember from the Workbench. If you press the right mouse button, you'll see what's available. There are four menus:

Project   Edit   Run   Windows

The **Project** menu lets you manage your BASIC programs. It contains items that erase, load and save programs. You already used one of these items when you saved the ball program.

The **Edit** menu helps you in editing programs.

The **Run** menu has several items to start programs, to stop running programs, and to affect program execution.

The **Windows** menu is used for the **LIST** and **BASIC** windows.

To start the program you could choose the Start item from the **Run** menu. To select it, press the right mouse button and move the pointer until the pointer is on top of the Start, then release the mouse button.

As soon as you do this, the program will run, and the listing will disappear again. Since you need to see the listing again, select the Show List item from the **Windows** menu. As the name indicates, this item will display the **LIST** window, whereas the Show Output item will display the **BASIC** window.

Keyboard shortcuts

You may have noticed an **A** on a blue background followed by a letter next to the items `Start` and `Show List`. The letters are R for `Start` and L for `Show List`. These abbreviations are alternate methods of running or listing a program:

Between the space bar and the right <ALT> key you'll find a key with an A printed on it, either as a **A** outline (Amiga 1000) or and italicized A (Amiga 500). This is one of the two Amiga keys which we'll simply call the open Amiga key. The corresponding key on the left, marked with either a solid red **A** (Amiga 1000) or a Commodore logo (C=) (Amiga 500) we'll call the C= key. You can use the abbreviations of `Start` and `Show list` by holding the <Amiga key> and pressing <R> or <L>. You will continue to find such abbreviations for important functions throughout this book. These are very convenient when you are using the keyboard a great deal. The method you use when you start a program or get the **LIST** window on the screen, is you choice.

Menu	Key combination
Edit menu:	
Cut	<open Amiga><X>
Copy	<open Amiga><C>
Paste	<open Amiga><P>
Run menu:	
Start	<open Amiga><R>
Stop	<open Amiga><.>
Step	<open Amiga><T>
Windows menu:	
Show List	<open Amiga><L>

1.6   BASIC commands, functions, and more

Now that you are familiar with both windows and the starting methods of programs, it's time to add to our video title program once more. Type the following lines in the **LIST** window:

```
?"Select:"¶
?"1 Enter Text"¶
?"2 Read Object"¶
?"3 Move Object"¶
?"4 Define Color"¶
?"5 Show Title"¶
```

These six new program lines, which you should understand, demonstrates that BASIC isn't nearly as difficult as you might have thought, and that the PRINT command is used very frequently. Here we have used it to create a menu. You'll be able to enter text or a title. Another item is to read objects, and another to give that object specific movement. The next selection allows you to add some color, and the last selection displays the whole thing so that you can see the title.

Test running the program

How does all this look on the screen? Simply type RUN to display the result. One more tip before you start the program: if you leave the **LIST** window active (if you don't click in the **BASIC** window) and then chose Start from the **Run** menu or use <Amiga key> and <R>, the listing of the program will appear on the screen immediately after the program is run. If you don't want this to happen, click in the **BASIC** window beforehand.

Making space

RUN the program. It looks all right, except it's kind of jammed together. That won't be difficult to change. Reactivate the **LIST** window. Now move the cursor past the quotation mark behind your name and press <RETURN>. This creates a blank line. (This is how you make yourself more room for programming).

At this location type:

```
?
```

This is simply a PRINT statement without a <RETURN> or anything else. If you press the cursor key with the arrow pointing down, the ? will be changed to PRINT.

When you RUN the program again, you'll see that there is a blank line between your name and the word Select :. Therefore, a PRINT command without anything following produces a blank line.

You can also get the opposite effect. Move the BASIC cursor in the LIST window behind the word video title program and type a semicolon (;) after the quotation mark. The first lines will then look like this:

```
PRINT "video title program";¶
PRINT "by John Doe"¶
```

Saving space

RUN the program again. If you look at the first line you'll notice that your name was displayed immediately after the program title. A semicolon after a quotation mark in a PRINT statement will display the next PRINT statement immediately at the end of the first. There still is a slight problem here. Our addition made program and by into one word, since we never told the Amiga to print a space in between. Enter a space before the quotation mark at the end of the first line in the LIST window. To do this, move the cursor between the m of "program" and the quotation mark and press the space bar. Whatever you enter in the LIST window will be inserted at the current cursor position.

We now have the menu selections on the screen. Next we need to instruct the Amiga so that it recognizes which selection we choose. Type the following in the LIST window:

```
?¶
? "Enter number:";¶
input a¶
```

INPUT

The only new command is INPUT. To see what this new command does, RUN the program again. You'll notice that the cursor is behind the text "Enter number:?". This looks right, but where did the question mark come from? The question mark tells you that the Amiga is waiting for you to enter something. This is the exact function of INPUT: you are asked for input. Enter a number and press <RETURN>. If this doesn't work and the screen flashes briefly, you must activate the BASIC window (click in the BASIC window). Whenever input is asked for, the BASIC window has to be active. The number that you typed is saved in a variable named a.

When the program is finished running an OK appears in the window.

INPUT is a command that allows you to enter data during a program, thus letting you "speak" to the Amiga. However, what does the Amiga do with this data? Type the following in the BASIC window (not in the LIST window):

```
? a ¶
```

The Amiga answers by displaying the number you entered and saved in variable a.

35

Guru meditations

If you are a cooperative person, you'll have entered a number between 1 and 5. Unfortunately, there are people who love to see computer programs get stuck or *crash*. When a program crashes, the Amiga gets "confused", for one of any number of reasons. It might be a power drop, or something in the program code, or incorrect input. When a crash occurs, the Amiga will display a big red and black box at the top of your screen that says Guru meditation as a signal. We've given the Amiga's system crash the nickname "guru". (If we say, "now it's doing the guru", don't expect to see a friendly Indian dressed in red driving by in a Rolls Royce). Don't worry, though, not everyone can cause an Amiga to crash by simply entering a number other than 1 through 5, such as 6; this will just result in an error message. This isn't as bad as a guru. Nevertheless, it is always wise to take user error into account when writing programs. So, we have to find out if a number smaller than 1 or larger than 5 has been entered. If this is the case, we'll simply restart the program.

In BASIC that looks like this:

```
if a<1 or a>5 then run ¶
```

Add this line to the end of your program in the **LIST** window.

IF...THEN

The BASIC command IF...THEN allows the computer to make decisions or "branch". You can put any condition between IF and THEN. The action taken by the computer once the condition is met following the THEN. Thus:

```
IF (condition is met) THEN (do something)
```

OR

In our example the condition is (a<1 OR a>5). The OR means that only one inequality has to be true for the condition to be met. After all, there are no real numbers that are smaller than 1 and larger than 5 at the same time. The RUN after THEN reruns the program if the condition is true. You already know this command from the **BASIC** window. The new fact is that it can be used within a program. From now on you can enter any number you like, such as 0, 6, or 10. The Amiga will keep on asking for input until you enter one of the correct numbers, no matter how many you enter. Unlike some programmers, a computer is inflexible. It will be satisfied only when the numbers are right.

BEEP

Maybe you'd like to wake up a sleeping user who just entered the wrong number and inform him of his error. Here you can use the tone the Amiga uses to alert you to an error. To do this, enter the following after the THEN.

```
beep:¶
```

The listing will then look like this:

```
IF a<1 OR a>5 THEN BEEP : RUN¶
```

Now it'll beep if the input is not correct, and the screen will blink; this blink is built into the BEEP function. (You'll remember that the colon after the BEEP separates different commands in a single line).

For now everything is still working fine. However, you don't want to restart a large program just because of a small error.

GOTO

We have the option of sending the program to a different point than its beginning. The GOTO command lets the program jump to any other program line. First of all, though, we need a way to tell the GOTO where to jump. In conventional BASICs you simply specify a line number. However, as we said before, the Amiga doesn't need line numbers. Instead it uses *labels*. This means that the place to which you want to jump has a name, or label. Get the LIST window on the screen and move the cursor to the beginning of the INPUT command. Create a new line by pressing <RETURN> and then enter:

query: ¶

The colon after the word is very important. It marks this word as a label. You could use hello:, la.de.da:, hum.de.dum: or program.start:, but none of these names would give you a clue as to what that part of the program does. You'll find it easiest to use names that indicate the part's function, so that everything makes sense when you get done.

Now we can change the RUN in the last line to:

goto query¶

This is also very easy. Position the cursor after RUN, press the <BACKSPACE> key three times, and enter the new text. You might run into the right border of the LIST window, in which case the whole window will scroll to the right. When you move the cursor back, the window moves also. The easiest solution is to enlarge the LIST window, with the gadget in its lower right corner. This is done in the same way as the Workbench windows.

Label and variable hints

Another thing about labels; letters and numbers are allowed, but spaces can't be used. Punctuation can be a little tricky and sometimes causes errors (commas or colons can make errors), and should be avoided. Labels can be up to 40 characters long; the Amiga will ignore any characters beyond that. This is also true of variables. So a variable doesn't have to be a; it could be Amiga as well. One comment about variables in this book: variable names will always be printed in courier typeface (for instance, the variable initialvalue...) to identify them as variables. It doesn't matter whether you enter the label or variable in upper or lowercase, either: Hello, hello and hELLO will all result in the same label or variable. AmigaBASIC will make sure that everything in the LIST window is written the same way throughout the program.

Try the following experiment and enter this in the last line:

```
goto Query¶
```

This time we used a capital as the first letter of the label. Press
<RETURN> and keep your eye on the label two lines above (here
query is still in lowercase.) AmigaBASIC adopts the last name
entered for all other identical names in the program. Above, query has
changed to Query as well.

If you like, you could add more labels to mark separate segments of the
program. AmigaBASIC strongly supports this method of structuring
your program. For example, mark the start of your program with a
label called Begin.

Our program looks like this so far :

```
Begin:¶
PRINT "Video Title program";¶
PRINT "by John Doe"¶
PRINT¶
¶
Select:¶
PRINT "Select:"¶
PRINT "1  Enter Text"¶
PRINT "2  Read Object"¶
PRINT "3  Move Object"¶
PRINT "4  Define Color"¶
PRINT "5  Show Title"¶
PRINT¶
PRINT¶
PRINT "Enter number:";¶
¶
Query:¶
INPUT a¶
IF a<1 OR a>5 THEN BEEP : GOTO Query¶
```

User errors

A little earlier we were talking about user errors, one of which you
might have already made. Typing a letter instead of a number. In that
case, you'll have noticed that the Amiga displays ?Redo from
Start on the screen. This simply means to type your input again.
We've already dealt with variables. Do you remember Hello or a?
We've just assigned numbers to these variables. This makes sense—
your math teacher would never have said something like, "the value of
y is Hello." For this reason, variables like a or Hello cannot be
assigned words or single letters.

String
variables

To store characters or words, we must use a *string variable*. You could think of these variables as strings of characters, after the name. String variables are indicated by a dollar sign following the variable name ($). You can assign the variables a$ or Hello$ any combination of characters you wish. To assign a string to a variable within a program, you must use quotation marks. If we change the last lines of the Query section along the following lines, even letters won't cause errors.

```
INPUT a$¶
IF a$<"1" OR a$>"5" THEN BEEP : GOTO Query¶
```

Why are we being so cautious about user errors? Because we can't anticipate how a user may respond to a prompt for input. The program must be able to handle most any user response.

1.7   Entering text in your video title program

Here's a potential problem. If the user continuously types an erroneous responses the screen will soon fill up with error messages and the original prompt will soon disappear. To avoid this problem we'll spend some more time on the menu routine.

There's another thing you should know about the **LIST** window. We have been using the cursor control keys to move the BASIC cursor, but the mouse can also be used. You may have noticed that whenever you opened the **LIST** window, the cursor appeared where you clicked the mouse. You can move the mouse around the window a little faster than the cursor control keys.

Highlighting   If you accidentally press the left mouse key and move the mouse, something completely different happens. An orange bar stretches from the line the BASIC cursor is on to the actual position of the pointer. Congratulations, you've just discovered another function of the screen editor—the orange bar is called a *highlight*. Type some text at any position in the program and move the pointer to that spot. Position the mouse pointer at the start of the new text, press and hold the left mouse key, and move the pointer to the end of the text. Be careful to stay within the same line so extra lines aren't included in the highlighting. When the text is completely within the orange highlight, release the right mouse button.

Using highlighting   Now type more text. The old text will disappear and be replaced by the text you are entering. Now highlight this new text and press the <BACKSPACE> key. The entire text will disappear from the screen. This is one way you can erase entire sections of a BASIC program. However, be careful when you use this function. It is quite easy to erase text, but it is time-consuming to retype it again. Always be certain that only the text you want erased is within the orange field. Keep in mind that once you erase text this way, it cannot be retrieved.

Cut *and* Paste   There are many other things we can do by highlighting a portion of text. Now activate the Cut item from the **Edit** pulldown menu. If you have only one drive, the Amiga asks you to take out the Extras diskette and insert the Workbench diskette. To perform this item of the **Edit** menu, AmigaBASIC needs a program that is located on the Workbench diskette. (This item is called Clipboard device).

Once this program is loaded you can re-insert the Extras diskette in the drive, since the routine is now in the Amiga's memory. The Amiga can detect which diskette is in the drive. Once the Cut function has been performed you will see that part of your program has disappeared. Don't worry—the text is in a special memory location called the *clipboard*. Without changing the position of the BASIC cursor, select Paste from the **Edit** menu, and the text will reappear. The contents of the clipboard can be inserted at any position.

Copy

The Copy function of this menu works almost the same as Cut, except that the highlighted text won't disappear from the screen. This is very helpful when you're duplicating parts of a program.

√√   USE THESE METHODS TO EDIT AND EXPAND THE PROGRAM SO THAT IT LOOKS LIKE THIS:

```
Begin: ¶
PRINT "Video Title program"; ¶
PRINT "by John Doe¶
¶
Select: ¶
PRINT "Select:"¶
PRINT "1 Enter Text"¶
PRINT "2 Read Object"¶
PRINT "3 Move Object"¶
PRINT "4 Define Color"¶
PRINT "5 Show Title"¶
PRINT¶
¶
Query: ¶
LOCATE 10,1¶
PRINT "Enter number:";¶
INPUT a$¶
IF a$<"1" or a$>"5" THEN BEEP : GOTO Query¶
IF a$="1" THEN EnterText¶
PRINT "Choice "a$" does not exist yet."¶
GOTO Query¶
```

Since we're still writing the program, we should note which menu selections aren't completed. We will write the EnterText: routine next. The other entries (2 through 5) will result in the message, "Choice a$ does not exist yet." The variable a$ contains the choice number. Here you can also see how text and variables can be mixed in PRINT statements by using quotation marks.

LOCATE

The LOCATE 10,1 command is also new. Normally, PRINT statement output is displayed on the next screen line. However, LOCATE allows you to specify an exact screen position at which to display text (in our case, 10 lines down in the first column). This way we can easily display the text "your choice:" at the same screen position even if an incorrect response is made. Try typing a LOCATE command in the direct mode (in the **BASIC** window). For example:

```
locate 5,20 : ? "hello"¶
```

Back to our video title program. If you run the program and choose any item except 1, you see exactly what happens. The program looks more polished, and it's foolproof as well. Only an entry of <1> causes an error message. This is expected, since the EnterText: label specified doesn't exist yet. If this is the first error message you've encountered in a BASIC program, note that AmigaBASIC will show the **LIST** window, and will highlight the line containing the error. By clicking the mouse in the OK box after the error message has occurred, you tell the Amiga that you have recognized the error.

There's only one way to correct the error: Write the missing EnterText: routine and add it to the program in the **LIST** window.

NOTE:

You will notice that there is a paragraph mark (¶) at the end of each line of program text. There are times when a program line simply wouldn't fit on one text line in this book. However, the line must be typed in as one program line, as in the FIELD command we'll see later. Press <RETURN> when you encounter these paragraph markers.

```
EnterText:¶
CLS : INPUT "How many lines of text (1-15)"; NoofLines$¶
IF NoofLines$="" THEN CLS : GOTO EnterText¶
NoofLines=VAL(NoofLines$)¶
IF NoofLines<1 OR NoofLines>15 THEN BEEP : GOTO EnterText¶
DIM text$(NoofLines)¶
FOR x=1 TO NoofLines¶
LINE INPUT "Text:";text$(x)¶
NEXT x : CLS : GOTO Begin¶
```

Here are several new commands. Before we examine them, here's one more tip: you don't have to enter all the following lines. Their only purpose is to demonstrate the functions of the commands, and they are not part of the video title program.

VAL

You already know the difference between numerical variables, such as a, and string variables like a$. Sometimes you need to change from one variable type to another. The VAL command allows you to change string variables into numerical variables. It is used this way:

```
z = VAL (z$) ¶
```

DIM

This introduces us to the third type of variable, the *array*. Arrays are commonly used when many different pieces of data are stored under one name. You have to tell BASIC beforehand how many elements the array is supposed to have, i.e. *dimension* the array. This is what the DIM statement does.

Arrays

Here's a mathematical example for arrays. You have dimensioned an array with DIM t$(10). This means that there can be 11 elements in array t$, namely t$(0), t$(1), t$(2), and so on up to t$(10). Each individual element can contain its own string of characters. Note however, that the array t$(z) is in no way related to the variable t$.

Multi-dimensional arrays

Arrays can also be multi-dimensional, such as DIM a$(2,2). This array would result in the following nine elements:

```
a$(0,0) a$(0,1) a$(0,2)¶
a$(1,0) a$(1,1) a$(1,2)¶
a$(2,0) a$(2,1) a$(2,2)¶
```

Here again, each element represents an individual string of characters that can be defined independently of one another.

A three-dimensional array can be visualized as a cube-shaped grid, with individual strings at the intersecting points. The Amiga will support arrays up to 255 dimensions. We'll deal with arrays more at a later time.

FOR...NEXT

This important command will increase the value of a variable from a starting value to an end value step by step. The following example will print all numbers from 1 to 50:

```
for x=1 to 50¶
? x¶
next x¶
```

In the first pass the value of x equals 1. When the program reaches the NEXT command it branches back to the corresponding FOR statement. The value of x is incremented by 1, making x equal to 2 in the second pass, and so on. Once the end value of 50 is reached, the program will go past the NEXT command instead of looping to the FOR again. Since there's nothing left to do in this example, it will stop after completing the loop.

**LINE
INPUT**

A normal INPUT a$ has several restrictions— For example, you can't use quotation marks or commas. On the otherhand, the LINE INPUT command allows you to enter any string without restrictions. Everything you enter until you press <RETURN> is included in the string.

Now we are familiar with the individual components of the EnterText: routine.

We use longer variable names in programs than z or t$. It's better to use names that give us a general idea of a variable's function (for example, text$, NoofLines). Using longer names doesn't change any characteristics of the variable types and functions that were just explained.

*How the
input
routine
works*

How does this part of the program function? First the program asks how many lines of text will be entered. The minimum number is 1, the maximum 15. Once this value is determined, the string array text$(x) will be dimensioned to this value. The same number of LINE INPUT commands are used to determine the text in the string array text$(x). From there the text can be recalled at any time. When all this is finished the screen is cleared and the program returns to the menu.

This routine lets you enter text that will be displayed in front of the moving object. To make a video title you would enter the title of a movie— For instance, Star Wars in the first line and Part I in the second line.

1.8

Safety first: saving your programs

Our video title program has already grown quite long and is only temporary. If you accidentally switched off the power to your Amiga, the program would be irretrievably lost, and all your work would be down the drain. This is why it is advisable to save a program frequently during its development. When a routine or program is completed, you must have a means to store it permanently.

Save *and* **Save As**

AmigaBASIC has two items in the **Project** pulldown menu called Save and Save As. Both will record the program presently in memory on a diskette. How do these commands differ from each other? Select the Save As item. (If you have only one disk drive and have taken the Extras diskette out of the drive, you will be asked to insert the Extras diskette in the drive). After that you will see a requester in the upper corner of the screen which says Save program as:. Below this is an empty box. Move the pointer into the empty box and click once. The box is now active, and a text cursor appears.

Programs saved to diskette need a name by which the Amiga can locate them at a later time. We could call our program video title. Type this name on the keyboard—it will appear in the box. If you make a typing error in the process, two keys allow you to correct your mistake: the <BACKSPACE> key erases the character to the left of the cursor, while the <DEL> key erases the character under the cursor. Once you have entered the name, click the OK gadget. The requester will disappear from the screen and the Amiga will start to save the program onto the diskette.

The Save item is quite simple. If a program already has a name, all you have to do is choose Save. You would use Save As if you wanted to change the name of the program. When you save a program under a new name, the old file is not erased.

AmigaBASIC gives you an alternative to the pulldown menu for saving a program. The SAVE command can be entered directly into the **BASIC** window:

```
save ¶
```

has the same effect as the pulldown item of the same name. The command:

```
save "name" ¶
```

has the same effect as the pulldown menu item Save As. You type the name of the program within quotation marks.

Now our program is on the diskette. If you were to turn the Amiga off at this point, you could re-load your program from the diskette any time you wanted to. Of course, who would want to turn it off now that things are getting exciting?

1.9

A clean slate:
erasing BASIC programs with NEW

Now that your program is safely on diskette, you can safely clear it from the Amiga's internal memory. The command that does this is called NEW. You can enter it directly in the **BASIC** window or select it from the **Project** menu. The Amiga clears both windows and places the text cursor into the window that was active last. The program has been completely erased; it is not in the internal memory of the Amiga anymore. (The term *internal memory* refers to the memory chips within the Amiga, while *external memory* refers to floppy diskettes, hard drives, etc.)

NEW

AmigaBASIC is now ready for new commands. You might be thinking, "Sure, but what if you guys forgot to tell me to save the program and then asked me to enter NEW?" As you might suspect, AmigaBASIC has a solution to this problem. Let's write a short BASIC program in the **LIST** window to demonstrate:

```
FOR x=1 to 100¶
PRINT x¶
NEXT x¶
```

Un-NEWing programs

The explanations in the last chapter should make the effect of this program clear. It displays numbers from 1 to 100 on the screen. This isn't very exciting, but it will do for our demonstration. If you like, RUN the program. Now erase it using NEW from either the **BASIC** window or the **Project** menu. Before clearing memory, the Amiga prints a requester on the screen which says Current program is not saved. Do you want to save it before proceeding? There are three gadgets that you can click for an answer:

YES   A requester asking you for the program name will appear

NO   The NEW command is executed

CANCEL   The requester and returns you to the program

This applies to old programs that have been edited as well as brand new programs. AmigaBASIC will know if you have made any changes in the program. If you try to erase it then, the Amiga will display the same requester as above. You can erase this short program now; it has served its purpose.

Exiting
BASIC

The NEW command isn't the only method of erasing a BASIC program. It is possible to exit AmigaBASIC completely. There are several different ways to do this:

Enter the command SYSTEM in direct mode, which exits AmigaBASIC and returns you to the Workbench. Or you can choose the Quit item from the **Project** menu. Both methods accomplish the same thing.

A third way to quit AmigaBASIC is to close the **BASIC** window and the **LIST** window by clicking their close gadgets. This also returns you to the Workbench screen. In every case, AmigaBASIC will ask you if you would like to save your program if it isn't already saved on diskette.

√√   NOW EXIT AMIGABASIC USING ONE OF THESE THREE METHODS.

Intermission 1

Clean up with:
program drawers

You will find intermissions like this one throughout this book. Intermissions describe important information that can't really be classified with anything else. In this intermission we will create a drawer for holding our BASIC programs. This doesn't really have much to do with AmigaBASIC graphics, but you need to know this before we can continue.

Editor's note: We have updated this book to include Workbench 1.2, Workbench 1.3 and Workbench 2.0. The Amiga Workbench is an ever expanding and improving system. Programs are changed and added to the Workbench to upgrade and improve the Amiga operating system. Therefore the programs listed in this book may not appear in the drawers or diskettes listed. If a program does not appear in the drawer mentioned, try looking in other drawers on the Workbench and Extras diskettes for the program. Most explanations will use Workbench 1.3 since this is the most popular operating system for the Amiga.

The Workbench will seem pretty empty compared to the recent commotion on the BASIC screen. The only thing you might see is the window of the Extras diskette. If this is the case, close this window by clicking the close gadget. Now open the **Extras** window again. You might be wondering why we're having you close the window and open the window. New icons are displayed only once a window is reopened. When you open it the second time you will see nine icons: the seven original ones (`Tools`, `FD1.3`, `ReadMe`, `AmigaBASIC`, `PCUtil`, `Trashcan` and `BasicDemos`) as well as two new ones. One of these is the ball program, the other is an icon with the name you gave your video title program. To understand these icons fully, you might need to enlarge the **Extras** window. You will see that the icons look like pieces of tractor-feed computer paper. The orange symbols on the paper are similar to those on the `AmigaBASIC` icon. These are used to identify BASIC program icons.

About drawers

If you have looked at the `BasicDemos` drawer beforehand, you have already seen many of these icons. We will deal more with the `BasicDemos` drawer in the next chapter.

A drawer's purpose is to help you organize your data storage. However, right now things look rather disorderly. Two programs are just floating around the otherwise organized surface. We want to make a separate drawer for the programs you will write during the course of this book.

CAUTION: We assume that you are working with a backup copy of your Extras diskette. You should not save any files onto the original Extras diskette. See the manual that came with your Amiga to find out how to make backup copies. To protect the original Extras diskette from being accidentally overwritten, slide the *write-protect tab* (move) to the locked position. (The small sliding tab at the corner of the backside of a diskette). The tab can have two positions. When the tab covers the little square hole, your Amiga can write on that diskette. When the tab exposes the square hole, the diskette is write-protected.

√√ NOW OPEN THE WORKBENCH.

Making a drawer

If you have a single drive system eject the Extras diskette and insert the Workbench diskette. However, be sure to leave the **Extras** window open! You'll find a drawer in the window called **Empty**. That drawer is there specifically to be copied.

√√ ACTIVATE THE **Empty** DRAWER, DRAG IT OVER TO THE **Extras** WINDOW AND RELEASE THE LEFT MOUSE BUTTON.

The drawer will be copied to the Extras diskette. The Amiga will do this automatically and you won't have to do anything else. If you have a single drive system, the Amiga will ask you to switch diskettes a total of three times. It will tell you which diskette to enter each time. Remember, do not eject the diskette until the light on the disk drive has gone out! This is true even if the message on the screen says to insert the next diskette while the drive light is on!

√√ WHEN THE COPYING IS FINISHED, CLOSE THE **Workbench** WINDOW. ACTIVATE THE NEW DRAWER AND CHOOSE THE RENAME ITEM FROM THE **Workbench** MENU.

A requester appears in the middle of the screen saying **Empty** with a text cursor. Before you can type the new name you must click into this requester. Delete the old name using the <DEL> key and type in a name (for example, my programs). Press <RETURN>.

Filling the drawer

We can put our ball program and video title program icons into this new drawer.

√√ MOVE THE BALL PROGRAM ICONS SO IT IS ON TOP OF THE DRAWER AND RELEASE THE LEFT MOUSE BUTTON.

This is how you put icons into drawers, the Trashcan, or other diskettes. The Amiga takes care of everything else. When the pointer returns to its normal shape you can repeat the process with the second icon.

Clean Up

Let's get organized with Clean Up before we go on to the next chapter. Clean Up neatly lines up the icons. There's more to it than that, though. You have to let the Amiga know that the order you have created is the final form you want.

Activate all icons in the **Extras** window. Here's a trick you can use: Hold the <SHIFT> key as you activate one icon after the other. As you'll see, all the icons stay active. Now we need to tell the Amiga that all active icons are in this order when the window is opened. You use the Snapshot item from the **Special** menu. This command directs the Amiga to "snap a picture" of the present order and record it on the diskette for later reference. The work area will remain the same until a new snapshot is taken or until more programs are added.

1.10 Something's moving out there: bobs and sprites

You've probably been curious enough to take a look at the BasicDemos drawer by now. This drawer contains a collection of interesting demonstration programs, all written in AmigaBASIC. There's quite a bit to see and hear in these programs. Go ahead and experiment with these programs. But don't be worried if you don't understand how these programs work and what they do. Your AmigaBASIC manual explains them in detail.

ObjEdit

At the moment we're interested in only one program. Open the BasicDemos drawer. This window takes longer to open, since it contains a lot of different programs. Find the program called ObjEdit. Once you have found it, start the program by double-clicking it with the left mouse button.

The name ObjEdit is short for Object Editor. We know what an editor is, from the **Edit** pulldown menu. But what are objects? And why do we want to edit them? Keep reading.

Loading the program ObjEdit will take a while since the Amiga has to load BASIC as well. Any time you click a BASIC program on the Workbench, the Amiga will load BASIC automatically. This simplifies the loading process. You can use the programs even if you don't know anything about AmigaBASIC.

Your Amiga then starts the ObjEdit program. You should see this displayed on the screen:

```
Enter 1 if you want to edit sprites¶
Enter 0 if you want to edit bobs¶
```

Objects

The cursor should be waiting for your entry. The Amiga has *objects* that can move independently on the background. You have been dealing with an object all along: the pointer. The pointer can move anywhere on the screen. Whether it's the **Workbench** window, an **AmigaBASIC** window or anything else in the background, you can move the pointer freely to any screen position. Objects that move independently of the background are invaluable for computer animation.

Early computer animation

What do we mean by "independent of the background?" Older computers didn't process movable objects. If movement was to be simulated on the screen, an object would have to be drawn in one spot, erased, drawn in another spot, erased, and so on. This process was then repeated rapidly to give the illusion of movement.

This method had one problem: The background, which ideally should remain constant, is changed as well. The spot where the object was erased would remain blank. Imagine if this happened with the pointer. Everytime you would move it, the cursor would erase everything in its path. Soon nothing would be visible on the screen. Thus, early animation was always quite simple.

Remember the old video games? One of the first was PONG, a table tennis game. The only things you could see were a white square, a center line and two narrow rectangles which could be moved by the players using paddles. When the little square came on your side of the center line, you would try to hit it back to the other side. The game was quite successful, and its inventor, Nolan Bushnell, went on to found another successful venture known as Atari Corporation.

The need for speed

PONG had no elaborate background because no affordable computer at the time was fast enough. For a long time, speed was the only thing that made animation with a background possible. Instead of simply erasing objects, the background would be memorized and redrawn once the object had moved past it. This process, however, requires a lot of computation, and thus more time. To make the animation look "real", the computers had to be very fast. Finally computer engineers thought it would be really neat to construct a graphic chip to handle this process. These chips were then developed and integrated into the home computers of that time. This made it possible to move smaller objects around the screen without having to worry about the background.

Different computers have different names for these objects. The most widely known are player missile graphics (Atari 400 and 800 computers) and sprites (Commodore 64). The Amiga also has graphic objects, but it has two different kinds: *sprites*, which function similarly to the Commodore 64's sprites; and *bobs* (blitter object blocks). We'll discuss the advantages and disadvantages of each later on.

This brings us back to the ObjEdit program. It allows you to define movable objects, both bobs and sprites. The one thing the program needs to know from you right now is whether you would like to draw a bob or a sprite. We'll start with bobs.

1.11

A star is Born: the object editor

Let's add some motion to our video title program. We want to make an object star, for example, fly across the title screen. We'll use a bob for this purpose.

Enter a 0 and press <RETURN>. A window, a choice of four colors and the text Bob size X:31 Y:31 Pen is displayed on the screen. If the set of lines in the upper left-hand corner doesn't look like a window to you, move the pointer to the lower right-hand corner (the sizing gadget) and hold the left button down. When you move the mouse you'll see an orange outline of the window moving with the pointer. When you release the button, the resized window is displayed. Our bob will be defined within this window. If you experiment a little further you'll find there is a limitation to the window's size. If you move either horizontally or vertically beyond these limitations, the orange outline will disappear. Also, if you keep an eye on the values of X: and Y: in the bottom line, you'll find that these numbers change as you change the window's size. These numbers specify the window's dimensions horizontally (X:) and vertically (Y:).

Now press the mouse's menu key. At the top of the screen you'll see the following menu titles:

File   Tools   Enlarge

Select the **Tools** menu. Here are each of the tools listed individually:

Pen

The tool you'll find active after starting the program is the Pen. The presently active mode is specified at the end of the line that displays the window size. You can draw freehand in Pen mode. The pen works like drawing programs such as Graphicraft™ or DeluxePaint™. If you move the mouse around the window while pressing the left button, the tip of the pointer draws a line. With a little time and patience, you can draw intricate objects.

Line

Since it's difficult to draw a straight line in pen mode, this item can be used to draw a line from one point to another. Click the mouse once at the line's starting point, hold down the button, and move the line to its endpoint.

Oval

This menu item draws circles and ellipses. You specify the four corners of a rectangle with the mouse. Once you release the left mouse button, the circle/ellipse will be drawn within the rectangle.

Rectangle

This menu item works the same as the circle. However, it draws a rectangle when the mouse key is released.

Erase

Since people do make mistakes, this function lets you erase graphics in the window by simply clicking the left mouse button.

Paint

With this item you can fill outlined areas with color. Simply move the pointer into the area and click once. Note, however, that you can easily ruin drawings with this function. The `Paint` command recognizes only lines that were drawn in the presently active color as borders (we'll talk about color selection in a minute). If there is the slightest break in the border lines, even one dot, the color will flow out of the area into the rest of the screen. When you work with `Paint`, you should save your project regularly.

Changing colors

Below the window you'll see four colored boxes (blue, white, black and orange). If you click one of these boxes you can change the active color. The word `Color:` is displayed in the presently active color. If you select blue as the active color, the word `Color:` disappears from the blue box, since you can't read blue on blue. Select white as the active color.

If you did some experimenting while we explored the `Tool` menu, you should now erase the drawing. To do this select `New` from the `File` menu. The following message box is displayed on the screen:

```
Current file is not saved
Do you want to save it?
 Press Y if you want to save it
 Press N if you don't want to save it
 Press C if you want to cancel command
```

If this seems familiar, think back to what BASIC does when you try to NEW a program that hasn't been saved. The only difference is that here you have to use the keyboard for input instead of the mouse. Press <N> to tell the computer that you don't want to save anything. After that you're presented with the question `bobs or sprites?` We'll stay with bobs, so type <0> <RETURN>. (If you haven't drawn anything yet, you won't need to do all this).

Now enlarge the window so that X reads approximately 140 and Y approximately 70. These values don't have to be exact. This is the size of the window in which we want to draw our star.

Drawing the star

Select the `Line` item from the `Tool` menu. Now we'll draw the outline of our star. Since we will want to color it, make sure there are no gaps in the lines. The easiest way to do this is not to move the mouse between lines. The picture below shows roughly how it should look:

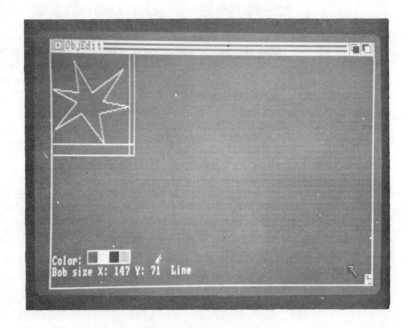

**Figure 3:
The object
editor**

If you're satisfied with the result you should save it, since you'll paint
it next. You should always be a little cautious using these drawing
programs. Select `Save As` from the **File** menu. You'll see `Enter`
`Filename >` on the screen. Type the name `Star`. Press
<RETURN>. The drive light will light; the bob is being saved. During
this time, don't do anything with the object editor. You could use the
Amiga when the disk drive is being accessed, but it's safer to leave it
alone during diskette operations.

*Coloring it
in*

Take one more look at your star. Are there any gaps in the lines? If
there are, "seal" them up with the `Pen` function. Now activate the
`Paint` item in the **Tool** menu. At the end of the last line on the
screen you'll see the word `Paint`. Move the pointer to the middle of
the star and click once. A white star should appear on the screen. If the
whole window turned white the lines weren't connected completely. If
there was a "leak", select `Open` from the **File** menu to reload your
star. Then you can search for the opening(s) and paint the star again
after you correct the problem.

If you accidentally type the wrong name for the `Open` requester, the
object editor stops and displays an error message. Click the `OK` gadget
and enter `RUN` in the **BASIC** window. Then the object editor restarts.

If the painting was successful, save the star with the `Save` item from
the **File** menu. Since the file has already been named, this command
automatically saves it under the same name.

56

*Enlarging
bobs*

This completes our star. If you would like to play some more with the object editor there's one more function we should tell you about. The **Enlarge** menu contains a 4 * 4 item that lets you enlarge bobs, but only if Y is less than 31 and X is less than 100. Larger bobs cause the Amiga to give a response which you'll have to acknowledge by pressing a key. Keep this in mind, otherwise the object editor will sometimes behave strangely. You can use only the Pen in **Enlarge** mode. The 1 * 1 item turns off this mode.

Exiting
ObjEdit

To exit the object editor, click the close gadget in the **BASIC** window. If an error occurred while the program was running, you might have to close the **LIST** window as well.

That's all there is to defining an object. The Amiga lets you simply draw an object, rather than forcing you to use PEEKs and POKEs as you would on other computers. If you think this is a nice feature, wait until you see how easy it is to make objects move with the Amiga.

If you have left the object editor you will see the Workbench screen again. Before we return to BASIC, let's get organized. Close and then open the **BasicDemos** window. Then move the new Star icon into the my programs drawer (or whatever you named the drawer). If you have drawn other bobs while experimenting, put them into the drawer as well. Then close the **BasicDemos** window for good. If you like, you can arrange your program drawer with Snapshot before closing the **BasicDemos** window.

1.12

Role assignments: more about graphic objects

Now we know that the Amiga has two different types of graphic objects: bobs and sprites. How are they both used? Does either have advantages or disadvantages over the other? We'll answer these questions in this section.

Birth of the Amiga

The history of the Amiga's development explains why it has two different types of graphic objects. When development began in 1983, the machine was envisioned as a game computer that would be far ahead of anything else on the market. The relatively small Amiga Corporation hired Jay Miner to design the special graphic chips. (Jay Miner really has to be mentioned, for we have to thank him for most of the Amiga's capabilities). Minor already designed the graphic chips for the Atari 400/800 series. His experience made it easy for him to design the video chip now called *Denise*, which has much more color and graphic power than the Atari chips. Denise can also create sprites.

While Denise is responsible for most of the Amiga's graphics, there are other chips that play a role in these processes. One of these, for example, is the *Agnes* chip. Agnes, in turn, has the components *Blitter* and *Copper*. It was these two components that created all the excitement when the Amiga was introduced. The main function of Blitter is to copy or manipulate memory or screen locations at high speed. This process is aided by Copper, but as a BASIC programmer you really don't need to know exactly how this works. The teamwork of Blitter and Copper also makes the fast window processing possible.

Now for a surprise: The highly advanced Blitter chip makes computer graphics' oldest concept feasible once more. If it is possible to quickly shift and copy screens, why shouldn't you be able to draw, erase, redraw and reconstruct the background? This is how the bobs (blitter object blocks) evolved as an alternative, (or rather a complement), to sprites. In short, bobs are graphic objects that are controlled by the Blitter.

Which are better–bobs or sprites?

If you ask which type of graphic object is "better", you have to keep in mind they differ quite a bit in some respects, since they are produced and controlled by two completely different chips. Both have advantages and disadvantages, depending on the application.

You should know the following about Amiga sprites: Their horizontal dimension is limited to 16 points on the screen—is about the same as the width of two text characters. However, their vertical dimension is unlimited. Their color selection is also somewhat limited, since only four different colors can be used at a time. Normally the maximum number of sprites is eight. Through various tricks, however, it is possible to display more than eight sprites on the screen at one time. Sprites also move faster than bobs.

Bobs, on the other hand, can be any size, horizontally as well as vertically. Bobs can be 32 different colors, and the number of different bobs is limited only by the availability of memory. Nevertheless, bobs are noticeably slower than sprites, especially if many bobs are moving at one time.

The following chart gives you an overview of the pros and cons for these two graphic objects:

graphic object	sprite	bob
controlled by:	Denise	Agnes/Blitter
maximum number:	8	unlimited
	(but can be duplicated)	(limited only by memory)
colors:	up to 4	up to 32
	(for 2 sprites of the	(from any
	same color)	available colors)
speed:	very fast	somewhat slower

Table 1: comparison of sprites and bobs

AmigaBASIC makes the displaying sprites and bobs quite simple. The same commands are used for both sprites and bobs, the only difference being in the creation of the object in the object editor.

1.13   Loading our STAR bob: reading graphic objects

Our star is a bob, simply because a sprite would have been too small for a proper star. Next we want to write a BASIC routine that will define the movement of the Star bob across the screen. Before we can do this, we have to load the video title program back into memory again.

Start up BASIC if it isn't up and running, and select the Open item from the **Project** menu. In the upper left hand corner you'll see the requester Name of program to load:. Click the mouse in the requester box, and enter the name of your program drawer in which you saved your video title program and star. Then press the </> key and enter the name of your video title program. This input should look something like this:

my programs/video title¶

Press <RETURN>. If the Amiga displays an error message saying File not found instead of loading, you have probably entered the wrong drawer or program name. If you don't remember the names, simply shrink the size of the **BASIC** and **LIST** windows and check the Workbench for the actual names. The loaded program will be displayed in the **LIST** window.

LOAD

The method we just used to load our program is the alternative to directly clicking it on the Workbench. Since there are two methods to save a program, you might suspect there is also a way to load a program in direct mode instead of the pulldown menu item. This command is LOAD, and uses the same syntax as the requester. So you could also have typed the following:

LOAD "my programs/video title"¶

Which method you use is up to you. If you like using the keyboard, you'll probably prefer this method. If you feel more comfortable using the mouse, the pulldown menu will probably suit you better. In any case, AmigaBASIC supports both items.

Subroutines

Now we would like to write our second routine—the first real routine was EnterText. We'll write the graphic object input the same way. First we have to include the corresponding point in our first menu. Until now you would get the response that this item did not exist yet, if you chose any point other than 1. From now on it should be possible to activate the ReadObject: routine with item 2.

Below the line

```
IF a$="1" THEN EnterText¶
```

enter this line:

```
IF a$="2" THEN ReadObject¶
```

Getting around the program

Then press <ALT><cursor down>. In other words, hold down the <ALT> key while pressing the bottom-most cursor key. This causes the cursor to immediately "jump" to the program end. <ALT><cursor down> will always jumps to the end of the program listing. Correspondingly, <ALT><cursor up> jumps to the beginning of the program. The combinations <ALT><cursor left> and <ALT><cursor right> allow you to jump to the left and right edges of a program line. These keyboard functions give you methods to move quickly through a program without using the mouse.

At the end of the program we can insert the next routine:

```
ReadObject:¶
CLS¶
PRINT "Please enter the name of the object you want to load"¶
INPUT Objname$¶
IF Objname$="" THEN CLS : GOTO Begin¶
OPEN Objname$ FOR INPUT AS 1¶
OBJECT.SHAPE 1, INPUT$(LOF(1),1)¶
CLOSE 1¶
ObjFlag=1 : CLS : GOTO Begin¶
```

This routine reads a graphic object from the diskette. There are three lines that consist of new material:

```
OPEN name of object FOR INPUT AS 1¶
OBJECT.SHAPE 1, INPUT$(LOF(1),1)¶
CLOSE 1¶
```

Files

The first line is responsible for opening the specified *file* (data on a diskette that isn't a program) so it can be read. The explanation and use of this first line can be found in Chapter 3 of this book, which deals with files and diskette management. At this point we want to concentrate on the graphics. What then happens at this command? The contents of a file are read. The program knows the name of the file through the input in the first three lines of the routine. Here we also have a safety feature: In case the user presses <RETURN> without entering a filename, the program will jump back to its start.

Now the data that was read from the diskette is assigned to INPUT$ (which is a string variable just like Hello$ or a$). The only difference is that you can assign the contents of a file to this specific variable. Again, more about this in the third chapter. This is possible because strings can be up to 32767 characters long. This is plenty of room for the files of a sprite or a bob. The file contains all the vital information of the object, in this case our star, in a specific order. Thanks to the object editor we don't have to worry about the composition of this string— the Amiga already took care of this.

**OBJECT
SHAPE**

The OBJECT.SHAPE command assigns the string to graphic object number 1 in the second line. This command gives the Amiga all the necessary information about the appearance of the object, such as its color, height, width, and other parameters. The third line closes the file that was just opened.

Then the variable ObjFlag is set to 1. This variable tells the Amiga if any file has been read yet. In a minute we'll discuss why it's important for the program to know this. After this formality the program returns to its start.

As soon as the object's appearance is defined, we can define its movement as well. Type the following line in the Query: routine below the two existing lines:

```
IF a$="3" THEN DefineMoveObject¶
```

Then enter the following lines at the end of the program listing:

```
DefineMoveObject:¶
CLS : IF ObjFlag=0 THEN BEEP ELSE Mover¶
PRINT "No object currently in memory!"¶
PRINT "Press any key"¶
Pause:¶
a$:INKEY$¶
IF a$="" THEN Pause¶
CLS : GOTO Begin¶
```

The last few lines comprise the beginning of the movement program. It checks if an object has been read in. If none has been loaded, then there isn't an object to move around. Then the Amiga displays an appropriate response on the screen and waits for you to press a key. It then returns to the main menu.

ELSE

There are two new commands in these lines: ELSE and INKEY$. The ELSE command is an expansion of the familiar IF...THEN function. Until now we only used the command in the context IF (something is true) THEN (do something). There are several additions to this command that we'll introduce step by step.

Let's take a closer look at the line:

```
IF ObjFlag=0 THEN BEEP ELSE Mover¶
```

The first part of the line consists of the familiar IF command. If the variable ObjFlag is equal to 0, then the Amiga will sound a beep. The new addition specifies an action that will apply if ObjFlag is not equal to 0. In this case the Amiga is supposed to go to the program routine called Mover:. IF...THEN...ELSE tells the Amiga what to do if something is true, and what to do if it isn't. This looks something like:

IF (condition) THEN (do something) ELSE (do something else)¶

To demonstrate the command in an everyday situation imagine this.

A friend has just bought a new Amiga and wants to learn to program in AmigaBASIC. He asks you where to get a good book on the subject. You'll say, or at least so we hope, "Go to a software dealer and look for *AmigaBASIC Inside and Out* by Abacus. If they don't have it, you can order it direct from Abacus." Or, in BASIC: "IF BASIC book is available at store THEN buy it, or ELSE order it."

This form of IF...THEN is especially interesting when—as in our case—you need to execute several commands if the condition is true, or send the program to a different point if the condition is not true. That wasn't too difficult, was it? If you don't understand this concept quite yet, you'll soon learn a way to enhance jumps and loops.

INKEY$

First, though, another command: INKEY$, which is actually quite simple. This string always contains the character that has just been entered on the keyboard. If no key was pressed, INKEY$ is empty. That's why the next line checks to see if the string is empty, and repeats the process if it is empty. This is how we get the delay loop; it waits until a$ has a value other than that of an empty string (""), i.e., until a key is pressed.

1.14   Tracking down your errors: the TRACE function

If you're confused by all these jumps, loops and inputs, the Amiga will be able to help once more. Click the **BASIC** window and type:

```
goto DefineMoveObject¶
```

Trace mode

This goto allows you to start programs at a specific point, instead of RUNning them right from the beginning. You'll hear a beep and the text which you previously programmed is displayed on the screen, since the object hasn't been read from the diskette. (If you can't see the **LIST** window on the screen, select Show List from the **Windows** pulldown menu). Then select the Trace On item from the **Run** menu. You'll now see the Delay: routine in the **LIST** window and a small orange field that quickly moves from one command to the next. To be more exact, it alternates between three lines each time. We have just turned the *trace* mode on. In this mode the Amiga shows us which line of the program is presently being executed. This function can be invaluable when you're troubleshooting your own programs, or figuring out someone else's programs. Now see what happens if you press a key (since this is what the Amiga is waiting for you to do). The program will return to its start, and will proceed to highlight commands in orange as they are executed.

When the **LIST** window suddenly disappears, at an INPUT command for instance, select Show List from the **Windows** menu again. If the program lines or the listing itself are very long, AmigaBASIC will often change the format of the program line displayed in the **LIST** window. If you need to, you can enlarge the **LIST** window accordingly. In the trace mode you should try to find the best placement of the **LIST** and **BASIC** windows on the screen. What this placement will look like depends mostly on where in the **BASIC** window the program output will appear. Since our program is displayed in the upper part of the **BASIC** window, position the **LIST** window in the lower portion of the screen. AmigaBASIC always adjusts the presently displayed program lines to fit the size of the **LIST** window.

Feel free to explore your program in trace mode. You might be able to clear up any uncertainties about the program's function. You'll notice the program runs quite a bit slower in trace mode than in normal mode. This is because the Amiga now has more to do between commands and because the execution has to be slow enough for the user to follow. After all, the function is designed for the testing of programs.

To turn the trace mode off, go to the **Run** menu once more. In the place of Trace On you'll now see Trace Off. This item turns the trace mode off.

TRON *and*
TROFF

AmigaBASIC also lets you use the trace function for specific parts of a program. The two TRON (TRace ON) and TROFF (TRace OFF) commands can be used just like any other BASIC command in the program. They can also be used in the direct mode instead of the pulldown menu items.

1.15   Moving on up to: the OBJECT commands

You might have noticed a slight bug in the EnterText: routine. If you call up the routine only once, there's no problem. As soon as you do it again, though, you get a Duplicate Definition error message. What happened? The problem lies in the DIM command that dimensions the text field once the number of text lines are determined. DIM is not allowed to dimension the same variable more than once. When you try to dimension it the second time, you'll get that error.

The easiest way to avoid this is to place all DIMs at the very beginning of the program. There they'll be executed once and won't be used again. When using this method, though, you need to know ahead of time how many elements the arrays are going to need. Our text$ array requires a maximum of 15 elements. Thus we'll dimension it to 15 elements at the beginning of the program. First erase the line:

```
DIM text$(NoofLines) ¶
```

DIM

in the EnterText: routine. You can highlight the command with the pointer and erase it by pressing <BACKSPACE>.

You can also dimension several arrays with one DIM statement. While we're at it, let's dimension the rest of the variables that will be required in the course of this program. The purpose each array serves will be explained when the particular array appears in the program.

Move the cursor to the beginning of the listing and type the following lines:

```
Setup: ¶
d=15 ¶
DIM Text$(d),Colormatrix(d,3),Move(d),Speed(d) ¶
```

NOTE:

Remember to save the program every once in a while. It's consistently getting larger, and you don't want to lose any of your work.

Move the cursor to the end of the program, and then type the following lines:

```
Mover:¶
PRINT "Move the object to it's starting point"¶
PRINT "using the cursor keys."¶
PRINT "When located press <RETURN>"¶
ox=100 : oy=100 : Destination=0¶
OBJECT.HIT 1,0,0¶
OBJECT.ON 1¶
OBJECT.STOP 1¶
Loop:¶
a$=INKEY$¶
IF a$=CHR$(13) THEN DestDef¶
IF a$=CHR$(28) THEN oy=oy-2¶
IF a$=CHR$(31) THEN ox=ox-5¶
IF a$=CHR$(30) THEN ox=ox+5¶
IF a$=CHR$(29) THEN oy=oy+2¶
OBJECT.X 1,ox : OBJECT.Y 1,oy¶
GOTO Loop¶
¶
DestDef:¶
CLS¶
Move(Destination*2+1)=ox : Move(Destination*2+2)=oy¶
Destination=Destination+1 : Move(0)=Destination¶
IF Destination=7 THEN Enddef¶
PRINT "Move the object to location"Destination¶
PRINT "<RETURN> = Set another location"¶
PRINT "<ESC> = End"¶
¶
Loop2:¶
a$=INKEY$¶
IF a$=CHR$(13) THEN DestDef¶
IF a$=CHR$(27) THEN Enddef¶
IF a$=CHR$(28) THEN oy=oy-2¶
IF a$=CHR$(31) THEN ox=ox-5¶
IF a$=CHR$(30) THEN ox=ox+5¶
IF a$=CHR$(29) THEN oy=oy+2¶
OBJECT.X 1,ox : OBJECT.Y 1,oy¶
GOTO Loop2¶
¶
Enddef:¶
Move(0)=Destination¶
OBJECT.OFF 1¶
CLS : GOTO Begin¶
```

Well, you deserve a little break after entering this. (Don't forget to use this break to save the program, too)!

Now that you are rested up, back to work. There are some new commands in this section that we would like to talk about that fall into two categories: OBJECT commands and other miscellaneous types of commands.

Bits, bytes and ASCII

Let's look at other types of commands first. CHR$ (x) is the only new command in this group. To explain this command we'll have to take a little look into the way the Amiga thinks. Feel free to sit back and relax while we take you on an imaginary voyage inside the Amiga's "brain".

Externally, it seems as though the Amiga deals with numbers and letters without any amount of effort. It can be said that the Amiga represents a completely new generation of computers. However, at the most basic levels of its functions, nothing has changed since the invention of ENIAC, the first real computer. The heart of the Amiga, the microprocessor chips, can work with only two different conditions: On and off. All of the computer's capabilities are based on these two states.

These conditions correspond to the digits 0 and 1, which make up the smallest unit of information, the *bit*. With various tricks and the concept of binary numbers, a computer can process several bits at once which in turn enables it to work not only with zeros and ones, but also larger numbers.

To make the transition from numbers to letters, another concept is needed: a letter is assigned to each number between 0 and 255. The reason behind 255 is that the original machines could not process higher numbers at an acceptable speed. (The highest number of the Amiga's 68000 processor can process directly is 4,294,967,294.) The order in which the characters are assigned has been standardized so that different kinds of computers can communitate. The name for this standard character assignment is the *ASCII code* (ASCII is the abbreviation for American Standard Code for Information Interchange).

CHR$

This brings us back to the CHR$ command. CHR$ is used to convert an ASCII code to its corresponding character. We'll perform an experiment in which we'll bring the Amiga's insides "outside". First enter the following line in direct mode (be sure to click the **LIST** window into the background so you have enough room on the screen):

```
width 80: for x=0 to 255 : ?chr$(x);: next x ¶
```

More about ASCII

Don't worry about the beep that you'll hear, since this is also included in the ASCII code. Here we have to be more specific; ASCII codes don't just contain text characters, but also control characters. CHR$ (7) is one of them. It produces the beep. CHR$ (12) will clear the screen. Even without these control characters there are quite a few other visible ones, too. After all, your screen should be filled with a variety of punctuation marks, numbers, upper and lowercase letters and other special characters. There are also several small boxes which indicate characters the Amiga can't display visually, such as the <HELP> key or one of the function keys.

Now back to our normal world where we deal completely with letters and numbers. After all that you now know, you'll be able to understand the CHR$ easily. In our program it is used to check if a specific key was pressed. The following program, for example, will wait until the <ESC> key is pressed:

This sample program is not a part of the video title program, so enter it separately. Make sure the video title program is saved, then enter NEW. NEW clears out the current program in memory. Now click in the **LIST** window and you can enter this simple program:

```
Delay:¶
If INKEY$<>CHR$(27) THEN Delay¶
```

The computer waits until you press the <ESC> key.

OBJECT. SHAPE

Now to the heart of our video title program, the OBJECT commands. In order to move objects (bobs or sprites), the Amiga has a separate group of commands, all of which begin with the word OBJECT followed by a period. The OBJECT.SHAPE command is one example you are already familiar with. This command is used to assign a particular shape to an object. Its syntax looks like this:

```
OBJECT.SHAPE object number, definition string¶
```

In BASIC, *syntax* refers to the correct composition of commands and their corresponding values. If you typed this in the **BASIC** window:

```
object.shape 1¶
```

Syntax errors

you're violating the syntax, since the second value (the definition string) was omitted. Try typing this example. The Amiga will tell you that you have just made a Syntax error. Imagine someone trying to speak a foreign language, but who isn't putting the words in the right order. In the same way, the Amiga cannot understand sentences that aren't structured correctly. The Syntax error message is the Amiga's way of saying that something in the command is either missing or incorrect.

Parameters

The values used in conjunction with a command are referred to as *parameters*. The value `object number` in the previous `OBJECT.SHAPE` command is a parameter. In the video title program this value will always be 1, since only the object with the number 1 will be used. You already know the definition string (in our case the bob). It was created with the object editor and saved on the diskette, and can be loaded into any BASIC program.

`OBJECT.X`
`OBJECT.Y`

`OBJECT.X` and `OBJECT.Y` are two other `OBJECT` commands that position an object at a particular spot on the screen, at a horizontal coordinate (X) as well as a vertical coordinate (Y). The coordinates specify the objects position from the upper left-hand corner of the screen. The visible region for X is 0 to 617, and for Y is 0 to 185. The object won't be visible on the screen if you specify larger coordinates. You can specify larger coordinates, but that will only be useful if the object is still partly visible. To specify a set of coordinates, the commands are used like this:

```
OBJECT.X object number, x coordinate¶
OBJECT.Y object number, y coordinate¶
```

`OBJECT.ON`

The object won't be visible quite yet after you enter these commands. Another command is required for this:

```
OBJECT.ON object number¶
```

`OBJECT.`
`OFF`

This "turns on" (displays) an object whose coordinates have been specified. The counterpart to this command is:

```
OBJECT.OFF object number¶
```

This command, in turn, will "turn off" the object and make it disappear from the screen.

`OBJECT.VX`
`OBJECT.VY`

Since these graphic objects are, after all, called "movable objects", there are commands that move the object. Two of these are the `OBJECT.VX` and `OBJECT.VY` commands. The V stands for velocity. These commands specify the object's velocity in the X and Y directions. Here again, VX represents the horizontal velocity, while VY represents the vertical. The speed is given in units of screen points per second.

In the standard resolution used by AmigaBASIC, the screen is comprised of 640*200 points (pixels). If you subtract the points that are included in the border, you'll get the visible region of the OBJECT.X and OBJECT.Y commands.

The starting coordinate is defined in screen points, too. An X-velocity of 1 means the object will move one point to the right each second. A Y-velocity of 2 means the object will move two points down each second. If you give both X and Y velocities, the object will move diagonally from the left top to the right bottom of the screen. "What if

I want to make the thing go from right to left, or from the bottom to the top?" Simple—just enter a negative velocity. An X-velocity of -1 is like a reverse gear. The following figure will be useful, when you later need to know the correct sign of the velocity for your own programs.

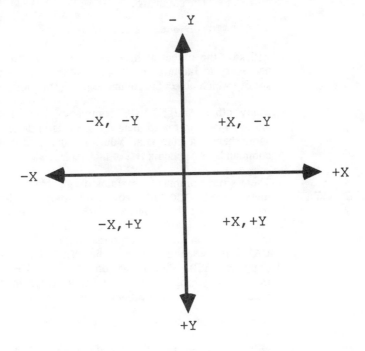

Figure 4:
The polarity
of OBJECT
velocities

If your object is supposed to move from the top right to the bottom left, the X-velocity will have to be negative and the Y-velocity will have to be positive. The values of the velocities will depend upon the desired speed of the object.

One more tip: when the X-velocity is considerably larger, the movement is mostly horizontal. Correspondingly, if the Y-velocity is much larger, the object will move vertically.

To press the Amiga's "accelerator", use the following two commands:

```
OBJECT.VX object number,x-velocity¶
OBJECT.VY object number,y-velocity¶
```

OBJECT.
START

However, as with the OBJECT.X and OBJECT.Y commands, these only define the object's velocity, it still won't start to move yet. For this you need another command:

```
OBJECT.START object number¶
```

**OBJECT .
STOP**

When the Amiga receives this command, the object starts to move. The best part is you don't have to do another thing from that point on. You can go on to something else in your BASIC program while the Amiga moves the object across the screen. But there has to be an "emergency brake", too. The command:

OBJECT.STOP object number¶

will stop the object at its present position. You can see why it is necessary to include an object number. It's the only way you can specify which object the command is referring to.

Many other AmigaBASIC commands control object movement, although we don't need them for our video title program. We will talk about them at a later point. You'll find an concise description of these commands in Appendix B.2 of this book.

**OBJECT .
HIT**

There's one command we almost forgot from the Mover: program routine: the OBJECT.HIT command. AmigaBASIC allows you to find out if an object is colliding with something else on the screen. This is known as *collision control*. The collision of objects is one of the events that can affect a program. This topic can also be found in the BASIC reference section under the ON COLLISION GOSUB command (Appendix B.2). Without this command, the object would stop as soon as it hit anything. This might be desirable in traffic control, but unfortunately not in our program. The command:

OBJECT.HIT object number, 0, 0¶

will specify that the object is allowed to collide with other graphic objects as well as the screen border.

Once this process is clear, you might ask, "How does the whole thing work together? What's behind this new part of the video title program?"

We've already checked if an object was really read into memory. If an object is in memory, the variables ox and oy are set to 100. These variables keep track of the coordinates at which the object is located. We just explained the OBJECT.HIT 1, 0, 0 command.

The Mover: routine also turns object number one on, and turns off any remaining movement. In later applications of the video title program, an object in memory from a previous program will start moving again once it is turned on.

Steering the object

Now you can steer the object with the cursor control keys. Depending on which key is pressed, the values of the X and Y coordinates will change. The `Loop` routine will repeat this process until the <RETURN> key is pressed. The actual position is then accepted as the starting point. The program then jumps to the `Destdef` (destination definition) routine. At this point the `move` array, which we dimensioned at the beginning of the program, is activated. The X and Y coordinates of the points of movement are repeatedly recorded. Their value is stored in the array's first position, namely `movement(0)`, since this number will be needed later. The number of points is limited to seven.

The definition of the destination points works the same way as defining the starting points. The cursor control keys are used, and <RETURN> accepts the specified point. The entry will end after the sixth point or when the <ESC> key is pressed. The `Enddef` routine brings the number of destination points up to date, removes the object from the screen and returns to the main menu.

If you would like to try the program out to this point, start it. Use item 2 (`Read Object`) to read your star into memory. Any graphic object could be used, if you have made others with the object editor. Item 3 (`Move Object`) will allow you to define the object's movement. Play around with the function, it's the easiest way to find any mistakes you might have made. The more complex a program becomes, the more difficult it becomes to fool around with it like this. Actually, use a more sophisticated term: you're *debugging*... just in case anyone in the family should ask.

1.16   Color comes into the game: color control

The Amiga can display 4096 different colors. This news created some excitement when the computer was introduced, but it's probably old news to you. Even so, this is an impressive display of colors, especially considering that a short time ago even the most advanced computers had trouble displaying more than 16 colors.

What is RGB?

One of the determining factors is the Amiga's monitor, an *analog RGB* monitor. What are "analog" and "RGB"? You may know how a television operates: an electron beam scans the screen line by line. A phosphorous layer on the screen is then illuminated where the electron beam hits it. Because this process is so fast, the human eye cannot detect how the picture is constructed dot by dot or line by line. The result looks like a complete picture.

So far, so good. If technology was still that simple today, we'd still have black and white television. For instance, green-screen (monochrome) monitors have been marketed by well-known computer companies for years. Even a black and white TV is technically more demanding than a monochrome monitor, since the intensity of the electron beam has to be varied in order to create different shades of grey on the television screen.

When a few ingenious scientists invented the color TV, they installed three electron beams next to one another. Each beam hit a different set of points on the screen. One set of these points glows red, one green and the third blue. Red-green-blue: RGB.

Other ingenious people discovered that these three colors can be used to create any other color of the spectrum. The three beams also vary in intensity and produce different shades of color. This concept was very successful with TV, but it took a while before the idea caught on in the computer field.

The manufacturers of monochrome monitors, now produced color monitors with three electron beams of constant intensity for red, green and blue. Because of the on/off mentality of computers, this concept is quite simple: there is simply three connections between the monitor and the computer for R, G and B. The system was restricted to only eight colors: black, white, red, green, blue, yellow, cyan and purple. This method is known as "digital color control". (As you might guess *digital* refers to the 0 or 1 technology: Power or no power)

*Amiga and
RGB*

What is so different about the Amiga's monitor technology? The Amiga also has only three connections to its monitor. But each of these three connections has 16 different intensity levels, not just one. The result is color quality that's almost identical to that of a TV. Even if you've owned your Amiga just a few days, you might be familiar with the RGB concept. Most Amiga programs allow you to adjust the color by varying the red, green and blue intensities. In this respect the Graphicraft drawing program behaves the same as the utility program Preferences. If you feel a great urge to see your 4096 different colors, reduce the size of the **BASIC** and **LIST** windows and activate the Preferences program on the Workbench. (Before doing this, be sure to save the current version of the video title program!) At the bottom of the Preferences screen you'll find three adjustable strips. When you are finished experimenting leave Preferences by simply clicking the Use gadget.

NOTE:

The present colors you set from Preferences remain in effect until you change colors again, or turn the Amiga off.

PALETTE

Well, what did you think of that? Maybe you're frantically searching for an **AmigaBASIC** window with three color adjustments in it. Sorry, but changing color in BASIC takes quite a bit more programming. Don't worry, though, it's not difficult at all. The PALETTE command is all you need to change colors in BASIC. The command requires four numbers. The first number represents the color you wish to change. Normally there are four colors available to you in AmigaBASIC. These colors, along with their respective numbers, are:

color	number
blue	0
white	1
black	2
orange	3

The next three numbers specify the percentages of red, green and blue that compose the particular color. This value must lie between 0 (0%) and 1 (100%). Type this line in the **BASIC** window:

palette 0, 0.6, 0.2, 0.4¶

Well? You probably don't think too highly of our color choice. All right, if you don't like it, try your own values. Taste is a very personal matter.

By the way, you can leave off the zero before the decimal point in BASIC. You could type the above PALETTE command like this, and it will work just as well:

palette 0, .2, .3, .6¶

Let's include the item `Define Color` in our video title program. First of all, enter the following line in the `Query:` routine, so we have another menu item:

```
if a$="4" then DefineColor¶
```

We also need a little more code in the `Setup:` routine. Type in the corrections, so that is looks like this:

```
Setup:¶
Colors=2¶
d=15 : MaxColors=(2^Colors)-1¶
TextColor=1¶
DIM Text$(d),Colormatrix(d,3),Move(d),Speed(d) ¶
Filler$=STRING$(16,"-")¶
Colormatrix(1,1)=15¶
Colormatrix(1,2)=15¶
Colormatrix(1,3)=15¶
```

Now to the end of the program. Here we have another lengthy part for you—Take a break whenever you feel like it. Just remember to press <RETURN> when you see the paragraph markers at the end of each line (¶). And <u>don't forget to save the program</u> regularly!

```
DefineColor:¶
CLS:PRINT "Color values:"¶
Colors:¶
FOR x=0 TO MaxColors¶
COLOR -(x=0),x¶
LOCATE 5,(x*4) + 1¶
PRINT x;CHR$(32);CHR$(32) ¶
NEXT x¶
¶
ColorChange:¶
LOCATE 7,1:COLOR TextColor,Background¶
PRINT "Enter the number of the color you want to
change."¶
PRINT " (e = End)"; : BEEP¶
INPUT Answer$¶
IF UCASE$(Answer$)="E" THEN AssignColor¶
Answer$=LEFT$(Answer$,2) ¶
ColorNumber=VAL(Answer$) ¶
IF ColorNumber<0 OR ColorNumber>MaxColors THEN BEEP: GOTO
ColorChange¶
RGBRegulator:¶
r=Colormatrix(ColorNumber,1) ¶
g=Colormatrix(ColorNumber,2) ¶
b=Colormatrix(ColorNumber,3) ¶
LOCATE 10,1: PRINT "Red:    <7>=- <8>=+ ";Filler$¶
LOCATE 10,20+r : PRINT CHR$(124);¶
LOCATE 11,1: PRINT "Green: <4>=- <5>=+ ";Filler$¶
LOCATE 11,20+g : PRINT CHR$(124);¶
LOCATE 12,1: PRINT "Blue:  <1>=- <2>=+ ";Filler$¶
¶
```

```
LOCATE 12,20+b : PRINT CHR$(124);¶
LOCATE 13,1: PRINT "        <0>=Color o.k."¶
PALETTE ColorNumber,r/15,g/15,b/15¶
¶
EnterKeys:¶
Key$=INKEY$¶
IF Key$="" THEN EnterKeys¶
IF Key$="7" THEN r=r-1¶
IF Key$="8" THEN r=r+1¶
IF Key$="4" THEN g=g-1¶
IF Key$="5" THEN g=g+1¶
IF Key$="1" THEN b=b-1¶
IF Key$="2" THEN b=b+1¶
IF Key$="0" THEN ColorChange¶
IF r<0 THEN r=0¶
IF r>15 THEN r=15¶
IF g<0 THEN g=0¶
IF g>15 THEN g=15¶
IF b<0 THEN b=0¶
IF b>15 THEN b=15¶
¶
Colormatrix(ColorNumber,1)=r¶
Colormatrix(ColorNumber,2)=g¶
Colormatrix(ColorNumber,3)=b¶
GOTO RGBRegulator¶
AssignColor:¶
a=Background : a$="Background"¶
GOSUB EnterColor:Background=a¶
¶
a=TextColor : a$="Text Color"¶
GOSUB EnterColor:TextColor=a¶
¶
a=TextBackground : a$="Text Background"¶
GOSUB EnterColor:TextBackground=a¶
¶
COLOR TextColor,Background¶
CLS : GOTO Begin¶
¶
EnterColor:¶
LOCATE 14,1¶
PRINT a$": ";a¶
Loop3:¶
LOCATE 14,1¶
PRINT a$; : INPUT Answer$¶
Answer=VAL(Answer$)¶
IF Answer$="" THEN Answer=.5¶
IF Answer<0 OR Answer>MaxColors THEN BEEP : GOTO Loop3¶
IF Answer<>.5 THEN a=Answer¶
RETURN¶
```

If you have any serious problems understanding the use of the commands we have discussed, please see the Appendices about command summaries. If that doesn't help, try to carefully reread the parts that deal with those commands.

STRINGS

Now for the new commands in this part: the command STRING$(16,"−") will produce a string consisting of 16 dashes ("-"). We need this string to make the color controller. The STRING$ function is extremely helpful when long strings that consist of one type of character. Type in this line in the direct mode of BASIC:

width 50 : ? string$(800,"!") ¶

WIDTH

All right, we admit that wasn't too nice. Your Amiga was rather busy for a while, wasn't it? You might have noticed that we used the WIDTH command here a second time already without explaining it. WIDTH is used to specify how many characters wide the lines will be. This is necessary because the Amiga doesn't automatically start a new line when it reaches the edge of the screen. Instead it will print out of the window, and the output will disappear from the screen. If you don't believe it, try this:

width 255 : ? string$(800,"!") <RETURN>¶

Depending on the margins used (60 or 80 characters per line, specified with Preferences), the maximum value is WIDTH 62 or WIDTH 77 with which all characters will be visible.

COLOR

Next there's the COLOR command. It is used to change the text color. COLOR is followed by two parameters. These values specify the color number of the foreground (first number) and the background (second number). Thus, if you wish to write with the background color on white, you'll have to enter the following:

color 0,1¶

UCASE$

The string function UCASE$ (. . .) stands for "uppercase". This function will change the entire content of the string into uppercase:

? UCASE$ ("WouLdN't YOu liKE To Know?") ¶

While we're explaining strings: another line down you'll find this command:

ColorNumber=LEFT$(Answer$,2) ¶

LEFT$
RIGHT$

The string Answer$ is a user-input string. It's possible that the user of the program might type a string longer than allowed. The program is only interested in the first two characters of the string. To isolate characters from the left or the right of a string. The LEFT$ and RIGHT$ commands are used. The first parameter specifies the string, the second parameter determines how many characters are included. If you would like to try:

?left$("Hello",3), right$("Amiga",2) ¶

"Wait a second, we could use this trick with LEFT$ in the main menu of our program, right?" True, we can use it to make the main menu selection foolproof. Enter the following in the Query: routine:

```
    •
    •
INPUT a$¶
a$=LEFT$(a$,1)¶
IF a$<"1" OR a$>"5" THEN BEEP : GOTO Query¶
    •
    •
```

GOSUB
RETURN

You'll find a command called GOSUB in the AssignColor: routine. Although it looks a lot like the GOTO command, there is a difference. The command stands for "GO to SUBroutine". A subroutine is a part of a program that performs a certain function for the program. When the Amiga reaches a GOSUB it remembers the line where it encountered the GOSUB and then proceeds to the line specified by the command. The subroutine is then executed until the Amiga reaches the RETURN command, after which it returns to the line following the original GOSUB command. RETURN and GOSUB work together, just like IF and THEN or like FOR and NEXT. The commands always appear together—otherwise you'll get an error message. If you don't quite understand how these two commands work together, the trace function can help you understand them.

Inequality

We're almost finished with this routine, except for one little detail. Do you see "IF answer<>0" in Loop3:? What does it mean? We know less than (<) as well as greater than (>), but it's impossible for a number to be both at once. Right. That's why <> means "not equal to" in BASIC. The command is checking to see if the the value is not equal to 0.

Color control

The variable Colors specifies which is the highest allowed color number. The program routine DefineColor: prints little boxes containing all of the valid color numbers on the screen. You're asked which color to change. You can then enter the desired number or the letter <E> to end the color changes. Thanks to the UCASE$ function it doesn't matter whether the <E> is entered in uppercase or lowercase. Once the color has been chosen the RGBRegulator: routine displays a color control system. This can be easily controlled with the numerical keyboard. The keys <7> and <8> change the red controller, <4> and <5> change the green controller, <1> and <2> control the blue. The <0> key signals that the color setting is satisfactory. In this case the program jumps back and asks whether you want to change another color. The variables r, g and b contain a number between 0 and 15 which represent the respective color intensities. These values are stored in Colormatrix.

How the
color
control
works

A word about the color control routine: It isn't quite as convenient to use as `Preferences`. One problem you might have noticed is that whenever a color is changed for the first time, the original setting is black. This is because AmigaBASIC is not able to read the actual value of the color register. As long as the array `Colormatrix` doesn't know the values, they are zero. For this reason we used the `Setup:` routine to assign the color white to the `Colormatrix` so at least the text color would have a value. Otherwise you would only see black.

Color control through the keyboard is slightly more tricky than using the mouse (in programs such as `Preferences` or Graphicraft). Most importantly, don't hold the keys down too long, since the number will be repeated after a short time (which can be adjusted with `Preferences`). In this case you might accidentally enter a huge number without knowing it, which would be stored in the keyboard buffer until the controllers react. At the end of the color adjustments the program will ask you for three more values: you can enter one color number each for the screen background, for the text and the text background. These colors will then be used for the output of the text which you entered in item 1 of the main menu. If you don't wish to change the normal settings, simply press <RETURN> three times.

1.17 The fruits of our labors: the display program

Our video title program project is getting ever closer to completion. The only subroutine that's still missing is the one that will display the result of our program.

How to write an output program

Imagine that the following section was not included and you had to write the output routine on your own. How would you go about it? First of all you would have to consider what the program is supposed to do. This is how we'd envision the output of the final program:

First the screen should clear, then the program would wait for you to press <RETURN>. During this time you'll be able to cue up your VCR, make the necessary connections and start the tape. After <RETURN> is pressed, there'll be a 10 second countdown, which will be quite helpful when you're trying to splice video sequences and make them look professional. Then we have to send the programmed text to the screen in the colors that were selected. Would it be possible to center it on the screen? That should look good. Once the text is displayed the object, (in this case our star), should execute its movement while the text remains on the screen. How about removing the text from the screen in some way at the end? For instance by scrolling it from the top and the bottom of the screen to the middle. This will give the same effect as in the title screen of the AmigaTutor program, which you might know from the Extras diskette. Once this is done, there will be a few more seconds of silence. "Cut! It's a wrap." This is how we pictured the function of the last part of the video title program.

The next step of developing the program is taking sort of an inventory. In other words, you need to see what you already have to work with, and what you need to create. Up to now we have put together the following program routines:

- A graphic object on diskette that currently resides in memory and is named object number 1.

- An array called Move (d) contains up to seven points of the specified movement. The array element Move (0) contains the exact number of points. This element is followed by pairs of coordinates of each point. The array is constructed in this manner: (number of points), x1, y1, x2, y2, etc.

- An array named Speed (d) where the x and y velocities are stored with which the object is moved from point to point. This array is constructed the same way as the Move (d) array. However, it is still empty.

•   An array called `Text$` which contains up to 15 lines of text to be printed on the screen.

•   The colors for the text and screen background are stored in the variables `Background`, `TextColor` and `TextBackground`.

•   There's also an array called `Colormatrix`. However, this is not needed anymore since the colors have already been taken over by the Amiga system.

•   There are other variables and data, but they are not important to this part of the program.

For the last part of the program we need more new commands so we'll introduce them now. Try to imagine how each of the following commands could be used to achieve the goals of this program routine.

The first new command will probably be useful only in the countdown routine. How will the Amiga know when 10 seconds have expired? Simple: the Amiga has several time/date functions in AmigaBASIC. Type the following command in the **BASIC** window:

`? date$¶`

DATE$ You see that `DATE$` does, indeed, display the month, day and year stored in the Amiga's memory. Yes, that's very nice, but we don't need days and months—we need seconds. Try this command instead:

`? time$¶`

TIME$ That's better. This command displays hours, minutes and seconds. The time is set with `Preferences`, and at the moment it's probably incorrect. You can isolate the seconds with the formula `(VAL(RIGHT$(TIME$,2)))`. However, this looks rather messy. There is an alternative:

`? timer¶`

TIMER   The variable `TIMER` will give you the time in seconds and in tenths of seconds. It specifies the number of seconds that have passed since 00:00:00 (midnight). Remember, this depends upon the time setting in `Preferences`.

INT   Sometimes when calculating or comparing numbers, the numerals to the right of the decimal point are unnecessary. Here we need only seconds, not tenths of seconds. The BASIC function `INT(x)` can help us in this case. The command stands for "INTeger":

`? INT (23.42143) ¶`

This omits the numbers to the right of the decimal point. The result is 23. Note that the function will not round off the number. I N T (9.99999) is 9, not 10. We'll introduce another command later for rounding a number.

To use these commands to make the Amiga pause for exactly one second, you would use the following procedure: The present value of INT (TIMER) is assigned to a variable. (In other words, it is assigned the number of seconds that have passed since midnight). A loop then continually compares the value of the variable to the actual value of the timer, until the two are not equal. After that, approximately one second will have passed. In a listing it might look like this:

```
Tim=INT(TIMER)¶
Wait2:¶
IF INT(TIMER)=Tim THEN Wait2¶
```

(after one second, the loop will stop)

CINT

The command for the rounding off of numbers is CINT ("Convert to INTeger"). The command rounds off numbers according to these rules: up to and including 4.5000... will be rounded to 4, larger numbers (from 4.5000...01 on) will be rounded up to 5. Compare this in BASIC:

```
?cint (4.6) : ? int (4.6)¶
```

ABS

We'll use the CINT function for calculating the object's velocity. Since we're already talking about mathematical functions, we'll throw in another one. What do you do if you need the value of a number, but aren't concerned with its sign? Distant memories of math class might help you out on this one. We're talking about *absolute values*, and in BASIC they look like this:

```
? abs(-3.5) : ? abs(3.5)¶
```

We'll need this function to calculate the X and Y velocities from the distance between two points in the path of our object's movement.

SCROLL

Because you so bravely suffered through all those mathematical functions, we'll throw another graphic effect at you. Do you remember how we were going to make the text disappear from the screen? The screen was to be divided into an upper and lower half, which would move toward the center and "swallow" the text. BASIC has its own command for shifting sections of the screen. Type the following example in the **BASIC** window:

```
for x=1 to 50 : scroll (0,0)-(630,150),2,2 : next x¶
```

The effect is clearly visible: the screen should be partially filled with text. Then a section of the screen slowly sinks toward the lower right. (You could program the sinking of the Titanic this way.) You have probably heard the expression *scrolling* which was derived from "screen rolling". When you enter text in the bottom line on the screen and then press <RETURN>, the screen will scroll upward. The top line will disappear from the screen, while a new line will appear at the bottom.

The Amiga is able to scroll the screen in all directions. The syntax of the SCROLL command looks like this:

```
SCROLL (x1,y1)-(x2,y2), x-direction, y-direction¶
```

The expression (x1,y1)-(x2,y2) specifies the corners of the rectangle that is scrolled. The coordinates (x1,y1) specify the upper left-hand corner, while (x2,y2) specifies the lower right corner of the rectangle. The values for the x-direction and y-direction specify, just like in the OBJECT command, how many dots the rectangle is moved in each direction. A single call of SCROLL will cause the rectangle to immediately jump to its destination. To create smooth movement, you must use a FOR...NEXT loop to repeat the SCROLL command. We can make the output of our program disappear from the screen with this function.

Those are all the new commands that we'll need in this part of the program. When you enter the next part of the video title program, please try to figure how each command works toward the goal of the program as you type it. You already know what we're trying to accomplish and what it's effect should be. Again, please don't forget to save the program regularly!

Move to the end of the program and type the following:

```
ShowTitle:¶
CLS¶
PRINT "Press the <RETURN> key"¶
PRINT "to begin showing the title."¶
WaitforKey:¶
a$=INKEY$¶
IF a$=CHR$(13) THEN CLS : c=10 :GOTO Countdown¶
GOTO WaitforKey¶
¶
Countdown:¶
LOCATE 10,39 : PRINT c¶
c=c-1:IF c<0 THEN StartDisplay¶
Tim=INT(TIMER)¶
Wait2:¶
IF INT(TIMER)=Tim THEN Wait2¶
GOTO Countdown¶
¶
StartDisplay:¶
WIDTH 80¶
COLOR TextColor,Background : CLS¶
```

```
COLOR TextColor,TextBackground¶
FOR x=1 TO NoofLines¶
Text$=LEFT$(Text$(x),80)¶
h=INT((80-LEN(Text$))/2)+2¶
LOCATE x+17-NoofLines,h : PRINT Text$¶
NEXT x¶
COLOR TextColor,Background¶
IF Move(0)=0 THEN MoveText¶
OBJECT.X 1,Move(1)¶
OBJECT.Y 1,Move(2)¶
OBJECT.ON 1¶
FOR x=1 TO Move(0)-1¶
OBJECT.STOP 1¶
GOSUB VelocityCalc¶
OBJECT.X 1,Move(x*2-1)¶
OBJECT.Y 1,Move(x*2)¶
OBJECT.VX 1,Speed(x*2-1)¶
OBJECT.VY 1,Speed(x*2)¶
OBJECT.HIT 1,0,0¶
OBJECT.START 1¶
Tst=TIMER¶
¶
Loop4:¶
px=ABS(Move(x*2+1)-OBJECT.X(1))¶
py=ABS(Move(x*2+2)-OBJECT.Y(1))¶
IF INT(TIMER-Tst)<18 AND (px>15 OR py>15) THEN Loop4¶
NEXT x¶
OBJECT.OFF 1¶
¶
MoveText:¶
Tst=TIMER¶
IF Move(0)<>0 THEN Finish¶
Wait3:¶
IF TIMER-Tst<(2*NoofLines+2) THEN Wait3¶
Finish:¶
FOR x=1 TO 30¶
SCROLL (1,1)-(630,100),0,3¶
SCROLL (1,100)-(630,180),0,-3¶
NEXT x¶
COLOR TextColor,Background¶
CLS : GOTO Begin¶
¶
VelocityCalc:¶
ox=OBJECT.X(1) : oy=OBJECT.Y(1)¶
Move(x*2-1)=ox : Move(x*2)=oy¶
zx=Move(x*2+1) : zy=Move(x*2+2)¶
FOR xx=1 TO 64 STEP .2¶
Speed(x*2-1)=CINT((zx-ox)/xx)¶
Speed(x*2)=CINT((zy-oy)/xx)¶
IF ABS(Speed(x*2-1))<40 AND ABS(Speed(x*2))<40 THEN
xx=64¶
NEXT xx¶
RETURN¶
```

If you got all that down, save it immediately—you probably don't need us to tell you that anymore.

How the program works

Do you understand approximately what the program does? We're now going to go over the individual program routines. Compare our explanations with the ones you have come up with on your own.

Displaying the title

The ShowTitle: routine waits until the <RETURN> key is pressed. The value CHR$(13) corresponds to this key. Then the variable c is set to 10. This is the counter for the countdown, which is why it is printed on the screen during the countdown. Each second its value is reduced by 1, until it reaches zero. The Wait2: loop waits one second until the next value of c is displayed.

Set colors

StartDisplay: first sets the screen width to 60 columns. Then it clears the screen in a predetermined background color and sets the color for the output of the text.

Text formatting

The loop that follows centers the text in the screen. The text is first limited to 60 characters with LEFT$. Note that the text entry routine will not accept more than 60 characters per line. The variable h calculates the horizontal position in the row where the text should begin. For this the remaining space on the line (60-LEN(text$)) is simply divided by two—one half for the left, one for the right. Finally the text is printed at the calculated position and the color is reset. If no movement was specified (the equation IF Move(0)=0 checks for this) the program jumps to MoveText: immediately.

Moving the object

Otherwise the object is brought to its starting position and the movement loop begins. At each pass the loop is interrupted to calculate the velocity values (more about that in a minute). The calculated values are transferred, and the OBJECT.HIT 1,0,0 command is used to turn the collision control off. The Loop4: runs until the object has reached its next destination point through 15 points. This value has proved practical in previous experiments. However, because of the rounding off, it is possible that the object will miss its destination. Because of this a time-check is built in: if the object takes more than 18 seconds to reach its destination, the movement is stopped, and the object starts toward the next destination point. 18 seconds is the time in which the object can move the longest possible distance, namely from one corner of the screen to the opposite corner.

Computing the speed

How does the `VelocityCalc:` routine work? First it determines the actual coordinates, which don't coincide 100% with the values in the `move(x)` array. Thus the actual values are assigned to the array instead of the theoretical ones. They are now the starting coordinates of the next movement, and are assigned to the variables `ox` and `oy`. The end coordinates are in the next two positions in the `move(x)` array. The following `FOR...NEXT` loop divides the distance between the X and Y coordinates by larger and larger numbers until both values are smaller than 40. Otherwise the star will move too fast. The fact that both are divided by the same number keeps the proportion between the X and Y distances constant. This ratio must be read by the velocities so the direction of the movement is correct. When the velocity is in the correct ratio, `xx` is set to 64 and the loop is ended. (`FOR xx=1 TO 64 STEP .2` increases `xx` by 0.2 until `xx` becomes 64. As soon as `xx` equals 64, the loop ends.) Then back to the main program (this is called `RETURN` in BASIC).

Moving the text

The `MoveText:` routine is the only one left. If no object movement took place, the viewer won't have time to read the text. Here the program waits for two seconds per line of text to give the viewer time to read it.

End program

This is followed by our `SCROLL` routine, which moves the top and the bottom sections of the screen toward the middle. In this way the text and background disappear from the screen. The color also gets reset and the screen is cleared, in case there's "leftover" text or background. After that, the program returns to the main menu.

That's how it works. Oh, we almost forgot: the new program routine must be included in the main menu, too. In the `Query:` routine, under the line:

```
IF a$="4" THEN DefineColor¶
```

Add the line:

```
IF a$="5" THEN ShowTitle¶
```

Run it!

You're probably dying to try out the program. Now's your chance:

Use item 1 to enter the text that you want displayed on the screen.

Use item 2 to read the object (star) from the diskette.

Select item 3 to determine its movement.

In case the present colors don't suit you, change them with item 4. Remember that you can still change the text color after you enter <e>. The first number entered will specify the screen color, the second determines the actual text color. The third one allows you to highlight the text with a colored bar. If you only press <RETURN>, the existing values will be accepted.

Item 5 produces the whole title.

You'll get more out of this program by playing around with it than by studying it. What you don't like, you can change in the menu selections.

Save it again

Once you have corrected the last errors, save the video title program one last time. In several places of this book we'll make a few changes and additions to the video title program, in order to make it more convenient or more powerful. For instance when we use graphics for the background from... No, never mind. We can't tell you about that just yet.

For now the video title program is finished. Until the next chapter, we wish you lots of fun with it.

Colors and resolution

2

2

It's all here in black and white: Amiga colors and resolution

Right now you might be saying, "OK, I've got a computer that's capable of displaying 32 of 4096 different colors at the same time, and what have I seen of them so far? All of <u>four</u> colors!"

You've got a point. The four colors that we used can be changed with the PALETTE command. We used this AmigaBASIC command in the Item 4 routine of the program (Define colors) allows you to do this. However, we haven't yet managed to display more than four colors on the screen at the same time in AmigaBASIC. This is about to change. This next chapter will introduce you to the Amiga's color in all of its splendor.

2.1

Amiga teaser:
A spectrum of color

You might remember that these "teasers" at the beginning of each chapter are meant to give you an idea of the Amiga's capabilities without requiring a lot of programming effort. You don't need to understand the program example right away. Just type it in exactly as it is printed out and enjoy the results.

If you are an Amiga 1000 owner with only 256K to work with, you'll need to incorporate some changes to this program, listed on the next page.

Type in the following program:

```
SCREEN 1,320,200,5,1¶
WINDOW 2,"This is as colorful as it gets",,23,1¶
FOR x=0 TO 7¶
FOR y=0 TO 3¶
co=x+y*8¶
LINE (x*38,y*45)-((x+1)*38,(y+1)*45),co,bf¶
NEXT y,x¶
WHILE INKEY$=""¶
PALETTE INT(31*RND)+1,RND,RND,RND¶
WEND¶
WINDOW CLOSE 2¶
SCREEN CLOSE 1¶
WINDOW 1¶
```

You might be wondering whether there's a typographical error in the second line of this program. Here's that line again, with the "error" underlined:

```
WINDOW 2,"This is as colorful as it gets",,23,1¶
```

Don't worry, this is not a mistake. The two commas after the quotation mark, followed by the number 23, are correct AmigaBASIC syntax.

Don't forget to Save the program on diskette after you've typed it in. You can use the program at a later time for experiments when you understand its concepts more clearly.

A few suggestions before you try the program out: You can change the size of the window and shift its position. Also, look closely at the appearance of the pulldown menus.

To end the program, simply press any key.

*Program
changes for
Amiga 1000
with 256K*

The lack of extra memory in a 256K Amiga 1000 becomes very restricting when you're working with many colors and high resolution. Without the RAM memory expansion, it's almost impossible to display more than eight colors on the screen at one time. If you have an Amiga 1000 with 256K of memory, change the first two lines:

Before:

```
SCREEN 1,320,200,5,1¶
WINDOW 2,"This is as colorful as it gets",,23,1¶
```

After:

```
SCREEN 1,320,200,3,1¶
WINDOW 2,"This is as colorful as it gets",,0,1¶
```

Also change the fifth line:

Before:

```
co=x+y*8¶
```

After:

```
co=(x+y*4) AND 7¶
```

Except for the few restrictions that we mentioned, this program version will give you the same results as the original program.

2.2   Pixels, colors and memory: Amiga screen resolutions

In the colorful demonstration program, you saw that it is possible to randomly change and select colors on your Amiga.

AmigaBASIC has commands that allow you to manage any number of windows. These windows can be on any one of a total of five screens. You can use various resolutions and different color combinations for screens and windows in BASIC. If what we've just said doesn't quite make sense to you, you'll find out more in just a minute.

Color and memory

Before we continue with our programming, let's get a little background on the subject of computer colors and resolution.

The display of colors and graphics are memory intensive. If you are or used to be the owner of a 256K Amiga 1000, you know that many graphic programs cannot run on your Amiga because of the limited memory space. This is understandable, since the computer must constantly load the information for the display of the screen in memory, and the process usually gobbles up a large amount of your free memory. This is the price you pay for the Amiga's easy to use mouse control and sophisticated graphics.

Do you remember the bobs? These also had to be loaded into memory first. Then they were copied into the actual screen display and removed from the screen before the next movement. In fact, your Amiga wouldn't be able to remember the location of any character or graphic on the screen. Because the computer can only remember the location of screen elements by keeping them in its memory, each graphic, each character—each and every dot displayed on the monitor screen—uses up part of your RAM.

Pixels

The screen display of a computer is composed of thousands of small dots called *pixels*. The picture on the screen is composed of pixels, just like a picture in a newspaper is made up of points of ink. When the points are small enough and the viewer is at a distance, the points form a whole picture. You've learned this principle stated in this book earlier, when we talked about the way a television works.

On a monochrome screen, a pixel can have only one of two values: either on or off (visible or invisible). Thus the pixels can very easily be displayed as bits in memory. Each point on a monochrome screen corresponds to one bit in the computer's memory.

Resolutions   The Amiga offers several levels of resolution. Each level displays a different number of pixels on the screen. The lowest resolution consists of 320 pixels horizontally and 200 pixels vertically. For an example, the demonstration program at the beginning of this chapter is displayed in low resolution. Multiply 320 by 200 pixels and you get a total of 64,000 individual pixels displayed on the screen.

Since the amount of memory used in programs and graphics are usually given in bytes, and one byte consists of eight bits, 8,000 bytes are required for this resolution. In other words, about 8 kilobytes (8K).

If you're curious as to why this equals "about" 8 kilobytes, refer to Appendix E under the word "byte".

The next level of resolution displays 640 pixels horizontally and 400 vertically. This is the resolution which the Amiga displays most of the time. The Workbench uses this resolution, as does AmigaBASIC. The 640 x 200 pixels yield a total of 128,000 pixels. Therefore, about 16K of memory is required to display a screen in medium resolution.

There are still two higher levels of resolutions. They are produced in the *interlace mode*, which we'll talk more about later. Their respective resolutions are 320 x 400 (128,000 pixels, or 16K) and 640 x 400 (256,000 dots or 32K).

Multiple colors   But the previous examples of resolution are quite simplified—we've assumed that the picture is displayed in only one color. (There are actually two colors, if you want to get technical. One color is used for the foreground, such as white for text and graphics, and one color for the background, such as blue). If a pixel is white, the bit is on (set). If a pixel is blue, the bit in memory is off (not set).

One bit per pixel is all that's needed for these "one-color" displays. However, how do we get four, eight, and even 32 colors on the screen at the same time? Simple: When one bit isn't enough, use more bits. For instance, if you have two bits for one point, you can already distinguish between four colors. If both bits are off, blue could be displayed. If the first bit is off and the second is on, the dot could be white. If, in turn, the first bit is on and the second is off, the dot could be black. If both bits are on, the dot could be a fourth color such as orange. Screens with four colors are then possible, such as those you've seen on the Workbench, or in the LIST and BASIC windows in AmigaBASIC.

But now with four colors, every screen requires 32K instead of 16K. If more colors are needed, more bits are used. For instance, using three bits per pixel, eight colors can be displayed. Think of the different combinations: off-off-off, off-off-on, off-on-off, off-on-on, on-off-off, on-off-on, on-on-off and on-on-on.

You're probably getting dizzy from all those ofns and ofs—excuse me, offs and ons. So let's use the standard way of representing this off/on system—by using *binary numbers*. The standard way to denote an "off" bit is with a 0. The standard way to denote an "on" bit is with a 1. So the eight possible combinations that result from three bits look like this:

```
000 001 010 011 100 101 110 111
```

This is our first real encounter with those mysterious binary numbers—you'll hear more about them in **Intermission 3**. This little game can be applied in the same way to four and five bits, and theoretically much further. In fact, all of the Amiga's 4096 colors could be encoded with only 12 bits, but the chips don't normally deal with producing video graphics. Usually 32 colors is the limit.

The following table shows all possible levels of resolution, the possible number of colors, and the amount of memory required by the Amiga to produce these colors:

Table 2: The Amiga's resolution levels

Resolution	Colors	Bits/pixel	Memory requirements
320 x 200 (low resolution, normal mode)	2	1	8 kilobytes
	4	2	16 kilobytes
	8	3	24 kilobytes
	16	4	32 kilobytes
	32	5	40 kilobytes
640 x 200 (high resolution, normal mode)	2	1	16 kilobytes
	4	2	32 kilobytes
	8	3	48 kilobytes
	16	4	64 kilobytes
320 x 400 (low resolution, interlace mode)	2	1	16 kilobytes
	4	2	32 kilobytes
	8	3	48 kilobytes
	16	4	64 kilobytes
	32	5	80 kilobytes
640 x 400 (high resolution, interlace mode)	2	1	32 kilobytes
	4	2	64 kilobytes
	8	3	96 kilobytes
	16	4	128 kilobytes

Bitplanes

Now can you see why there's been such intense competition among the computer makers to offer as much memory for as little money as possible? The table on the previous page also explains why it's so easy to fill 512K bytes of memory with just two graphics.

Some more general theory on computer resolution and memory:

The bits that control a specific pixel aren't located consecutively in memory. They are located in *bitplanes*, since this is a more efficient way for the Amiga to store them. Only one bitplane is needed for two colors. Two bitplanes are needed for four colors. The first bit of each pixel is located in the first bitplane, and the second bit in the second plane. If a third, a fourth, or a fifth bit is added, a corresponding third, fourth, or fifth bitplane is added as well.

To understand the concept of bitplanes a little better, imagine this: the planes are stacked on top of each other, and the more planes present, the more colors that can be displayed. Take a look at Figure 5:

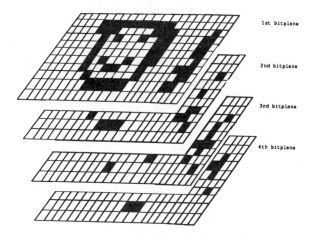

1st bitplane

2nd bitplane

3rd bitplane

4th bitplane

Figure 5: Together the "layered" bitplanes produce a color picture

Technically this illustration isn't quite correct, since the planes are actually located one after the other in memory. In other words, the Amiga stores the bits in the first plane, then the bits in the second plane, and so on. Nevertheless, Figure 5 should make it easier for you to visualize the concept.

If at this point you are saying, "Whoa—I only understood about half of this, and not even that half very well either," don't worry. It is not essential to know the details of memory management to program colors in AmigaBASIC. It's enough that you know how many bitplanes are required for a certain number of colors, and approximately how much memory a graphic will need. After all, you'll eat up 512K in a hurry if you use colors and screens wastefully.

What exactly are these "screens", anyway? You'll find the answer in the next section.

2.3   "Motion" graphics:
        The Amiga's screens

You might have used a graphic program where you pulled down the entire screen with the mouse, and behind that screen a completely new screen is visible—for instance, the famous bouncing ball demo. The Amiga can "stack" different graphic screens one on top of the other, and their order can be changed with the front and back gadgets. Once you've closed all of the screens, you're left with an empty blue background.

What are
screens?

Don't confuse screens with windows—they're two very distinct Amiga features. In this context, the term *screen* refers to the entire "frame" displayed on the video monitor. In turn, the windows and icons are displayed within this screen. Try the following little experiment:

√√ REDUCE THE **LIST** AND **BASIC** WINDOWS IN SIZE SO THAT THE WORKBENCH SCREEN IS VISIBLE (CLICK THE SIZING GADGETS IN THE LOWER-RIGHT CORNER OF THESE WINDOWS).

√√ MOVE THE POINTER TO THE WHITE TITLE BAR AT THE TOP OF THE WORKBENCH SCREEN.

√√ MOVE THE MOUSE DOWNWARD WHILE HOLDING THE LEFT MOUSE BUTTON UNTIL THE ENTIRE SCREEN, INCLUDING ALL ICONS AND WINDOWS, SLIDES DOWNWARD AND DISAPPEARS AT THE BOTTOM OF THE MONITOR.

You've just moved the Workbench screen. Usually there won't be any other screen behind it, unless other programs are running on your Amiga, or another screen is still active from one of your BASIC experiments.

A screen can theoretically contain an unlimited number of windows and icons. However, the screen resolution and the maximum number of colors is constant throughout the screen. This is because these values must be specified when a screen is created. These parameters remain constant until the screen is redefined or closed. For example, you cannot specify a different resolution or a different number of bitplanes for one particular window in the screen, since the parameters stay the same throughout the screen.

Drag the Workbench screen back into view. Then type the following line in the **BASIC** window:

```
screen 1,320,200,3,1¶
```

SCREEN

As soon as you press <RETURN>, an empty screen is displayed. This screen has a resolution of 320 x 200 pixels and has a maximum of eight colors. Screens are actually independent video graphics, except that all of the different screens can be displayed on the same video monitor. You'll see that your new screen has a back gadget and front gadget, just like the Workbench screen. If you click the back gadget, the Workbench screen will come back into view. This back/front system works exactly the same way with screens as with windows.

As soon as you create a screen, you can define windows in it. Type the following line in the **BASIC** window:

```
window 1,"Hello",,0,1¶
```

WINDOW

On the new screen you'll now see a window called **Hello**. AmigaBASIC automatically makes this the new **BASIC** window (the reason for this in a minute).

In any case, your Amiga is now displaying two screens: The Workbench screen , and the Hello screen that you just created. Most of the time you'll be working on the Workbench screen—for instance, when you're programming in AmigaBASIC. You'd use the other screens in the background to run other programs.

It's often difficult to use the front and back gadgets, because they are usually covered by windows. So there's another way of bringing the Workbench screen to the foreground. The key combination <C=><N> (<Amiga key><N>for Amiga 1000) positions the Workbench in front of all other screens. To position the Workbench in back of all other screens, use the <C=><M>or <Amiga key><M> combination.

**SCREEN
CLOSE**

To close the new screen, type the following command in the **BASIC** window:

```
screen close 1¶
```

However, this closes the screen containing our **BASIC** window. Now we're stranded without a **BASIC** window. Don't worry—simply select the Show Output item from the **Windows** menu and the **BASIC** window is redisplayed on the Workbench screen.

Now you know the most important commands you need to program screens and windows in AmigaBASIC. But what do those numbers after the commands mean? Let's look at our first example above:

```
screen 1,320,200,3,1¶
```

Parameters
with
SCREEN

The first number after the SCREEN command is the *screen ID* number. AmigaBASIC can manage up to four screens, so the screen ID number must be between 1 and 4.

You might know what the next two values are: The first is the number of horizontal pixels and the second is the number of vertical pixels. However, these numbers don't specify the screen's resolution, only the actual size of the screen within the current resolution. For example, try this:

```
screen 1,200,200,3,1¶
```

When you type a vertical value below 200, you won't be able to move the arrow past the bottom of the window. If you move this screen, you'll only be able to pull it up to the defined height. Try this:

```
screen 1,200,100,3,1¶
```

The fourth value in the SCREEN command specifies the number of bitplanes that the screen will have. This way you control the number of colors that the screen will be able to display.

The last number specifies the screen's resolution. The following four values are permitted:

Table 3:
Possible
resolutions
for SCREEN

Value	Resolution level	Pixels
1	Low-res, normal	320 x 200
2	High-res, normal	640 x 200
3	Low-res, interlace	320 x 400
4	High-res, interlace	640 x 400

The values that you give for the screen's horizontal and vertical sizes must be within its resolution, otherwise you'll get all sorts of strange results. For instance, don't select a size of 440 x 200 when your resolution is 320 x 200 (resolution 1). Even though AmigaBASIC won't display an error message, your should still avoid these "out-of-bounds" values.

Interlace
mode

The table above uses the term *interlace*. It's about time we explain that word. First, let's demonstrate the effect of the interlace mode on the screen. Type this line:

```
screen 1,640,400,1,4 : window 1,"Test",(0,0)-
(400,300),15,1¶
```

You'll notice two things right away: The characters on the screen are extremely small, and the monitor screen is flickering. The advantage of interlace mode is that it achieves a higher vertical resolution, and produces graphics up to 400 pixels in height. The disadvantage of interlace mode is that it causes the screen to flicker. Let's refer back to television technology to discover how the higher vertical resolution is produced, and why the picture is flickering.

You already know that the motion of objects on the monitor is animated rather than "real". The picture is simply displayed over and over at high speed (approximately 30 times a second). To the human eye this animation looks continuous and fluid. However, the picture still flickers considerably at 30 frames per second.

So that it wouldn't have to use more frames per second for higher resolution graphics (which would complicate the transmission), the Amiga uses a trick to stabilize the picture. In the first 1/60 second the monitor shows only every second line of the picture. In the second 1/60 second, the picture is constructed again, this time displaying the lines that were left blank during the first half. To the naked eye it seems as though 60 frames per second are drawn, which is enough to stabilize the picture and prevent it from flickering.

Stabilizing the picture

The Amiga uses the same trick, regardless of whether you use an Amiga monitor or a television set. In normal mode, a resolution of 200 lines (or vertical pixels) is used. To double this number in interlace mode, the Amiga sends a different picture when the monitor is constructing the second set of lines. The two half graphics are combined to form a picture with twice the vertical resolution. However, the picture is quite unstable, because only 30 frames per second are now being displayed.

Also, the higher the contrasts between bordering colors, the stronger the flickering will be. The amount of flickering also depends upon the shape of the object. Whether you use the interlace mode is up to you.

If you need an absolutely stable picture, there is an alternative. Special monitors are available that have a slightly longer illumination time, which minimizes the flickering. By the way, if you think that this flickering is very unprofessional for a computer like the Amiga, take a close look at the projection behind the newscasters during your local 11 o'clock news. Notice any similarities?

2.4   Creating your own Amiga windows

Once you've defined your screens, the next step is to create the windows in those screens. As you might have noticed in our examples, the WINDOW command performs this task. If the interlace screen from the last chapter is still active (indicated by the slight flickering of the other screens), close it now:

```
screen close 1¶
```

To return to the **BASIC** window, select the Show Output item from the **Windows** menu. Then type the following line in the **BASIC** window:

```
window 2,"Hello",(320,20)-(615,150),31,-1¶
```

Owners of 256K Amiga 1000s must make another compromise here. Type the following line instead:

```
window 2,"Hello",(320,20)-(580,120),15,-1¶
```

WINDOW

A window named **Hello** is displayed in the Workbench screen. Now type the following line:

```
for x=1 to 100 : ? x : next x¶
```

As you'll see, the numbers are displayed in the new window. The command:

```
window output 1¶
```

displays the output in the **BASIC** window.

Well, it's time to make this a little more systematic. First the parameters of the WINDOW command:

```
window 2,"Hello",(320,20)-(615,150),31,-1¶
```

for 256K Amiga 1000:

```
window 2,"Hello",(320,20)-(580,120),15,-1¶
```

WINDOW
parameters

The first number after the command specifies the window ID number. AmigaBASIC allows you to open any number of windows—at least until you run out of memory. The number 1 is reserved for the **BASIC** window, so you should use numbers starting at 2 to identify the windows you create. If you type 1 for a new window, you can change the size, resolution and colors of the **BASIC** window. However, if you wish to display more than four colors or a higher resolution than 640 x 200 pixels, the window will have to be moved to a new screen, since the settings of the Workbench screen can't be changed. The present version of AmigaBASIC is limited to a resolution of 640 x 200 and two bitplanes (four colors).

The second parameter of the WINDOW command is the window's name. It is entered as a string, either within quotation marks or in a string variable.

The third parameter set of the WINDOW command specifies the position and size of the window. If these values are missing, the window will cover the entire screen. To display a window that's smaller than the screen, you specify the coordinates of the upper left-hand corner and the lower right-hand corner in the format (x1,y1)-(x2,y2). For example: (100,10)-(500,140)

The fourth value determines the features of the window. The individual values are added together to form a single number that specifies the properties you want the window to have. The following single values are used:

**Table 4:
Parameter
values for
the WINDOW
command**

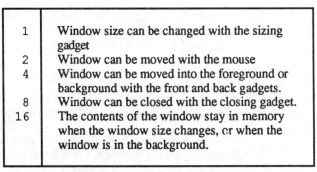

1	Window size can be changed with the sizing gadget
2	Window can be moved with the mouse
4	Window can be moved into the foreground or background with the front and back gadgets.
8	Window can be closed with the closing gadget.
16	The contents of the window stay in memory when the window size changes, or when the window is in the background.

For instance, if you want a window that can be moved (2) and clicked closed (8), as the fourth value you type 10 (2+8). A window whose size can be changed (1), which can be moved (2) and can be clicked into the background (4), requires 7 (1+2+4) as the fourth value. If the window is to have all the available items, the fourth value will be 3 1 (1+2+4+8+16). However, note that the last item (16) uses up a lot of memory, since the Amiga must store the entire window's contents at the same time it's manipulating another window. A 256K Amiga 1000 really doesn't have enough memory to utilize this item.

If the window's contents are not to be kept in memory (no value 16), the window's contents are erased as soon as the window is moved, or when another window is moved into the foreground. Therefore, if you don't give a window the value 16, make sure that it remains in the foreground and is not shifted—use the value 0 (no items) to be safe. Depending on which value you type, the corresponding window icons may or may not appear in the window frame.

The last value in the WINDOW command specifies the screen in which the window is displayed. If you don't specify a value here, or else specify the value -1, the window is displayed in the Workbench screen.

WINDOW OUTPUT

From the time that it's created with the WINDOW command, a window automatically becomes the output window. This means that any output of a running BASIC program is displayed in the newly-created window. To redirect the BASIC output back to another window, you use the following command:

window output *window_number*¶

WINDOW OUTPUT simply redirects the output to another window, and does not change the window sizes or positions. AmigaBASIC even lets you switch the output to a window that isn't open or visible. To display the new output window in the foreground, you'd use this command:

window *window_number*¶

WINDOW CLOSE

The WINDOW CLOSE command closes the window you specify. It has no other parameters. However, this command works only with windows that were previously defined:

window close *window_number*¶

"Cleaning" windows

The command above clears a defined window from the screen without deleting it. AmigaBASIC has no command that will erase a single window from memory once it is opened. Even the SCREEN CLOSE command will not erase the screen's windows. Only a RUN command or clearing a program from the corresponding pulldown menu item can close those windows and screens.

As a result, you should not use too many windows when you're programming. This impractical aspect of AmigaBASIC often disables a WINDOW command that previously worked fine, which results in an Illegal function call error message (although other errors display this error message too). If this problem arises, either use another window number or erase all windows by restarting the program.

Feel free to experiment with all the WINDOW commands you've just learned. Use examples of your own.

Even though you might have tried all the examples, this section has still probably seemed a little dry and boring. Let's use the new knowledge about AmigaBASIC screens and windows to do something useful.

We've used only four colors in our video title program up to now—let's change this. Open your video title program and edit the Setup: routine so that it looks like this:

```
Setup:¶
Colors=2¶
d=15 : Colors=(2^Colors)-1¶
TextColor=1¶
SCREEN CLOSE 2¶
IF Colors>2 THEN SCREEN 2,640,200,Colors,2 : WINDOW 2,
"Videotitle",,28,2¶
DIM Text$(d),Colormatrix(d,3),Move(d),Speed(d)¶
Filler$=STRING$(16,"-")¶
Colormatrix(1,1)=15¶
Colormatrix(1,2)=15¶
Colormatrix(1,3)=15¶
```

Don't forget to save the new program version immediately. If you don't want to lose the original version, then save the altered version under a new name.

The Colors variable contains the number of bitplanes that are used. The standard setting is 2. If you want to use more colors (and if your Amiga has at least 512K of memory), you can type in 3 (for 8 colors) or 4 (for 16 colors). If the value of Colors is greater than 2, the program will define a corresponding screen and window. You can see this clearly when you select item 4 in the menu (Define Color).

Things are starting to get fun... Now that you can create and program screens and windows, we can move on to the AmigaBASIC commands that use windows for graphic output.

2.5

Versatility:
the first graphic commands

This section details the Amiga's graphic commands. One thing you'll notice right away is that each graphic command has a complete set of options, which makes them extremely versatile.

Click the **BASIC** window into the foreground for the following experiment, so that you can see it completely.

Let's start out doing something small. Try this:

```
pset (400,100) ¶
```

PSET

You may not notice it unless you look for it, but a small white dot is now displayed in the middle of your screen. It is in the location where the **LIST** window usually starts, about halfway up the screen. If you still can't see it, let's make it a little bigger. Type in this command:

```
pset (401,100) ¶
```

This displays another dot next to the first. Now you should be able to see them both clearly. The BASIC command P SET is used to produce individual points of a graphic. Since two points on the screen aren't very exciting, let's place a series of points adjacent to each other:

```
for x=1 to 184 : pset (x,x),3 : next x¶
```

This displays an orange line on the screen.

The PSET command specifies where the point is placed using a set of X and Y coordinates. These coordinates are enclosed within parentheses (x, y) just like in the WINDOW command. It's the same concept used in the popular game **Battleship**® (from Milton-Bradley). A set of two coordinates specifies the target, and the Amiga draws a dot at that target location. The only difference is that the Amiga won't say "You sank my battleship!" (Incidentally, you could write a Battleship program in AmigaBASIC—but you might want to get a little more programming experience first).

In a normal window on the 640 x 200 screen, the X value can be between 0 and 184 (part of the screen is used by the frame and the window symbols). The color can be specified after the coordinates. The complete syntax looks like this:

```
PSET (x,y),color¶
```

The BASIC command line above which produced the diagonal line is quite simple. The variable x is increased from 1 to 184 in steps of 1. The values of the X and Y coordinates will always be the same—in fact, they'll both have the value of x. Thus a point is drawn at (1,1), at (2,2), (3,3), and so forth, up to (184,184), and draws a line across the screen at a 45-degree angle.

However, AmigaBASIC gives you a much simpler method of drawing lines: the LINE command. The line that we just drew with PSET can also be drawn this way:

```
LINE (1,1)-(184,184) ¶
```

LINE

The LINE command's parameters are the starting point of the line, a dash and the end point of the line. The final value specifies the color of the line. You can also omit the first pair of coordinates; the line will then start at the endpoint of the previous line:

```
LINE -(500,10),2¶
```

RND

An easy way to create interesting graphics is to use random values. The RND (RaNDom) variable is used for this. RND always contains a random number in the range between 0 and 1. Let's look at some sample values:

```
for x=1 to 10 : ? rnd : next x¶
```

Now type the following demonstration routine in the **LIST** window and immediately save it to diskette. We'll experiment with the RND command by changing this routine bit by bit. Also, don't hesitate to experiment on your own. If you particularly like one of the effects you get, be sure you save the version under a unique name.

The first version draws colored dots at random locations:

```
CLS¶
Loop:¶
PSET (617*RND,184*RND),3*RND¶
GOTO Loop¶
```

One thing about random numbers: When you multiply RND with a number (for example, 617), you'll get a value between 0 and the specified number (617). This determines the X and Y coordinates as well as the color. Soon the screen will be covered with more and more colored dots. To stop the program, press <Amiga> and <.> simultaneously, or use the pulldown menu.

If you have plenty of free memory, you can do this on a higher resolution screen with more colors:

```
Colors=4¶
Cmax=2^Colors-1¶
SCREEN 1,640,200,Colors,2¶
WINDOW 2,"Dots",,31,1¶
CLS¶
Loop:¶
PSET (617*RND,184*RND),Cmax*RND¶
GOTO Loop¶
```

You can make the RGB composition of the colors random as well. Simply insert these lines preceding the CLS command:

```
FOR x=1 TO (2^Colors)-1¶
PALETTE x,RND,RND,RND¶
NEXT x¶
```

You'll use the formula (2^Colors)-1 quite frequently. It calculates the highest possible number of colors from the number of available bit-planes (in the variable Colors). The ^ symbol signifies an exponent, i.e., 2^4 would be 2^4 in AmigaBASIC.

The RND command is very easy to use in conjunction with the PALETTE command, since PALETTE requires numbers in the range between 0 and 1. That's exactly the numbers RND produces.

Now replace the line containing the PSET command with this:

```
LINE -(617*RND,184*RND),Cmax*RND¶
```

This version creates a "haystack" of colored lines.

The LINE command is actually more powerful than you might suspect. Type the following command line in the **BASIC** window:

```
LINE (10,10)-(300,100),1,b¶
```

As we said before, AmigaBASIC's graphic commands are very powerful and versatile when taken advantage of their additional parameters. The b stands for box, or rectangle. How did the Amiga know where and how large to make the rectangles? The starting coordinate determines the upper left corner, while the end coordinate is the lower right corner. This might remind you of the format used to specify window sizes. In fact, AmigaBASIC uses the same format to determine the coordinates for points, lines, windows, rectangles and other graphic objects.

Add a ,b to the LINE command in our little demonstration program:

```
LINE -(617*RND,184*RND),Cmax*RND,b¶
```

The results are again quite interesting. Hold on—the LINE command has another surprise in store. You can also color in these rectangles. To do this you replace the b parameter with bf (block fill). Try this demonstration program:

```
LINE -(617*RND,184*RND),Cmax*RND,bf¶
```

Not bad!

However, some of you like to retain control and calculate everything down to the finest detail. If you're one of these people, you might not like the random functions very much. Another method to produce computer graphics is mathematical formulas—this is easy in AmigaBASIC, too.

At this time, save the demonstration program, then type NEW to clear the memory. Do you remember all of those sine curves back in high school math class? Type in this program routine for a refresher course:

```
FOR x=0 TO 617¶
y=90+80*SIN(x/40)¶
PSET (x,y)¶
NEXT x¶
```

SIN

Do you still remember what the sine function does? Well, for starters, it has values in the range between -1 and +1. The formula in the second line of the routine converts the SIN function into screen coordinates. The X value is divided by 40 so that the curve doesn't get too "narrow". The result is multiplied by 80 (producing numbers between -80 to +80) and added to 90. This produces Y coordinates between 10 and 170.

If all this sounds too mathematical for you, simply plug different values into the formula and see what happens. (Note: you may change the 40; you may only reduce the 80; leave the 90 alone).

To produce a continuous curve instead of the series of dots that we now have, you can use the LINE command again. First you'll have to specify a starting point, so that the first line doesn't start at any point on the screen. Because of this the first PSET command is retained:

```
PSET(0,90)¶
FOR x=0 TO 617¶
y=90+80*SIN(x/40)¶
LINE -(x,y)¶
NEXT x¶
```

COS

If you use COS (*cosine*, the counterpart of sine) you'll see how the curve changes. SIN and COS can produce many interesting effects. We've put together a few demonstration programs for you to quickly type in:

```
FOR x=0 TO 617¶
y=90+80*SIN(x/40)¶
LINE (0,90)-(x,y)¶
NEXT x¶
```

When you connect the points on a sine curve with some other fixed point, an intricate line formation will result. Let's add some more color:

```
Colors=4¶
SCREEN 1,640,200,Colors,2¶
WINDOW 2,"sine lines",,15,1¶
FOR x=0 TO 617¶
co=co+1 : IF co>7 THEN co=0¶
y=90+80*SIN(x/40) ¶
LINE (0,90)-(x,y),co¶
NEXT x¶
```

Experiment with other values—for example, in the LINE statement:

```
LINE (320,90)-(x,y),co¶
```

Or:

```
LINE (320,184)-(x,y),co¶
```

Now use the block and block-fill items in the LINE command:

```
LINE (320,184)-(x,y),co,b¶
```

You're only limited by your own imagination. Remember, these are only demonstration examples—try experimenting on your own! If you use more complicated formulas, you might end up with something like:

```
Colors=4¶
SCREEN 1,640,200,Colors,2¶
WINDOW 2,"sine lines",,15,1¶
FOR x=0 TO 617¶
co=co+1 : IF co> 7 THEN co=0¶
y1=90+80*SIN(x/40) ¶
y2=90+70*SIN(x/60) ¶
LINE (x,y1)-(617-x,y2),co¶
NEXT x¶
```

Or:

```
Colors=4¶
SCREEN 1,640,200,Colors,2¶
WINDOW 2,"sine lines",,15,1¶
FOR x=0 TO 617¶
co=co+.5 : IF co>7 THEN co=1¶
y1=90+80*SIN(x/40) ¶
y2=90+70*SIN(x/60) ¶
x2=320-300*SIN(x/50) ¶
LINE (x,y1)-(x2,y2),co¶
NEXT x¶
```

Hopefully these examples will give you some incentive to start experimenting with these commands. Remember, the worst thing that can happen is that you'll get an error message, or that the output won't be very pretty. In the process you'll learn how to use these graphic commands to produce impressive displays.

Have you thought about spicing up the video title program with these routines?

Intermission 2

Chaining your different programs together

You might find that once you've played around with sine waves and LINE commands, you produce a graphic that you modestly think is astounding. Wouldn't it be nice if you could include it in the background in your video title program? After all, even though the flying objects and the colored text are impressive, the program still lacks that little something in the background. You'll learn how to change that in this intermission.

Appending programs

The Amiga has several different methods to display a background. First, we'll use a simple method: we'll just append the program that draws the sine curve onto the end of the video title program. Then we'll have the program execution jump to that routine just before the text and moving objects are displayed. Sine wave graphics are interesting enough in and of themselves to be displayed as the background of the program. (By the way, if you use this program to create a title for video, be sure to time the title so you know how long it is. After all, you wouldn't want to erase the footage on the cassette when you record the video title).

Back to the future: It would be senseless to save or print out the sine wave program routine, then retype it at the end of the video title program. Instead, AmigaBASIC can "chain" your programs together.

Load the sine wave program routine into memory. (It might still be in memory, since it's the last one we typed in; otherwise, load it from diskette).

Now it has to be resaved on diskette in a special format. Type the following command line in the **BASIC** window:

```
save "videographic",a¶
```

ASCII

The new ,a at the end represents ASCII. Haven't we heard of that before? ASCII codes are the numbers that are used with the CHR$ command. ASCII stands for American Standard Code for Information Interchange. The a following the SAVE command instructs the Amiga to save the program in ASCII values. If this is a special parameter for the SAVE command, what is its normal format for saving programs?

Normally you type the SAVE command without this item, or you simply chose Save from the **Project** menu. In this case, the program is saved on the diskette in a special memory-conserving format (for more info about this, look under "Tokens" in **Appendix E**). But if a program is saved in this format, it cannot be chained to another program. Chaining only works if the program is saved in ASCII format. Here's another item that you can use with SAVE:

```
SAVE "test",p¶
```

Protecting files

The p stands for "protect". This is used to save a program so that it can be run, but not listed or altered. For example, say you wanted to sell your own BASIC software program. The buyer of the program should be able to run and use the program, but should not be able to look at its listing. You can accomplish this by saving programs in the protect format. The program is encoded when it is written on the diskette, and AmigaBASIC will not be able to decode it again. Once you click or LOAD such a program, the **LIST** window is blocked, and the program can only be run.

However, this protection won't take a professional pirate very long to "*crack*" (decode). If a commercial program was protected with this format, it would be only a matter of time until some pirate wrote a counter program to crack the protection. However, this format is quite adequate for home use.

MERGE

Now that we've briefly discussed the pirating and program cracking controversy, let's return to harmless applications. Once you've saved the videographic program in ASCII format, load the video title program. When you chain two programs, the first program must be in memory while the second is loaded from diskette. The command that chains a program saved in ASCII format is very simple:

```
merge "videographic"¶
```

(If your program has a different name, you'll have to use that name instead).

Now the graphic program is chained to the end of your video title program. That was pretty easy, wasn't it?

Now we just have to make sure that the sine wave subroutine is also executed. First, give the subroutine a label, such as Graphics:. If your new program still contains SCREEN, WINDOW and COLOR commands, you should delete them now. The largest number of colors can be found in the variable Colors.

Make sure that you don't use any variables in the subroutine which are already being used in the main program. This would be a confusing source of errors.

At the end of the program you still need a RETURN command. In our case it would look like this:

```
Graphics:¶
FOR x=0 TO 617¶
co=co+.5 : IF co>Colors THEN co=1¶
y1=90+80*SIN(x/40)¶
y2=90+70*SIN(x/60)¶
x2=320-300*SIN(x/50)¶
LINE (x,y1)-(x2,y2),co¶
NEXT x¶
RETURN¶
```

The only thing still missing is the command that will call the subroutine. Type the following lines in the program routine StartDisplay: of the video title program:

```
StartDisplay:¶
WIDTH 80¶
COLOR TextColor,Background : CLS¶
GOSUB Graphics¶
COLOR TextColor,TextBackground¶
```

That's it. Run the altered program to see the results. And don't forget to save the new version if you like it.

With the method introduced here, you can chain any number of programs in any order you like. This can be very helpful when you're writing larger programs.

You can merge several background graphics for your video title. For instance, you could present several graphic routines from which the user can chose.

So that you have enough graphic programs to offer, you should learn a few new commands. This is why we'll move right along to...

2.6

Full circle: more graphic commands

The next command that we'll learn about will draw circles. Here's a preview of the command's capabilities:

```
CIRCLE (320,90),160¶
CIRCLE (260,50),15,,,,.5¶
CIRCLE (380,50),15,,,,.5¶
CIRCLE (260,53),8¶
CIRCLE (380,53),8¶
CIRCLE (380,50),45,,.2,2.2¶
CIRCLE (260,50),45,,.8,2.8¶
CIRCLE (320,80),20,,,,.7¶
CIRCLE (320,110),80,,3.1,0,.2¶
CIRCLE (320,10),10,,4.7,1.5,.9¶
CIRCLE (320,15),5,,5,1.8,.7¶
```

CIRCLE

This example isn't quite as easy to type in as previous examples. Be careful to include the correct number of commas! Hopefully, you'll find the result is well worth the effort. After all, this program looks pretty neat when you run it. If you like, save it on diskette for later use.

The AmigaBASIC command CIRCLE created this entire graphic without the aid of any other commands. This in itself proves how powerful CIRCLE is. Of all the AmigaBASIC commands, CIRCLE offers you the most items. The face that we drew in our sample program consists of circles, ellipses and arcs. All these graphic objects can be created with parameters of the CIRCLE command.

This is the most simple form of the CIRCLE command:

```
CIRCLE (x,y),radius¶
```

This command line creates a circle with a centerpoint at (x,y) and the specified radius. The value of the radius is given in number of pixels. However, the number of pixels is valid only in the X-direction. We'll talk about the Y-direction later.

Of course, we can use different colors, too:

```
CIRCLE (x,y),radius,color¶
```

Arcs and ellipses

Not only can CIRCLE create full circles, but also parts of circles, or arcs. The next two values specify the angles. The first angle determines the start of the arc, the second is the end of the arc.

```
CIRCLE (x,y),radius,color,angle1,angle2¶
```

The values of the angles must be in the range between 0 and 2*π, since the angles are specified in radians. A quarter of a circle ranges from 0 to 1.57; half of a circle from 0 to 3.14; three-quarters of a circle from 0 to 4.71; and a full circle from 0 to 6.28—although for a full circle you can simply omit this parameter. The following figure should help you find the correct angle values:

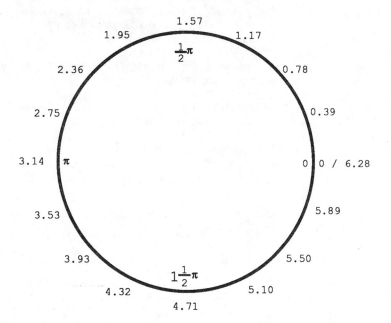

Figure 6:
Angles as
coefficients
of π

AmigaBASIC also gives you a method to draw sectors of circles, e.g., for a pie chart. If you type a negative value for an angle, the corresponding point will be connected to the center by a line. Try this in the **BASIC** window:

```
circle (320,100),200,3,-1.57,-3.14¶
```

The seventh and last value determines whether the circle is to become an ellipse. It specifies the relationship between the X-radius and the Y-radius.

```
circle (x,y),radius,color,angle1,angle2,x/y-ratio¶
```

If you want to draw a perfect round circle the x/y ratio will depend on adjustment of your monitor. The leftmost of the three knobs on the back of the Amiga monitor determine the height of the picture. If this adjustment is not normal, your circle will be displayed as an oval, and vice versa. A value of 0.44 will be the correct x/y ratio at the normal monitor setting. This is also the default value used by AmigaBASIC if this parameter is not specified. Smaller values will compress the circle into a horizontal ellipse. Values larger than 0.44 will stretch the circle into a vertical ellipse.

Armed with this knowledge, let's take on the listing for our demonstration program:

Making a face

The first line CIRCLE (320,90),160 draws a round circle with its center at (320,90) and a radius of 160 pixels.

The next two lines CIRCLE (260,50),15,,,,.5 and CIRCLE (380,50),15,,,,.5 draw the eyes. Two slightly egg-shaped ellipses are formed, since the x/y ratio is slightly above the normal value.

The fourth and fifth lines CIRCLE (260,53),8 and CIRCLE (380,53),8 create the pupils within the eyes.

The following two lines draw the eyebrows:

```
CIRCLE (380,50),45,,.2,2.2¶
CIRCLE (260,50),45,,.8,2.8¶
```

Here we used normal circles with a radius of 45 pixels. However, only segments of the circles are used (arcs), with starting angles of 0.2 and 0.8, and with ending angles of 2.2 and 2.8. To see where these angles are, refer to Figure 6.

Now for the nose: CIRCLE (320,80),20,,,,.7 is positioned exactly in the middle of our face, and its shape is definitely elliptical.

CIRCLE (320,110),80,,3.1,0,.2 is a half circle from π to 0 (where 0 is identical to 2*π) that forms a smile.

The last two commands draw a bit of hair:

```
CIRCLE (320,10),10,4.7,1.5,.9¶
CIRCLE (320,15),5,,5,1.8,.7¶
```

The two hairs are arcs from a vertical ellipse. Again, compare the starting and ending angles to Figure 6.

Maybe you'd like to follow the face's construction step by step on the screen. Unfortunately, the Amiga makes this difficult for us because it's so fast. Even Trace mode won't help much in this case. For this purpose there's another item on the **Run** pulldown menu that simplifies the testing of programs. The Step menu item notifies the Amiga to execute one command and pause before executing the next command. The Amiga pauses until you select the Step item from the Run menu again, or until you press the <right Amiga><T> key combination.

This Step item available from the menu does not have a corresponding BASIC command. Try it out with this "face" program: Everytime you select Step or press the key combination, another part of the face is drawn. This way you can see how the graphic is constructed step by step, and see the order in which the commands are executed. If you look at the LIST window, you'll see that each command is highlighted as it's executed, just as in trace mode. <Amiga> <.> disables the step mode.

PAINT

Whether it's drawn fast or slow, the drawing of this program still reminds you of something you'd find scribbled on a schoolroom blackboard. To make it look more Amiga-like, we need another command.

PAINT lets you color in the outlined areas. Change your program listing so that it is identical to the listing below. Save this new version as soon as you're done typing:

```
CIRCLE (320,190),200,1,,,.6¶
PAINT (320,170),1¶
CIRCLE (320,90),160,3¶
PAINT (320,90),3¶
CIRCLE (260,50),15,1,,,.5¶
CIRCLE (380,50),15,1,,,.5¶
PAINT (260,50),1¶
PAINT (380,50),1¶
CIRCLE (260,53),8,2¶
CIRCLE (380,53),8,2¶
PAINT (260,53),2¶
PAINT (380,53),2¶
CIRCLE (380,50,45,2,.2,2.2¶
CIRCLE (260,50),45,2,.8,2.8¶
CIRCLE (320,80),20,2,,,.7¶
CIRCLE (320,110),80,2,3.1,0,.2¶
CIRCLE (320,10),10,2,4.7,1.5,.9¶
CIRCLE (320,15),5,2,5,1.8,.7¶
CIRCLE (160,70),40,3,,,.6¶
CIRCLE (480,70),40,3,,,.6¶
PAINT (160,70),3¶
PAINT (480,70),3¶
CIRCLE (160,60),30,2,1,3,.3¶
CIRCLE (480,60),30,2,.3,2.2,.3¶
CIRCLE (150,65),25,2,4,1,.7¶
CIRCLE (490,65),25,2,2.2,5.4,.7¶
```

Painting the face

Besides having new broad shoulders and a pair of ears, our little guy now also has a more colorful face.

If you examine the construction of these graphics, you'll get an idea of how the PAINT command really works: You specify a point within a completely enclosed area. You also specify a color. AmigaBASIC then fills the entire area within the boundary of the graphic with that color. The Blitter chip makes the fast execution speed of this command possible—its specialty is moving, filling or changing graphic objects.

Note one important characteristic of this command: PAINT recognizes the outline only if it is drawn in one specified color. In the sample program you might have seen that the body is drawn and painted before the head, then the head is drawn and painted, covering up parts of the body. The parameter for painting outlined areas has the following syntax:

```
PAINT(x,y),color,outline color¶
```

Saving the face

If no outline color is specified, the command assumes that it is the same as the paint color. Therefore, PAINT (320,90),3 will paint everything around the point (320,90) until it reaches an orange outline. If the outline was white (color number 1) and the paint color black (color number 2), you'd need the following command:

```
PAINT (x,y),2,1¶
```

Please remember this aspect of the PAINT command—otherwise our little guy would quickly lose his face.

A note about **PAINT**

The outline of the area that is filled with PAINT can be created by any graphics command. The outlines do not have to consist of circles or ellipses. The important thing is that the outline has absolutely no gaps in its boundaries. Otherwise the color will "leak" beyond the intended area. You might remember that we have already encountered this problem in the object editor which we used to define our objects. That's because the object editor is also a BASIC program, and uses the PAINT command.

The next program demonstrates another method to create outlines. It uses the LINE command to draw a grid whose individual segments are randomly filled with color. After a while it'll really starts to look like Battleship...

Now to the listing:

```
FOR x=0 TO 615 STEP 15¶
LINE (x,0)-(x,185)¶
NEXT x¶
FOR y=0 TO 180 STEP 10¶
LINE (0,y)-(635,y)¶
NEXT y¶
FillIn:¶
PAINT (635*RND,180*RND)¶
GOTO FillIn¶
```

The STEP in the FOR...NEXT loop might be new to you. This command is used to change the size of the steps. The command line:

```
FOR x=0 TO 615 STEP 15
```

counts in increments of 15 from 0 to 615, in effect, 0, 15, 30, 45, etc. The program uses this method to assure the correct spacing between the bars of the grid. Try changing the STEP value and see what happens.

Pyramids in BASIC

Now you know commands to create points, lines, rectangles, circles, ellipses and arcs, and you know how to paint outlined areas in color. However, AmigaBASIC offers you even more tools for programming computer graphics. As you know, the Blitter chip can fill areas incredibly fast. The next BASIC command we'll introduce uses this feature to maximum advantage. First, another demonstration program for you to type in:

```
COLOR 3,0¶
AREA (100,150)¶
AREA (400,150)¶
AREA (250,20)¶
AREAFILL¶
COLOR 2,0¶
AREA (100,150)¶
AREA (400,150)¶
AREA (200,180)¶
AREAFILL¶
COLOR 1,0¶
AREA (250,20)¶
AREA (400,150)¶
AREA (450,100)¶
AREAFILL¶
```

This little program takes us back into the days of pyramids and pharaohs. As you can see, you can create a pretty convincing optical illusion with three differently colored triangles.

AREA
AREAFILL

Don't think that you can only create triangles with the AREA command. You can specify the vertices of a polygon with several AREA commands. The Amiga stores the specified points of your polygon until it encounters the AREAFILL command. Then the specified object is almost instantly drawn on the screen by the Blitter chip. However, there is a restriction: Not even AmigaBASIC can remember more than 20 points at one time. Any points that are defined after the 20th point are ignored. This shouldn't cramp your style, though, since a polygon with 20 vertices is complex enough already.

If you draw random areas, you can again get some interesting results. The next program is a good demonstration. (But don't forget to save your pyramid first).

```
Colors=4¶
SCREEN 1,640,200,Colors,2¶
WINDOW 1,"Areas",,15,1¶
Start:¶
COLOR ((2^Colors)-1)*RND,0¶
FOR x=1 TO 3+17*RND¶
AREA (617*RND,184*RND)¶
NEXT¶
AREAFILL¶
GOTO Start¶
```

The program's structure is pretty simple. First a random color is chosen from the available set of colors. The FOR...NEXT loop will "cycle" between 3 and 20 times. (The minimum value is three, because that's the minimum number of vertices needed to create a visible area... two points would only create a line). Once the polygon is drawn, the program jumps back to the label Start: and repeats the procedure.

Since all vertices are chosen randomly, you'll get some pretty strange, twisted—interesting—creations. But the AREA can also be determined with mathematical equations too:

```
Colors=4¶
SCREEN 1,640,200,Colors,2¶
WINDOW 1,"Areas",,15,1¶
FOR x=0 TO 617¶
co=co+1 : IF co>(2^Colors)-1 THEN co=0¶
COLOR co,0¶
y1=90+80*SIN(X/49)¶
y2=90+70*COS((617-x)/25)¶
x2=ABS(320-x)¶
AREA (x,y1)¶
AREA (x2,y2)¶
AREA (x,x/4)¶
AREA (320,90)¶
AREAFILL¶
NEXT x¶
```

122

AREA and AREAFILL are the last of the major graphics commands. In the following sections we will apply all the commands we've leaned about so far in a major program. This will give you a practical application apart from the mere learning experience. First we'll tackle programming with statistics, for those of you in business and economics. After that we'll have a treat for those of you with artistic tendencies. But thanks to the Amiga's graphic capabilities, these two areas don't have to be entirely exclusive.

2.7   The turning point: bar graph and pie chart utility

You've seen bar graphs and pie charts before. T.V. reporters represent election results in bar graphs. Your state government uses pie charts to show who's getting each slice of the annual budget. The national newspaper *USA Today* has taken bar graphs and pie charts to their extreme by using them to replace intelligent journalistic commentary altogether. Whatever the application, computer graphics are a popular method of creating graphics to represent statistical information. The Amiga was made to order for this.

Pie charts

As the name implies, *pie charts* is a circle divided into "pieces", like in a pie. The size of a piece (sector) corresponds to the percentage of the total. Whenever percentages (for instance, in the stock exchange), composition (the membership of political parties), or relationships (profit versus total sales) are used, pie charts can help us visualize the numbers and gain a better understanding of the information.

Bar charts

Another method of graphically depicting statistical data is the *bar chart*. The term has nothing to do with alcohol consumption, although a bar chart could be used to convey this. A bar chart is composed of vertical bars of different heights, with each bar representing an amount (value). Bar charts are helpful in visualizing the relationships between different values, or the development of a single value. You could display the dollar amount of sales in a month, the rising or dropping cost of living, price changes, or the progress of an investment with the help of bar charts.

These charts can be used for as many applications as your imagination can suggest.

The program

You could create bar charts and pie charts on your Amiga using the standard graphic commands, but typing in a series of commands each time you wish to make a chart takes too much time. To make the task easier, we've written a program that will accept your statistical values, then automatically create a bar chart or pie chart for you. The listing begins on the next page:

```
Graphics:¶
  IF Array(0)=0 THEN RETURN¶
  IF UCASE$(Array$(0))="B" THEN GOSUB BarGraph¶
  IF UCASE$(Array$(0))="P" THEN GOSUB PieChart¶
RETURN¶
¶
PieChart:¶
  Total=0¶
  FOR x=1 TO Array(0)¶
    Total=Total+Array(x)¶
  NEXT x¶
  Divi=Total/6.283 : Angle1=.0001 : BColor=1¶
  FOR x=1 TO Array(0)¶
    LColor=BColor¶
    IF LColor>(2^Colors)-1 THEN LColor=1¶
    BColor=LColor+1¶
    IF BColor>(2^Colors)-1 THEN BColor=1¶
    Angle2=Angle1+Array(x)/Divi¶
    CIRCLE (320,100),156,BColor¶
    CIRCLE (320,100),150,BColor,-Angle2,-Angle1¶
    PAINT (320,32),LColor,BColor¶
    CIRCLE (320,100),150,BColor¶
    PAINT (320,32),0,BColor¶
    CIRCLE (320,100),150,BColor,-Angle1,-Angle2¶
    MidAngle=(Angle1+Angle2)/2¶
    px=320+165*COS(MidAngle)¶
    py=100-80*SIN(MidAngle)¶
    Distance=0¶
    IF MidAngle>1.57 AND MidAngle<4.72 THEN Distance =
LEN(Array$(x))¶
    IF Distance>15 THEN Distance=15¶
    COLOR LColor,0¶
    LOCATE (py/8.75)+1,(px/7.9)+1-Distance¶
    PRINT Array$(x);¶
    Angle1=Angle2¶
  NEXT x¶
  CIRCLE (320,100),156,0¶
RETURN¶
BarGraph:¶
  Max=.0001 : LColor=0¶
  FOR x=1 TO Array(0)¶
    IF Array(x)>Max THEN Max=Array(x)¶
  NEXT x¶
  BarWidth=INT(600/(Array(0)))¶
  IF BarWidth>100 THEN BarWidth=100¶
  Factor=160/Max¶
  LOCATE 1,1 : PRINT Max;¶
  LOCATE 10,1 : PRINT Max/2;¶
  FOR x=0 TO 10¶
    LINE (1,170-x*16)-(5,170-x*16)¶
  NEXT x¶
  FOR x=1 TO Array(0)¶
    LColor=LColor+1 : IF LColor>(2^Colors)-1 THEN
LColor=1¶
    LINE (30+(x-1)*BarWidth,170-Array(x)*Factor)-
(25+x*BarWidth,170),LColor,bf¶
```

```
      COLOR LColor,0¶
      LOCATE 23,(5+(x-1)*(BarWidth/7.9))¶
      PRINT Array$(x);¶
   NEXT x¶
RETURN¶
```

You should immediately save this graphics program on diskette.

Well, hopefully this wasn't too much work for you. The explanation for this program follows:

Structured program code

The first thing you might have noticed about this listing is that it looks "different" from the previous ones. Most of its lines are indented a few spaces. What does this mean? The concept behind this is called *structured programming*. Typical BASIC programs tend to be very difficult to read, which is the result of unstructured, ineffective programming. Often even the program's author won't quite recognize a program's structure after it's been laid aside for a short time.

Since AmigaBASIC has the tools needed to structure programs (labels, subroutines, etc.), the program should be structured visually. If you want to figure out how a program works from its listing, the listing above will be much easier to understand than an normal unstructured program. We've delayed discussing this method until now, since this is the first time that you've typed an entire program all at once.

The rule for structured programming is simple: Wherever a new loop, a new subroutine or any new logical unit begins, the lines of that unit are indented one or two places to the right. Wherever the distinct unit ends, the lines are moved back one or two spaces to the left. That's it— that's the only rule.

If you'd like to structure it even a little more, you can insert blank lines between separate units of the program.

Calling the program

In its present state, the new program is useless. After all, it's only a subroutine—and we still don't have a routine that will call the utility up. For the first experiments, include the following little test program at the start of your bar graph and pie chart utility. Move the cursor to the beginning of the program, and type the following lines:

```
Setup:¶
  Colors=3¶
  SCREEN 4,640,200,Colors,2¶
  WINDOW 99,"Graphics",,8,4¶
  PALETTE 7,.8,.2,.1¶
  DIM Array(50),Array$(50)¶
TestEntry:¶
    WINDOW 1¶
    INPUT "B=bar, P=pie: ",Array$(0)¶
```

```
Entry:¶
     Array(0)=Array(0)+1¶
     PRINT "Value number "Array(0)":";¶
     INPUT Array(Array(0))¶
     PRINT "Title:";¶
     INPUT Array$(Array(0))¶
     IF Array$(Array(0))<>"" THEN Entry¶
Jump:¶
     Array(0)=Array(0)-1¶
     WINDOW 99¶
     GOSUB Graphics¶
     END¶
```

When you save this new version, select a different name from the original program so that you'll have both the test version and the subroutine on diskette. Do this in direct mode (SAVE "program") or from the Save As item in the **Project** pulldown menu.

A dry run

If you want to test out the program right away, decide whether you want to display your data as a bar graph or a pie chart. First click in the window then type a <b> for the bar graph or a <p> for the pie chart, then press <RETURN>. Then the program will ask you for the first value. Type any value, such as 850. After you press <RETURN> the program asks you for the value's title. This title will be printed under the bar or next to the pie segment. You could type "Amiga", for instance. In the last month 850 Amigas were sold. The next number could be 400, with the title "Atari ST". A third number can represent the total of all other computers, 1200, with the title "others". Then press <RETURN> twice without typing any more values. These three entries alone can create an informative picture of home computer sales. (However, we don't take any responsibility for the statistical validity of our sample numbers).

Using the program

The subroutine requires three types of data from the main program. First it requires the number of possible bitplanes. This number is contained in the variable Colors. The numbers that will be displayed in the picture are contained in the array Array(x). This array can have any number of elements, but so that you'll be able to read the graph, use no more than 50 values. The number of values is stored in the variable Array(0). If the value of this variable is 5, the data from Array(1), Array(2), up to Array(5) will be used. You may type any desired numbers for both types of graphics. This means that you don't have to make sure that your values add up to 100%—the subroutine will automatically convert your data into percentages.

127

The titles of your values are stored in the array `Array$(x)`. Each number in the array `Array(x)` has a corresponding title in the `Array$(X)` array. Therefore the title to `Array(1)` would be in `Array$(1)`, etc. The variable `Array$(0)` contains the character which identifies what type of chart your picture is. For bar graphs this will be a `b`. For pie charts it will be a `p`. If you type any other characters, the program quits without drawing a picture. You'll have to substitute your own numbers for this sample data in your program.

For clarification, here's a list of the variables and the values in our example:

Table 5: Transferred variables in the bar graph/pie chart utility

Name	Sample contents	Remarks
`Colors`	4	number of bitplanes for the Workbench screen: 2
`Array(0)`	3	number of elements in `Array` and `Array$`
`Array(1)`	850	1st number
`Array(2)`	400	2nd number
`Array(3)`	1200	3rd number
`Array$(0)`	p	p = pie chart b = bar graph
`Array$(1)`	Amiga	title of 1st number
`Array$(2)`	Atari	title of 2nd number
`Array$(3)`	others	title of 3rd number

The routine doesn't need any other value entries except for those listed above. If you were to write your own data management program, you might have to define the screen and the window in which you'd like the graphic to appear.

Before the subroutine is called, a chosen window is made the output window with the following command:

```
WINDOW window number
```

Then the subroutine is called up with this line:

```
GOSUB Graphics
```

This can be followed by separate program routines.

How it works

The previous section gives you all you'll need to operate the utility program. Now we'll discuss how the "nuts & bolts" of the program work. If things get a little too mathematical here or there, keep in mind that you don't have to understand the program completely to use it.

Initialization

First, in the `Setup:` routine, the test program sets the number of bitplanes, opens a 640 x 200 screen with the desired number of colors and opens a window with the number 99. We chose this high window number so that it wouldn't get in your way in case you decided to make some alterations.

Color

The `PALETTE` command specifies a color. You can change all colors if you'd like. Remember that `PALETTE` works only on the screen in which the actual output window is positioned. We redefined the color 7 because it is of the same value as the color 1 when you turn the Amiga on (white). If the pie chart has seven sectors and the sector with the color 1 was placed next to the sector with the color 7, you'd have white on white, which wouldn't be visible. Therefore we changed the color 7 to red. Next `Array` and `Array$` are dimensioned to 50 elements each.

Checking input

You type values in both arrays into the `TestEntry:` routine until a title receives a blank entry. This signifies that all values are full.

The `Jump:` routine gives the content of `Array(0)` which contains the number of data elements. Then window 99 is designated the output window and the graphics subroutine is called up. After returning from the subroutine, the program is ended.

Drawing graphics

The subroutine begins with the `Graphics:` routine, and first checks to see if any values are present. If none are present, it jumps back to the program start. The value of `Array$(0)` decides whether a bar graph or a pie chart is drawn. Thanks to the UCASE$ function it's irrelevant whether an upper or lowercase letter is typed. Then, within the subroutine, another subroutine is called to draw the specified chart type.

Making a pie

Let's look at the `PieChart:` subroutine. The first four lines add up all existing values to get the total sum. This total corresponds to 100%. Each value can then by divided by a constant to calculate the size of its arc. This number is assigned to the variable `Divi`. The number 6.283 is $2*\pi$—the largest possible angle. The starting value of `Angle1` is set slightly above 0, since the `CIRCLE` command cannot tell the difference between +0 and -0. If it were an angle of 0, the first sector wouldn't be connected with the center point correctly. The border color `BColor` is assigned the starting value of 1 (white).

129

Coloring in the chart

The following FOR...NEXT loop contains the drawing commands. It is executed until no more values are left. At the beginning of the loop the line color LColor takes on the old value of BColor. If one of the colors is above the allowed maximum, it is set back to 1. (We don't use the background color 0 for the chart). Then the border color is also raised by one. So what's the deal with these two colors? As you probably remember, PAINT accepts outlines of areas only in a specific color. Since we want to paint the sectors of our pie chart in different colors, we need a line color LColor and a border color BColor.

The trick used for painting the areas isn't mathematically elegant, but it's quite practical. Practicality sometimes takes precedence. The problem? PAINT always requires a point within the outlined area in order to paint that area. Since the sectors are often of very different sizes, this point isn't easy to calculate. The solution: we use two concentric circles to construct the pie chart, the outer circle being slightly larger (radius: 156) than the smaller (radius:150). The border color protects those parts of the circle that are already finished. Then the area between the two circles is colored with PAINT and in the process the color also spills into the rest of the circle. This is why we always use a border color that is one number above the paint color. At the end of the routine the outer circle is erased. If you watch very closely you'll be able to recognize this process while the chart is being drawn.

Computing all the angles

Now let's see how the program executed our theoretical concept. The fifth line in the loop calculates the new value of Angle2, the larger of the two border angles. Its new value is the starting angle plus the size of the arc allotted to the specified value. First the outer circle is drawn in the present border color. Then the outline that will protect the previously-drawn sectors is drawn. The PAINT command in the next line paints in the color LColor and recognizes the outlines in the color BColor as borders. Its starting point is exactly in the free area between the concentric circles. After the areas are painted, the entire inner circle is outlined in the border color and the area between the circles is erased with the background color 0. Lastly, the sectors are separated with the border color.

Adding text

The remaining commands outside the loop have mainly one purpose: print the appropriate titles next to the corresponding sectors. We had to come up with another trick for this, too. First we calculate the angle that exactly bisects each sector. This angle is called Midangle. To be honest, this is where it starts getting tricky. How can you calculate a point from just a radius and an angle? After all, we need to know the location of this point to know where to place the titles. Figure 7 might help you visualize this problem:

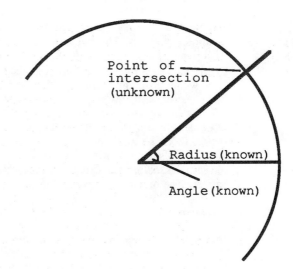

**Figure 7:
The angle
that
intercepts
the arc—
finding the
intersection**

Well, Hannes Ruegheimer finally came up with the answer after paging
through heaps of formulas that he had kept from his college exams.
There he found a ingenious equation under the heading *"Geometric and
trigonometric functions"*:

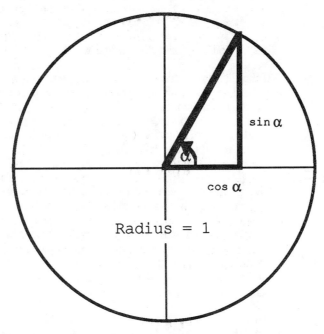

**Figure 8:
Sine and
cosine in the
circle**

131

SIN and COS can be used for straight calculations, not just pretty computer graphics! The radius multiplied by the cosine of the angle will give us the X coordinate of our point, while the radius multiplied by the sine of the angle will give us the Y coordinate. Simple, huh? Now we have to convert the coordinates into actual screen coordinates (the center is (320,100)), and we'll have the variables px and py.

Let's get to the next problem. If the text is positioned to the right of a sector, it can be any length. At the worst it'll be cut off by the right edge of the screen. However, a title that's to the left of its sector will run into the sector after only a few characters, which you don't want to happen. The line that starts with the:

```
distance=0¶
```

LEN

command gives the title the room it needs. When the angle is between 1.57 (1/2 * π) and 4.72 (1 1/2 * π), the title is displayed to the left of the pie chart. In this case the length of the string is determined and the text is moved over by that length. The last letter is displayed to the immediate left of the circle. Here's another new AmigaBASIC command: LEN(a$). This command counts the number of characters contained in a string.

```
LEN("hello")¶
```

would be 5, and

```
LEN("Antidisestablishmentarianism")¶
```

is 28. (You can count them if you want).

If the distance of the title's first character from the circle is more than 15, it'll have to be restricted to 15. Unfortunately there's no more room on the screen than that.

Finally, the coordinates in px and py (which are presently in pixels) are converted to rows and columns for the LOCATE command. Then the text is printed on the screen.

This program is set up to run at 80 characters per line. Please select only this value in Preferences.

For the next execution of the loop the starting angle (Angle1) is assigned the value of the end angle (Angle2). Then the whole procedure is repeated for the next sector. As we mentioned, the outer circle is erased once all sectors are drawn. Then the subroutine jumps back to the line from which it was called.

Hopefully you don't have a bad headache by now. Don't worry if you didn't catch every math angle in this section—it won't really matter.

The rest of the equations...

The `BarGraph:` subroutine isn't as hard to understand. Its first four lines look for the largest values that were typed in. This value is then stored in the variable `Max`. The lowest possible value for `Max` is 0.0001, since two lines down we'll have to divide 600 by `Max`, and division by zero is illegal. Try this:

```
? 1/0¶
```

and you'll see that the Amiga will give you a `Division by zero` error.

The variable `BarWidth` contains the width of the bars. This value depends on the total number of bars that will be displayed. However, `BarWidth` shouldn't be any larger than 100 pixels. After all, we're drawing a bar graph—a bar that fills the whole screen isn't really a bar graph anymore, but more like the Empire State Building.

The variable `Factor` contains the number by which each value has to be multiplied to get the correct height. The maximum is 160 pixels. All other values should be less than 160.

Scaling the bar chart

We'll draw a scale for the height of the bars at the left border of the screen. The following five lines take care of this. The maximum value and the halfway mark are printed along with 11 increment marks. The last six lines of the subroutine contain the loop that draws the individual bars. Like its counterpart in the pie chart program, the loop is executed until all values have been displayed. The `LINE` command is used to actually construct the bars on the screen. Each bar changes color by one color number within the display limits. Again, the background color is omitted.

Below the bars we'll print the text titles with the `LOCATE` and `PRINT` commands. The position of the titles is dependent on the width of the bars. The whole process is repeated for each bar, and then the program jumps back to the beginning with `RETURN`.

Congratulations! You've finally made it through this mathematical theory section. Take some time to experiment with your new utility program. You won't believe the range of the statistics you can display.

In the course of this book we'll improve the input routine most of all—for example, so that you can save values on diskette and keep track of your finances over a length of time. If you're not interested in economics and statistics, don't despair. In the next section we'll show you a program that will bring out the true *artist* in you. After all, what better canvas than your Amiga?

2.8   Illusion or reality: the mouse and menus in BASIC

How do you think your own BASIC programs differ from the professional software like Graphicraft™ or Textcraft™? Sure, these two packages are faster and more powerful. However, the most distinguishing feature is that professional programs are almost entirely mouse driven. The entire program is controlled with the pointer and the pulldown menus. You'll probably say, "Well, but those guys are professionals..." Fine. From here on out, we'll uncover some more AmigaBASIC programming secrets and promote you to a professional standing in the process. In fact, it isn't difficult to write a BASIC program that looks very professional.

Try typing in the following lines, for instance:

```
MENU 1,0,1,"Selection"¶
FOR x=1 TO 9¶
      MENU 1,x,1,"Option "+CHR$(48+x)¶
NEXT x¶
FOR x=2 TO 4¶
      MENU x,0,0,""¶
NEXT x¶
ON MENU GOSUB Selection¶
MENU ON
Delay:¶
  GOTO Delay¶
Selection:¶
  LOCATE 10,20¶
  PRINT "You chose option";MENU(1);¶
  RETURN¶
```

MENU

If you try the program, you'll probably think that it doesn't even do anything. However, if you press the menu key of the mouse you'll see that instead of the usual menu titles, there's only one new title in the menu bar. Select this menu and take a look at its contents. As an example there are 9 menu items. Select one of them and you'll see that the corresponding number is displayed on the screen.

**MENU
RESET**

This program isn't very practical, but it's an indication of how easy it is to program menus in BASIC, and how professional the results can be. We don't have a pulldown item to stop the program, and the Run menu with its Stop item is not available at the moment. Therefore, press the <CTRL><C> combination. This key combination will let you stop almost any BASIC program dead in its tracks. As you'll notice, the usual pulldowns won't return to the screen even after the program has been stopped. Since we need them to program, there has to be some way of getting them back. The following BASIC command will do this:

```
menu reset¶
```

Type this command in the **BASIC** window. The pulldown menus will be available once more. Let's take a closer look at the individual commands and their functions.

MENU requires three numerical values and the name to be assigned to the menu. The command at the beginning of our sample program is:

```
MENU 1,0,1,"Selection"¶
```

Specifying menus

The first parameter after the MENU command specifies the number of the menu. At the normal setting, the **Project** menu is number 1, the **Edit** menu is number 2, the **Run** menu is number 3 and the **Windows** menu is number 4. A maximum number of 10 pulldown menus can be defined in the **BASIC** window.

The second parameter determines the item number in the menu. Number 0 is the title of the menu. Numbers 1 through 19 are items in the menu.

The third parameter can be one of the following numbers:

- 0 *disables* (turns off) the specified menu item. The item will not be available and will be displayed in difficult-to-read lettering. This is also known as a *ghost menu item*. If the second number is a 0, the entire menu will be disabled.

- 1 has the opposite effect of 0: it enables the menu item/menu. The specified menu item or the entire menu is enabled and available for use.

- 2 has the same effect as a 1, except for one difference: the selected menu item is marked with a checkmark. This indicates to the user of the program if this menu item is currently active.

Any string expression can be used for the title of a menu item: text within quotation marks, or a string variable containing text. If you omit this string parameter, the MENU command changes the parameters of an existing pulldown item (but usually you'll be changing the third number). The CHR$ command also lets you specify single characters or add to text. (If you're wondering why we added the value x to the number 48, take a look at the ASCII table under the CHR$ command in **Appendix B**).

WARNING:

Type the following command line, but do <u>not</u> test out the resulting pulldown! If no items are defined for the menu and the menu selected, it might cause AmigaBASIC to crash. If you haven't saved your program before this time, it would be lost with the crash.

```
menu 1,0,1,"Test"¶
```

This line defines pulldown menu number 1 with the name Test. As we said above, <u>don't</u> try the menu right now—you can see it after you type in the next command. Type the next command right now. Leave two spaces before the word Number (you'll see why in just a moment).

```
menu 1,1,1," Number 1"¶
```

Now you can take a look at the pulldown menu without risk. The second command line created an item in the menu. However, AmigaBASIC can't do much with this item in direct mode, since there isn't any supporting program.

To disable menu number 1 entirely, type:

```
menu 1,0,0¶
```

To reverse this command, use:

```
menu 1,0,1¶
```

The next command marks the first item with a check mark:

```
menu 1,1,2¶
```

As you can see in our example, if you define fewer than four menus, the predefined menus must be erased. The following line performs this:

```
for x=1 to 4 : menu x,0,0,"" : next x¶
```

This line erases all existing pulldown menus from the screen. This could be quite useful in some programs. However, you already know how to get them back:

```
menu reset¶
```

Event trapping

The MENU command arranges all menus just the way you want them. Up to now we haven't talked about the monitoring and evaluation of the menus. The method used to monitor the menus is one of AmigaBASIC's most fascinating capabilities. If you take a closer look at our example (or follow it with TRACE) you'll see that the main program actually consists of only the Delay loop. This loop continually jumps back to itself.

This works by the *event trapping* principle. If a certain event for which AmigaBASIC has been waiting occurs, the running program is immediately interrupted and a subroutine is called. Once the subroutine has been executed, AmigaBASIC will continue program execution where it was first interrupted. This method of programming is not only practical, but very effective as well. You can write various subroutines that deal with collision of graphic objects, error messages, menu and mouse control or timers (timed intervals), while the main program is doing something completely different.

The following command tells AmigaBASIC which subroutine to jump to when an item is selected:

ON MENU GOSUB...¶

This command lets you specify a line number or a label. Each variation of event trapping has its own safety device, or *trigger*, that activates the function. For the menu event trapping this trigger is:

MENU ON¶

MENU ON,
MENU OFF,
MENU STOP

If you want to interrupt the menu trapping, you can use the MENU STOP command. To disable it completely, use the MENU OFF command. The difference between these two commands is in the "recognition" of the event: with MENU STOP the Amiga still registers any menu selection, but does not react to it. It will wait until event trapping is activated again. Once event trapping is reactivated, it will still register the selections that were made while the event trapping was inactive. However, MENU OFF instructs the Amiga to stop trapping events completely. No selections made during this time are registered when the event trapping is turned back on.

These principles of ON, OFF and STOP are the same for all other event trappings. We'll refer back to them several times in the course of this book. Then you'll be able to tell the difference more clearly from some direct examples of OFF and STOP.

ON MENU
GOSUB

The last question that we need to answer is, "What can I make the subroutine do that I called with ON MENU GOSUB?" As we said, each time a user selects a menu item, the item will call up its corresponding subroutine. However, first the subroutine needs to find out which item was actually selected. For this we have two new functions: MENU(0) and MENU(1).

MENU(0)
MENU(1)

The MENU(0) command determines the number of the selected pulldown menu, which corresponds to the first value in the MENU command. The MENU(1) command determines the number of the selected item within the selected pulldown menu. This value corresponds to the second parameter of the MENU command.

The following demonstration routine will expand our sample program by one menu item. Type this line exactly between the two FOR...NEXT loops in the first part of the original menu program:

```
menu 1,10,1,"Quit"¶
```

Revise the Selection: subroutine so that it matches this:

```
Selection:¶
  IF MENU(1)=10 THEN MENU RESET : END¶
  LOCATE 10,20¶
  PRINT "You chose option";MENU(1)¶
  RETURN¶
```

It works like this:

First the Selection: subroutine checks to see if you chose item number 10. Number 10 represents Quit. If this item was selected, the MENU RESET command is used to recall the default menus and the program is ended with the END command. In all other respects, the program will perform the same as before.

Since our example has only one pulldown menu, we don't have to worry about the number of the menus or the MENU(0) value. In larger programs with more than one pulldown menu, you'll have to determine the number of the menus with MENU(0) before you can determine the individual items with the MENU(1) command.

MOUSE

Is everything clear so far? If you still want more applicable demonstrations, it won't be long until we'll be able to show you all these functions in an expanded, more powerful BASIC utility program. But first we need one more basic concept: the mouse input and programming. To demonstrate this, we'll present you with possibly the shortest paint program ever written for the Amiga:

```
ON MOUSE GOSUB Draw¶
MOUSE ON¶
Delay:¶
GOTO Delay¶
Draw:¶
      WHILE MOUSE(0)<>0¶
              PSET (MOUSE(1),MOUSE(2))¶
      WEND¶
RETURN¶
```

Considering how short it is, the program is quite impressive, don't you think? As you can see, error trapping for the mouse is essentially the same as error trapping for menus. The command:

```
ON MOUSE GOSUB...¶
```

specifies the subroutine that responds to the mouse.

MOUSE ON¶

This command activates the entire process. The infinite loop represents a running program.

**WHILE...
WEND**

Only the Draw: routine contains something really new and worth explaining: the WHILE...WEND command. These two commands are another way to program loops. This type of loop is used to repeat an operation while a specified condition is met. A simple loop that waits for any input would look like this:

WHILE INKEY$="" : WEND¶

You can try this example in the **BASIC** window. The WHILE...WEND loop is often more practical and more elegant than FOR...NEXT or IF...THEN, even though the three are fairly interchangeable. The condition for which the WHILE...WEND loop tests in our demonstration program is:

MOUSE(0)<>0¶

You probably noticed that you were able to draw only when you pressed the left mouse button. The MOUSE(0) function supplies information about the status of the mouse button. If the button is not depressed, its value will be 0. If it is pressed, there are several possibilities, which we'll discuss later. Should we come across any particular variables, we'll explain them at that time. (If you want to know everything right away, you can look under MOUSE(x) in the command descriptions of the **Appendix B**). In addition to MOUSE(0), MOUSE(1) and MOUSE(2) are used in our example. These two are actually more simple than MOUSE(0):

MOUSE(1) contains the mouse's X coordinate.

MOUSE(2) contains the mouse's Y coordinate.

The two values are in pixels, and AmigaBASIC automatically counts them in the corresponding screen. This is what makes drawing with the mouse so simple.

What would be the best way to fully demonstrate all the capabilities of the mouse and the pulldown menus, and at the same time create a practical program that's interesting to use? Maybe you've already guessed the kind of program our new program utility will be. In the next section we'll write our own painting program—one that utilizes almost all of AmigaBASIC's commands, is easy to use, and can produce stunning graphics. It even has a few goodies...read on.

2.9   The AmigaBASIC paint program

This section introduces you to an AmigaBASIC utility that produces top-notch graphics and drawings on your Amiga. A lot of work went into developing this program. We're not saying this because we lack modesty, but only to explain the program's great size. You'll want plenty of time to tackle the biggest project in this book yet (you might want to go get some snacks and something to drink before you start typing). Are you ready? Say so long to your family and friends, close the door and let's get started. We think the results and the learning experience will be well worth the effort.

Of course, this program is contained on the Abacus optional program diskette—complete, error-free and ready to run. If you dislike typing, seriously consider purchasing the program diskette from your dealer or directly from Abacus. (Suggested retail price is $14.95).

Compatible programs

If you've been typing in all the previous examples in this book, you'll already have two major utility programs: The video title generator to create titles for video segments out of text and objects, and the bar graph and pie chart utility to display statistical data in graphic form. With these examples we are trying to accomplish one main goal: To give you programs that you will enjoy as much as possible, but programs that have real use other than for the learning process. There's one important characteristic that these programs should have in common, particularly for graphics: they should be *compatible*. This means that you could produce a picture with the paint program and later use that picture as a background in the video title program. After, all graphics from "real" graphic programs like Graphicraft™ or DeluxePaint™ should be readable and usable in AmigaBASIC (which they are).

Our paint program is an important link in this compatibility chain. We think it's a sophisticated, powerful utility program, with many features found in commercial graphic programs. Of course, a program this versatile will not be as short as our previous demonstration programs. This means that the next two sections contain many pages of listings that have to be entered. We'll be up front about it: it's going to take you a while to enter it all. Take your time. It's fine if want to enter the program in "modules," and then stick the book back on the shelf for a while. But don't forget to save the program each time you stop!

When you're finished, we'll explain the program thoroughly and point out special commands, items and tricks.

Copy the program structure as much as possible. The final program
will be more clear this way, and you'll be able to find and correct
mistakes much faster.

```
Setup:¶
  Colors=5 : MaxColors=2^Colors-1¶
  DIM Pointer(4,1),AltColor(4),Colors%(31,2)¶
  DIM FillPattern%(7),AllPatterns%(8,7),Solid%(1)¶
  DrawType=1 : DrawColor=1 : FillColor=2 : Mode=1¶
¶
  Solid%(0)=&HFFFF : Solid%(1)=&HFFFF¶
  FOR x=0 TO 7¶
    FillPattern%(x)=&HFFFF¶
    AllPatterns%(0,x)=&HFFFF¶
  NEXT x¶
  FOR x=1 TO 8¶
    FOR y=0 TO 7¶
      READ AllPatterns%(x,y)¶
    NEXT y¶
  NEXT x¶
¶
  DATA 24672,1542,24672,1542,24672,1542,24672,1542¶
  DATA -13108,13107,-13108,13107,-13108,13107,
-13108,13107¶
  DATA 26214,13107,-26215,-13108,26214,13107,-26215,
-13108¶
  DATA -13108,-26215,13107,26214,-13108,
-26215,13107,26214¶
  DATA -258,-258,-258,0,-4113,-4113,-4113,0¶
  DATA -8185,-8197,-18019,-20491,-20467,-8197,-8185,-1¶
  DATA 0,0,1632,4080,4080,2016,384,0¶
  DATA 960,1984,3520,6592,16320,25024,-3104,0¶
¶
  SCREEN 1,320,200,Colors,1¶
  WINDOW 2,"AmigaBASIC Draw Program",,16,1¶
  WINDOW CLOSE 3¶
  WINDOW CLOSE 4¶
  WINDOW 2¶
```

The program begins with a Setup: routine. Here all variables are set
to their starting values, the arrays are filled and the screens and windows
used for output are activated.

The variable Colors again contains the number of active bit-planes.
The values 2 (8 colors), 4 (16 colors) or 5 (32 colors) are available.
Normally you'll be working with 32 colors, since our program operates
in low resolution. Therefore, you shouldn't have any memory problems
with your 512K Amiga 1000 or standard Amiga 500 or 2000 models.

Integer arrays

You probably noticed in the `Colors$` array the unusual percentage symbol following the array's name. AmigaBASIC offers different types of variables. You already know two of these: the normal numerical variables (a, b, c, hello...) and the *string variables* (a$, b$, c$, hello$). String variables are identified by the dollar signs following their names. The percentage symbol (%) works similarly. It identifies *integer variables*. You already know about the BASIC functions `INT` and `CINT`. Therefore you probably know that integers are always whole numbers—they never have any digits to the right of the decimal point.

It's possible to declare certain variables as integer variables before they are used. Since these numbers will never have digits to the right of the decimal point, they use less memory. This is because of the method by which the Amiga manages numbers in RAM. Integers can only assume values between -32768 and 32767. We'll take a closer look at this in Intermission 3. Also, we'll be introducing other types of variables in the next section of the book.

Try typing this line in the **BASIC** window:

```
a=7/3 : a%=7/3 : ? a,a%¶
```

You'll see that the variable a% has no numbers to the right of the decimal point. Since the paint program contains numbers that can only be whole numbers, we use integer arrays for them. The `Colors%` array is dimensioned as (31,2), so it can contain 32 x 3 elements. Remember multidimensional arrays? It's easiest to visualize these arrays as tables where each individual position represents a particular element of the array. We can use up to 32 colors in the program, where three values have to be specified for each color (R, G and B).

Fill patterns

We also define the fill pattern in the `Setup:` routine. Fill patterns in AmigaBASIC will be discussed in detail in the next section. For now you only have to know one thing: the fill pattern process requires integer arrays in which the patterns are stored. In our program we use the arrays `FillPattern%`, `AllPatterns%` and `Solid%` for this purpose. The `FillPattern%` array contains the structure of the actual pattern, while `AllPatterns%` contains (as the name suggests) all available patterns. Our paint program offers a choice of nine patterns to fill areas. The definitions of all nine patterns are in the `AllPatterns%` array. `Solid%` contains a special pattern that produces solid, single-colored areas. We'll need this from time to time.

Hexadecimal numbers

These arrays are filled with their default values in the `Setup:` routine. But there's something special about the commands used in this routine: look at the format for numbers. What's the meaning of that weird looking `&HFFFF`? This is a *hexadecimal value*. This type of number is especially useful for programmers. (You'll find further explanations of hexadecimal numbers in **Intermission 3**). AmigaBASIC can work with hexadecimal numbers as well as regular decimal values.

The value &HFFFF performs a pattern definition in which all points are turned off. This results in a solid, single-colored area. This pattern is then assigned to the Solid% and FillPattern% arrays, as well as the first of the nine pattern choices. Before we start the program, you should chose from a selection of patterns. We've prepared nine of them for you.

READ
DATA

The required values are read in with DATA and READ. But "read in" with what? The commands DATA and READ are a team that lets you enter values in a program, then reads them in and uses them in the program. Values can be numbers or words or any desired combination of characters. The data is written in a line that begins with the DATA statement. The statement is followed by the data, separated by commas. The READ command then reads the data into the variables. The DATA and READ combination is used only within a program listing, and cannot be entered in direct mode.

The following five lines are <u>not</u> part of the paint program. If you'd like to try the example, be sure to save your paint program in its present form before typing these lines in:

```
READ a$,b$,c$,d¶
PRINT "I bought an ";a$¶
PRINT "It's a great ";b$;" that's a lot of ";c$;"."¶
PRINT "With it you can do ";d;" things."¶
DATA Amiga,computer,fun,1000¶
```

Do you see how it works? The values in the DATA line are assigned to the corresponding variables in the READ line. In a program, the reading always begins in the first DATA line, regardless of where it is located. Then the values are read consecutively. Be careful that the variable types and the values correspond. If you tried to read a character into a numerical variable, you'd get a Type mismatch error message. If all data have been read, and another READ command is encountered, the Amiga would display an "Out of DATA" error message.

The first block of DATA statements contain the structure of the nine patterns. These values are read into the AllPatterns% array.

Next we define the output screen and output window.

Low-res...
and why

As mentioned before, this paint program runs in low resolution (320 x 200 pixels), mostly because we want our graphics to be compatible with commercial programs like Graphicraft™. Almost all commercial paint programs use low resolution, since it makes 32 colors available. If you've seen sample graphics on the Amiga, you'll probably agree that the variety of color makes up for the slightly rougher resolution. The next two program lines deactivate windows 3 and 4. In case they are already displayed on the screen (which could happen if the program is interrupted and then restarted).

143

Now go to the end of the program code you've typed so far, and enter the next part of the paint program:

```
FOR x=0 TO 31¶
    READ r,g,b¶
    PALETTE x,r/16,g/16,b/16¶
    Colors%(x,0)=r : Colors%(x,1)=g : Colors%(x,2)=b¶
    NEXT x¶
¶
    DATA 0,0,3, 15,15,15, 0,3,12, 15,0,0¶
    DATA 0,14,15, 15,0,15, 3,10,1, 15,14,0¶
    DATA 15,8,0, 10,0,14 ,8,5,0, 11,8,3¶
    DATA 2,11,0, 15,10,15, 0,0,9, 7,15,0¶
    DATA 14,12,0, 15,2,3, 0,0,0, 15,11,10¶
    DATA 0,6,8, 3,3,3, 4,4,4, 5,5,5¶
    DATA 6,6,6, 7,7,7, 8,8,8, 9,9,9¶
    DATA 11,11,11, 13,13,13, 0,0,15, 12,15,12 ¶
```

In this section the array Colors% is assigned its values. Throughout the program, Colors% will contain the R, G and B content of the available colors as numbers ranging from 0 to 15. At first, however, a problem arises: you might remember from the video title program that there is no AmigaBASIC command to read the actual values of the color registers. The color registers can be changed with PALETTE, but we know of no way to find out their values with BASIC.

If you changed the colors in the program for the first time, the default setting would change to black (R=0, G=0, B=0). This would make the program difficult to use—black drawings can be very hard to see on a black background. So we've put the RGB values for 32 colors in the Colors% array. They'll remain there until they are changed when the program is running.

Go to the end of your program listing and type in the next section:

```
Pulldown:¶
    MENU 3,0,0,""¶
    MENU 4,0,0,""¶
    MENU 1,0,1,"Program"¶
    MENU 1,1,1,"Draw            "¶
    MENU 1,2,1,"Color Palette"¶
    MENU 1,3,1,"Fill Pattern "¶
    MENU 1,4,1,"Load Screen   "¶
    MENU 1,5,1,"Save Screen   "¶
    MENU 1,6,1,"Clear Screen "¶
    MENU 1,7,1,"End           "¶
    MENU 2,0,1,"Drawing tools"¶
    MENU 2,1,2,"  Draw freehand  "¶
    MENU 2,2,1,"  Draw thick     "¶
    MENU 2,3,1,"  Points         "¶
    MENU 2,4,1,"  Spray          "¶
    MENU 2,5,1,"  Lines          "¶
    MENU 2,6,1,"  Frame          "¶
    MENU 2,7,1,"  Box            "¶
```

```
MENU 2,8,1,"  Connected lines"¶
MENU 2,9,1,"  Oval          "¶
MENU 2,10,1,"  Fill          "¶
MENU 2,11,1,"  Eraser        "¶
MENU 2,12,1,"  Text          "
```

Here we define the pulldown menus. First the default menus 3 and 4 are erased, since we only need two menus in our program. Menu 1 contains the items that control the program: you can select the individual items for color, screen and fill pattern control, as well as handling your files. Menu 2 contains the individual tools that are used in the drawing process.

The currently active tool is indicated with a checkmark to the left of its item name. Be absolutely certain you leave two blank spaces when you're entering the menu item names, so that the checkmark will fit on the line without overlapping the item name.

Now that we've taken care of all the preliminaries, we're ready to type the actual drawing program, MainLoop:

```
MainLoop:¶
  ON MENU GOSUB MenuSelect¶
  ON MOUSE GOSUB EvalMouse¶
  MENU ON¶
  MOUSE ON¶
¶
  WHILE -1¶
  WEND¶
```

Using event trapping

This routine activates event trapping for the menus and mouse control, and assigns the proper subprograms. Then you'll see a WHILE...WEND loop. This is not a typo. The number -1 after the WHILE represents a true condition in AmigaBASIC. (We'll take a closer look at this in the next **Intermission**). This configuration results in an infinite loop. As long as you don't use the mouse (select a menu or click a mouse button), the program will simply run in this loop. All functions in our drawing program are controlled by event trapping. If you have programmed BASIC on another computer before, this method might seem strange to you. Nevertheless, it makes possible some very flexible and powerful programs. Event trapping and "normal" programming methods can be used in conjunction with one another. How you structure a program depends on its requirements.

The main program is followed by the subprograms needed for the menu control:

```
MenuSelect:¶
  Men=MENU(0)¶
  MenChoice=MENU(1)¶
  ON Men GOTO Project,DrawTools¶
¶
EvalMouse:¶
  IF Mode=1 THEN ON DrawType GOSUB
DrawThin,DrawThick,Points,Spray,DrawLines,Frame,Box,Conne
ctedLines,Oval,Fill,Eraser,Text¶
  IF Mode=2 THEN GOSUB ColorPalette : IF EndOK=1 THEN
GOSUB ColorDone¶
  IF Mode=3 THEN GOSUB DefinePattern : IF EndOK=2 THEN
GOSUB PatternDone¶
  IF Mode=4 THEN GOSUB RGBDef : IF EndOK=3 THEN Mode=2 :
GOSUB SelectColor¶
RETURN¶
¶
Project:¶
  IF MenChoice=1 THEN GOSUB ColorDone : GOSUB
PatternDone¶
  IF MenChoice=2 THEN GOSUB PatternDone : MENU 2,0,0 :
Mode=2 : GOSUB SelectColor¶
  IF MenChoice=3 THEN GOSUB ColorDone : MENU 2,0,0 :
Mode=3 : GOSUB PatternEditor¶
  IF MenChoice=4 THEN GOSUB ColorDone : GOSUB PatternDone
: GOSUB DrawLoad¶
  IF MenChoice=5 THEN GOSUB ColorDone : GOSUB PatternDone
: GOSUB DrawSave¶
  IF MenChoice=6 AND Mode=1 THEN OK=0 :GOSUB Query : IF
OK=1 THEN Adef=0 : AREAFILL: CLS¶
  IF MenChoice=7 THEN GOSUB ColorDone : GOSUB PatternDone
: OK=0 : GOSUB Query : IF OK=1 THEN EndIt ¶
RETURN¶
¶
DrawTools:¶
  MENU 2,DrawType,1¶
  DrawType = MENU (1)¶
  MENU 2,DrawType,2¶
RETURN¶
```

ON...GOTO
MenuSelect: determines the selected menu item. The variable men contains the menu number, and the variable menupoint contains the selected menu item. Depending on which menu was selected, the program jumps to either Project: or DrawTools:. Here we encounter a new variation of the GOTO command. The ON...GOTO command jumps to a specific label or line number depending on the value of a variable.

Don't enter the following line—it's not part of the paint program. We'd just like to show you how this command operates:

```
ON x GOTO cocktail,appetizer,soup,maincourse,dessert¶
```

If x has a value of 1, the program will jump to the routine labeled cocktail:. If x = 2, appetizer: is called up. If x = 3 it'll be the soup:. x = 4 brings us to the maincourse: and x = 5 completes the meal with dessert:. If x is less than 1 or greater than 6, the program will simply skip the ON...GOTO command and continue with the next line.

ON...GOSUB

The EvalMouse: routine is responsible for the control and evaluation of the mouse. At the beginning of the EvalMouse: routine you'll find a relatively long ON...GOSUB command. This command works the same way as the ON...GOTO command. The only difference is that at the next RETURN statement the program will return to the line were the ON...GOSUB was given.

If you click the left mouse button when the program is running, the program will jump to this label first. Clicking the mouse is a common action, so what the click will accomplish depends on which mode the program is in. The variable Mode determines this. The various subprograms supply it with the correct values. If Mode has a value of 1, the program will be in drawing mode. This mode is selected with the first item in the first pulldown menu.

The variable DrawType contains the active drawing type. When you select an item in the second pulldown menu, you specify a particular drawing action. There's a separate subprogram for each different type of drawing. The program jumps to this subprogram as soon as the left mouse button is clicked, and then that particular subprogram is executed. If Mode has a value of 2, the color selection routine is active. In this case, control of the program is handed over to the ColorControl: subprogram. The variable EndOK tells us whether the color adjustments are complete (indicated by clicking the OK gadget). If EndOK is 1, AmigaBASIC executes the ColorDone: subprogram.

If Mode has a value of 3, the procedure is the same, except that this routine is responsible for the definition of the fill patterns. The subprogram DefinePattern: will be called up. If the pattern definition is ended, EndOK must have a value of 2.

Mode 4 isn't much different from the other three. It's a special function of the color subprogram. A color isn't simply selected—the R, G and B components of a color are selected with slide controllers with the routine RGBDef:. There's a separate mode to distinguish between color definition (the adjustment of colors with the RGB controllers) and the selection of colors (picking the colors that will be used for drawing). Once this mode is ended when EndOK=3, the program will return to mode 2 (the color selection).

Since EvalMouse: is a subprogram, it must be ended with a RETURN statement. This will return the program to the place where the subprogram was called up.

The `Project:` routine is responsible for the operation of the first pulldown menu. The variable `MenuChoice` contains the menu selection that was captured by the `MenuSelect:` routine. Depending on the value of `MenuChoice`, the individual subprograms are now called up and carry out the specified functions. Menu item 1 is used to return the drawing mode from the color or pattern subprogram. In the beginning of the program, the drawing mode is automatically active (remember `Mode=1` in `Setup:?`). So, for the first menu item, the program needs to call up only those parts that end the color and pattern subprograms (namely the `ColorDone:` and `PatternDone:` routines).

Menu item 2 calls the color selection subprogram up. In case the pattern definition program is already running, it is first switched off through a `GOSUB PatternDone` command. The second pulldown that offers the selection of drawing types should be inaccessible while the color program is running. Thus, `MENU 2,0,0`. The variable `Mode` is assigned the number 2, and the program jumps to the `SelectColor:` subprogram.

The third menu item activates the pattern editor. In this subprogram it is possible to define fill patterns. First the color program is turned off, in case it was still running, the drawing tool items are deactivated again and the value 3 is assigned to `Mode`. After these preparations we continue with the `PatternEditor:` routine.

Menu items 4 and 5 are not available at this point. They'll allow you to save and load graphics from diskette. We'll wait until the next chapter to add this part of the program. You'll find detailed information about peripherals and data management in that chapter.

Menu item 6 is allowed only in mode 1. It erases the present picture from memory. Prior to erasing the picture, the `Query:` routine displays a requester that asks you if you're sure you want to erase the graphic. When you click the OK gadget, the erasing begins. The `Adef=0` and `AREAFILL` commands remove any area that might be in construction. (This is the only type of drawing that isn't drawn immediately, but constructed step by step). This process has to be stopped before the screen can be cleared. Then the screen is finally cleared with `CLS`.

The seventh and last menu item exits the paint program. The color and pattern definitions are switched off first, and a requester similar to the one for the erase item is displayed. If it is confirmed, the program jumps to the `EndIt:` label, where the program is finally exited.

The `Project:` subprogram ends with a RETURN statement.

`DrawTools:` takes care of the second menu. The previous menu item loses its check mark, the variable `DrawType` is updated and finally the new menu item receives a check mark. That's it for `DrawingType:`.

Now to the subprograms that produce the individual drawing modes. We'll start with the first version of freehand drawing, the thin pen:

```
DrawThin:¶
  Test= MOUSE(0) : x=MOUSE(1) : y=MOUSE(2)¶
  WHILE MOUSE(0)<>0¶
    LINE (x,y)-(MOUSE(1),MOUSE(2)),DrawColor ¶
    x=MOUSE(1) : y=MOUSE(2)¶
  WEND¶
RETURN¶
```

Drawing a thin line

You might be wondering why we assigned the value of MOUSE(0) to the variable Test, which isn't even used. There's a pretty good reason for this—as you might remember, you can find out if the left mouse button was pressed or is being pressed with MOUSE(0). MOUSE(1) gives you the X-coordinate of the pointer, and MOUSE(2) gives you the Y-coordinate of the pointer. Technically, MOUSE(1) and MOUSE(2) give you the X- and Y-coordinates of the point at which MOUSE(0) was last called. So, to get the most recent point, we need to call MOUSE(0) just before we read the coordinate values. The WHILE...WEND loop connects the last point drawn with the position of the pointer as long as the left mouse button remains pressed. As a result, a line is drawn freehand with the mouse.

The following subprogram for drawing freehand with the thick line is almost identical:

```
DrawThick:¶
  Test=MOUSE(0) ¶
  WHILE MOUSE(0)<>0¶
    x=MOUSE(1) : y=MOUSE(2) ¶
    LINE (x,y)-(x+5,y+5),DrawColor,bf¶
  WEND¶
RETURN¶
```

Drawing a thick line

To produce a thick line, larger squares are drawn at the actual pointer position. When you drag the mouse relatively slow, a thick line is drawn. However, when you drag the mouse fast, the squares are drawn spaced farther apart, producing a kind of dashed line.

If you purposely want to draw a dashed line, you use the next drawing type:

```
Points:¶
  Test=MOUSE(0) ¶
  WHILE MOUSE(0)<>0¶
    PSET (MOUSE(1),MOUSE(2)),DrawColor¶
  WEND¶
RETURN¶
```

This draws a point at the position of the pointer. If you hold the button down and drag the mouse slowly, you'll get a smooth line. If you drag the mouse faster, the line will become dashed. This little subprogram is the same one we used to earlier demonstrate the mouse .

The spraycan effect is also pretty easy to program:

```
Spray:¶
  Test=MOUSE(0)¶
  WHILE MOUSE(0)<>0¶
    x=MOUSE(1)+14*RND : y=MOUSE(2)+7*RND¶
    LINE (x,y)-(x,y),DrawColor,bf¶
  WEND¶
RETURN¶
```

Spray effects

The spraycan draws a cluster of small dots within a specified area. The coordinates for the dots are created randomly. Horizontally, the dots can be as far as 14 pixels from the position of the pointer, and seven pixels vertically. Wait a second! Why use a complicated LINE command with the block fill item for a simple point? After all, only one point is drawn, since the upper left-hand and the lower right-hand corners of the rectangle are identical. We did this for a good reason. This method has a great advantage over using the PSET command: the block fill item uses the presently active fill pattern, regardless of the graphic's size. If you've selected a fill pattern and hold the spraycan on one spot for a longer period of time, the pattern will build up in that area. You can draw many interesting effects with this technique.

While we're talking about LINE, here are more routines that utilize this command:

```
DrawLines:¶
  Test=MOUSE(0)¶
  x1=MOUSE(3) : y1=MOUSE(4)¶
  PSET (x1,y1),DrawColor¶
  WHILE MOUSE(0)<>0¶
  WEND¶
  LINE (x1,y1)-(MOUSE(5),MOUSE(6)),DrawColor¶
RETURN¶
```

More about lines

This routine lets you draw lines between two points. The procedure is very simple: move the pointer to the starting point, press the mouse button and hold it while you drag it to the end point. Then simply release the mouse button. There's your line.

You probably noticed the new parameters of MOUSE: MOUSE(3) and MOUSE(4), MOUSE(5) and MOUSE(6) are used in this routine. These values work like this:

If the mouse button is pressed and then released, these values result in the following:

MOUSE(3) =the X-coordinate of the starting point

MOUSE(4) =the Y-coordinate of the starting point

MOUSE(5) =the X-coordinate of the ending point

MOUSE(6) =the Y-coordinate of the ending point

Mouse coordinate checking

One more time: MOUSE(1) and MOUSE(2) give you the coordinates of the point where the pointer was located when MOUSE(0) was called last. However, MOUSE(3) to MOUSE(6) give you the starting and ending coordinates of the movement. This movement begins with the pressing of the left mouse button and ends with its release. The starting coordinates are stored in x1 and y1 in the program. So that you can see the point, it is marked on the screen with the PSET command. The empty WHILE...WEND loop waits while the mouse button is pressed. Once the button is released, the line is drawn from the starting point to the end point where the mouse was released.

MOUSE(3), MOUSE(4), MOUSE(5) and MOUSE(6) are especially useful when you're drawing lines and polygons (for which more than one point is required). They can be used for the drawing of rectangles, which is what our next routine does. Scroll to the end of your program listing and type in the following lines:

```
Frame:¶
  Test=MOUSE(0)¶
  x1=MOUSE(3)  :  y1=MOUSE(4)¶
  Pointer(0,0)=x1 : Pointer(0,1)=y1¶
  Pointer(1,0)=x1 : Pointer(2,1)=y1¶
  Value=4¶
  WHILE MOUSE(0)<>0¶
    Pointer(3,0)=MOUSE(5)¶
    Pointer(3,1)=MOUSE(6)¶
    Pointer(1,1)=Pointer(3,1)¶
    Pointer(2,0)=Pointer(3,0)¶
    GOSUB PlacePoint¶
  WEND¶
  LINE (x1,y1)-(Pointer(3,0),Pointer(3,1)),DrawColor,b¶
RETURN¶
```

Rectangles

Most of this routine defines values of the Pointer array. Only at the very end do we have a LINE command. What's going on? With some functions, such as the drawing of rectangles, colored rectangles and circles, you can specify the object's size before it is finally drawn. But you must have some way of seeing what the actual size of the object is. Commercial programs show the object as it is being constructed. We won't build this feature into our program, partly because we don't have enough memory available, and partly because the program would be too slow.

Instead, we've found another solution: our program displays only the vertices (corners) of the object. These vertices are in the `Pointer` array in the following order:

`Pointer(0,0)` contains the X-coordinate of the first point

`Pointer(0,1)` contains the Y-coordinate of the second point

`Pointer(1,0)` contains the X-coordinate of the second point

`Pointer(1,1)` contains the Y-coordinate of the second point

The variable `Pointer(2,0)` is the third X-value and `Pointer(2,1)` is the third Y-value, and so forth. The variable `Value` contains the number of points. The subroutine `PlacePoint:` then converts the values contained in `Pointer` into movable points on the screen.

Drawing
rectangles

To draw a rectangle, the user presses the mouse button and thus defines one of the corner points. Now, while pressing the mouse button, he can move to the diagonally opposite corner point and release the mouse button to complete the rectangle. Throughout this process the corners will be indicated by dots on the screen.

You might also notice something peculiar. In the WHILE...WEND loop we read in MOUSE(5) and MOUSE(6), even though the mouse button is still depressed and the movement is still not completed. If you used MOUSE(5) and MOUSE(6) before the mouse button was released, their values will be the same as MOUSE(1) and MOUSE(2). This means that the last time MOUSE(0) was called is crucial in this case, as well.

Blocks

The block routine is identical to the rectangle routine except for one symbol: the LINE command uses the bf (block fill) parameter instead of b.

Duplicate the previous program routine listing with Copy and Paste from the **Edit** pulldown menu, and make the necessary changes:

```
Box:¶
  Test=MOUSE(0)¶
  x1=MOUSE(3) : y1=MOUSE(4)¶
  Pointer(0,0)=x1 : Pointer(0,1)=y1¶
  Pointer(1,0)=x1 : Pointer(2,1)=y1¶
  Value=4¶
  WHILE MOUSE(0)<>0¶
    Pointer(3,0)=MOUSE(5)¶
    Pointer(3,1)=MOUSE(6)¶
    Pointer(1,1)=Pointer(3,1)¶
    Pointer(2,0)=Pointer(3,0)¶
    GOSUB PlacePoint¶
  WEND¶
  LINE (x1,y1)-(Pointer(3,0),Pointer(3,1)),DrawColor,bf¶
RETURN¶
```

The block item lets you draw rectangles the same way as before, except that the rectangles are filled with the active fill pattern. To fill other kinds of areas (objects other than blocks), you use the AREA command:

```
ConnectedLines:¶
  Test=MOUSE(0)¶
  x1=MOUSE(3) : y1=MOUSE(4)¶
  IF y1>186 THEN y1=186¶
  IF x1>311 THEN x1=311¶
  AREA (x1,y1)¶
  IF Adef=0 THEN Adef=1 : xa=x1 : ya=y1¶
  IF Adef<>1 AND x1=xa AND y1=ya THEN DoFill¶
  Adef=Adef+1 : IF Adef=20 THEN DoFill¶
  LINE (xa,ya)-(x1,y1),DrawColor¶
  xa=x1 : ya=y1¶
RETURN¶
¶
DoFill:¶
  Adef=0 : COLOR DrawColor,0 : AREAFILL¶
RETURN¶
```

Drawing other polygons

Once you chose the Connected lines item in the **Drawing tools** pulldown menu, you position the pointer where you want the first vertex of the polygon. Click the mouse once and move the pointer to the second vertex. The previously defined points will be connected with lines, so that you can see the outlines of the polygon. You can repeat this process for as many as 20 points. After 20 points the polygon is automatically displayed on the the screen, since the AREA command cannot accept any more points. To draw the polygon before the 20th point, you simply click the mouse twice without moving it, and, voilà, there's your polygon.

Keep it in the area

The AREA command would display an error message if you chose a point outside the specified area. The maximum area in the window is 186 points high and 311 points wide, automatically determined by the ConnectedLines: subprogram. (The two IF...THEN lines are responsible for this.) Then the program furnishes the Amiga with the points of the actual clicks with the AREA command.

The variable Adef stores the number of previously defined vertices. If Adef is 0, it is changed to 1, and AmigaBASIC uses the coordinates that the mouse had when the item was called. These coordinates are stored in xa and ya. These two coordinates are needed to make a line from the previous point to the new point. The next program line checks to see if the X- or Y-coordinate has changed since the last click. If they didn't change, the definition is finished (DoFill:). At the definition of each new point, AmigaBASIC increments the variable Adef by one. If Adef reaches the value of 20, the definition is ended by the execution of the DoFill: routine. Finally, the old values are assigned to xa and ya. The DoFill: routine sets Adef back to 0, sets the chosen color with a COLOR command for AREAFILL, and draws the desired object.

See how easy it is to start talking computerese?

Circles and ellipses

On to the next round! Up until now we've been working with square and rectangular shapes. It's about time to produce something more curvacious. The following routine draws the circles and ellipses:

```
Oval:¶
  Test=MOUSE(0)¶
  x1=MOUSE(3) : y1=MOUSE(4)¶
  Pointer(0,0)=x1 : Pointer(0,1)=y1¶
  Pointer(1,0)=x1 : Pointer(2,1)=y1¶
  Pointer(3,0)=x1 : Pointer(4,1)=y1¶
  Value=5¶
  WHILE MOUSE(0)<>0¶
    r1= ABS(x1-MOUSE(5))¶
    r2= ABS(y1-MOUSE(6))¶
    Pointer(1,1)=y1-r2 : Pointer(2,0)=x1+r1¶
    Pointer(3,1)=y1+r2 : Pointer(4,0)=x1-r1¶
    GOSUB PlacePoint¶
  WEND¶
  IF r1=0 THEN r1=.1¶
  IF r1<r2 THEN Factor=(r2/r1) : r1=r1*Factor :
r2=r2*Factor¶
  CIRCLE (x1,y1),r1,DrawColor,,,(r2/r1)¶
  RETURN¶
```

To create circles and ellipses with the drawing program, you move the pointer onto the center point of the desired circle. Press the right mouse button and drag the mouse. The horizontal distance of the mouse to the center point determines the X-radius of the circle (ellipse). The vertical distance determines the Y-radius. At the points of the circle (ellipse) that are the farthest from the center point, you'll see four pointers. The fifth pointer indicates the center point. The position of the individual points of the circle are illustrated in Figure 9.

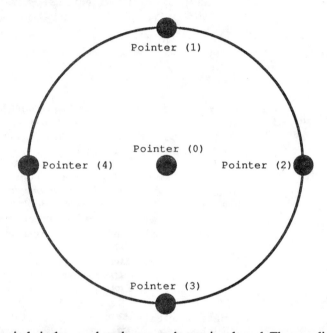

Figure 9: Pointer positions in a circle

The circle is drawn when the mouse button is released. The coordinates of the center point are stored in x1 and y1. If you compare the figure above with the values stored in the Pointer array, you'll see how it works: each point has either a X-value or a Y-value in common with the center point. The other value is determined in the WHILE...WEND loop. The variable r1 is the absolute value (always positive) of the X-radius, and r2 is the same for the Y-radius. As long as the mouse button remains pressed, only the pointers are displayed. If the X-radius is equal to 0, it will be increased to 0.1, since you might get a Division by Zero error otherwise.

We still have to figure out the ratio between the two radii, which we need for the CIRCLE command. Normally the whole thing works only if the X-radius is larger than or equal to the Y-radius. If this is not true (If r1<r2 ...), we need to reverse this ratio. Once this is done, the CIRCLE command finally draws the circle (ellipse).

Now we're going to add a routine that's responsible for coloring in the outlined areas. The key command is PAINT:

```
Fill:¶
Test=MOUSE(0)¶
IF Click=0 THEN¶
  Click=1¶
  SOUND 440,6,200¶
  x=MOUSE(1) : y=MOUSE(2)¶
  RETURN¶
ELSE¶
  Click=0¶
  IF ABS(x-MOUSE(1))=0 AND ABS(y-MOUSE(2))=0 THEN¶
    PAINT (x,y),FillColor,DrawColor¶
  ELSE¶
    SOUND 440,6,200¶
  END IF¶
END IF¶
RETURN¶
```

Filling in objects

You've probably notice the unusual combination of IF...THEN...ELSE and END IF statements. Actually you already know the individual components: IF...THEN allows you to test conditions. An ELSE after IF...THEN specifies what happens if the condition is false.

Often you'll need to execute more than one command in an IF...THEN statement. Up to now you'd have to write those commands all in one line. This will work as long as you don't have too many commands, but the **LIST** window limits the program lines to 255 characters. Also, too many commands on one line can be very confusing.

Because of this, AmigaBASIC gives you a way to increase the scope of the IF...THEN...ELSE statement, and enter program parts of any length in the statement. However, it's important that no commands are entered on the same line after the IF...THEN and after the ELSE statement. The commands that are executed simply start on the next line. The whole block is completed with a END IF statement. The structure looks like this:

```
IF (condition) THEN¶
  (program section¶
   that is to be executed¶
   if the condition¶
   is true.)¶
ELSE¶
  (program section¶
   that is to be executed¶
   if the condition¶
   is false.)¶
END IF¶
```

As you can see in the paint program, we can integrate IF...THEN/ELSE/END IF structures within each other. But if you want to be able to make sense of it all, be sure to indent all of the lines correctly.

More about filling in

Why do we make such a big production of a simple PAINT command? Do you remember the object editor? It's also a sort of paint program, written in AmigaBASIC. If you color an area with the object editor, it is very easy to destroy your entire window. Either you chose the wrong border color, or you simply forgot that the PAINT function was active. After we went through this agonizing experience, we wanted to safeguard our program against such mistakes as much as possible. We had a pretty good idea how to do it:

The Workbench uses a double click to finalize a selection. We adopted this feature. Consequently, when you want to paint an area, you must place the pointer within that area and click the mouse twice. At the first click you'll hear a warning beep (we'll discuss the SOUND command later in this book). If you have forgotten that the Fill mode was active, this sound will remind you. At this point you can simply chose another drawing type, and nothing will happen. Only if you click the mouse a second time in the same position will the area be filled.

Reading the mouse status

To determine how many times the mouse has been clicked, the number of clicks is stored in the variable Click. The routine works like this:

At the first execution, Click=0. You click once at the pointer. Now Click is raised to 1, the warning beep sounds, the program notes the coordinates of the pointer's position and jumps back. The fill color FillColor and the drawing or border color DrawColor can be specified in the color selection subprogram.

When you click the mouse a second time, the Fill: routine is called up. This time, since Click has the value 1 (not equal to 0), the program will execute the ELSE subprogram. Click is set back to 0. If the pointer position has not changed (simply compare the present values with the ones stored in x and y), the area is colored. However, if the coordinates have changed, another warning beep will sound and the program will jump back. If you still want to fill the area, you must click twice at the new position. It takes a little practice to hold the mouse perfectly still while you're clicking it, but it's a small price to pay for such a convenient safety feature. Should you want to permit a slight movement of the mouse (technically known as *slop*), change the second IF...THEN line in the Filling: routine like this:

```
IF ABS(x-MOUSE(1))<11 AND ABS(y-MOUSE(2))<6 THEN¶
```

This revised line will allow a horizontal movement from the original position of 10 points, and a vertical deviation of 5 points. Of course, your chances of making a mistake are then increased.

Erasing errors

Since we're now familiar with all the methods required to create a graphic masterpiece, let's come up with an eraser to correct rough drafts. For this we use the `Eraser:` routine:

```
Eraser:¶
  Test=MOUSE(0) ¶
  WHILE MOUSE(0)<>0¶
    x=MOUSE(1):y=MOUSE(2) ¶
    PATTERN ,Solid%¶
    LINE (x,y)-(x+10,y+5),0,bf¶
    PATTERN ,FillPattern%¶
  WEND¶
RETURN¶
```

You'll need the eraser to remove unwanted portions of your drawing. The program works the same way as the thick pen, except that the color number 0 (the background color) is used. As a result, graphics that are "erased" will receive the same color as the background, and therefore become part of the background.

PATTERN

Another unknown command pops up in this routine: `PATTERN`. As its name implies, `PATTERN` pertains to our fill pattern. We'll save the explanation of exactly how this command works for later. However, you should know that `PATTERN, Solid%` instructs the program to use a solid pattern. On the other hand, `PATTERN, FillPattern%` will activate the pattern chosen in `DefinePattern:`.

Before the command that displays the eraser on the screen, we'll choose the solid pattern, since otherwise you'd just erase in the presently active pattern. The result would just be an inverse of the pattern. However, we want everything in the particular spot to disappear. The opposite of "everything's here" (`Solid%`) is "everything's gone"; that is why we have the two `PATTERN` commands.

Don't panic if all this is confusing to you. Believe us, behind all this clever advice are countless test-runs and even a few deletable expletives.

The next subprogram, which manages the different drawing modes, is `PlacePoint:`. It creates the blinking pointer dots used by `Frame:`, `Box:` and `Oval:` and displays them on the screen. The `PlacePoint:` routine receives the coordinates in the `Pointer` array from these subprograms.

```
PlacePoint:¶
  FOR x=0 TO Value-1¶
    xz=Pointer(x,0) :yz=Pointer(x,1)¶
    IF xz<0 THEN xz=0 : Pointer(x,0)=0¶
    IF xz>311 THEN xz=311 : Pointer(x,0)=311¶
    IF yz<0 THEN yz=0 : Pointer(x,1)=0¶
    IF yz>186 THEN yz=186 : Pointer(x,1)=186¶
    AltColor(x)=POINT(xz,yz)¶
  NEXT x¶
  FOR x=0 TO Value-1¶
    PSET (Pointer(x,0),Pointer(x,1)),-(AltColor(x)=0)¶
  NEXT x¶
  FOR x=0 TO Value-1¶
    PSET (Pointer(x,0),Pointer(x,1)),AltColor(x)¶
  NEXT x¶
RETURN¶
```

The entire section consists of three FOR...NEXT loops. The first loop calculates the points and stores what was there before. The second loop sets the points, the third one erases them again. The routine loops the same number of times as there are points. Since the counting starts at 0, the last point has the number Value-1. The four IF...THEN lines in the first loop check if the coordinates of the actual point are outside of the legal area. If the X-value is smaller than 0 or larger than 311, or if the Y-value is smaller than 0 or larger than 186, the values are set to the corresponding maximum/minimum number.

Next, the program stores the color of the point that was at the particular position originally, in the AltColor array. The BASIC function POINT(x,y) tells you which color a certain pixel is. It gives you the color number of the specified point, or the number -1 if the point is outside the legal area.

1 equals 1...
or does it?

The task of the second loop in the above routine is to place the actual point onto the screen. The only thing worth mentioning is the color to be used: is calculated with the expression -(AltColor(x)=0). The reason behind this is quite simple: we want the pointer to contrast clearly with the background. Should the point that was originally at this position have had the background color (number 0, black in the default setting), the pointer should be in the color number 1 (white). If the original point had some other color, the pointer will take on the background color.

Now you know what the formula is supposed to accomplish, but you still don't know how it works. The entire process has to do with how AmigaBASIC conducts logical comparisons. An incorrect expression has the value 0. A correct expression has a value of -1. We'll talk more about this in **Intermission 3**. If you like, you can try typing this in the **BASIC** window:

```
? (0=1)¶
```

In essence, we're asking the Amiga "Is zero the same as one?" The Amiga will answer, "No, zero is not the same as one." In its own language this is:

0

If the question is:

? (1=1)

then the answer will be:

−1

This last answer says, in effect, "Yes, one is equal to one." That's because a true expression has the logical value of -1.

The formula − (AltColor (x) =0) gives the following results:

0   AltColor (x) is not equal to zero, since − (false expression) is -0, or 0.

1   AltColor (x) is equal to zero, because − (true expression) is -1), or 1.

As you can see, a rather complicated concept can be disguised by a simple formula. Albert Einstein, for instance, said simply $e=mc^2$. Einstein's little equation was expressing a formula for a concept most of us will never fully grasp.

The last FOR...NEXT loop supplies the pixels with their original colors, and the pointers disappear from the screen.

Now to the last subroutine which deals with the drawing types. Actually you can't call it a "drawing" type, since this routine is responsible for text entries.

We placed this routine immediately after the Placepoint:routine in our final version of the program. Because of the way that our programming is structured, it really doesn't matter where it goes. You can type it in at the end of the program, or you can insert this routine right after Placepoint:.

```
Text:¶
  Test=MOUSE(0)¶
  x=MOUSE(1) : y=MOUSE(2)¶
  MENU OFF : MOUSE OFF¶
  MENU 1,0,0 : MENU 2,0,0¶
  WINDOW 5,"Enter Text:",(0,177)-(311,185),18,1¶
  CLS¶
  LINE INPUT Text$¶
  WINDOW CLOSE 5¶
  WINDOW 2¶
  MENU 1,0,1 : MENU 2,0,1¶
  MENU ON : MOUSE ON¶
  LOCATE INT(y/8.86)+1,INT(x/10)+1 : COLOR
DrawColor,FillColor¶
  PRINT Text$;¶
  COLOR DrawColor,0¶
RETURN¶
```

This menu selection can be used to label parts of your drawings. Click the pointer at the location you want the label displayed. Then you'll see a window appear at the bottom of the screen. You can drag this window anywhere on the screen. Type the desired text and press <RETURN>. The window will close and the text will be displayed at the position you specified.

Text entry

The Text: subprogram first determines the coordinates of the pointer. The event trapping and both pulldown menus are disabled while the window is on the screen for the text entry. The text is read in with LINE INPUT, which means that any characters may be used. After the text has been entered, we get rid of window 5, and turn window 2 back on. Also, the two pulldown menus and event trapping are turned back on. Before the text can be printed on the picture, the pixel-coordinates must be converted into rows and columns for the LOCATE command. To make the text colors more flexible, the actual text color is contained in DrawColor, while the text background color is stored in FillColor. This way you can use colored text highlighted by colored bars. If you don't want a colored background for your text, simply chose the background color (number 0) as your fill color. Before we leave the subroutine, we have to use COLOR DrawColor,0 to reset the background color to 0. Otherwise if you tried to clear the screen, it would be erased in the fill color.

This concludes the topic of drawing. Remember, don't forget to save the program every once in a while.

Color control

Now we move on to the color subroutine. This routine is called up when you chose the Color Palette item from the **Program** pulldown menu. There are two sections to the color routine. The first subroutine is where you select the colors for drawing. The second subroutine is where you define the RGB composition of the individual colors.

Type in the first program section as follows:

161

```
SelectColor:¶
  ColorChoice=0 : EndOK=0¶
  MOUSE OFF : MENU OFF¶
  WINDOW 3,"Color Palette",(4,20)-(245,160),18,1¶
  PATTERN ,Solid%¶
  FOR x= 1 TO (MaxColors+1)/8¶
    FOR y= 0 TO 7    ¶
      LINE (y*30,(x-1)*16)-((y+1)*30,x*16),(x-1)*8+y,bf¶
    NEXT y¶
  NEXT x¶
  LINE (10,72)-(50,95),DrawColor,b¶
  LINE (15,75)-(45,93),DrawColor,bf¶
  LOCATE 14,3 : COLOR 0,1 : PRINT "Draw";¶
  LINE (70,72)-(110,95),FillColor,b¶
  LINE (75,75)-(105,93),FillColor,bf¶
  LOCATE 14,10 : COLOR 1,0 : PRINT "Fill";¶
  LINE (135,72)-(235,95),1,b¶
  LOCATE 10,16: PRINT "Palette";¶
  LINE (190,109)-(230,132),1,b¶
  LOCATE 14,21 : PRINT "OK";¶
  PATTERN ,FillPattern%¶
  MOUSE ON : MENU ON¶
RETURN¶
¶
ColorPalette:¶
  Test=MOUSE(0)¶
  x=MOUSE(3) : y=MOUSE(4)¶
¶
  GOSUB ChooseColor¶
¶
  PATTERN ,Solid%¶
  LINE (10,72)-(50,95),DrawColor,b¶
  LINE (15,75)-(45,93),DrawColor,bf¶
  LINE (70,72)-(110,95),FillColor,b¶
  LINE (75,75)-(105,93),FillColor,bf¶
  PATTERN ,FillPattern%¶
¶
  IF WINDOW(0)=3 AND 72<y AND y<95 THEN¶
    IF 70<x AND x<110 THEN ColorChoice=1¶
    IF 10<x AND x<50 THEN ColorChoice=0 ¶
    IF 135<x AND x<235 THEN¶
      PATTERN ,Solid%¶
      PAINT (137,74),3,1¶
      PATTERN ,FillPattern%¶
      GOSUB PaletteDef¶
      RETURN¶
    END IF¶
  END IF¶
  GOSUB OKCheck¶
¶
```

```
    IF ColorChoice=0 THEN¶
      LOCATE 14,3 : COLOR 0,1 : PRINT "Draw";¶
      LOCATE 14,10 : COLOR 1,0 : PRINT "Fill";¶
    ELSE¶
      LOCATE 14,3 : COLOR 1,0 : PRINT "Draw";¶
      LOCATE 14,10 : COLOR 0,1 : PRINT "Fill";¶
    END IF¶
RETURN¶
¶
ChooseColor:¶
  IF WINDOW(0)=3 AND x<240 AND y<(2^(Colors+1)) THEN¶
    fx=INT(x/30) : fy = INT(y/16)¶
    IF ColorChoice=0 THEN¶
      DrawColor=fy*8+fx¶
    ELSE¶
      FillColor=fy*8+fx¶
    END IF¶
  END IF¶
RETURN¶
¶
OKCheck:¶
  IF x>190 AND x<230 AND y>109 AND y<132 THEN¶
    PATTERN ,Solid%¶
    PAINT (192,111),3,1 : EndOK=1¶
    PATTERN ,FillPattern%¶
  END IF¶
RETURN¶
¶
ColorDone:¶
  MENU 2,0,1 : Mode=1¶
  WINDOW CLOSE 3¶
  WINDOW OUTPUT 2¶
RETURN¶
```

Quite a chunk, huh? As always, we'll go through and explain the
routine bit by bit (or at least byte by byte).

When `ColorPalette:` is first called up, it displays a new window
smaller than the drawing window. The new window contains colored
squares, one per available color. A click in one of these squares selects
its corresponding color.

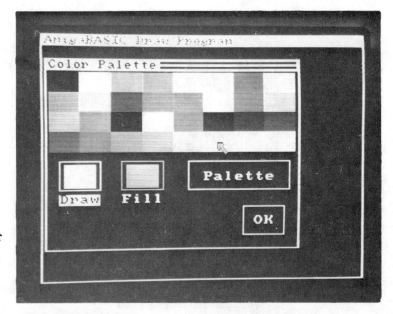

The Color
Palette
window in
the paint
program

Below the color squares are four more boxes. The first two indicate the current drawing and fill colors. The fill color is important only for the PAINT command, since in its case, a border color and a fill color can be specified.

If you click in one of these two boxes, you're specifying whether you will change the drawing color or the fill color. The label of the chosen box is printed in reverse video. The boxes themselves are displayed in the active colors.

The Palette box will activate color definition. Since this part of the program doesn't exist yet, you'll just have to wait. A click in the OK box will exit the color subroutine.

How did we program all this?

How the color routines work

The SelectColor: routine constructs the window and its contents and makes all necessary preparations. The variables ColorChoice and EndOK are set to zero. The variable ColorChoice determines if the drawing color (ColorChoice=0) or the fill color (ColorChoice=1) is changed. Event trapping must be disabled while a window is being constructed. That's because if the output window is changed during construction, part of the text and graphics would end up in the wrong window. Therefore, we disable the monitoring of MOUSE and MENU with the MOUSE OFF and MENU OFF commands. Now the new window appears on the screen. It can be shifted with its contents intact.

To construct the colored squares, we'll need the solid pattern again, so we use the PATTERN, Solid% command. The next two nested FOR...NEXT loops bring the color into the window. If there are eight available colors (3 bitplanes), one row of eight squares are drawn. If there are 16 colors (4 bitplanes), two rows of eight squares are drawn. If there are 32 colors, four rows are drawn. The expression (Colors+1)/8 results in 1 for three bitplanes, 2 for four bitplanes and 4 for five bitplanes. After that, the two boxes for the drawing and fill colors are drawn, and the corresponding text is printed. The Palette and OK boxes are also constructed in this routine. Before the RETURN, the fill pattern is set back to the original pattern, and event trapping is reactivated.

The mouse and Color- Palette:

While mode 2 is active, the ColorPalette: subroutine is responsible for the evaluation of mouse clicks. First of all, the coordinates of the mouse when the routine begins are determined. Then the ChooseColor: subroutine is called up. It checks if one of the color squares has been clicked. If one has been clicked, that color becomes the new drawing or fill color, depending on the value of ColorChoice.

Once the program returns from the ChooseColor: routine, ColorPalette: will redraw the drawing color and fill color squares, in case either was changed. The fill pattern from the Solid% variable is used for this. Whenever areas outside the picture area are drawn, we switch back to this solid pattern with the PATTERN command. Otherwise these areas would be colored with one of the fill patterns.

If this doesn't make a lot of sense to you right now, don't worry—soon we'll get to the Fillpattern subroutine, where all of your questions will be answered.

You already know the function of the ChooseColor: routine: it checks if one of the color squares has been clicked. If so, it changes either the drawing or the fill color. In the IF...THEN statement you'll find the function WINDOW(0). Like MOUSE, the WINDOW command can transfer different types of data. The statement WINDOW(0) will give you the number of the selected window. This is the window that the user has selected by clicking the mouse. After all, we have to check if the user clicked in the correct window, since he could just as well have clicked in another one. One computer rule is that the programmer should make all possible errors, before the user makes them. The subroutine is only executed if a point within window 3 or within the color squares was clicked.

Checking
bitplanes

We compare the Y-coordinate with the formula $(2 \wedge (\text{Colors}+1))$, which depends on the number of available colors. The lower limit differs from one row of squares to two rows to four rows of color squares. If there's only one row, y must be less than 16. If there are two rows, 32 is the border, and with four rows the limit is 64. The color squares have a height of exactly 16 pixels. The variable Colors contains the number of bitplanes. If you don't trust our formula, simply plug the possible values (3,4 or 5) into the formula. You'll see that it works.

The variable fx is assigned the horizontal position of the square that was clicked—in other words, how many squares from the left border the mouse was clicked. The variable fy specifies the row where the square is located. From these two values the color number can then be calculated with the formula fy*8+fx.

Depending on the value of ColorChoice, the new color is assigned either to DrawColor or FillColor. The label OKCheck: is self-explanatory. This routine checks if the OK box has been clicked. In this case, EndOK is set to 1, and the program jumps back with RETURN. The color program is then exited with the ColorDone: routine. The **Drawing tools** pulldown menu is again displayed and mode is set to 1. The color window (window 3) disappears from the screen, and window 2 (in which the drawing is located) becomes the output window once again.

Color
selections

Once you've entered all these program lines, you can chose from 8, 16, or 32 standard colors. However, maybe you don't quite like these colors, or you need a lot of different shades of green for a country landscape, and can do without the orange, dark blue and pink shades. Whatever your needs, the following section of the program lets you use the Palette box to change the RGB display of all available colors.

At this time insert the following program routine between the subroutines ChooseColor: and ColorPalette:.

```
PaletteDef:¶
  IF ColorChoice=0 THEN NewColor=DrawColor ELSE
NewColor=FillColor¶
  PATTERN ,Solid%¶
  LINE (0,71)-(240,107),0,bf¶
  COLOR 1,0¶
  LOCATE 10,2 : PRINT "R";¶
  LOCATE 11,2 : PRINT "G";¶
  LOCATE 12,2 : PRINT "B";¶
  LOCATE 14,2 : PRINT STRING$ (15, " ")¶
  LINE (24,70)-(218,78),1,b¶
  LINE (24,80)-(218,88),1,b¶
  LINE (24,90)-(218,98),1,b¶
  LINE (222,70)-(238,98),NewColor,bf¶
  Mode=4¶
  PATTERN ,FillPattern%¶
```

```
RETURN ¶
¶
RGBDef:¶
  Test=MOUSE(0)¶
  x=MOUSE(3) : y=MOUSE(4)¶
  GOSUB ChooseColor¶
  IF ColorChoice=0 THEN NewColor=DrawColor ELSE
NewColor=FillColor¶
  GOSUB RGBRegulator¶
  GOSUB OKCheck : IF EndOK=1 THEN EndOK=3¶
  WHILE MOUSE(0)<>0¶
    x=MOUSE(1) : y=MOUSE(2)¶
    IF WINDOW(0)=3 AND x>26 AND x<218 AND y>70 AND y<98
THEN¶
      Colors%(NewColor,INT((y-71)/8.7))=INT((x-26)/12)¶
      GOSUB RGBRegulator¶
    END IF¶
  WEND¶
RETURN¶
¶
RGBRegulator:¶
  PATTERN ,Solid%¶
  LINE (25+r*12,71)-(37+r*12,77),0,bf¶
  LINE (25+g*12,81)-(37+g*12,87),0,bf¶
  LINE (25+b*12,91)-(37+b*12,97),0,bf¶
  r=Colors%(NewColor,0)¶
  g=Colors%(NewColor,1)¶
  b=Colors%(NewColor,2)    ¶
  LINE (25+r*12,71)-(37+r*12,77),1,bf¶
  LINE (25+g*12,81)-(37+g*12,87),1,bf¶
  LINE (25+b*12,91)-(37+b*12,97),1,bf¶
  PALETTE NewColor,r/16,g/16,b/16¶
  LINE (222,70)-(238,98),NewColor,bf¶
  PATTERN ,FillPattern%¶
RETURN¶
```

The first of the three subroutines, PaletteDef:, is again responsible for preparations and the screen construction. Depending on the value of ColorChoice, the variable NewColor is assigned the color number of the drawing color or the fill color. This will be changed, as long as the user doesn't chose another color. The sliders for red, green and blue appear in the Color window. Because we need to make a little room for the sliders, we have to eliminate the color squares for the drawing and fill colors, as well as the Palette box. To erase these squares, we'll just let the Amiga draw a block in the background color (number 0). At this empty sqaure we'll draw the three sliders and display the letters R, G and B as labels. We'll also draw a little box next to the sliders which will display the current selected color, so that you can tell at a glance which color you're adjusting.

Mode now has a value of four. We already determined in the EvalMouse: routine that mode 4 is subordinate to mode 2. The program needs the choice of modes so that it can tell what the user is presently trying to specify with a mouse click.

Checking mouse input

The RGBdef: routine evaluates mouse input as long as the color definition program remains active. Once the mouse coordinates have been determined, the ChooseColor: routine checks if one of the color squares was clicked. You can then determine which color is going to be changed. The new color is also immediately assigned to the variable NewColor.

The subroutine RGBRegulator: is next. It will adjust the sliders according to the actual color values.

To check if the OK field was clicked, we'll borrow the OKcheck: routine (which actually belongs to the ChooseColor: subroutine). If the user is done, EndOK will be set to one. Then we switch this value to three, and the end-signal for the color definition program is set. If you click the OK box in mode four, the program will go one step back into mode 2, the color selection. After clicking OK once more, you'll be returned to the drawing mode again.

If this is a little too cumbersome for you, you can also simply select the Draw item from the **Program** menu. This will put you in the drawing mode immediately.

Moving the sliders

The WHILE...WEND loop in the RGBDef: routine shifts the sliders automatically. One of the color components (R, G or B) in the Colors% array is constantly adjusted—as long as the mouse button remains pressed, the active window is number three and the pointer remains within the bar controller. Which color component will be adjusted depends on the Y-position of the pointer. The value of the color component is determined by the pointer's X-position. Before the IF...THEN statement and the WHILE...THEN loop are completed, the RGBRegulator: routine is called up. This subroutine uses the variables r, g and b to draw the controllers in their correct positions.

First the routine erases the old controller by redrawing it in the background color. Then it reads the values of r, g and b from the Colors% array. The result is always a number between 0 and 15. Zero signifies "no color", while 15 means "full color". The sliders are redisplayed at the new position if necessary. A PALETTE command informs AmigaBASIC of the new color definition. Finally the new color is drawn in the square representing the active color. Finally the program jumps back with RETURN.

Select which color is redefined by clicking in one of the color squares. The R, G and B sliders are dragged with the mouse, just like in Preferences and other "professional" programs. Once all colors are to your liking, exit the color definition with a click in the OK box.

You see that it's a lot easier to actually use the program than to listen to our explanations. After all, that's the way it is with almost everything in life. Imagine how much documentation you could write on toothbrushes, refrigerators, or bicycles!

Intermission 3

Bits, bytes and other mysteries

Time to interrupt the flow of the learning process once again. Feel free to take a break and rest your fingers before you read on—but <u>after</u> you've saved all of your work to diskette.

The next part of the painting program involves the definition of fill patterns. So that you'll understand the programming of these patterns, first you need to know some fundamental mathematical principles. This intermission explains binary numbers, hexadecimal numbers, and all of the wonderful things that you can do with them.

Binary numbers

You already know that a computer can only distinguish between two conditions: 0 and 1—power on and power off, logically "true" and logically "false". All operations of a computer are derived from these two fundamental conditions.

We're interested in finding out how the Amiga can remember numbers other than 0 and 1. The number 2 should give it quite a bit of trouble, since it can't distinguish between no power, low power and high power. Actually, you should already be able to guess the solution. What did we do when one bit wasn't enough for all the colors? We simply added another bit. The Amiga uses the same strategy to deal with larger numbers. With one bit it can deal with 0 and 1. With two bits it can already distinguish between 0, 1, 2 and 3. The numbers 0 through 7 look like this to the Amiga:

Table 6: Decimal numbers and binary numbers

number	in bits	number	in bits
0	000	4	100
1	001	5	101
2	010	6	110
3	011	7	111

These combinations are identical to the ones we know from bitplanes. Maybe you've heard of the *binary system* in school. This number system uses only the the digits 0 and 1, but can represent all numbers of the *decimal system*. You may want to know why you'd want to use the binary system, when you had enough trouble figuring out the decimal system.

*Using
binary
numbers*

The binary system, which probably looked like a waste of time in math class, is actually a very useful number system for computing. Our standard decimal system uses ten numbers (0, 1, 2, ...,9). When ten numbers aren't enough, another digit is added: one digit is sufficient for 9, but for 10 we need two digits. The values of each digit are always powers of the base number (1=10^0, 10=10^1, 100=10^2, etc.).

You might wonder why exactly the number 10 was chosen for the base number. Thinking it over, there really isn't any particular reason. It's probably because we humans have always needed some sort of help in the field of mathematics. Since we have ten fingers and toes, 10 seems to make logical sense. However, you can build number systems on any base number: 3, 8, even 127, if you really wanted to.

*As easy as
1,10,11*

Computers know only two numbers (0 and 1), and therefore must operate with the binary system. A second digit is needed to represent the decimal number 2 in binary. The same goes for all other exponents of 2: 2^0=1, 2^1=2, 2^2=4, 2^3=8, 2^4=16, etc. The binary system requires a new digit for each of these numbers. The disadvantage is that even relatively small numbers require a lot of digits. But aside from that drawback, the whole thing works just as well as the decimal system. If you want to calculate the value of a binary number, you simply add up the values of each occupied digit.

For example, look at the binary number 10011011. This is what its value looks like when split up into exponents of 2:

value:	128	64	32	16	8	4	2	1
	(2^7)	(2^6)	(2^5)	(2^4)	(2^3)	(2^2)	(2^1)	(2^0)
content:	1	0	0	1	1	0	1	1

The binary number 10011011 corresponds to the decimal value of 128+16+8+2+1, or 155.

*Bytes,
words and
longwords*

For technical reasons, eight bits are commonly grouped into one unit called a *byte*. A byte has eight bits, and so it has a maximum value of 255. If you want to check, simply add up all the decimal values in our example above.

Each of the Amiga's memory cells can store one byte. This is a holdover from the times when microprocessor chips could only handle eight bits at a time (the Amiga's immediate predecessors at Commodore—the C-64, C-128, etc.—used eight-bit chips). The Amiga's main processor, the 68000, can handle 16 bits at a time. A 16–bit value is referred to as a *word*. A word consists of two bytes that are stored in consecutive memory cells. With 16 bits you can display numbers up to 65535. The 68000 processor can even handle 32-bit values. These values are called *longwords*, and have values between 0 and 4,294,967,294. Quite a number, huh? Don't worry, you don't need to remember it.

You won't be seeing the terms *word* or *longword* in this book. We mentioned them simply so that you'd recognize them if you saw them anywhere else.

Hexadecimal numbers

Often only 15 or 31 bits are used to store a number, and the highest bit is then used to store the sign of the number. Under these circumstances, a 0 means positive, and a 1 means negative. AmigaBASIC works this way, as well: 16-bit numbers are between -32768 and +32767, while 32-bit numbers range from -2147483647 to +2147483646. These decimal numbers can get pretty lengthy, and aren't recognizable at a glance anymore. This is one of the reasons why programmers came up with another numeral system besides binary numbers. This is called the *hexadecimal system*. This system is based on 16. The letters A to F are used to count up from 10 to 15 decimal and reach hexidecimal 10. Here's a comparison of the three number systems:

Table 7: A comparison of the three number systems

decimal	binary	hex.	decimal	binary	hex.
0	0000	0	8	1000	8
1	0001	1	9	1001	9
2	0010	2	10	1010	A
3	0011	3	11	1011	B
4	0100	4	12	1100	C
5	0101	5	13	1101	D
6	0110	6	14	1110	E
7	0111	7	15	1111	F

Advantages of hex

The hexadecimal system has a few advantages over other number systems when you work with computers. First, you can represent larger numbers with fewer digits. The gain of one or two digit places may not seem like much, but every little bit counts (no pun intended). Also, 16 is a power of two. This means that hexadecimal and binary numbers can be easily interchanged. Four digits of a binary number always coincide with one hexadecimal digit, as shown in the chart above.

For example, which way is easier to tell how many bits will be used: with decimal 65535 or with hexadeciaml FFFF? See, hexadecimal isn't all that bad...

Hex notation

If you're going to use hexadecimal numbers in AmigaBASIC, you'll need to identify them some way. It's done by preceding the number with an ampersand and an h:

```
? &h7fff
```

Octal notation

While we're on the subject of numbers, AmigaBASIC also recognizes another number system: the *octal system*. In this system, the base is 8, and digits range from 0 to 7. For example:

```
? &o7777
```

You'll almost never use octal numbers. On the other hand, you'll commonly use hexadecimal and binary numbers. Unfortunately, AmigaBASIC has no way of directly displaying binary numbers. You'll use mostly decimal and hexadecimal numbers in your AmigaBASIC programs. You can execute any mathematical function with them:

```
? &hf + &ha02
```

This line corresponds to 15+2562 and results in 2577. The line notation is unimportant to AmigaBASIC—only the value itself counts. You can even use other number system types in conjunction with one another:

```
? 15 + &ha02
```

Logical operators

Actually, there's a lot more you can do with these kinds of numbers. There are *logical operators*, for example. That sounds awfully mathematical, but really isn't bad. You already know the AND and OR commands. So far we've used them mainly in conjunction with the IF...THEN statement:

A logical AND means "as well as": Both conditions have to be true for the statement to be true.

OR stands for "either one of the two". Only one of the conditions needs to be true for the statement to be true.

Commands like AND and OR are used to perform logical operations. In this process individual bits are compared with each other. You already know that AmigaBASIC expresses the value of a logical expression with 0 and -1. Now we'll bring a little coherence to these explanations:

AND

Let's start with AND. Type the following line in the **BASIC** window:

```
? 59 AND 93
```

The Amiga will reply with the number 25. How does this happen? It's all very simple:

```
              00111011        (59)
      AND     01011101        (93)
              00011001        (25)
```

In the result, a bit is set only when both of the two corresponding bits are set. The following scheme demonstrates the possible AND combinations and their results.

```
      0 AND 0 = 0
      0 AND 1 = 0
      1 AND 0 = 0
      1 AND 1 = 1
```

When you perform logical operations on numbers, AmigaBASIC compares them bit for bit and puts together a resulting number, as you could see from the above example of AND. You'll see how this works with the rest of the operators.

OR

The next logical operator is OR. A logical OR sets a bit if either one of its corresponding two bits are set. The following example:

? 77 OR 132

results in 205. Take a look at how this is done:

```
        01001101    (77)
    OR  10000100    (132)
        11001101    (205)
```

The following combinations are possible with OR:

```
    0 OR 0 = 0
    0 OR 1 = 1
    1 OR 0 = 1
    1 OR 1 = 1
```

XOR

There are still more logical operators. One of these is XOR, pronounced "eksor" and short for "exclusive or". This is not an exclusive comparison in the sense that it can only be used by the rich and famous—it means that either one bit or the other must be set for the logic to be true. If both bits are set, then the resulting bit is not set:

90 XOR 213

results in 143.

```
         01011010    (90)
    XOR  11010101    (213)
         10001111    (143)
```

Here are the possible XOR combinations:

```
    0 XOR 0 = 0
    0 XOR 1 = 1
    1 XOR 0 = 1
    1 XOR 1 = 0
```

EQV

The next logical operand is EQV, which is short for "EQuiValent". The resulting bit is set if its two corresponding bits have the same value. This function isn't used very often. It's also not quite as simple as the previous functions, since in this case the leading characters (positive or negative signs) of the numbers have to be taken into account:

? 106 EQV −42

results in 67:

```
        0001101010      (106)
EQV     1111010110      (-42)
        0001000011      (67)
```

Combinations possible:

```
        0 EQV 0 = 1
        0 EQV 1 = 0
        1 EQV 0 = 0
        1 EQV 1 = 1
```

IMP

The next comparison is a little exotic. IMP stands for the mathemicial expression "IMPlied." Comparing the values sets the second bit according to the first. There is an even clearer definition, but since you'll almost never use this in practice, we won't go any further. Here are the tables to demonstrate:

```
370 IMP -474
```

results in -337.

```
        0101110010      (370)
IMP     1000100110      (-474)
        0001000011      (-337)

        0 IMP 0 = 1
        0 IMP 1 = 1
        1 IMP 0 = 0
        1 IMP 1 = 1
```

NOT

The last logical operator is NOT. This function turns logical values around. The value 0 becomes -1 and -1 becomes 0. After all, "true" is expressed through the number -1. This isn't quite consistent (up to now, 1 was the counterpart to 0), but we can't change that. NOT calculates the values by this formula:

```
new value = -old value-1
```

Thus, 0 can be changed into -1 and vice versa. This operation doesn't make too much sense when used with all other numbers. Why should NOT 2 be –3, anyway? Therfore, NOT is used almost exclusively in IF...THEN statements or similar conditions. The following two BASIC lines have exactly the same result:

```
IF NOT (a$="Hello") THEN...
```

and

```
IF a$<>"Hello" THEN...
```

Well, you've done it. Now you know everything about bits, bytes, number systems and logical operators. All this knowledge will come in handy later in this book and when you're programming on your own. You'll already see this in the next section.

If this intermission was a little dry for you, we'll try to make up for it. The next section deals with the Amiga's fill patterns, and brings us to the completion of your paint program.

2.10

Blitter & the paint program: defining your fill patterns

Fill patterns, like so many other Amiga graphic operations, are handled by the Blitter chip. Besides just copying and coloring areas, the Blitter chip can also execute complex area and pattern operations. It uses the same logical operands that we looked at in the previous Intermission to perform these operations. It's quite simple for Blitter to fill a block or polygon created by AREA with any sort of graphic symbol, such as little hearts or "Amiga A's", instead of a solid color. You can design these patterns yourself form scratch. All that the blitter requires is the data describing the particular pattern.

Designing patterns with **PATTERN**

How does AmigaBASIC handle pattern operations? It has a special PATTERN command for this purpose—you've seen it plenty of times in the previous listings. The data that describes the pattern is entered after PATTERN:

```
PATTERN (value for lines),(array for areas)
```

You can specify a pattern in the first position that will be used to draw the individual lines. This pattern is specified with a 16-bit number. There are 16 points across in which to specify your pattern. For instance, if you want to draw the lines in a "point on/point off" pattern, the bits and values would look like this (we added the decimal and hexadecimal values):

```
bits:          01010101 01010101
dec:           21845
hex:           &H5555
```

Type this in the **BASIC** window:

```
pattern &h5555
```

Patterned lines

After this line is entered, the new pattern will be used to draw the lines. A bit with the value of 1 represents a set (visible) pixel. A bit with the value of 0 is an unset (invisible) pixel. Try typing in the **BASIC** window this command to draw a few lines:

```
for x=1 to 1000 : line (635*rnd,185*rnd)-
(635*rnd,185*rnd) : next¶
```

You'll have to look awfully close to see the individual pixels. Try it again with a different pattern:

```
pattern &hcccc
```

Now you should be able to see the pattern better.

The PATTERN command allows you to enter a bit pattern and then use this new pattern with the normal AmigaBASIC graphic commands. Your Amiga will do the rest.

By the way, you've just learned something new: A fill pattern or a line pattern remains active until it is replaced by another one. The Amiga's default pattern is "all points on", which corresponds to the hexadecimal value &HFFFF.

Line
patterns vs.
fill patterns

Be very careful when you're filling areas, because the "invisible" points in the line really aren't there. We're now drawing with a group of pixels rather than a continuous line, and the color will just spill through our line. This is why we didn't include a pattern definition for lines in the program, since lines are mostly used to create the outlines of colored areas. Instead, you can define fill patterns for drawing in our paint program. We use the second parameter of the PATTERN command for this. The only difference is that for surface patterns, a whole array of integer values is needed instead of a single number:

PATTERN, (array name)

Now you see why all our PATTERN commands have a comma before the arrays Solid% and FillPattern%. This is because we simply omitted the value for the line definition.

What values must the array have? Well, you already know that they have to be integer values. This is obvious, since fractions would be very hard to convert to bits. The fill pattern used to fill enclosed areas and draw surfaces and blocks can be drawn, is also 16 pixels wide. The patterns can be of any desired height. But there is one rule: The height of the pattern in bits must always be a power of 2 (that is, 2, 4, 8, 16, etc.). We'll use a height of 8 pixels (16*8 pixels) per pattern in our paint program. The areas that are filled can be much larger, since the pattern will simply repeat itself within the area.

You can choose from nine different patterns in the paint program. You may change any pattern in any way you like.

We can now enter the next lines in our program:

```
PatternEditor:¶
    MOUSE OFF : MENU OFF¶
    EndOK=0¶
    WINDOW 4,"Fill Patterns",(54,30)-(300,130),18,1¶
    LINE (0,0)-(132,66),3,b¶
¶
    FOR x=0 TO 2 ¶
        FOR y=0 TO 2 ¶
            FOR i=0 TO 7¶
```

```
                FillPattern%(i)=AllPatterns%(y*3+x,i)¶
       NEXT i¶
       PATTERN ,FillPattern%¶
       LINE (144+x*34,y*25)-(175+x*34,23+y*25),1,bf¶
     NEXT y¶
   NEXT x¶
   GOSUB MarkPattern¶
¶
   LINE (5,68)-(65,82),1,b¶
   LOCATE 10,3 : PRINT "Clear";¶
   LINE (75,68)-(135,82),1,b¶
   LOCATE 10,12: PRINT "Inv.";¶
   LINE (5,85)-(65,100),1,b¶
   LOCATE 12,3 : PRINT "Load";¶
   LINE (75,85)-(135,100),1,b¶
   LOCATE 12,12: PRINT "Save";¶
   LINE (162,77)-(222,92),1,b¶
   LOCATE 11,24 : PRINT "OK";¶
¶
   FOR i=0 TO 7¶
     FillPattern%(i)=AllPatterns%(PtrnNumber,i)¶
   NEXT i¶
   GOSUB DrawPattern¶
¶
   MENU ON : MOUSE ON¶
 RETURN¶
¶
 DefinePattern:¶
   Test=MOUSE(0)¶
   x=MOUSE(3) : y=MOUSE(4)¶
   IF WINDOW(0)=4 AND x<132 AND y<66 THEN¶
     px=INT(x/8.25) : py=INT(y/8.25)¶
     Bit=FillPattern%(py) AND 2^(15-px)¶
     IF Bit=0 THEN¶
       FillPattern=FillPattern%(py) OR 2^(15-px)¶
     ELSE¶
       FillPattern=FillPattern%(py) AND (65535&-2^(15-
 px))¶
     END IF¶
     IF FillPattern>32767 THEN FillPattern=FillPattern-
 65536&¶
     FillPattern%(py)=FillPattern¶
     PATTERN ,Solid%¶
     LINE (px*8+4,py*8+2)-(px*8+9,py*8+8),-(Bit=0),bf¶
     PATTERN ,FillPattern%¶
     y1=INT(PtrnNumber/3) : x1=PtrnNumber-y1*3¶
     LINE (144+x1*34,y1*25)-(175+x1*34,23+y1*25),1,bf¶
     FOR i=0 TO 7¶
       AllPatterns%(PtrnNumber,i)=FillPattern%(i)¶
     NEXT i¶
     RETURN¶
   END IF¶
¶
   IF WINDOW(0)=4 AND x>142 AND x<244 AND y<75 THEN¶
     px=INT((x-143)/34) : py=INT(y/25)¶
     IF px+py*3=PtrnNumber THEN RETURN¶
```

```
        PtrnNumber=px+py*3¶
        FOR i=0 TO 7¶
          FillPattern%(i)=AllPatterns%(PtrnNumber,i)¶
        NEXT i¶
        GOSUB MarkPattern¶
        GOSUB DrawPattern¶
        PATTERN ,FillPattern%¶
        RETURN¶
      END IF ¶
  ¶
    IF WINDOW(0)=4 AND x<222 AND x>162 AND y<93 AND y>76
  THEN¶
        PATTERN ,Solid%¶
        PAINT (164,78),2,1¶
        PATTERN ,FillPattern%¶
        EndOK=2 : RETURN¶
      END IF ¶
  ¶
    IF WINDOW(0)=4 AND x<135 AND y>68 AND y<100 THEN¶
        PATTERN ,Solid%¶
        IF x<66 AND x>4 AND y<82 THEN¶
          PAINT (6,69),2,1¶
          LINE (1,1)-(131,65),0,bf¶
          FOR i=0 TO 7 : AllPatterns%(PtrnNumber,i)=0¶
            FillPattern%(i)=0¶
          NEXT¶
          PAINT (6,69),0,1¶
          PATTERN ,FillPattern%¶
          y1=INT(PtrnNumber/3) : x1=PtrnNumber-y1*3¶
          LINE (144+x1*34,y1*25)-(175+x1*34,23+y1*25),1,bf¶
        END IF ¶
  ¶
        IF x<136 AND x>74 AND y<82 THEN¶
          PAINT (76,69),2,1¶
          FOR i=0 TO 7¶
            FillPattern%(i)=FillPattern%(i) XOR &HFFFF¶
            AllPatterns%(PtrnNumber,i)=FillPattern%(i)¶
          NEXT i¶
          GOSUB DrawPattern¶
          PAINT (76,69),0,1¶
          PATTERN ,FillPattern%¶
          y1=INT(PtrnNumber/3) : x1=PtrnNumber-y1*3¶
          LINE (144+x1*34,y1*25)-(175+x1*34,23+y1*25),1,bf¶
        END IF¶
        IF x<66 AND x>4 AND y>84 THEN GOSUB PtrnLoad¶
        IF x<135 AND x>75 AND y>84 THEN GOSUB PtrnSave¶
      END IF¶
  RETURN¶
  ¶
  MarkPattern:¶
    y1=INT(AltPattern/3) : x1=AltPattern-y1*3        ¶
    LINE (143+x1*34,y1*25-1)-(176+x1*34,24+y1*25),0,b¶
    y1=INT(PtrnNumber/3) : x1=PtrnNumber-y1*3¶
    LINE (143+x1*34,y1*25-1)-(176+x1*34,24+y1*25),3,b¶
    AltPattern=x1+y1*3¶
```

179

```
RETURN¶
¶
DrawPattern:¶
  MOUSE OFF : MENU OFF¶
  PATTERN ,Solid%¶
  LINE (1,1)-(131,65),0,bf ¶
  FOR y=0 TO 7¶
    FOR x=0 TO 15¶
      Bit=FillPattern%(y) AND 2^(15-x) ¶
      IF Bit<>0 THEN LINE (x*8+4,y*8+2)-
(x*8+9,y*8+8),1,bf¶
    NEXT x¶
  NEXT y¶
  PATTERN ,FillPattern%¶
  MOUSE ON : MENU ON¶
RETURN¶
¶
PtrnLoad:¶
  MOUSE OFF : MENU OFF¶
  PAINT (6,86),2,1¶
  GOSUB EnterName¶
  IF Nam$="" THEN EndPtrnLoad¶
  OPEN Nam$ FOR INPUT AS 1¶
    FOR x=0 TO 8¶
      FOR y=0 TO 7¶
        AllPatterns%(x,y)=CVI(INPUT$(2,1)) ¶
      NEXT y¶
    NEXT x¶
  CLOSE 1¶
¶
EndPtrnLoad:¶
  WINDOW CLOSE 5 : WINDOW 4¶
  PAINT (6,86),0,1¶
  MOUSE ON : MENU ON¶
  FOR x=0 TO 8¶
    FOR y=0 TO 7¶
      FillPattern%(y)=AllPatterns%(x,y) ¶
      PATTERN ,FillPattern%¶
      y1=INT(x/3) : x1=x-y1*3¶
      LINE (144+x1*34,y1*25)-(175+x1*34,23+y1*25),1,bf¶
    NEXT y¶
  NEXT x¶
  FOR i=0 TO 7¶
    FillPattern%(i)=AllPatterns%(PtrnNumber,i) ¶
  NEXT i¶
  GOSUB DrawPattern¶
RETURN¶
¶
PtrnSave:¶
  MOUSE OFF : MENU OFF¶
  PAINT (78,86),2,1¶
  GOSUB EnterName¶
  IF Nam$="" THEN EndPtrnLoad¶
  OPEN Nam$ FOR OUTPUT AS 1¶
    FOR x=0 TO 8¶
      FOR y=0 TO 7¶
```

```
              PRINT #1,MKI$(AllPatterns%(x,y));¶
          NEXT y¶
        NEXT x¶
      CLOSE 1¶
¶
EndPtrnSave:¶
  WINDOW CLOSE 5 : WINDOW 4¶
  PAINT (78,86),0,1¶
  MOUSE ON : MENU ON¶
RETURN¶
¶
PatternDone:¶
  MENU 2,0,1 : Mode=1¶
  WINDOW CLOSE 4¶
  WINDOW OUTPUT 2¶
  PATTERN ,FillPattern%¶
RETURN¶
¶
EnterName:¶
  Altname$=Nam$¶
  WINDOW 5,"Enter Name:",(0,80)-(311,88),0,1¶
  CLS¶
  LINE INPUT Nam$¶
  IF Nam$= "=" OR Nam$="*" THEN Nam$=Altname$¶
RETURN¶
```

You should be getting very familiar with the AmigaBASIC graphic commands.

How the pattern editor works

As in the Color subroutine, the first lines construct the window and its contents. PatternEditor: is responsible for this procedure. During these preparations, event trapping is disabled. You'll see the nine available fill patterns displayed in the new window. They are stored in the AllPatterns% array and are displayed on the screen by the nested loops. The % symbol after the array names indicates that the elements of the arrays will be integer values. You've already encountered this with normal variables—it works the same way for arrays. The eight pattern data items are first copied from the AllPatterns% array to the FillPattern% array. The FillPattern% array always contains the currently active pattern. The subroutine then draws a small filled-in box for each pattern. Since we read default values into all arrays from the DATA statements in the beginning of the program, there are already nine patterns available.

Next the subroutine MarkPattern: is called up. It draws an orange frame around the currently active pattern, so you can clearly recognize it. The next lines construct the boxes for Clear (erase pattern), Inv. (inverse pattern), Load, Save and OK. To activate one of these functions the user clicks the corresponding box with the mouse.

181

Lastly, the DrawPattern: routine is called up. This subroutine draws the magnification of the active pattern. Here you can then click the individual points of the pattern on or off, thus changing or defining a pattern.

The event trapping is reactivated at the end of the subroutine, and the program jumps back with RETURN. The following illustration shows what the **Fill Patterns** window will look like:

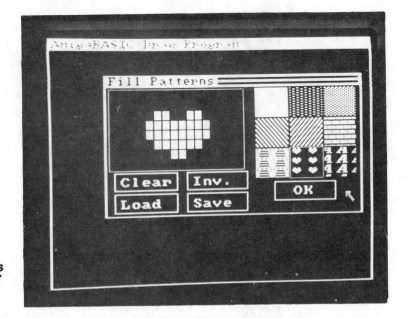

Figure 11: The Fill Patterns window of the paint program

You can compare your results to this picture to see if your version is correct. If one or another pattern isn't quite the same as ours, even though you haven't changed it, look closely at the DATA statements at the beginning of the program. It's very easy to miss a DATA statement, or type one in incorrectly.

Defining patterns

Now for the DefinePattern: routine. This subroutine responds to mouse input as long as mode 3 (the pattern definition) is active. First we determine the coordinates of the mouse and store them in the variables x and y. Then we check step by step the field in which the click occurred, and what operations the program must follow. This starts with the work grid in which the magnified pattern is visible.

182

As mentioned before, each pixel of the pattern is enlarged and displayed as a square on the screen. You can turn individual pixels on or off by clicking the mouse. If the selected window is number 4 and the click occurred within the work grid, we have to find out which particular pixel was clicked. The variables `px` and `py` convert the mouse coordinates into columns and rows to specify the location of the square that was clicked.

The variable `Bit` isolates the bit corresponding to the selected pixel in the `FillPattern%` array. For this we use the AND operand. The resulting bit is set <u>only</u> when the same bit is set in the output number (`FillPattern%(py)`) as in the reference number (`2^(15-px)`). Otherwise the resulting bit will have a value of zero. If `bit` has a value of 0, the pixel that was clicked will be turned on. If the result is not 0, the pixel will be erased. For this we use another AND operand with a number in which all bits are set except the one that corresponds to the chosen pixel. (We use this formula: `65536&-2^(15-px)`). As a result, all bits except the selected one remain unchanged while the chosen bit will be erased.

The variable `FillPattern` contains a new value that is assigned to the `FillPattern%` array. To assign the new value to the integer array, there is one more thing we must take care of. Although the new number will be 16 bits, it will always be positive. To get the corresponding integer, we need to subtract 65535 from the numbers that are larger than 32767. This way we'll receive a negative value which will then be assigned to the `FillPattern%` array.

You're probably wondering why AmigaBASIC attaches a & character to the number 65535 in the **LIST** window. This is done with all integer numbers outside of the range -32768 to +32767.

From high math to low-res

This completes the mathematical explanation of the pattern definition. However, you'll want to see the results of the definition displayed on the screen as well. Depending on the status of the pixel, it will be set or erased in the work grid. The statement `-(bit=0)` reverses the value of a bit. (Remember how true and false expressions are expressed?) If `bit` has a value of 0, then the result is 1, and vice versa.

We'll use the result of this formula as the drawing color. With the color 0 (background; invisible) or the color 1 (first drawing color; visible) a LINE command draws a solid square. This way the status of the pixel that was clicked will be reversed. If the pixel was off to begin with, it will be turned on. If it was originally on, it will be erased. First, the fill pattern has to be reset to `Solid%`, since we need a solid square, not one filled with a pattern. This explains why we used the PATTERN, `Solid%` command before any block-fill operations throughout the program. `Solid%` deposited a solid pattern at the beginning of the program. When we need areas outside of the picture being drawn by the user, no pattern is read.

183

So that the user can see what the pattern will look like in actual size, we reproduce the edited version in the rectangle where the original was. Just changing the contents of the the FillPattern% array won't change anything that's already been displayed on the screen. We need to redraw the square with a LINE command and block-fill.

You can make use of this principle in designing your graphics. When you choose a new pattern, or load a new set of patterns from diskette, the patterns on the screen will remain unchanged. The reason for this is that the blitter chip simply adopts the local pattern in the picture when it draws the screen. You could achieve the same result by setting each pixel of the pattern by hand, but this would take too much time and effort.

The subroutine DefinePattern: also places the new contents of the FillPattern% array in the appropriate elements of the AllPatterns% array, upon which the program jumps back.

Changing the current pattern

The next section of the program allows you to redefine the actual pattern. Simply click in the rectangle of the pattern you wish to use or modify. The square will then be identified by an orange frame and its contents will be copied into the work grid. The variable PtrnNumber is assigned the number of the actual pattern. If the click occurred on the already active pattern, the program simply jumps back with RETURN, in order to save time.

The eight bits of data are copied from the AllPatterns% array to the FillPattern% array, and MarkPattern: and DrawPattern: are called. Again, an orange frame is drawn around the active pattern, and the pattern is copied pixel by pixel into the work grid. This latter operation takes the most time, so just sit back for a second. The new pattern is then activated with PATTERN.

The next section requests a click in the OK gadget. This is simple: the variable EndOK will equal 2, and then jump back. The routine MouseControl:, which called this subroutine up, will take care of the rest.

Testing for gadgets

Now all that's missing are the four gadgets for Clear, Inv., Load and Save. The outer IF...THEN statement checks if the mouse coordinates at the time of the click were within one of the four gadgets. If not, the program simply continues execution. The inner IF...THEN statements then check the coordinates for each gadget, one after the other.

Click the `Clear` gadget. The selected square is filled. As always, the `Solid%` pattern is activated first. Within the work grid the `LINE` command draws a box in the background color to erase the contents. Erasing part of a picture simply consists of drawing over a particular area using the background color. The eight values of the erased pattern are set to zero in the `FillPattern%` and `AllPatterns%` arrays. Then the `Clear` box that was just filled is returned to its normal condition. Lastly, the new pattern (an empty field) is drawn at its place in the pattern squares.

Inverted patterns

The routine for the `Inv.` gadget works in the same way. You can use the `XOR` function to receive the negative value of a pattern: the 0 and 1 values are simply exchanged. The `XOR &HFFFF` function does this for us, since when comparing all bits with the number 1, 1 will become 0. (1 `XOR` 1 = 0). Also, 0 will become 1 (0 `XOR` 1 = 1). The new values are then assigned to `FillPattern%` and `AllPatterns%` right away. Next the `DrawPattern:` routine is called up to display the inverted pattern in the work grid. Everything else should be familiar to you: clear the `Inv.` gadget and redraw the corresponding pattern square.

If the `Load` or `Save` gadgets were clicked, the `LoadPattern:` or `SavePattern:` subroutine would be called up and after returning, the program would simply jump back to the main program. We will look at how both `LoadPattern:` and `SavePattern:` work in a little bit.

We've already heard of the next routine, `MarkPattern:`. It first clears the frame around the old pattern and then draws a frame around the new one. The number of the new pattern is found in the variable `PtrnNumber`. To remember the value of the old pattern the next time around, the program places this number in the variable `AltPattern`.

You're also familiar with the function of the `DrawPattern:` routine. It displays a fill pattern in the work grid pixel by pixel. The construction of the work grid takes about three seconds. The event trapping is disabled so that the subroutine is not interrupted during this process. Also, the old contents of the work grid are erased by drawing a block in the background color. To construct the grid, the individual values of the `FillPattern%` array are checked—for each bit that is set a square is drawn. Then the event trapping is turned back on and the program returns to the main routine.

By the way, when was the last time you saved your program?

Saving and loading patterns

There's only one detail left: Your most thrilling pattern definition won't be worth much unless you can save and retrieve patterns from diskette. We've included the ability to load and save a complete set of nine fill patterns on diskette.

*Loading fill
patterns*

The next routine of the paint program, `PtrnLoad:`, is responsible for loading the fill patterns. The event trapping is first disabled, since the Amiga doesn't want any interruptions during the execution of this routine. The `PAINT` command in the second line fills the `Load` gadget box to visually confirm the selection. When `EnterName:` is called up, the Amiga asks you for the name of the file to be read or written to diskette. The filename is stored in the variable `Nam$`. If you press <RETURN> without entering a filename, `Nam$` will be empty. In this case we simply end the subroutine and return to `PtrnLoad:`.

The `EndPtrnLoad:` routine takes care of this. If you do enter a name, the corresponding file is opened for reading. You'll learn more about this and the `OPEN` command in **Chapter 3** (Loading and saving graphics) and **Chapter 5** (All about data) of this book. For now, all you need to know is that the numbers that determine the patterns are read into the `AllPatterns%` array little by little off the diskette. This is done in the two nested `FOR...NEXT` loops. The `CLOSE` command is a required companion to `OPEN`. (We'll discuss these commands later on, also). `EndPtrnLoad:` ends the loading routine.

Window 5 was opened by `EnterName:` and must now be closed again so that Window 4 is the output window again. Also, event trapping is reactivated, which brings the new patterns to the screen. Up to now they are simply stored in the `AllPatterns%` array—they have not been displayed. To correct this, two nested loops copy the values for pattern 1 through pattern 9 into the `FillPattern%` array. It draws each of the nine pattern squares at the same time. After these two loops, the `FillPattern%` array is assigned the new pattern that replaces the last active pattern.

*Saving fill
patterns*

The two subroutines for saving fill patterns aren't difficult to follow, either. The `PtrnSave:` routine disables event trapping, fills the `Save` box, uses `NameEntry:` to determine the input filename, opens the specified file for writing, and then writes the contents of `AllPatterns%` to this file value by value. The file is closed, and the patterns are saved. `EndPatternSave:` ends the saving of the patterns. Window 5 must be closed and window 4 must be active. The `Save` gadget is cleared, and then event trapping is turned back on. We'll discuss the commands `CVI`, `MKI$` and `INPUT$` in detail in **Chapter 3** and **Chapter 5**.

*Saving
patterns*

Now we'll find out how to use AmigaBASIC's loading and saving functions. All nine patterns are saved at the same time in one file on the diskette. A file is a set of records, just like a program, except that it contains data. After you click the `Save` gadget, a requester will be displayed in the center of the screen. This requester is the same width as the screen, but only one line high. You type the name that you want the file saved under in this line.

Use the same rules for names that you use for programs. Choose short but meaningful names, like `Pattern1`. This way you'll recognize the file much faster. Pressing <RETURN> inputs the entry. After you type a name and confirm it with <RETURN>, you'll see the disk drive light turn on.

Remember: <u>do not take the diskette out of the drive while this light is on</u>. After the file is written, the program returns to the pattern definition routine.

Loading patterns

To load a file of nine patterns, simply click the `Load` gadget. The requester for the name entry is displayed. Enter the name of the pattern file you want to load and press <RETURN>. The program then reads the patterns from the file and displays them in the nine pattern squares. You can then use these patterns just like the default patterns of the program. After you use your paint program for awhile, you'll build a large selection of fill patterns from which to choose.

Let's continue with the program. There's the `PatternDone:` routine, which is virtually the same as the `ColorDone:` routine in the color section. The pattern definition ends, and the program returns to drawing mode. You execute this routine when you click the `OK` gadget.

`PatternDone:` reactivates the second pulldown menu that contains the drawing tools, and sets the mode to number one (`Draw` mode). It closes the pattern subroutine window, makes window 2 (where your graphic is) the active window, activates the last chosen pattern and then returns to the main program. Now you're ready to continue your drawing or select any other tool.

We still need the `EnterName:` routine, which asks for a filename during the `Load` and `Save` functions. The variable `AltName$` contains the previous contents of `Nam$`. Then it activates the requester in which you're to enter the name, and displays the cursor in the requester with the `CLS` command. The program asks for input with the `LINE INPUT` command. If you simply enter an equal sign (=) or an asterisk (*), the filename that was last used will become the current filename (the name found in the variable `AltName$`).

That's it... the program returns to the place from which it was called.

Your typing marathon is almost finished. Go to the end of the program you have typed in so far. Enter these last few lines, and you'll have a complete drawing program.

```
Query:¶
  MENU 1,0,0 : MENU 2,0,0¶
  MENU OFF : MOUSE OFF¶
  WINDOW 5,"CAUTION!",(43,70)-(270,120),0,1¶
  COLOR 0,1 : CLS : LOCATE 2,2¶
  PRINT "Do you really want to"¶
  PRINT " lose your picture?"¶
  PATTERN ,Solid%¶
  LOCATE 5,12 : PRINT "Yes";¶
  LOCATE 5,21 : PRINT "No";¶
  LINE (77,31)-(127,46),0,b¶
  LINE (145,31)-(195,46),0,b¶
  SOUND 880,6,100¶
Pause:¶
  Test=MOUSE(0)¶
  WHILE MOUSE(0)=0¶
    x=MOUSE(1) : y=MOUSE(2)¶
  WEND¶
  IF (y<46 AND y>31) THEN¶
    IF (x<127 AND x>77) THEN PAINT (79,33),3,0 : OK=1 :
GOTO EndQuery ¶
    IF (x<195 AND x>145) THEN PAINT (147,33),3,0 : OK=0 :
GOTO EndQuery¶
  END IF¶
  GOTO Pause ¶
EndQuery:¶
  MENU ON : MOUSE ON : MENU 1,0,1 : MENU 2,0,1¶
  WINDOW CLOSE 5 : WINDOW 2¶
RETURN¶
¶
EndIt:¶
  MENU RESET¶
  SCREEN CLOSE 1¶
END¶
```

Confirming deletes

This final routine executes the safety check for erasing a picture or exiting the program. As usual, we construct a window that is displayed on top of the screen. Event trapping is deactivated, as are the pulldowns, so that the user knows that nothing else can be selected at this time.

The window is titled **CAUTION!** to make sure the user knows that this is his/her last chance to save the program. In the window you'll see the message Do you really want to lose your picture? and two gadgets for Yes and No. While the window is being constructed, you'll hear a warning sound generated by a SOUND command (more about this command later). The Pause: loop runs until one of the two gadgets is clicked. Depending on your decision (yes, erase or no, don't erase) the variable OK receives the value 1 or 0. The subprogram that called the routine (Project:) then reacts accordingly.

The EndQuery: routine is again quite simple. It ends Query: by enabling the event trapping and reactivating the pulldown menus.

*End
program*

All that remains of the program is one small routine, `EndIt:`. The program will jump to this routine when it is exited. The `MENU RESET` command establishes the default pulldowns, `SCREEN CLOSE 1` closes the screen that our paint program operates in. The `END` command then terminates the program.

Actually, the `END` command is only cosmetic, because if the program reaches the last line without further `GOTO` or `GOSUB` commands, it's done anyway. Nevertheless, there are two reasons to use the `END` command in this place. First, as in this case, it's used to mark the end of the program in listing; second, it ends the program even if more lines follow (e.g., subroutines).

You're back in direct mode... there's nothing but silence. The paint program is finished. Congratulations, you've finished the longest program yet! We hope you feel it was worth the trouble. After all, you now have a powerful utility program at your disposal. In the next chapter you'll learn how the graphics that you draw are stored on diskette and how they can be retrieved. We'll also show you how to use the graphics in other programs, such as the video title program.

Feel free to experiment with the paint program. We've told you all you need to know to run it, but we'll give you some suggestions now.

*Debugging
your final
program*

But first: While you're trying out the program, you'll most likely come across errors you made while entering the program. Most of the time, the program will stop and display the error in the **LIST** window. In that case, compare the specified line with the listing in this book, and then correct the error.

If the program doesn't perform the way it's supposed to, the troubleshooting becomes much more difficult. Most likely you'll have to go over the whole program until you find the error. In any case, don't be angry with yourself—it's almost impossible to enter so many program lines without making a mistake. Even in the final phases of the publishing of this book, we had to hammer out some errors that were still hiding in there.

In any event, if you've understood everything we described here, you have a solid knowledge of graphic programming on the Amiga.

Paint program tricks and tips

In closing we want to give you some tips. After starting the program, it will take a moment before it is operational. During this time all the preparations will be carried out. After just a few seconds the program will be ready to use.

A word about the pointer. You'll notice that the standard form of the pointer doesn't work well for drawing. This is mainly because you can't see the point with which you're drawing. If you like, you can use Preferences to create your own pointer. For example, a pair of cross hairs would be practical.

A note on patterns: you can use the fill patterns to fill areas and draw thick lines. However, if the fill pattern used for drawing has any "holes" in it, you won't be able to create an enclosed area. If you try to fill an area created with such an outline, the color will spill onto the rest of the picture. Because of this, one of your nine patterns should always be a solid one (like our Solid% pattern) so that you can use it in conjunction with PAINT.

About using text

Finally, something about writing text in the picture. This item should be used sparingly, since it can easily clutter up the picture.When text is printed, the drawing color is used for the text, while the fill color is used for the text background. This way you can fit text into filled areas. However, the text item cannot use fill patterns. Therefore, text will cover any object behind it, since text has priority over graphics. If you want to write text on the blank screen, just choose the background color as your fill color.

These tips should help you to use the paint program more effectively. They conclude **Chapter 2** and the graphic section of this book.

You did remember to save the pr—no, never mind. You're almost a professional programmer by now—you don't need reminding.

Diskettes and
file management

3

3   Organizing your data:
Diskettes and file management

Now that we've worked with AmigaBASIC's graphics and animation, we need to look at commands that are important when we work with large amounts of data.

Usually data is stored on a *diskette*, sometimes referred to as a floppy diskette. Your Amiga can use different types of diskettes. We'll look at them later, and we'll work on some useful programs. First we want to create a diskette that can be used exclusively by AmigaBASIC and its programs. Up to now we've been using the Extras diskette, but we can't continue this for too long—we'd run out of storage space in a hurry.

Editor's note: We have updated this book to include Workbench 1.2, Workbench 1.3 and Workbench 2.0. The Amiga Workbench is an ever expanding and improving system. Programs are changed and added to the Workbench to upgrade and improve the Amiga operating system. Therefore the programs listed in this book may not appear in the drawers or diskettes listed. If a program does not appear in the drawer mentioned, try looking in other drawers on the Workbench and Extras diskettes for the program. Most explanations will use Workbench 1.3 since this is the most popular operating system for the Amiga.

3.1   Saving it for posterity: making your own BASIC diskette

We've put quite a few programs on the Extras diskette since we first opened it. We created a program drawer a few pages ago, and then we started saving our programs in there without giving the process too much thought.

In the meantime, the Extras diskette has been getting full. It was fairly full to begin with, because AmigaBASIC, the BasicDemos drawer and the other files on the diskette take up a large amount of storage space.

Requesters   We hope you haven't had problems because of this. But perhaps when you tried to save a program, you found that the Extras diskette was full. In this case a requester is displayed. Requesters are produced by the Workbench. The specific requester you get when you've run out of room on your diskette is Volume Extras is full. The diskette has no room for your program, so it can't carry out your command.

You confirm that you've read the message when you click the Cancel gadget. If the window is displayed a second time, it's probably an error in the current version of Workbench. Click the Cancel gadget again.

As if that wasn't enough warning, AmigaBASIC will give you the Disk full error message. Just click the OK gadget.

Making a work diskette   If this has happened to you, you'll want to know how to make enough disk space to store your program. Even if it hasn't happened to you yet, it's bound to happen soon.

The solution to the problem is easy. We can make a seperate diskette for AmigaBASIC and its programs. For this you'll need a blank diskette, or a diskette that can be erased without destroying anything important.

You can't make a diskette in AmigaBASIC itself; you need to exit AmigaBASIC and return to the Workbench. If you don't have a program in memory, select Quit from the **Project** menu, or type the SYSTEM command in the **BASIC** window.

Trapped?

But what do you do when you have an important program in memory that you want to save, and you get a Disk full error? You haven't stored your program on diskette yet. If you leave AmigaBASIC, you'll lose your entire program. You must leave the current BASIC program in memory.

Thanks to the Amiga's multitasking abilities, it's easy to get around this problem. Click the close gadget in the LIST window to close it, and use the sizing gadget to shrink the BASIC window to its smallest possible size. Drag this window with the drag gadget so that you can see all of the Workbench window. AmigaBASIC will run in the background while you use the Workbench.

To activate the Workbench, click anywhere outside of the BASIC window. The title bar will display Workbench release 1.x. (or whatever version number Workbench you own), followed by the amount of memory available to you.

√√   REMOVE THE EXTRAS DISKETTE FROM THE BUILT-IN (INTERNAL) DISK DRIVE, AND INSERT A BLANK DISKETTE.

Formatting diskettes

First you need to *format* the new diskette. If this is the first time you're doing this, you may not know why formatting is necessary. A diskette is essentially a piece of magnetized plastic in a protective case. The Amiga uses 3.5" diskettes. That means that the plastic magnetic media of the diskette is about three and a half inches in diameter. Almost all the latest personal computers use this type of diskette. A few years back, personal computers used 5.25" disks, but these are more easily damaged, harder to work with, and have less storage space than the newer 3.5" diskettes.

The piece of plastic inside the diskette is magnetized. A magnetic head in the disk drive, the *read/write head*, moves over the diskette as it spins in the drive at high speed. The read/write head writes bits to diskette and later reads them off the diskette. Positive magnetization means that the bit is on; negative means that it is off. Groups of bits form bytes, and bytes combine to form files and programs.

The bits are written on concentric *tracks* (concentric means that the circular tracks lie inside of one another). You might think of a computer diskette as a combination of a LP record and a magnetic tape.

Tracks need to be placed on the diskette before it is used, so that the read/write head can do its job properly. These tracks need to be arranged in a distinct format. Therfore, you need to *format* each diskette before it is used.

Different formats

Maybe you're wondering why the tracks aren't already on the diskette. This is because 3.5" diskettes are used by different types of computers. Different computers have different diskette formats. Even though the diskettes are the same size and material, the information on the diskette is organized differently. The number of tracks, their distance from one another, the coding of information and the diskette control information vary greatly from one computer to another. For example, an Atari ST computer can't do anything with an Amiga diskette, and vice versa.

AmigaDOS

Your Amiga can work with several disk formats. Normally, diskettes will be accessed using AmigaDOS. The abbreviation DOS stands for *Disk Operating System*. AmigaDOS is a program that is responsible for disk input, output and maintenance. If your Amiga is running under another DOS, it can read diskettes in a different format. The Amiga 1000 can, for instance, read IBM PC diskettes by using a software MS-DOS adapter, as can a fully-equipped Amiga 2000. As long as you're working with AmigaBASIC, however, you don't need to worry about other disk formats.

Technical information

Here's the technical data for those of you who are interested. The AmigaDOS disk format uses 80 tracks on each side of the diskette (160 tracks total) to store 880K per diskette. Since we read and write on both sides of the diskette, Amiga disk drives have two read/write heads. Remeber this when you shop for blank diskettes—make sure that you buy *double-sided* diskettes (diskettes which have been checked for defects on both sides).

If you put in an unformatted diskette, a disk icon with the name DF0:BAD will appear in the **Workbench** window. Since AmigaDOS can't read the diskette, it calls it "bad." The diskette is either unformatted or it has a format that AmigaDOS doesn't understand (like an Atari ST diskette).

NOTE:

Make sure that the diskette you are going to format doesn't have any important programs or data on it. The old information will be destroyed, and you will not be able to recover any of it. You should put labels on each of your diskettes so that you know what they contain. At least write the diskette's name on the diskette. Blank diskettes that you buy usually have labels in the package.

√√ IF YOU'RE SURE THAT YOU WANT TO FORMAT THE DISKETTE, THEN ACTIVATE THE DF0:BAD ICON. CLICK THE ICON ONCE SO THAT IT TURNS BLACK.

√√ CHOOSE THE INITIALIZE ITEM FROM THE **DISK** PULLDOWN MENU.

Initializing and formatting are two items that describe the same process: writing tracks on a new diskette.

Your Amiga displays a window that tells you to insert the Workbench diskette. If you have two drives, you should insert the Workbench diskette into the second drive. If you only have one drive, eject the blank diskette and insert the Workbench diskette.

After a short while, the Amiga will ask you to insert the blank diskette back into the drive.

To make sure that you know what you are doing, a requester asks if it is OK to Initialize disk in drive DF0 (all data will be erased)? If the diskette has a name, it will ask if it is OK to Initialize disk ... , followed by the diskette's name.

√√   YOU NEED TO CONFIRM THAT IT'S OK TO FORMAT THE DISKETTE IN DRIVE 0.

AmigaDOS calls the internal disk drive DF0, and the first external drive DF1.

The formatting process starts when you click the Continue gadget— there's no way to cancel once it begins.

√√   IF YOU'RE READY, CLICK CONTINUE.

The 80 tracks are written to diskette and then checked. The **Initialize** window displays which track is being formatted, as well as how many tracks still need to be formatted. The first track is number 0, and the last track is number 79. The message Formatting will appear while tracks are being written. Verifying means that they are being checked for errors, or verified.

If the format
goes wrong

If the Amiga finds an error while checking the tracks, an error message is displayed. Several things might cause this. Try to format the diskette once or twice more. If it still doesn't format, then the diskette might have a material defect in its plastic disk. Try another diskette. If you have problems here as well, talk to your Amiga dealer. But chances are everything will work correctly.

The formatting isn't completed when the 80 tracks are created on the diskette. Your Amiga warns you of this by displaying the following message in the **Initialize** window:

WARNING: Initialize Still in Progress. DO NOT REMOVE DISK.

Wait!!!

The drive light will go out for a couple of seconds, but <u>do not remove</u> <u>the diskette yet</u>. Some important control information will be written on the diskette. Only then is the Amiga finished formatting the diskette.

The formatted diskette is given the name `Empty`. Click the `Empty` disk icon. The window that appears will have a trashcan in it, and nothing more. The *disk gauge* on the left side of the window shows that the diskette is completely empty. We'll want to fill it step by step.

`Rename`

`Empty` is not a good name for your BASIC diskette, so we'll change it. If the `Empty` disk icon isn't black any more, click the icon to re-activate it.

√√   CHOOSE RENAME FROM THE **WORKBENCH** MENU.

This displays an input line in the center of the screen. Position the pointer in this line and click. To delete the word Empty, press the <DEL> key until the line is blank. Then you can type in the new name. We should use a name that has some meaning. How about "BASICDisk"?

√√   ENTER THE NAME BASICDISK AND PRESS THE <RETURN> KEY.

Empty will be renamed BASICDisk. Notice that the title in the window changes when you change the name.

√√   DON'T CLOSE THE **BASICDISK** WINDOW YET.

Copying
programs

We want to copy some programs to our new diskette. First let's put AmigaBASIC on the diskette. Insert the Extras diskette.

√√   TAKE THE WORKBENCH DISKETTE FROM DRIVE 1 (THE SECOND DRIVE) AND PUT IN THE EXTRAS DISKETTE.

It's a lot easier to make backups with two drives. If you only have one drive, you'll need to change diskettes several times during the copying process. <u>Remember not to remove a diskette while the disk drive's light</u> <u>is on</u>. To be safe, you might wait until the disk drive stops spinning (the noise will stop). If you don't follow this advice, you may lose all the data on the diskette.

√√   CLICK THE EXTRAS ICON.

The corresponding window is displayed in the **Workbench** window.

√√   MOVE THE POINTER ONTO THE AMIGABASIC ICON, PRESS AND HOLD THE LEFT MOUSE BUTTON, AND DRAG THE ICON INTO THE **BASICDISK** WINDOW.

To copy objects while in the Workbench, just move the icon from the old window (**Extras**) into the new window (**BASICDisk**).

If you've got two drives, the copying will be done by now. The pointer will turn into a wait pointer (a cloud with a few Z's drawn in it) during the copy process.

Copying with a single disk drive

If you've only got one drive, you need to exchange Extras and BASICDisk several times. The Workbench will inform you which diskette to insert by displaying a requester.

When the copying is done, the AmigaBASIC icon will appear in the **BASICDisk** window.

Copying drawers

Now we need to copy our BASIC programs. You can copy a drawer that contains programs in the same way you copy a single program. The number of times you'll need to exchange diskettes will depend on how much memory you have available, and how many files and programs are in the drawer.

√√   COPY YOUR PROGRAMS DRAWER FROM THE EXTRAS DISKETTE TO THE BASICDISK DISKETTE.

The programs are copied from one diskette to another, rather than actually moved—copies of the programs can be found on both diskettes now. It works differently when you move files and drawers inside a single diskette. For instance, when you move a BASIC program from one drawer into another. In this case they are not copied, they are really moved.

Now you've copied your programs and demos. The programs are not arranged in your drawer, though. We should clean up the Workbench now.

Leave the **BASICDisk** window open:

√√   CLOSE THE **EXTRAS** WINDOW, THEN OPEN THE **WORKBENCH** WINDOW.

As you know, if you have only a single drive, you'll be asked to put the Workbench diskette in the drive. We're not going to spell out the procedure anymore, since by now you should understand what you need to do. Besides, the Amiga tells you what it wants.

In one of the earlier Intermissions, we made a drawer for your BASIC programs. Perhaps you don't remember how we did that. You'll find a drawer called Empty in the **Workbench** window. Any time you need a fresh empty drawer, simply copy the Empty drawer.

*Copying
into drawers*

Move the drawer icon from the old window into the new window by holding down the left mouse button and then letting it loose. You've copied things from the Workbench so many times by now, that we don't need to say anything more about this.

Now click the `close` gadget for the **Workbench** window; we don't need it any more. We'll do the rest of the clean-up work on our new BASICDisk.

*Putting your
drawers in
order*

Since you'll be writng many AmigaBASIC programs in the future, it makes sense to organize the drawer so that it's easier to find them.

We thought about what kinds of programs we'll be writing, and so we suggest that you organize drawers in the following categories:

- Video
- Drawing programs
- Graphics
- Data
- Music
- Speech
- Miscellaneous

We need a total of seven drawers. We want to divide the current contents from my `programs` (or whatever this program drawer is called) into several subdrawers. We'll do the same with programs we write later.

Now we'll create seven drawers:

Duplicate

√√ CLICK ON THE EMPTY DRAWER AND CHOOSE DUPLICATE FROM THE **WORKBENCH** PULLDOWN MENU.

Now we have two copies of a drawer. To prevent confusion, rename the new drawer <u>immediately</u>.

√√ CLICK THE NEW DRAWER AND CHOOSE RENAME FROM THE **WORKBENCH** PULLDOWN MENU.

Here's a trick to save you time. Since you'll need to delete the text `Empty` or `copy of Empty` several times, instead of using <DEL> to get rid of the old text, use the <Amiga key><x> key combination.

Move the drawers you just renamed out of the way, so that you'll have enough room for the next one. Make five more copies in the same way. When you are finished, move the drawers around in the **BASICDisk** window. You can move them wherever you want using the mouse pointer.

Snapshot

If you'll remember our first Intermission, or you have some experience working with the Workbench, you know that these operations are not remembered by the Amiga unless you tell it to remember what you've done. You make it remember this by pressing the <SHIFT> key in the BASICDisk icon, clicking all the icons inside the window, and then choosing the Snapshot item from the **Special** pulldown menu.

The following illustration shows how our **BASICDisk** window looked after this. You can arrange yours any way you want.

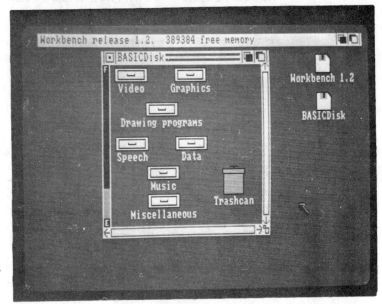

**Figure 12:
Our
BASICDisk
window**

*Rearranging
the drawers*

All the drawers are in place. Now we need to move the programs from the my programs drawer into the new drawers. Open this drawer, but don't worry too much about how messy it is. The Amiga isn't big on neatness. Now move the programs into the various drawers. This way we can organize them by category. For instance, move the ball program from the first chapter into the Graphics drawer. The Workbench takes care of copying programs from one drawer to another on the same diskette.

If you've had a BASIC program in the background since the beginning of this chapter, you can take care of saving it now. You need to use a BASIC command to do this. Click the **BASIC** window that is still in the Workbench level and use the sizing gadget to enlarge it. Then type the following command.

```
chdir "BASICDisk:
```

followed by the name of the drawer the program should go in. For graphics programs, you would type:

```
chdir "BASICDisk:Graphics"
```

Then you can use the SAVE command or the corresponding pulldown menu item to save your program. Then close the **AmigaBASIC** window by clicking on the close gadget.

A place for everything

Return to the Workbench and drag the rest of the programs into the seven drawers. Put all your video programs in the Video drawer. Put the drawing programs and pattern files that you've saved in the Drawing programs drawer. Move the bar chart/pie chart utility into the Graphics drawer. We also put all the sample programs in the drawer that worked with graphics or animation. The Data, Music, and Speech drawers are still empty. We'll have programs in them before we're done with this book, though. The Miscellaneous drawer contains programs that won't fit into any other category.

After moving your programs into the subdrawers, click the individual drawers and select the Snapshot item. When you've finished with this, you've completed your BASIC diskette. We'll use it from now on to store your BASIC programs and files.

Close all the windows except **BASICDisk** and click the AmigaBASIC icon. The next section will describe the AmigaBASIC disk commands available to you.

3.2

Directories, trees, and more: disk commands in AmigaBASIC

We needed to return to the Workbench to format and organize our new BASIC diskette, since AmigaBASIC doesn't support these operations.

SAVE *and* **LOAD**

However, AmigaBASIC does have a number of disk commands that you can use. You have learned a couple already. To save programs, you use the SAVE command. To load programs, you use the LOAD command. You can also use pulldown menu items to load and save, but these are really BASIC commands. It doesn't matter whether the command is called Open in the **Project** pulldown menu or LOAD in the **BASIC** window; you'll get the same result using either one.

Look it up

The first new command we'll look at is important if you want to display the files or programs contained on a diskette. After a while you'll probably forget the names of some of the programs. You can look at your files by going to the Workbench level, but this method is inconvenient, and takes too much time and memory.

It's easier to use a BASIC command. Type this command in the **BASIC** window:

```
files
```

FILES

The FILES command shows you the names of all the files in the current *disk directory*. A file is anything that you can store on a diskette: a program, data, a graphic, etc. A *directory* is the "table of contents" of a diskette.

What's a current directory? Look at the output we got in response to the FILES command. The first line says:

```
Directory of [BASICDisk]
```

AmigaBASIC lets you know which directory is being displayed. If you're in the Workbench and look at the contents, you'll only see the things that are in the **BASICDisk** window.

Info files

However, there are more than just program names (like AmigaBASIC) found here. If you look carefully, you'll notice that most names seem to come in pairs. For instance, there is the file AmigaBASIC and the file AmigaBASIC.info. We need to look at the way the Workbench operates to understand what these *info files* do.

Every file on the diskette is assigned an icon by the Workbench. The icons don't all look alike; you've probably seen programs that have their own icons. Maybe you've worked with the `IconEd` program that is on the Workbench diskette. (You can use `IconEd` to edit the appearance of icons in any way you want).

The directory also displays names in square brackets. These are *subdirectories*, also called *drawers*. They're displayed in the Workbench as drawer icons. There are also info files for these drawers. You can use them to store custom icons.

Sub-directories

Subdirectories are fairly easy to understand. Programs and files are stored in a subdirectory by category to keep them organized, just as we did with our BASICDisk. You can nest drawers inside of drawers inside of drawers, etc., or at least until you run out of memory.

Subdirectories can be explained graphically using a tree structure. Tree structures illustrate how subdirectories are organized and how you can move around subdirectories.

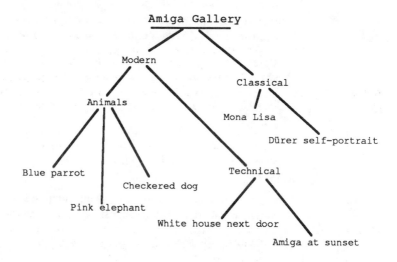

Figure 13: Disk directory tree structure

Suppose we have a diskette named `AmigaGallery` that we use to store graphics. The disk name is the root of the tree. Two directories are contained on the diskette: `Classics` and `Modern` (the tree has two large limbs). If you want to load a graphic named `Pink elephant`, you need to follow the path from `Modern` to `Animals`.

204

You can only load programs and data from the current directory. If the program is in another location on the diskette, AmigaBASIC won't find it. Programs can be identified by the path you must follow to get to them. This means you can save several programs on the same diskette under the same name, just as long as they are stored in different directories.

CHDIR

To put this theory into practice, we need a BASIC command introduced in the last chapter—CHDIR (CHange DIRectory).

If you want to know the programs on the BASICDisk which are stored in the Graphics directory, you use:

```
chdir "Graphics"
```

Now you've changed from the main directory, BASICDisk, to the Graphics directory. If you use the FILES command to view its contents, you'll see the new directory name in the first line:

```
Directory of: [Graphics]
```

This followed by the names of all the programs stored in the Graphics directory. If the list contains another directory, you can use CHDIR to climb higher in the tree.

Returning to the root

What can you do when the program you're looking for isn't in the directory you're in? There are two solutions: either you can retrace the path you followed, or you can jump back to the root of the tree and start over.

There are two types of commands you can use. Typing the following line:

```
chdir "/"
```

CHDIR "/"

moves you back one directory. In our example, you'll move from the Animals directory into the Modern directory. If you type CHDIR "/" again, you'll end up in AmigaGallery.

If you use a CHDIR "/" command when you are in the AmigaGallery level, you'll get a File not found error message.

If you don't want to retrace your path, type the following command:

```
chdir ":"
```

CHDIR ":"

This command returns you to the root of the tree. From here, you can start climbing the tree again to find the program you're looking for.

Multiple drives and `CHDIR`

One more thing we need to know. What happens if you've got more than one disk drive? Up to now, we've just worked with one diskette, (BASICDisk). If you've got two drives and would like to see the root directory of drive 1, type:

```
chdir "df1:"
```

AmigaBASIC refers to the internal disk drive as `DF0:` and the first external drive as `DF1:`. The D stands for "Drive" and F for "Floppy." If you have a third drive, it's called `DF2:`. If you own a hard disk drive, the system will call it `DH0:` (Drive Harddisk 0).

Drive designation

You can precede the name of a directory with the drive designator. For instance:

```
chdir "df1:Text"
```

designates the `Text` directory on drive 1 as the current directory. This only makes sense if the drive is really connected. If AmigaBASIC can't find the drive, it will ask you to insert a diskette with that name (`Please insert volume df1 in any drive`).

By the way, you can use diskette names instead of drive designators:

```
chdir "BASICDisk:Graphics"
```

This line designates `Graphics` as the current directory, regardless of which drive BASICDisk is in. If this diskette isn't already in a drive, the Amiga will ask you to insert it into one of the drives.

Here's one more form of the `CHDIR` command:

```
chdir "df1:Amiga-Gallery/Modern/Animals"
```

Moving through the sub-directories quickly

This is the fastest method to get at your `Pink elephant` graphic. You can type the names of the directories you need to pass through on the way to your destination, separating them with slashes (`/`). If you type a nonexistent path or mistype a directory name, AmigaBASIC displays a `File not found` error message. With a little bit of practice, you'll get to be very good at climbing through the directories on your AmigaBASIC diskettes.

AmigaBASIC can do more than this, though. You can load and save programs and choose and display directories, but you can also rename and delete your programs from the **BASIC** window.

We'll go through an example. First type a couple of program lines in the **LIST** window (nothing special—we're going to delete this program in a short while anyhow).

Now save your program with the Save As item in the **Project** menu. Type in the name Test and press <RETURN>. Your Amiga stores the file on the diskette. You can verify this using the FILES command. You'll find the files Test and Test.info in the list.

Let's say that you don't like the name Test. Maybe you think the name doesn't describe the program's contents well enough, and the name Worthless is more appropriate. You could save the program under another name, since it's still in memory, but that's a waste of memory—you already have a copy of the program under the name Test on the diskette.

NAME

A new BASIC command comes in handy here. Its called NAME, and you can use it to rename your programs. To rename Test as Worthless, type the following in the **BASIC** window:

NAME "Test" AS "Worthless"

The drive runs for a short while. Now your file has a new name. The info filename was also changed—Test.info is now called Worthless.info. If your info file is still called Test.info, then you have an older version of AmigaBASIC. For temporary relief, use the NAME function again:

NAME "Test.info" AS "Worthless.info"

Then everything will be OK. However, you should visit your dealer immediately to get the newest version of AmigaBASIC.

KILL

The next command is useful for getting rid of unwanted files (like our Worthless program). You can get rid of programs from the Workbench by putting them in the trashcan, but you need to Empty Trash yourself. It's quicker to use AmigaBASIC to delete files. This is often an advantage, but it can be hazardous: Make sure that you really want to get rid of a file. Once you have used the KILL command, you can't get the file back. If you're sure that you want to delete Worthless, type:

KILL "Worthless"

AmigaBASIC deletes the program quickly and painlessly.

We'd like to tell you about a little trick we learned. When you delete an info file only, its corresponding program file is not displayed in the **Workbench** window, but AmigaBASIC knows it exists. You'll be able to see the filename using the FILES command, and you can still execute the program. This is a good way to protect your program from curious people. To produce this effect, you use this syntax:

```
KILL "Junk.info"
```

You can KILL an info file from any filename to test this out. Start experimenting with program and file structures using the disk commands you already know. But the best is yet to come. We'll look at managing data on diskettes. We're going to look at storing address lists, stock prices, graphics and much more.

3.3 The data collector: a BASIC address book

Up to this point we've simply saved AmigaBASIC programs to diskette. The two previous times we saved files that were <u>not</u> programs (for example, the object editor's object file and the paint program's fill patterns), we told you we'd tell you more later. That time is now.

Storing data

Obviously, you can store more than AmigaBASIC program files on a diskette. You can also store *data files*. Data can be many things: Numbers, text, pictures, and more. Most commercial programs save data files to diskette, since the data would otherwise be erased when the computer is turned off. For example, a data file contains information about the characters created with a word processing program, so that you can work with a document you typed in months ago.

We'll look at the simplest way that AmigaBASIC saves data and reads it back later. The following program creates an address file on the diskette:

```
OPEN "AddressFile" FOR OUTPUT AS 1¶
¶
Entry:¶
  PRINT¶
  INPUT "Name";Nam$¶
  INPUT "Address";Address$¶
  INPUT "City";City$¶
  INPUT "Phone";Phone$¶
  PRINT#1,Nam$¶
  PRINT#1,Address$¶
  PRINT#1,City$¶
  PRINT#1,Phone$¶
  x=x+1¶
  PRINT "Record"x" ("Nam$") stored."¶
  PRINT "Add more records?"¶
  INPUT "Y/N:";Ans$¶
  IF UCASE$(Ans$)="Y" THEN Entry¶
¶
CLOSE¶
PRINT "File closed. Program ended."¶
```

We'll put all our data management programs in the Data drawer. Type:

```
chdir "BASICDisk:Data"
```

Save the program under the name Write Addresses. (Program filenames can use blank spaces).

How the program works

OPEN

The OPEN command first opens the AddressFile file. A file must be OPENed before a BASIC program can use it. This makes sense—you can't read a book unless you open it.

You also use the OPEN command to declare whether you are going to write to the file (OPEN...FOR OUTPUT) or read from it (OPEN...FOR INPUT). You can either read from a file or you can write to the same file, but you cannot do both at once. However, you can open several files at once, some for input and others for output.

This is the reason that every open file is assigned a number (number 1 in our example) so that the Read and Write commands will know which file to work with.

When an output file is opened for the first time (as in our example), the OPEN command stores the file on diskette in the current directory. The command's syntax looks like this:

```
OPEN "(File name)" FOR (Mode) AS (File number)
```

This command also has a second syntax. It contains the same information, but in a different order:

```
OPEN "(Mode)", #(File number), "(File name)"
```

We could have written our first line like this:

```
OPEN "O",#1,"AddressFile"
```

You can use either form. Depending on the situation, one of the command forms may be better than the other. We'll come back to this later.

Now we have a file called AddressFile with the number 1 into which we can write data. Now let's write some data to the file.

PRINT#

The Entry: subroutine starts by asking the user for the values of the variables Nam$, Address$, City$, and Phone$. These strings contain the information that comprise our electronic address book. To write this data in the file, we use the PRINT# command. We put the file number behind the PRINT# command. The command PRINT#1,Nam$, writes the variable Nam$ in file number 1—i.e., in AddressFile. The PRINT# command works like the regular PRINT command, except that the output is sent to a file, not the screen.

Sequential files

We store the addresses in a *sequential* file. Sequential files store data items one after the other, or in sequence. The file stores the first name, then the address, city, and finally the telephone number. Then it stores the second name, the second address, second city, etc.

Sequential files are one kind of file used by AmigaBASIC. Other filetypes include random (or relative) files, which we'll discuss later.

The rest of the program should be easy for you to understand. We increment the variable x so that we can display the number of addresses that have been typed. Then the program asks the user if he wants to enter more addresses. If <y> is pressed, the program will jump back to the Entry: section.

More about
INPUT

You may not have noticed something about the INPUT line, or you may have thought this was a typographical error. Look carefully at the difference between these two commands:

INPUT " (Text) ";Variable   (uses a semicolon)

INPUT " (Text) ",Variable   (uses a comma)

We use both versions of the INPUT command in our example program. If there is a semicolon between the text and the variable, AmigaBASIC will display a question mark after the Text. If you use a comma, a question mark is <u>not</u> displayed. We don't want a question mark displayed when the program asks for <y> or <n>, so we use the comma syntax.

CLOSE

If you press <n> or any key other than <y>, the program executes a CLOSE 1 command. The CLOSE command closes a file that was opened with the OPEN command. The following happens along the way:

When we issue a command to store data to diskette, the information isn't written on the diskette character by character as we type it in. That would take too long, and would tie up the disk drive. For instance, the Amiga might be multitasking and trying to access another program on the diskette, but couldn't access the other program as long as AmigaBASIC had one or more disk files open in this way.

To avoid this conflict, a *buffer* is set up for each open file. A buffer is a range of memory (usually 128 bytes long) in which characters are stored until the buffer is full. When the buffer is eventually filled with 128 characters, these characters are transferred from the buffer and then written to diskette. The CLOSE command ensures that the buffer contents will be saved, even if the buffer isn't full yet.

The CLOSE command is also necessary before you issue some other AmigaBASIC disk commands. You can't open a file again to read or write until it has been CLOSEd. And you can't KILL a file or reNAME it while it is open. The CLOSE command also frees up the file number so that you can use it for another file.

If you try to read from or write to a CLOSEd file, you'll get a Bad file number error message.

How to operate the program

Working with this demonstration address program is pretty easy. The Amiga will ask you for the address information item by item. After typing an address, you need to press <y> to continue.

Type in the names of a couple of friends to try it out.

However, it doesn't do us a whole lot of good just to have the addresses stored on a diskette. We still need a program that will read the addresses from the diskette. Before typing in the new program following, save the `Write Address` program if you haven't done so already. Use NEW to clear the memory. Then type in the following program:

```
OPEN "AddressFile" FOR INPUT AS 1¶
¶
ReadData:¶
  INPUT#1,Nam$¶
  INPUT#1,Address$¶
  INPUT#1,City$¶
  INPUT#1,Phone$¶
  PRINT¶
  PRINT "Name: ";Nam$¶
  PRINT "Address: ";Address$¶
  PRINT "City: ";City$¶
  PRINT "Phone: ";Phone$¶
¶
  IF EOF(1)=0 THEN ReadData¶
CLOSE 1¶
```

When you run this program, the addresses are read from the file and written to the screen. Save this program under the name `Read Address`.

The OPEN command opens `AddressFile FOR INPUT`. You should recognize this command from the graphics chapter, since we read in graphic object data there.

To read in the data, AmigaBASIC must be able to find the file. If it can't, it will give you a `File not found` error message. If you get this error, and you're certain that the name you typed is correct. Also, you may have to use CHDIR to change the current directory.

INPUT#

We can use INPUT# to read in information from a file just as we can use PRINT# to write out information to a file. It's important to read the information in the order that it was written. Otherwise, you may get someone named 10538 with a zip code of 949-4449 and who lives on John Doe street!

The INPUT# command reads in variables just like the INPUT command. The difference is that the information is read in from a file, and not from the keyboard. The data from the file is then displayed on the screen.

EOF

The EOF (End of File) function tells us whether there is more data to be read from the file or not. You type the file number in parentheses. If there is still more data to be read, EOF (File number) returns a 0. If the last character has been read, it returns a -1. This way you can see whether there's more information to be read or whether you should close the file.

If you try to read from a file that doesn't have any more data, you'll get an Input past end error message. This means that you tried to read past the end of the file.

Reading sequential files

Reading a sequential file works much like READing DATA lines: the pointer is moved one position over so that you always read the next unread value. Remember, the sequential file displays the addresses on the screen in the same order that they are stored in the file.

This is the most distinguishing characteristic of a sequential file: its records must be read one after the other. If you only want to read the tenth address, you must first read the first nine before you can get to the tenth. It's impossible to jump over the data in between. Therefore, sequential files are most useful when you're working with data that is always processed in the same order.

FOR OUTPUT/ INPUT/ APPEND

If you wanted to expand the sequential file, it would be a hassle to read in all the old data and then store it again. There's a way to avoid this: you can open a file FOR APPEND to expand the file.

Load the Write Address program. Change the OUTPUT in the first line to APPEND, like this:

```
OPEN "AddressFile" FOR APPEND AS 1
```

Start the program and type one or two addresses. Don't let it bother you that the program thinks it is writing the first and second record—it is actually writing the first and second records being appended. When you finish, load the Read Address program and run it. You'll see that the new addresses are stored at the end of the file, after the old addresses.

NOTE: You can append data to sequential files at any time, but you cannot put
                     data at the beginning or the middle of the file. You cannot change or
                     delete information with this command, either.

                     If you want, you can use APPEND mode everytime you write to the
                     file. If the file doesn't exist, AmigaBASIC will respond as it does in
                     OUTPUT mode—it will create a new file.

                     Now that you know a little about sequential files, let's apply this
                     knowledge in a larger program. In the graphics chapter of this book, we
                     promised to include a utility for working with data for bar charts and pie
                     charts. This complementary program is listed in the next section.

3.4 Information for bar and pie charts: managing statistical data

You need groups of data available to create pie charts and bar graphs. Previously, we typed in this data on the keyboard, but that's a poor solution. Say you wanted to chart the daily price fluctuations of Commodore's stock . You'd get tired of the stock market in a hurry if you had to type in all this data every day, beginning with the initial price. Next you'll write a program that will store these prices, so that all you need to do is add one price number each day.

You already wrote the program that creates bar graphs and pie charts from statistical data. It should be stored in the `Graphics` drawer of your BASIC disk. You've also saved the address program. Use NEW to erase the BASIC memory area. Now load the version of the bar graph/pie chart program that was stored without the text input part. Type `CHDIR: "BASICDisk:Graphics"` to get into the `Graphics` drawer.

Look for the name of the program file using the `FILES` command. Load the program. Move into the Data directory using the command `CHDIR ":Data"`.

Now we need to save the program as an ASCII file. You'll remember we have already worked with chaining, or merging, programs in a previous Intermission. Once again we have two programs that we can either combine into one, or else we'll have to retype the code from one program into the other. If you dislike typing as much as we do, you'll want to `MERGE` the bar graph/pie chart program with our new program. Therefore you need to save the chart program in ASCII format:

```
SAVE "NewBarPie",A
```

Now clear the memory using the NEW command. Type in the first section of the new program:

```
Setup:¶
  DIM Number$(58),Desc$(58),Value$(58) ¶
  DIM Array$(50),Array(50) ¶
  FOR x=1 TO 58¶
    IF x>4 AND x<55 THEN Number$(x)=STR$(x-4) ¶
  NEXT x¶
  TopLine=1 ¶
¶
  Colors=3¶
  SCREEN 4,640,200,Colors,2¶
  WINDOW 99,"Graphics",,20,4¶
  PALETTE 7,.8,.2,.1¶
¶
```

```
WINDOW 1,"Statistical-Data-Manager",(0,12)-
(631,111),22,-1¶
¶
  MENU 1,0,1,"Data   "  ¶
  MENU 1,1,1,"Load   "¶
  MENU 1,2,1,"Save   "¶
  MENU 1,3,1,"Delete"¶
  MENU 1,4,1,"Quit   "¶
  MENU 2,0,1,"Graphics"¶
  MENU 2,1,1,"Bar Graph"¶
  MENU 2,2,1,"Pie Chart"¶
  MENU 3,0,0,""¶
  MENU 4,0,0,""¶
¶
  ON MENU GOSUB MenuControl¶
  MENU ON¶
¶
GOTO MainLoop¶
```

Arrays

The program begins by dimensioning the arrays that we'll need for the program. `Number$` is the number of the data line. `Nam$` is the description of a value. It might be the name of the company whose stock you're charting. `Value$` is the number that we need for statistical purposes; it might be a percentage. We use a string array for numbers because that makes the input routine simpler—it lets you type whatever you want to type. The array's contents will be converted to numbers when we call the graphics routine.

You should recognize `Array$` and `Array` from the bar graph/pie chart utility. We use these arrays to pass data to the subroutine.

The array `Number$` will always have the same contents. As we said earlier, it contains the numbers of the data lines. We allow up to 50 values, so we number things from 1 to 50. Why did we set the array up to have 58 elements? Is that for safety reasons? Those are good questions. Let's talk about them.

The basic idea is that you'll only be able to see a few of the 50 data lines—you can't fit all 50 on the screen. A data line contains three elements: The number of the data line at the beginning; the name of the item; and the number that corresponds to the name.

Cursor placement

You'll always see 9 data lines on the screen. Your work (input, correction, insertion, deletion, etc.) will always be displayed on the fifth line. The values 1 to 4 and 6 to 9 are for orientation—so that you can see what values lie in the immediate vicinity of the present line. You scroll the lines up and down with the cursor keys, while the cursor stays in the middle line.

Since you'll want to work on the first and last lines of the file, we put in some blank array fields to precede the first element and follow the last element. The first real data line is in the fifth position in the array. That's why we use 58; 4 + 50 + 4 = 58.

216

STR$

The FOR...NEXT loop sets the values for the Number$ array. The first four positions are empty. Then we insert the numbers 1 to 50. Finally we insert four more blank positions. You can use the STR$ command to convert numbers into strings. STR$ is the opposite of VAL. The following line:

```
? VAL(STR$(5))
```

VAL

returns the number 5. It converts the number 5 to a string and then back to a number. Converting from one data format to another is very important, so we'll discuss more of these commands later.

The variable TopLine is set to 1. TopLine -1 is the last line that contains data. Since there isn't any data in the arrays at the beginning, line 1 is the first line that doesn't contain any data.

You can set up one to four bitplanes, depending on how many colors you want in your graphics.

Now we produce the screen and window for the Graphics: subprogram. We define color number 7 from white to red. Sound familiar? It should—we described these preparations in the description of the bar graph/pie chart utility in Section 2.7.

Window 1 (the **BASIC** window) will be reduced and named Statistical-Data-Management. If you don't like this name, you can easily change it. We typed -1 as the screen. While screen 1 to 4 are just for the user, -1 is the number of the Workbench screen.

Defining the
pulldown

Next we define the pulldown menu. We want to put this program under menu control. We have Load, Save, Delete (erase the data in memory), and Quit available as items in the **File** pulldown menu. The **Graphics** menu lets you choose between a Bar Graph and a Pie Chart.

Menus 3 and 4 have items **Run** and **Window** disabled.

Next we activate event trapping for the menu control and jump to MainLoop:.

In contrast to drawing programs, this program isn't controlled just by event trapping. The pulldown menu functions are breaks in the MainLoop: and TypeText: program sections. Handling event trapping this way is a typical method. It always makes sense when the possible results (menus, mouse, timeouts, error handling, break control, and collision checks) improve or expand on the things in the main program.

Here's the subroutine that takes care of menu choices.

```
MenuControl:¶
   Men=MENU(0)  : MenuPoint=MENU(1) ¶
   IF Men=1 THEN¶
      IF MenuPoint=1 THEN GOSUB LoadData¶
      IF MenuPoint=2 THEN GOSUB SaveData¶
      IF MenuPoint=3 THEN GOSUB ClearData¶
      IF MenuPoint=4 THEN Quit¶
   END IF¶
   IF Men=2 THEN¶
      IF MenuPoint=1 THEN Array$(0)="B"¶
      IF MenuPoint=2 THEN Array$(0)="P"¶
      Array(0)=TopLine¶
      IF Value$(Array(0)+4)="" THEN Array(0)=Array(0)-1¶
      FOR x=1 TO Array(0)¶
         Array$(x)=Desc$(x+4)¶
         Array(x)=VAL(Value$(x+4))¶
         IF Array(x)=0 THEN Array(x)=.01¶
      NEXT x¶
      MENU OFF¶
      MENU 1,0,0 : MENU 2,0,0¶
      WINDOW 99 : CLS¶
      ¶
      GOSUB Graphics¶
      ¶

      WINDOW 2,"Please press a key!",(350,0)-(631,0),20,4¶
      COLOR 0,1 : CLS¶
      WHILE INKEY$=""¶
      WEND¶
      WINDOW CLOSE 2¶
      WINDOW 1¶
      MENU ON¶
      MENU 1,0,1 : MENU 2,0,1          ¶
   END IF¶
RETURN          ¶
```

The number of the chosen menu is placed in the variable Men. The number of the chosen menu item is placed in the variable MenuPoint. We did it the same way in the paint program. As you can see, it's often smart to use old solutions to solve new problems.

If the first menu is used, the corresponding subroutines will be called directly from the routine responsible for menu control. If the second menu is chosen, one of the two sorts of graphics figures is chosen. The first element in the array is Array$. This can be either a B (for Bar chart) or P (for Pie chart) to identify which sort of chart is desired.

Line adjustments

The first position in Array must contain the number of data items when the Graphics: subroutine is called. The variable TopLine contains this value, which is handled by an assignment statement. Sometimes, TopLine will be a little too big. If you press <RETURN> after the last data input, the cursor will move one line below the last data line. In this case, the value 0 without a description would appear in the graphic figure if left alone. That would look silly. To avoid this, the program checks if there is a number in the numerical column of the last line. If there isn't, the line will be treated as an empty line, and Array(0) will be decremented by one.

The following FOR...NEXT loop copies the contents of the the arrays corresponding to data lines into the Array and Array$ arrays. Remember that the field Desc$ and Value$ have four blank elements at the beginning (thus we use Array$(x)=Desc$(x+4)). The loop will be executed until it runs out of data lines.

The VAL function is used to convert the contents of Value$ into numbers for the Array array. If it encounters a 0 in the file, the value will be incremented by 0.01. This way we avoid a Division by Zero error message in the Graphics: subroutine.

Menus while drawing

The menus are disabled during the drawing process with MENU OFF. The two pulldown menus become ghost menus, which visually informs you that none of the items are presently available.

The window in which the graphics will appear, WINDOW 99, is then activated. First we erase it using CLS, since earlier graphics will still be displayed in the window (if you've called it previously).

Everything else is taken care of in the Graphics: subroutine, which is called using the GOSUB command.

Creating a requester

After drawing the graphic, the program returns. We create a requester that displays Please hit a key! The window itself is only two pixels high, since the title explains all.

The WHILE...WEND loop waits for you to hit a key. Once you do this, the requester will be closed and Window 1 (the **BASIC** or data entry window) will be activated. Next the event trapping for menu selection and the two pulldown menus are reactivated. Program control will RETURN to the program line where the Amiga was interrupted by a menu call.

Unfortunately, you can't try this new program out yet, since we're missing the Graphics: subroutine. Also, we can't use this with certain types of data yet.

Type the next section of the program:

```
MainLoop:¶
  CLS¶
  IF TopLine>50 THEN TopLine=50¶
  IF LineOne>TopLine THEN LineOne=TopLine : BEEP¶
  IF LineOne<1 THEN LineOne=1 : BEEP¶
  PRINT "Number";TAB(10);"Description";TAB(45);"Value"¶
  FOR x=LineOne TO LineOne+8¶
    COLOR 1,0¶
    PRINT Number$(x);TAB(10);Desc$(x);TAB(45);Value$(x)¶
  NEXT x¶
  IF DescData=0 THEN StartSlice=10 : EndSlice=40¶
  IF DescData=1 THEN StartSlice=45 : EndSlice=55¶
  xp=StartSlice¶
¶
  GOSUB TypeText¶
  in$=""¶
¶
GOTO MainLoop¶
¶
¶
TypeText:¶
  IF xp<StartSlice THEN xp=StartSlice¶
  LOCATE 6,xp¶
  COLOR 0,3 : PRINT " "; : COLOR 1,0¶
  i$=INKEY$¶
  IF i$="" THEN TypeText¶
  IF i$=CHR$(2) THEN LineOne=1 : RETURN¶
  IF i$=CHR$(5) THEN LineOne=TopLine : RETURN¶
  IF i$=CHR$(4) THEN DeleteLine : RETURN¶
  IF i$=CHR$(14) THEN InsertLine : RETURN¶
  IF i$=CHR$(28) THEN GOSUB AcceptText : xp=StartSlice :
LineOne=LineOne-1: RETURN¶
  IF i$=CHR$(29) THEN GOSUB AcceptText : xp=StartSlice :
LineOne=LineOne+1: RETURN¶
    ¶
  TextPos=xp-StartSlice+1¶
  IF DescData=0 THEN Text$=Desc$(LineOne+4)¶
  IF DescData=1 THEN Text$=Value$(LineOne+4)¶
¶
  IF i$=CHR$(30) THEN¶
    IF TextPos<=LEN(Text$) THEN i$=MID$(Text$,TextPos,1)¶
  END IF ¶
¶
  IF i$=CHR$(13) OR i$=CHR$(9) THEN¶
    GOSUB AcceptText¶
    DescData=1-DescData¶
    IF DescData=0 THEN LineOne=LineOne+1¶
    xp=StartSlice¶
    IF TopLine<LineOne THEN TopLine=LineOne¶
    RETURN¶
  END IF¶
  IF i$=CHR$(8) OR i$=CHR$(31) THEN¶
    LOCATE 6,xp¶
    IF TextPos<=LEN(Text$) THEN¶
      PRINT RIGHT$(Text$,LEN(Text$)-TextPos+1);¶
    ELSE¶
```

```
          PRINT " ";¶
        END IF¶
        xp=xp-1 : IF xp<StartSlice THEN xp=StartSlice : BEEP
: GOTO TypeText¶
        in$=LEFT$(in$,(LEN(in$)-1))¶
        GOTO TypeText¶
      END IF¶
    IF i$=CHR$(34) THEN i$=CHR$(39)¶
    IF i$ > CHR$(31) AND i$ < CHR$(127) THEN¶
      IF xp>=EndSlice THEN xp=EndSlice : BEEP : GOTO
TypeText¶
      LOCATE 6,xp¶
      PRINT i$;¶
      in$=in$+i$¶
      xp=xp+1¶
    END IF¶
GOTO TypeText¶
¶
AcceptText:¶
  IF in$<>"" THEN¶
    IF DescData=0 THEN Desc$(LineOne+4)=in$¶
    IF DescData=1 THEN Value$(LineOne+4)=in$¶
    in$=""¶
    AltData=1¶
  END IF¶
RETURN¶
¶
DeleteLine:¶
  FOR x=LineOne+4 TO 54¶
    Desc$(x)=Desc$(x+1)¶
    Value$(x)=Value$(x+1)¶
  NEXT x¶
  TopLine=TopLine-1¶
  IF TopLine<1 THEN TopLine=1¶
RETURN¶
¶
InsertLine:¶
  IF TopLine>=50 THEN BEEP : RETURN¶
  FOR x=TopLine+4 TO LineOne+4 STEP -1¶
    Desc$(x+1)=Desc$(x)¶
    Value$(x+1)=Value$(x)¶
  NEXT x¶
  Desc$(LineOne+4)=""¶
  Value$(LineOne+4)=""¶
  TopLine=TopLine+1¶
RETURN¶
```

The routine is divided into the following sections: TypeText: is responsible for the data that is input; MainLoop: is responsible for scrolling the lines. When you scroll, some information disappears at the bottom of the screen and new data becomes visible at the top of the screen, or vice versa. This allows the user to display at least a portion of the entire file.

221

Everytime the screen is moved, `MainLoop:` redisplays the text on the screen. First it uses `CLS` to erase the screen. The value of `TopLine` may not exceed 50. The variable `LineOne` contains the number of the first line on the screen. More accurately, `LineOne` contains the array position in the first of the nine data items that will be displayed on the screen.

An example should make this clear. If `LineOne` equals 1, then the first line will contain the values of `Number$(1)`, `Desc$(1)`, and `Value$(1)`. As you know, these are empty, so the first line is blank. The fifth line is the first line that can be reached by the cursor. It is input line one. `Number$(5)` contains the number one. Thus, `LineOne` also contains the number of the current input line.

This may be a bit confusing. Don't worry about it though—all theory is confusing until you apply it. You've got enough of the program typed in that its rudimentary functions will now run.

Don't forget to save the program as you go along. If errors crop up, correct them by comparing this listing to your listing, and insert the corrections.

Trying out the program

When everything runs correctly, hit <RETURN> a couple times. You can also type in a few words so that the scrolling is easier to see. End each input word by pressing <RETURN>.

You see that the cursor jumps between the column `Desc` and `Array`. Type <RETURN> until the cursor is in input line five.

Now experiment with the <cursor up> and <cursor down> keys. You'll see that the lines move up and down. When you've moved the cursor to the top of the file, you'll see that input line one is preceded by four blank lines. Right now, `LineOne` has the value 1—you're working with input line one, and the first line on the screen is filled with the first elements of the `Number$`, `Desc$`, and `Value$` arrays.

If the cursor is on input line five, `LineOne` has the value five. That's all there is to it. Once you understand this, the rest of the program should be easy to follow.

The next two lines keep the scrolling from moving too far up or down. The cursor cannot move further up than the first line or further down than the last line (`TopLine`). We use a `BEEP` to remind the user of that.

TAB

The program displays the column titles (`Number`, `Description`, and `Value`) and the nine data lines. We use a new BASIC command to do this: `TAB`. The term `TAB` comes in deed from the word tabulator). You've probably used tabs on typewriters or word processors previously. The `TAB` command is used for the same thing: to jump to a specified column on the screen:

```
PRINT TAB(10);"Hello!"
```

prints "Hello!" starting at column 10 on the screen. You'll use TAB to easily create tables and lists.

The variable DescData comes into play at the end of the Mainloop:. The variable DescData lets the program know whether a label (in the text column) or a number (in the numeric column) will be input.

We use StartSlice and EndSlice to specify the boundaries of the allowed input field for the TypeText: subroutine. The value xp is also used in the TypeText: subroutine. It indicates the horizontal position of the cursor. When input begins, it is equal to the start column.

After these preparations, we call the TypeText: subroutine. After returning, the input string in$ is erased. This is done so that it can be used the next time. Finally, MainLoop: jumps to its own beginning. As long as there is no interruption, the program will run indefinitely.

Changing keyboard input

Now let's take a look at the TypeText: subroutine. First we'll look at its basic functions. We wrote our own routines for keyboard input here. Normally, we can use the AmigaBASIC commands INPUT and LINE INPUT, but we can't use them here. While these commands are being executed, AmigaBASIC can't check which keys were hit. Since we want full control over all keys, we'll read each key with INKEY$ and then put words and numbers together later.

The program starts with one restriction on xp—it may not be smaller than the StartSlice variable. This isn't possible at the beginning since we've just made xp and StartSlice equal. However, during input, you may move the cursor left or erase characters, and the cursor may try to leave the input field on the left side. The first line of TypeText: prevents this.

LOCATE

The cursor stays on one screen line, and can't be moved up or down. Line 6 uses LOCATE 6,xp to set the cursor on the right line in the correct horizontal position.

We create our own cursor in the shape of an orange box. We use COLOR 0,3 to specify orange as the background color and blue as the foreground color. If we type a blank, an orange box is the default. After this, the colors for all other text are returned to their normal settings.

INKEY$

The central command in the input routine i$=INKEY$ follows. The variable i$ contains the current character input. If i$ is empty, then a key wasn't pressed yet. In this case the TypeText: program will jump to its beginning and wait until a key is pressed.

Keyboard buffer

If you type faster than the Amiga can process the characters, the characters won't be lost. AmigaBASIC has a 15-character long *keyboard buffer*. The Amiga uses this "holding tank" to store characters for which it isn't ready. The INKEY$ command reads from this buffer. If the buffer is full and you type more, a short blip on the screen will warn you that any characters typed at this time will be ignored. It's the same blip you hear when AmigaBASIC doesn't have a window that it can use for keyboard input.

The rest of the TypeText: subroutine is used to evaluate the characters that are input. If you want to compare the contents of INKEY$ (or a copy of it in in$), you need the CHR$ command. The CHR$ command takes an ASCII code number and converts it into the number's corresponding character. Now we can compare characters with characters (INKEY$ with CHR$(x)). If they are equal, the program responds.

Control characters

A CHR$(2) is a <CONTROL><B> character. This is the character produced when you press and hold down the <CTRL> key and then press the <B> key. The <CONTROL><B> character is not displayed on the screen—most *control characters* aren't displayed. But this doesn't mean that they have no effect. Many can greatly affect the execution of a program. You'll notice that if you press <CONTROL><G> when you're in the **BASIC** window, you'll hear a BEEP sound. You also have some experience with <CONTROL><C>, the combination that terminates the current BASIC program.

Start of file

We use <CONTROL><B> to jump to the first line of the data list. The variable LineOne is set to one and then we RETURN from the subroutine. MainLoop: takes care of displaying the lines.

End of file

We use <CTRL><E> (CHR$(5)) in a similar fashion. It can be used to jump to the end of your file. The end of the file is the last line to contain input. It may also be a line containing no input at all.

Deleting lines

We use <CONTROL><D> (CHR$(4)) to delete a line. You can use this key combination to delete the line on which the cursor is currently located. The DeleteLine: routine handles this. After executing this routine, the program returns to the MainLoop: routine.

Inserting lines

We use <CONTROL><N> (CHR$(14)) to insert a new line. The new line is inserted at the current cursor position in the InsertLine: subroutine.

We tried the four control functions in a way that you can remember. Here are short descriptions of their use:

<CONTROL><B>	beginning of text
<CONTROL><E>	end of text
<CONTROL><D>	delete a line
<CONTROL><N>	insert a line

Assigning control codes

When you program control codes, you should strive to assign easily remembered values to the control characters. Whenever possible, you should replace <CONTROL> sequences with pulldown menu items since you can include explanatory text. Also, it's often much easier to work with the mouse than with the keyboard.

The next two program lines handle the <cursor up> and <cursor down> keys.

Moving up a line

The <cursor up> key is CHR$(28). When the user presses this key, he leaves the current input field. The input there should be inserted into the list. The AcceptText: routine handles this. The cursor position pointer, xp, is set to the start column so that it will be at the beginning of the new input field. The variable LineOne is decremented by one, and then we're ready to RETURN to the MainLoop: to scroll up one line.

Moving down a line

The <cursor down> key is CHR$(29). This line is constructed exactly like the previous line. The only difference is that it scrolls down.

The variable TextPos calculates the cursor's position in the current input text. For example, if the cursor is located in column 14 and the value of StartSlice is 10, we are in the (14-10+1)th position (the fifth position) in the input text.

The Text$ string contains the text that we are typing or correcting. The value will be read from the field Desc$ or Value$ at the beginning (the variable DescData decides which one).

The <cursor right> key corresponds to CHR$(30). If the cursor is located in a section of text that was typed previously (the IF TextPos<=LEN(Text$) checks to make sure) and the user presses <Cursor right>, i$ is assigned the value of the character in Text$ on which the cursor is located.

<RETURN> and <TAB>

The <RETURN> key is CHR$(13); the <TAB> key is CHR$(9). The <TAB> key is marked on Amiga 500 models by a pair of arrows (|← and →|). The <RETURN> and <TAB> keys have the same function in our program: terminate input to the current field. The AcceptText: routine is called. The variable DescData (alternates between 1 and 0) determines whether we are in the Description or the Value column. The formula (Variable)=1-(Variable) "toggles" the value of a variable between zero and one.

If DescData has the value zero, the program jumps from the Value column to the Description column. A linefeed will be executed. The variable xp is reset to the value of the first column. A new TopLine is set. (The variable TopLine is the largest line number that contains an input). If the new value of LineOne is larger than TopLine, then TopLine will be reset equal to the LineOne variable. Now that the `TypeText:` routine has done its job, it RETURNs to the `Mainloop:` routine.

Backspacing and moving left

The next program section searches for the <BACKSPACE> and <cursor left> keys. The two keys have the same effect in our program: delete the character to the left of the cursor.

There are two cases to consider. If the cursor is located on text that is in the original string (IF `TextPos<=LEN(Text$)....`), the old text should show up when you erase what was just typed. If there isn't any text under the new input, a blank space will be displayed. The following expression:

`RIGHT$(Text$,LEN(Text$)-TextPos+1)`

returns the segment of `Text$` that is "behind" the current cursor position.

Editing input

If you make an error with an editor like this, you need to press <BACKSPACE> until you've erased the incorrect character and all those in front of it. You've got experience with this sort of editing already in the **BASIC** window and the INPUT and LINE INPUT commands.

If you are in a field that already contains text, you can move left and right over the text. When you type a new character, the old character is replaced. Move the cursor back over the new input and the old character reappears. When you press <RETURN>, the new text up to the current cursor position will be accepted. The text that follows the cursor will be erased.

Incidentally, the Apple II's editor works in the same way. Steve Jobs and Steve Wozniak developed the Apple II in a garage, and created almost every piece of hardware and software themselves. They developed this somewhat simple but functional mode of cursor control. This isn't comparable to a screen-oriented editor, but it's not bad once you get used to it. It's difficult to write a better editor in AmigaBASIC.

Deleting characters

The actual characters are deleted like this: The cursor position xp is decremented by one. If we reach the value of `StartSlice`, a beep sounds and the cursor won't move any further. The input string in$ is set so that it's equal to the segment of the string to the left of the cursor (`in$=LEFT$(in$,(LEN(in$)-1))`). Once this is done, the program jumps to the beginning of the `TypeText:` section so that you can input characters.

You may have noticed that you can't put quotation marks (") in the string. All other characters are allowed, but quotation marks are replaced by apostrophes ('). Quotation marks in text cause problems when you store data. We'll explain later why this is so.

Limiting input

The last lines of the `TypeText:` loop are responsible for the input of normal characters. We don't want control characters or function keys displayed, so we only allow ASCII codes from 32 to 126. If you are interested, you can look at the table in the Appendix for a description of these characters. If `i$` is one of these characters and `xp` is less than or equal to `EndSlice` (in which case, the Amiga will beep and refuse to accept other characters), the characters will be printed on the screen and the input string `in$` will receive another character. The cursor position `xp` is incremented by one. Then the program jumps to the beginning of the `TypeText:` loop.

So far so good. Now we need to look at the subroutines that help out the `TypeText:` routine. We'll look at the `AcceptText:` routine.

Assigning text to an array

The `AcceptText:` routine is called when it's time for the current input text to be assigned to its corresponding array. The routine is only executed when the input string `in$` isn't empty. If there's nothing there, there's nothing to assign. By the way, if the cursor is located in the first position of an input field (where it always is when the cursor first types an input field) and either <RETURN>, <TAB>, <cursor up>, or <cursor down> are pressed, the field contents won't be changed. This makes it possible to search through lists.

If `in$` contains a string, its contents will be put into the `Desc$` or the `Value$` array. The variable `DescData` determines which one. Then we erase `in$` so that it can be used for the next input. The variable `AltData` is set to one.

Changing saved text

The data can be changed only in the `AcceptText:` routine. If the user wants to leave the program without having saved the modified data, a warning window is displayed. At the beginning of the program `AltData` has the value zero. Once data is changed, the value of `AltData` is changed. The program knows that `AltData` equal to one means that modifications have been made. Once `AcceptText:` has performed its tasks, it returns to the line from which it was called.

The next subroutine `DeleteLine:` deletes a data line. Each of the lines from the one after the current line to the last line of the file are copied over the lines that precede them. The elements of the `Desc$` and `Value$` arrays are assigned the contents of the next higher array element.

The line which the cursor is on disappears and is replaced by the next higher line. The `TopLine` is decremented by one. If we've reached the top of the file (IF `TopLine<1` THEN...), then `TopLine` is set to one. Once done, the subroutine RETURNs to the routine from which it was called.

227

Inserting lines of data

DeleteLine:'s complementary subroutine is InsertLine:. It is used to insert data lines. Before it tries to insert the lines, it checks if there is room for another line. If TopLine equals 50, the list is already full, and no more lines can be inserted. A beep sounds to indicate this.

If TopLine is less than 50, InsertLine: moves the elements one position forward starting at the end of the file (TopLine+4) and going back to the current line. We use STEP −1 to make the FOR...NEXT loop count backwards. After the loop is complete, the last line moved forward is erased so that new data can be inserted. The variable TopLine is incremented by one. Then a RETURN is executed.

Now we're ready for the most important routines of our program: the routines for reading from and writing to the diskette:

```
SaveData:¶
  MENU 1,0,0 : MENU 2,0,0 ¶
  MENU OFF¶
  GOSUB TypeName¶
  WINDOW 1¶
  IF Nam$="" THEN EndSave¶
  OPEN Nam$ FOR OUTPUT AS 1¶
    PRINT#1,TopLine+4¶
    FOR x=1 TO TopLine+4¶
      WRITE #1,Desc$(x)¶
      WRITE #1,Value$(x)¶
    NEXT x¶
  CLOSE 1¶
  ¶
EndSave:¶
  MENU 1,0,1 : MENU 2,0,1¶
  MENU ON¶
  AltData=0¶
RETURN¶
¶
LoadData:¶
  IF AltData=1 THEN GOSUB Query¶
  MENU 1,0,0 : MENU 2,0,0¶
  MENU OFF¶
  GOSUB TypeName¶
  WINDOW 1¶
  IF Nam$="" THEN EndLoad¶
  FOR x=1 TO 58¶
    Desc$(x)=""¶
    Value$(x)=""¶
  NEXT x¶
  OPEN Nam$ FOR INPUT AS 1¶
    INPUT #1,NmbrData¶
    TopLine=NmbrData-4¶
    FOR x=1 TO NmbrData¶
      INPUT #1,Desc$(x)¶
      INPUT #1,Value$(x)¶
    NEXT x¶
    LineOne=TopLine¶
  CLOSE 1¶
```

```
                 ¶
       EndLoad:¶
         WINDOW 1¶
         COLOR 1,0¶
         CLS¶
         PRINT "Number";TAB(10);"Description";TAB(45);"Value"¶
         FOR x=LineOne TO LineOne+8¶
            PRINT Number$(x);TAB(10);Desc$(x);TAB(45);Value$(x)¶
         NEXT x¶
         MENU 1,0,1 : MENU 2,0,1¶
         MENU ON¶
         AltData=0¶
       RETURN¶
                 ¶
       TypeName:¶
         Altname$=Nam$¶
         WINDOW 2,"Type filename:",(50,80)-(580,88),0,-1¶
         CLS¶
         LINE INPUT Nam$¶
         IF Nam$= "=" OR Nam$="*" THEN Nam$=Altname$¶
         WINDOW CLOSE 2¶
       RETURN¶
```

When you choose the Save item from the **File** pulldown menu, the program executes the SaveData: subroutine. Event trapping makes it possible to save at any time. Remember that the modifications you make to the current cursor line won't be saved in the file unless you press the <RETURN> or <TAB> key first. Modifications won't be transferred to disk until you save the file.

The SaveData: routine first disables the menus. All the pulldown menus are displayed as ghost menus now. Then the subroutine TypeName: is called. It is used to receive the name of the file. If the filename Nam$ is empty, nothing will be saved; instead the program will jump directly to the EndSave: label.

WRITE

Next the subroutine opens the file matching the name in Nam$ for output. First we write the number of data items, TopLine+4, to the file. The FOR...NEXT loop will be executed this many times. The loop writes Desc$ and Value to the file. We use the WRITE command for this.

You've seen PRINT before, but what does WRITE do? Basically they do the same thing—they write data (numeric or text) to the screen or to a file. They differ in just a couple of details. Let's compare the two commands in the **BASIC** window. Type the following lines:

```
PRINT 1,2,3;4;5;6
```

and

```
WRITE 1,2,3;4;5;6
```

229

WRITE
vs.
PRINT

When commas are used as dividing characters for the PRINT command, numbers are printed in columns. Each column is 15 characters wide. The WRITE command simply outputs the commas as well. When colons are used as divider characters for the PRINT command, data items are printed right after each other (positive numbers are proceeded by a blank space since they don't have a sign). The WRITE command converts semicolons to commas. Try these examples:

```
PRINT "Hello, ";"how are you?"
```

and

```
WRITE "Hello, ";"how are you?"
```

They do different things. The WRITE command puts quotation marks around strings, while PRINT doesn't.

Why is this important? Maybe you've done some thinking about how AmigaBASIC works with characters in sequential files. A sequential file is just a bunch of characters that follow one right after the other. So how can AmigaBASIC tell where a data element begins and ends when it reads from the file? AmigaBASIC uses various separators to do this.

Carriage
returns and
linefeeds

We'll take a look at typewriters to explain. The carriage return code (CHR$(13)) is a separator character. The <RETURN> key gets its name from the typewriter key that executes a carriage return and a linefeed. Computer engineers used this idea for the characters that end a line: the carriage return code (CHR$(13)). The CHR$(10) character has a similar function. It is the linefeed character. It causes the screen or printer to go down one line without returning to its beginning. Thus carriage return and linefeed need to be used together.

Now back to programming. The PRINT statement puts this code behind an input if the expression doesn't end with a comma or a semicolon, whether you're printing on the screen or into a file. Writing to a sequential file with the following commands:

```
PRINT #1, "Hello"¶
PRINT #1, 1,2,3¶
PRINT #1, 4;5;6¶
```

produces:

```
Hello<LINEFEED> 1<13 SPACES> 2<13 SPACES> 3 <LINEFEED> 4
5 6 <LINEFEED>¶
```

What can we learn from this example? First, if a PRINT statement is not ended with a separator, a linefeed is automatically appended to the input. When a comma separates two data items, AmigaBASIC inserts enough blanks to move to the next tab column. When a colon separates two data items, data items are written directly following each other, except that blanks will be used instead of +'s for positive numbers.

Problems
with
INPUT#

We have problems when we try to read values from a sequential file with the INPUT# command, since INPUT# reads to the next separator. Commas are treated as separators for this command.

Experiment with this by creating a file in the **BASIC** window:

```
open "Textfile" for output as 1¶
a$="Hello, how are you?"¶
b$="Test"¶
print #1, a$¶
print #1,b$¶
close 1¶
```

We've written two strings to a sequential file. Now we want to read them:

```
open "Testfile" for input as 1¶
input #1,a$¶
input #1,b$¶
?a$¶
?b$¶
```

What's wrong? The string a$ has the value Hello. The string b$ has the value how are you?. The comma in the string was interpreted as a separator. We don't see "Test" anywhere. But we can change that easily enough:

```
input #1,c$¶
?c$¶
close 1¶
```

Finally we've read all the data items. The comma causes problems with reading the string. This will cause our program to get all confused, since the field contents read and written will be different.

More about
WRITE

What does BASIC do to neutralize separators inside strings? It puts quotation marks around the strings. That's why WRITE is so useful. When we write data to disk using WRITE, we can be sure that the strings will be read back correctly.

WRITE lets you put anything except quotation marks in strings. If you use quotation marks, things will hit the fan. For this reason, the TypeText: routine won't permit quotation marks—it automatically converts them into apostrophes.

Wow! That was quite an explanation for just two lines of the program. But hopefully you've learned a lot about sequential files. This will be useful when you start writing your own data management programs.

Closing the file

The `SaveData:` program section doesn't contain any more surprises. The file is closed with the `CLOSE` command. The `EndSave:` procedure reactivates menu event trapping and sets `AltData` to zero. `AltData` must be zero because the data in the file and in memory are identical at present, and will remain so until you modify the data in memory. We need to be able to read in the data that we wrote, so we have the `LoadData:` subroutine.

Deleting the old file

Reading in new data means deleting the old data. To protect modified data, we check `AltData` first. If modifications have been made, the program section `Query:` gives the user the opportunity to save the data (`Query:` is the program routine on the next page). We deactivate menu trapping so that nothing gets screwed up.

The subroutine `TypeName:` furnishes a filename. If no name is input, loading will be halted and the program branches to `EndLoad:`.

The following `FOR...NEXT` loop deletes the current data from the arrays. Otherwise, if you read in a file that's shorter than the file currently in memory, part of the old data will be appended to the list. We don't want that to happen, so we delete all the data before we load the new file.

Now we open the file for reading. First we read the number of data items in the file. Since the four blank array elements are stored at the beginning of the file, `TopLine` is given the value `NmbrData-4`. All the data is read into the `Desc$` and `Value$` arrays using a `FOR...NEXT` loop.

After loading, the cursor is positioned to the last line of the file so that you can append data. This is useful for lists which expand over time—for instance information about stock prices. To do this, we set `LineOne` equal to the value of the `TopLine` variable.

The `EndLoad:` routine has a couple lines that can also be found in the `MainLoop:` of the program. The current list is displayed on the screen. This is necessary because the `MainLoop:` is only activated by a keystroke. However, the user should see the new data on the screen before this occurs. Menu trapping is turned on again, and `AltData` is set to zero. The data that was just read is identical to the data on the diskette. Then we return from the subroutine.

Wildcards

The subroutine `TypeName:` is almost identical to a routine in the paint program. When you type the = or * wildcards, the last filename that was accessed is used again. After this input, the window disappears from the screen.

Now that we've typed and discussed routines for loading and saving data, all we need is the `Query:` subroutine. It warns the user that the current data hasn't been stored yet:

```
Query:¶
  WINDOW 2,"Attention!",(155,50)-(475,135),0,-1¶
  COLOR 0,1¶
  CLS¶
  LOCATE 2,3¶
  PRINT  "      Your data has not"¶
  PRINT  "         yet been saved."¶
  PRINT : PRINT  "          Save it now?"¶
  LOCATE 9,15 : PRINT "Yes"¶
  LOCATE 9,26 : PRINT "No"¶
  LINE (95,57)-(148,74),0,b¶
  LINE (183,57)-(236,74),0,b¶
  BEEP¶
WaitforMouse:¶
  Test=MOUSE(0)¶
  WHILE MOUSE(0)=0¶
  WEND¶
  x=MOUSE(1) : y=MOUSE(2)¶
  IF 95<x AND x<148 AND 57<y AND y<74 THEN¶
    PAINT (97,59),3,0¶
    GOSUB SaveData¶
    PAINT (97,59),1,0¶
    WINDOW CLOSE 2¶
    RETURN¶
  END IF¶
  IF 183<x AND x<236 AND 57<y AND y<74 THEN¶
    PAINT (185,59),3,0¶
    WINDOW CLOSE 2¶
    RETURN¶
  END IF¶
  GOTO WaitforMouse¶
¶
ClearData:¶
  IF AltData=1 THEN GOSUB Query¶
  RUN¶
  ¶
Quit:¶
  IF AltData=1 THEN GOSUB Query¶
  COLOR 1,0¶
  MENU RESET¶
  CLS¶
END¶
```

The Query: routine is easy to understand. It creates a requester with a white background and blue text. The requester displays the message Your data has not yet been saved. Save it now? and gadgets for Yes and No. A BEEP also sounds to alert you.

The WaitforMouse: subroutine waits for a Yes or No click. As you can see, you can use the MOUSE commands without using event trapping. If the user clicks in the Yes gadget, the field is painted orange and the SaveData: routine is called.

WARNING: If you leave an empty string for the filename, your data will be completely lost be careful.

After the program is finished saving, it paints the gadget to its original color, closes the window, and returns. If you click the No field, the square paints the gadget orange, closes the window, and returns. If the click occurs elsewhere in the window, the WaitforMouse: subroutine is called again.

Finally, we use two small functions. The function DeleteData: erases memory—all data items are cleared. The quickest and most effective method to restore all variables to their original values is to restart the program with the RUN command.

Using RUN inside a program starts the program at the beginning—all variables and arrays are cleared. We may wish to do this occasionally but certainly not all the time. Normally you should use GOTO when you want to branch to the beginning of the program. It's the same for the End: routine. This routine is used to end the program. Here we set that background and text colors back to their original values, reactivate the **BASIC** pulldown menus, and erase the screen. The END command returns us to direct mode.

Now we're finished programming the data management section. But we're still missing a vital link. We've got numbers—but no graphics! Don't worry. You won't need to do much more.

At this time save the current version of the statistical data program to the diskette. We saved the graphics routine in ASCII format before we typed this program. Now we'll append it to this program using MERGE.

If you followed the instructions at the beginning of this section, you'll have an ASCII version of your bar chart/pie chart utility in your Data drawer. Use the FILES command to make sure it's there. Type the following in the **BASIC** window:

```
merge "New BarPie"¶
```

After a couple of seconds, the Graphics: routine will be written at the end of your new program. Save the program immediately. (You can use the same name that you used for the non-graphic version).

Now you should test the program for typing errors. Can you load and save? Are the graphics displayed correctly? As you know, when you see an error message, compare the line in which the error occurs with the listing at the error-free program Appendix.

Running the program

This new program displays a window that fills about half a screen. You'll see an orange cursor at the beginning of the column Description in line one. This is where you type the data to be graphed. This text will be printed with the pie segment or under the bar in the diagram that is drawn. You confirm the input by pressing <RETURN>, <TAB>, or a <cursor up/down> key. You type the value (number, percent, etc.) in the Value column. If the cursor is located on the first character of an input, the input will not be changed. Otherwise the program accepts the text up to the cursor position. Text behind the cursor is erased. You use <BACKSPACE> or <cursor left> to erase characters. The text that was typed over will reappear.

The screen will always contain nine lines of the data list. The entire list may contain a maximum of 50 elements. You use <CONTROL><B> to jump to the beginning of the list, <CONTROL><E> to jump to the end, <CONTROL><D> to delete a line, or <CONTROL><N> to insert a new line.

Saving a list

To save a data list, choose Save from the **Data** menu. The Load item reads in data that was previously stored. You use Delete to clear the program's work area and Quit to return to BASIC direct mode.

Selecting graphics

To choose either a pie chart or a bar graph, choose the desired form from the **Graphics** pulldown menu. The graphic is constructed, and then a small requester asks you to press a key. To hide this requester, you can click it into the background. Press any key to return to the input screen.

Tricks & Tips

Here are a few tips to help you get the most out of this program:

- Add an extra line to your file containing a round number that is larger than all the others, to serve as a comparison value. For example, if your largest value is 898, type 1000 in another line. That makes the scaling much cleaner.

- If you've got many small values in your pie chart, type them between the large ones. If all the small values come at the end, the label of one may overlap one another.

- Keep your labels short in the pie charts. If the labels are too long, they'll trail off the right edge of the screen or overlap the graphic figure. Also, keep your description labels short for bar charts, since there isn't much room per bar.

- If you want to use specific colors, just write more PALETTE commands behind the PALETTE command in the Setup: section of the program.

3.5 Amiga and friends: peripheral devices

This section introduces you to the Amiga's *peripheral devices*. These are hardware components that are connected to your Amiga (usually with cables), but are not directly part of a computer—they're "optional equipment." You can connect many different kinds of peripherals to your Amiga. Even if you don't have a printer and haven't used the various interfaces on your Amiga, you can learn about some interesting possibilities.

The first peripheral we'll look at is the Amiga's *RAM disk*. You actually have one more disk drive than you thought—or at least, it's a reasonable substitute for a disk drive, and much cheaper.

RAM disk pros and cons

Both AmigaBASIC and AmigaDOS allow you to use part of the Amiga's memory as a *virtual disk drive*, or RAM disk. As you already know, RAM stands for Random Access Memory. A RAM disk has no moving parts; information is stored in memory instead of on a diskette. That means you can write and read programs and data to the RAM just like you would a floppy diskette. A RAM disk can even have a directory and drawers.

The effectiveness of a RAM disk depends on how much memory you have available. The RAM disk uses dynamic memory allocation. In other words, it uses the barest minimum amount of memory, only what it actually needs. The memory used by the RAM disk can't be used by AmigaBASIC or other programs at the same time. If you delete a program that is stored in the RAM disk, the memory occupied by that program is immediately freed up for other uses.

Let's see all this theory in practice. Type the following command in the **BASIC** window:

```
chdir "ram:"¶
```

RAM:

When you type this command the first time, your Amiga may request the Workbench diskette for the RAM disk utility program.

Use FILES to look at the directory of the RAM disk. It doesn't have a disk name. You'll see Directory of [] displayed. The RAM disk directory may contain the BasicClip file. If you use Cut, Copy, and Paste from the **Edit** pull-down menu, AmigaBASIC puts the Clipboard's contents in the RAM disk.

Type a few program lines in the **LIST** window—nothing special, a couple lines of text will suffice for this example. Now save the lines you've input.

Type the following line in the **BASIC** window:

```
save "test"¶
```

Almost as soon as you press <RETURN>, OK will appear on the screen. This is one great feature of RAM disks: they're super fast. Very little time is required to read from or write to a RAM disk, because the files are simply juggled around in main memory.

Back to info files

Take a look at the RAM disk's directory. It will contain the files test and test.info. AmigaBASIC automatically produces an info file when it saves a file. Workbench 1.2 puts an icon for the file in the Workbench screen. This icon exists as long as the RAM disk is used.

Note: Workbench 1.1 can't open a window for the RAM disk. Type:

```
kill "test.info"
```

Then see your dealer about getting Version 1.2 of Workbench.

Now erase the memory with NEW and load test from the RAM disk:

```
load "test"
```

RAM disks are not forever...

It's impressive to see the RAM disk in operation. Even lengthy BASIC programs can be loaded in seconds—a bare fraction of the time it takes for a floppy disk drive. One advantage is that you can type program data on a RAM disk, and not to copy it to disk until the program is done. Your work will be speeded up immensely.

There are many good applications for a RAM disk. However, you should remember that unlike data that is stored on floppy diskettes, all data on a RAM disk is temporary. A power surge, power failure or a system crash will destroy that data.

NOTE:

Many Amiga programs do not work with the RAM disk running. If you own an unexpanded Amiga 500, you will have to disable the RAM disk. We showed you how to do this earlier, but we'll reiterate:

√√ TURN ON THE AMIGA, AND INSERT THE WORKBENCH DISKETTE WHEN THE COMPUTER ASKS YOU TO.

√√ WHEN THE BLUE SCREEN APPEARS, PRESS <CTRL><D>. A 1> PROMPT WILL APPEAR (YOU ARE NOW IN THE CLI).

√√ TYPE LOADWB¶. WAIT UNTIL ANOTHER 1> PROMPT APPEARS ON THE SCREEN.

√√ TYPE ENDCLI¶.

Printers

Next we'll look at another of the Amiga's peripheral devices: *printers*. Even if you don't have the hardware described, you should read the next few pages for two reasons: First, you'll probably get your hands on some of this hardware sooner than you think (that's why they invented credit cards). Second, it can't hurt you to know the printer commands.

Before you can work with a printer, you need to make some preparations. First you need a cable to connect your Amiga to your printer. You can get a printer cable at any Amiga dealer.

NOTE:

There is a major difference between the printer cable available for the Amiga 500 and 2000, and the cable sold for the Amiga 1000. Be absolutely sure that you have the correct cable for your machine when you buy it—the wrong cable will damage your Amiga.

Next, you need to set Preferences in the Workbench to inform the Amiga which *printer driver* should be used. Printer drivers are utility programs that control the format in which data is sent to specific models of printers. The Workbench contains driver files for the most popular makes and models of printers. Commodore and various printer manufacturers are presently working on other driver files, if your printer isn't listed. (You can find out more about this in your Amiga manual). After you select the correct printer driver, all you need to do is turn the printer's power switch on.

LPRINT

The simplest command for sending data to the printer is the LPRINT command. The L in LPRINT stands for Line. The LPRINT command works like the PRINT command: the only difference is that this command sends output to the printer, not to the screen.

```
LPRINT "Hello, how are you?"
```

The Amiga needs to load the printer driver from the Workbench diskette before the first printing can take place. Once the driver is loaded, your printer prints the line Hello, how are you?. AmigaBASIC now has all the information that it needs to about the printer.

LPRINT lets you use the same separators that PRINT normally uses:

```
LPRINT "Hello",5,"Amiga";"Test"
```

Separators and LPRINT

In the last chapter, we discussed control codes and separators. You'll remember that when the line is ended with a semicolon, the output data won't be printed immediately. Instead, the data will be stored in the printer buffer until a linefeed (CHR$(10)) code is encountered. The following line executes two linefeeds:

```
LPRINT chr$(10)
```

The first linefeed is produced by the CHR$(10), and the second is automatically produced by LPRINT. Your printer might not respond correctly to the linefeed code, and print everything in the same line. If this is the case, check the printer settings in Preferences and look in your printer handbook. You may need to adjust the DIP switches in your printer. If you can't figure out what to do, your computer dealer should be able to help you out.

LLIST

You can use the LLIST command to produce program listings on your printer when you develop and test programs. For a demonstration, load a short program and then type:

```
LLIST
```

Your printer prints out the program listing. AmigaBASIC is disabled during printing. The printing can take a long time if the program is large (such as your paint program). Multitasking can be a real timesaver printing, because you won't have to wait for the printer to finish. For example, you can click AmigaBASIC into the background and work with another program during printing. Multitasking is dependent on how much free memory you've got.

Your printer may have *buffer memory*. This buffer stores the output data in its own RAM and then signals the Amiga that the printing is already done, so it can move on to the next task—even though the printer still might have 15 minutes worth of printing ahead of it. You can terminate printing at any time using the <CONTROL><C> key combination.

These are the fundamental AmigaBASIC printer commands. But AmigaBASIC has many more commands for printing flexibility.

PRT:

A device name (similar to RAM:) called PRT: (printer) offers you another way to print out a program listing:

```
LIST ,"PRT:"
```

LIST

You can tell the LIST command where to redirect the listing by appending more information to it. You can also write a file to disk using this method. We'll demonstrate on the RAM disk:

```
LIST ,"RAM:Test"
```

DELETE

This command produces a file called Test to which the program is written in ASCII format. You can use the LIST command as an alternative to the SAVE ,A command.

SCRN:

Another interesting device is SCRN: (screen). Typing the command:

```
LIST ,"SCRN:"
```

displays an entire program listing in the **BASIC** window.

LPT1:

Back to printer output. You can use both PRT: and LPT1: as device names for the printer—they produce almost identical results. Microsoft used two names to make AmigaBASIC as compatible as possible with its other versions of BASIC. Microsoft's IBM PC BASIC uses LPT1: (Line Printer 1) the first printer connected to the computer. To make it easier to convert a BASIC program that runs on the IBM PC to one that runs on the Amiga, Microsoft designed AmigaBASIC so that it understands this device name and sends the output to PRT:, the standard printer.

Output files

You can also use device names to open an output file, so that you can send data to various devices:

```
OPEN "PRT:" for output as 1
```

This line sends all the output that is written to file 1 to the printer. If AmigaBASIC responds with File already open, the device PRT: is already being used for this. AmigaBASIC may refuse to build a second connection. If you have some problems, and since we're only experimenting now, clear all files and connections with the NEW command. Then try typing:

```
PRINT#1, "Hello!"
```

Don't be surprised if this text isn't printed immediately. AmigaBASIC always sets up a buffer for files, to avoid having to individually transfer each character. The contents of the buffer are transferred when you use the CLOSE command, or when the buffer gets full. This is the only difference between LPT1: and PRT:—LPT1: prints immediately, while PRT: uses a buffer. Typing the following line will start the printer:

```
CLOSE 1
```

I/O

With these commands you can open files for any device. Of course, you need to choose the correct mode. Opening the printer FOR INPUT causes AmigaBASIC to respond with an error message like Bad file mode or Device I/O error. The I/O stands for Input/Output. You'll see this abbreviation a lot when you work with data transfer.

Since we've been using device names without paying too much attention, AmigaBASIC may refuse to open some device. You can always reload the Workbench in this case—this sets everything back to the default settings.

KYBD:

You can use the keyboard (KYBD:) FOR INPUT to a program. The following listing is a very simple program that accepts the characters that you type in on the keyboard, displays the characters on the screen, and then outputs them to your printer:

```
OPEN "KYBD:" FOR INPUT AS 1¶
OPEN "SCRN:" FOR OUTPUT AS 2¶
OPEN "LPT1:" FOR OUTPUT AS 3¶
WHILE i$<>CHR$(138)¶
 i$=INPUT$(1,1)¶
 PRINT#2,i$;¶
 IF i$=CHR$(13) THEN i$=CHR$(10)¶
 IF i$=CHR$(8) THEN i$=CHR$(127)¶
 PRINT #3,i$¶
WEND¶
CLOSE 1,2,3¶
```

We open the keyboard for reading and open the screen and printer for writing (it can't be the other way around).

Hitting <F10> (CHR$(138)) ends the program.

You may recognize INPUT$ from reading in object files. We'll discuss it in more detail shortly.

We convert two special characters before we output to the printer. If the user presses <RETURN> (CHR$(13)), the character is converted to CHR$(10), so that the printer will execute a linefeed. If the user types CHR$(8) <BACKSPACE>, the character is converted to CHR$(127) for the printer. This is the code that most printers use to delete characters in the buffer. Each character is sent to the printer as soon as it is input. However, as long as it hasn't been printed, we can easily take care of errors by erasing the last character in the buffer.

If this doesn't work on your printer, take a look at your printer manual. Most manuals contain a table of the character set. These tables give you information about which control characters change the printer's print style, the distance between lines, and much more.

Escape codes

There are a lot of *<ESC> codes* that you can use on your printer if it's an Epson or an Epson-compatible. You may have discovered the <ESC> key on the Amiga keyboard. The <ESC> character (CHR$(27)) can be used to produce many interesting effects. First we'll take a quick look at the developments of printer standards.

Printer history

When ASCII was developed many years ago, there were virtually no powerful printers available for small computers. Hobbyists were happy if their printers could print uppercase and lowercase letters. No one thought about having them print in italics, bold, wide, or near letter-quality text.

241

Adding codes for printer control

Consequently, the positions in the ASCII code table weren't occupied by letters, numbers, and miscellaneous characters (totaling about 30 codes unused) were enough to activate the primitive special printer effects. For example, CHR$(14) was used to enable extra-wide characters on many printers. Today many codes, like CHR$(10) and CHR$(13), have been usurped for other tasks, and there aren't nearly enough unused codes to do this.

What escape codes do

Computer specialists needed to expand the number of control codes. For this reason, the engineers decided to use character 27 to form escape codes. Character 27 instructs the printer not to print the character that follows it, because it's a control character. For example, when the printer encounters a CHR$(69) alone, it prints out an E. But when it encounters a CHR$(27) and then a CHR$(69), in other words <ESC><E>, the printer knows that the 69 is a control character. It then looks to find what <ESC><E> means.

The Japanese printer maker, Epson, developed a greatly extended printer code standard to be used with dot-matrix printers. The <ESC><E> sequence enables the bold print for Epson and Epson-compatible printers. Many printers use this standard to handle control characters.

"Other" escape codes

But for various, complex reasons, many printers are not Epson-compatible. A printer manufacturer might have thought that they had a superior method of escape code layout, or that their printer could out perform the Epson standard using a simpler method. Or, more commonly, the manufacturer chose to toe the line of another printer standard, such as IBM's.

Normally, printer drivers work only with their specified printer. It required a great effort by the user to convert the printer driver to work with another printer. When he bought a new printer, the odds are it wasn't compatible with the last. This means that he'd have to change the printer driver and insert new control codes.

Printer drivers

The developers of the Amiga found a better solution: They set up a standard printer code table that is included in all Amiga programs. These standard printer codes are then converted by the various printer driver programs to the special character sequences required by each printer. This way, the standard Amiga printer codes can be adapted to a wide range of printers, each supported by its own printer driver program.

Before you print for the first time, select the printer driver that corresponds to your printer from the Preferences printer menu and save your choice to the Workbench diskette. If your printer is not on the list, don't panic: Many printers are designed to "clone" popular models, and you should be able to print using a compatible driver for another model. The Epson driver works with most dot-matrix printers. The best thing to do is ask your dealer. However, if you have an "oddball" printer, you should get in contact with Commodore or the printer manufacturer for advice. (Luckily for you, most manufacturers use the Amiga printer codes on the following pages).

Each separate printer driver in Preferences acts as kind of an interpreter: It gets information in one language (Amiga's standard control characters), and translates the information immediately into another language (control characters which your specific printer can understand). As long as the right printer driver can be found in Preferences, the Amiga can handle the translation.

Tables 8a and 8b on the following pages are a complete overview of the Amiga control codes. See your printer manual for more information on the effect each code has on your printer.

Control character	Effect
CHR$(27)"c"	Printer initialization
CHR$(27)"#1"	Deactivate all other modes
CHR$(27)"D"	Linefeed, like CHR$(10)
CHR$(27)"E"	Linefeed + carriage return, like CHR$(13)
CHR$(27)"M"	Up one line
CHR$(27)"[0m"	Normal printing
CHR$(27)"[1m"	Bold on
CHR$(27)"[22m"	Bold off
CHR$(27)"[3m"	Italic on
CHR$(27)"[23m"	Italic off
CHR$(27)"[4m"	Underline on
CHR$(27)"[24m"	Underline off
CHR$(27);x;"m"	Background color (x from 30 to 39), Foreground color (x from 40 to 49)
CHR$(27)"[0w"	Normal font size
CHR$(27)"[2w"	Elite type on
CHR$(27)"[1w"	Elite type off
CHR$(27)"[4w"	Condensed on
CHR$(27)"[3w"	Condensed off
CHR$(27)"[6w"	Enlarged on
CHR$(27)"[5w"	Enlarged off
CHR$(27)"[2"CHR$(34)"z"	NLQ on
CHR$(27)"[1"CHR$(34)"z"	NLQ off
CHR$(27)"[4"CHR$(34)"z"	Double-strike on
CHR$(27)"[3"CHR$(34)"z"	Double-strike off
CHR$(27)"[6"CHR$(34)"z"	Shaded print on
CHR$(27)"[5"CHR$(34)"z"	Shaded print off
CHR$(27)"[2v"	Superscript on
CHR$(27)"[1v"	Superscript off
CHR$(27)"[4v"	Subscript on
CHR$(27)"[3v"	Subscript off
CHR$(27)"L"	Superscript (half-step)
CHR$(27)"K"	Subscript (half-step)
CHR$(27)"[0v"	Return to normal
CHR$(27)"[2p"	Proportional type on
CHR$(27)"[1p"	Proportional type off

Table 8a: Standard printer control characters

Control character	Effect
CHR$(27)"[0p"	Delete proportional spacing
CHR$(27)"[";x;"E"	Proportional spacing=x
CHR$(27)"[5F"	Move left
CHR$(27)"[7F"	Move right
CHR$(27)"[6F"	Block characters
CHR$(27)"[0F"	Block characters off
CHR$(27)"[3F"	Adjust character width
CHR$(27)"[1F"	Centering
CHR$(27)"[0z"	Line spacing 1/8 inch
CHR$(27)"[1z"	Line spacing 1/6 inch
CHR$(27)"[";x;"t"	Page length at x lines
CHR$(27)"[";x;"q"	Page break at line x (tractor-feed)
CHR$(27)"[0q"	Page break (tractor-feed)
CHR$(27)"(B"	American character set
CHR$(27)"(R"	French character set
CHR$(27)"(K"	German character set
CHR$(27)"(A"	English character set
CHR$(27)"(E"	Danish character set (no.1)
CHR$(27)"(H"	Swedish character set
CHR$(27)"(Y"	Italian character set
CHR$(27)"(Z"	Spanish character set
CHR$(27)"(J"	Japanese character set
CHR$(27)"(6"	Norwegian character set
CHR$(27)"(C"	Danish character set (no.2)
CHR$(27)"#9"	Set left margin
CHR$(27)"#0"	Set right margin
CHR$(27)"#8"	Set page header
CHR$(27)"#2"	Set page footer
CHR$(27)"#3"	Margin release
CHR$(27)"[";x;y;"r"	Set page header x lines from top & page footer y lines from bottom
CHR$(27)"[";x;y;"s"	Set left margin (x) and right margin (y)
CHR$(27)"H"	Set horizontal tabulator
CHR$(27)"J"	Set vertical tab
CHR$(27)"[0g"	Clear horizontal tab
CHR$(27)"[3g"	Clear all horizontal tabs
CHR$(27)"[1g"	clear vertical tab
CHR$(27)"[4g"	Clear all vertical tabs
CHR$(27)"#4"	Clear all tabs
CHR$(27)"#5"	Set standard tabs

**Table 8b:
Standard
printer
control
characters**
(continued)

For an example of the use of these codes: If you wanted to tell your printer to print bold type, you would type:

```
lprint chr$(27);"[1m";"Hello!"
```

Of course, some printers can do more than others. When you use a control character that the printer doesn't understand, then that control character is simply ignored.

About
interfaces

You could create your own printer driver with your own control codes. But converting control codes involves a lot of programming. There is a solution, however. You can filter out characters directly through the *interface* connected to your printer.

We haven't said anything about interfaces yet. Your Amiga has "ports" through which data is transferred to and from peripheral devices. The device name for the parallel interface is PAR:. The device name for the serial interface is called SER:.

PAR:

Most printers are connected to the Amiga's parallel interface, but they could also be attached to the serial interface. A *parallel* interface has many more data lines, because the bits that comprise characters are transferred all at once (in parallel). A *serial* interface has only one data line, and the bits are transferred one at a time (in serial). This is the major difference between the two. We'll assume that you're using a parallel interface with your printer.

To send control characters, open a file to the device PAR::

```
OPEN "PAR:" for output as 1
```

AmigaBASIC will refuse to open this file and will display File already open. This is because data for the printer PRT: and LPT1: is already being sent to the parallel interface. AmigaBASIC thinks that if a printer is connected to the parallel interface, there can't be a second device on the same interface—therefore PAR: is unavailable.

Your only option is to reload the Workbench. We can do this with the <CTRL><C=><Amiga key> combination (Amiga 1000 users: <CTRL><left Amiga key><right Amiga key>). When you work with AmigaBASIC you must decide at the beginning whether you want to work with the filtered or the unfiltered printer connection. Once the Workbench is loaded, insert your BASICDisk again and click the AmigaBASIC icon. Then type in the command line above. Now you can send data to the printer:

```
PRINT #1,CHR$(27);CHR$(69);"Bold print!"¶
CLOSE 1¶
```

If there isn't any bold print on the printer paper, then your printer doesn't understand these particular control characters.

COM1:

We've looked at RAM:, PRT:, LPT1:, PAR:, SER:, SCRN:, and KYBD: so far. There's one device name that we haven't mentioned yet: COM1: is used to activate an RS-232 standard on a serial interface. Since you probably won't use device, we put information about it in **Appendix B** (look under the OPEN command).

Joysticks

We're not quite finished. There's another peripheral device that we haven't mentioned: *joysticks*. A joystick can move in four directions, and has one or more fire buttons. They are better suited for video games than for business programs. You're likely to find joysticks on a game machine or a low-end home computer, but you can also use them on the Amiga. You can use joysticks with AmigaBASIC—if you have a joystick, get it out so we can experiment.

The right edge or back of the Amiga has two connectors named JOY1 and JOY2. The mouse is already plugged into the JOY1. Connect the joystick to the JOY2 connector (we still need the mouse to work with the Amiga).

If you move the joystick or hit the fire button, nothing happens. AmigaBASIC doesn't "see" the new input device. We can change that by entering the following program:

```
OPEN "Extras:BasicDemos/Ball" FOR INPUT AS 1¶
    OBJECT.SHAPE 1,INPUT$(LOF(1),1)¶
CLOSE 1¶
x=320 : y=100¶
OBJECT.ON 1¶
WHILE 1¶
    OBJECT.X 1,x¶
    OBJECT.Y 1,y¶
    x=x+STICK(2)¶
    y=y+STICK(3)¶
WEND¶
```

Save the program to disk and then try it out.

Using the joystick

Let's use the joystick to move a graphic object around the screen. To this end, load Ball from the BasicDemos directory of the Extras diskette. It's alright to use your own sprite from the video program.

Now for a brief explanation of the joystick program. The variables x and y contain the screen position of the graphic object. They are set at the beginning of the program so that the object is in approximately the middle of the screen. We use OBJECT.ON to make the object visible.

STICK

The infinite WHILE...WEND loop is used to move the object. You'll see a new command, STICK(x), that is used to read information from the joystick. How does it work?

The Amiga can have two joysticks connected to it—one can be attached to the first connector (JOY1), the other to the second connector (JOY2).

Each joystick can be moved in an X-direction and a Y-direction. The number in parentheses following STICK determines which direction is being monitored:

STICK(0)   checks the X-movement of joystick one
STICK(1)   checks the Y-movement of joystick one
STICK(2)   checks the X-direction of joystick two
STICK(3)   checks the Y-direction of joystick two
STICK(x)   is a BASIC function which can take on three values

Value	Meaning
0	no movement in the direction checked
1	movement up or to the right
-1	movement down or to the left

If we move joystick up two, STICK(3) returns a one. The joystick program adds the function values to the X- and Y-variables so that they change when the joystick is moved. OBJECT.X and OBJECT.Y are used to construct the object at its new screen position. Moving in the X- and Y-direction at the same time produces diagonal movement. You should remember how this works from working with the OBJECT commands before.

Experiment with this demonstration program to discover how joystick movement affects the movement of the graphics object.

The fire button

Now let's play with the fire button. We'll expand the program by adding a line inside the WHILE...WEND loop:

```
IF STRIG(3) =-1 THEN BEEP
```

STRIG

Now the Amiga beeps when you press the fire button. The STRIG(x) command determines if the fire button was pressed. The command is an abbreviation for Stick Trigger. You need to instruct STRIG(x) what to monitor. STRIG(1) returns -1 when the fire button of JOY1 is pressed, while STRIG(3) returns a -1 when the fire button of joystick two is pressed.

That still leaves STRIG(0) and STRIG(2) available. The way they work is similar to the way MOUSE(0) works. They return a -1 when the fire button was hit since the last check. In this way, you can check if the button was hit while the program was busy with other tasks.

At this stage of your BASIC education, you're probably confident enough to write your own video game. First one piece of advice: Feel free to experiment with JOY1. But be careful—if even one joystick command is issued to connection one, AmigaBASIC will expect a joystick, and won't recognize the mouse any more. The mouse cursor will lock in its position and can only be moved by holding down one of the <Amiga> keys and then using the cursor keys.

We'll show you how hard it is to work without a mouse. Save your work and then type:

```
? stick(0)
```

Can't use the mouse, can you? The only way to solve this problem is to type the NEW command—and sometimes even NEW doesn't work. If not, all you can do is reload the Workbench. Sometimes it makes you wonder about this version of Microsoft BASIC...

3.6

Getting it down on paper:
a print routine for the statistics program

Now you can use your new knowledge about printer commands to expand the statistics program. Let's write a routine that will print out the statistics file so you have a paper copy of collated data (for example, your stock prices).

First load your statistics program. You won't need to make many changes to it. We'll take care of the printouts by adding another menu item. Accordingly, you'll need to change Setup: a little:

```
MENU 1,0,1,"Data   "¶
MENU 1,1,1,"Load   "¶
MENU 1,2,1,"Save   "¶
MENU 1,3,1,"Print "¶
MENU 1,4,1,"Delete"¶
MENU 1,5,1,"Quit   "¶
```

You also need to make a few changes in the MenuControl: routine:

```
MenuControl:¶
  Men=MENU(0)  : MenuPoint=MENU(1)¶
  IF Men=1 THEN¶
    IF MenuPoint=1 THEN GOSUB LoadData¶
    IF MenuPoint=2 THEN GOSUB SaveData¶
    IF MenuPoint=3 THEN GOSUB PrintData¶
    IF MenuPoint=4 THEN GOSUB ClearData¶
    IF MenuPoint=5 THEN Quit¶
```

Now we need the new print routine. Insert it under the EnterName: section of the program.

```
PrintData:¶
  MENU 1,0,0 : MENU 2,0,0¶
  MENU OFF¶
  OPEN "PRT:" FOR OUTPUT AS 1¶
    PRINT #1,"File:";Altname$;CHR$(10)¶
    PRINT #1,"Number";TAB(10);"Description";TAB(45);
"Value"¶
    FOR x=4 TO TopLine+4¶
      PRINT #1, Number$(x); TAB(10); Desc$(x); TAB(45);
Value$(x)¶
    NEXT x¶
  CLOSE 1¶
  MENU 1,0,1 : MENU 2,0,1¶
  MENU ON¶
RETURN¶
```

This program is fairly simple to understand. First we suppress event trapping, open a printer file, print the name of the file that was loaded (Altname$ contains the name of the last file that was used), print the title line, and then print the individual data lines. Then we close the printer file, reactivate the menu, and return to the line where execution was interrupted when PRINT was chosen.

You can have the data printed in several type styles if your printer supports them.

When we expand and improve programs, it's easy to see the advantages of AmigaBASIC—its modular construction makes it easy to add new features to a program.

Hardcopy

You need a hardcopy utility program to print the pie charts and bar graphs on paper. We can't write one here, since graphic programming varies widely from one printer to another, and so there's no solution that works for all printers. Besides that, AmigaBASIC is simply too slow for the calculations needed for printing out graphics. A normal BASIC print routine would take about 40 minutes.

However, you should be able to make a hardcopy with the GraphicDump utility that is being shipped with the latest versions of the Workbench diskette. Consult the Amiga manual for instructions.

The next chapter discusses some possibilities for preserving your works of art for all posterity. With a couple tricks, we'll get to graphic hardcopies.

Loading and saving graphics

4

4   A picture's worth a thousand bytes: Loading and saving graphics

You may have noticed that something vital was missing from our drawing program: there's no way to save the graphics! It's no fun devoting all that time to designing a graphic that's going to disappear when you turn the computer off. We're now going to show you how to save graphics to disk and call them back later.

4.1

Give and take:
the GET and PUT commands

Let's begin by introducing two new BASIC commands: GET and PUT. The best explanation would be a demonstration program:

```
DIM Array%(563) ¶
           ¶
CIRCLE (50,20),40¶
CIRCLE (35,12),5¶
CIRCLE (65,12),5¶
CIRCLE (50,20),8¶
CIRCLE (50,18),30,,3.5,5.8¶
PAINT (50,20),3,1¶
GET (0,0)-(99,39),Array%¶
           ¶
CLS¶
FOR x=0 TO 5¶
  FOR y=0 TO 4¶
    PUT (x*100,y*40), Array%¶
  NEXT y¶
NEXT x¶
```

An army of little faces is displayed on the screen, drawn with the CIRCLE commands. But the two new commands are the really important part of this demonstration program.

GET

The GET command lets you save part of a graphic in a data array. This example uses the data array Array%. The PUT command positions the saved graphic segment anywhere on the screen. GET simply reads the bits from the different bit patterns, puts these together into bytes and stores the bytes in the array provided. PUT copies the bytes from the given array into the bitplanes.

The GET command syntax is divided into coordinates reaching from the upper left corner of the area selected to the lower right corner. The screen area must be rectangular. After the coordinates goes the name of the data array into which the data should be placed:

GET (*xstart,ystart*)-(*xend,yend*),array

Before you can use GET, you must first dimension a data array. You can compute how many elements are needed for a given screen area with a simple formula. We'll give this same formula to you in a moment.

PUT

The saved graphic can be displayed anywhere on the screen by using the PUT command, followed by the upper left corner coordinates and the name of the array:

```
PUT (xtarget,ytarget),data array
```

Memory and graphic data

Here's the formula to compute the memory requirements of a graphic area:

```
bitplanes * height * 2 * INT((width+16)/16) + 6
```

The values for width and height are given in pixels. The last part of the formula calculates the number of bytes needed for a graphic segment of the given size. This number must be multiplied by the number of bitplanes, since a color point is made up of several bits, and there are different bitplanes. Last, we add 6 bytes which contain other control information. The result is the memory requirement in bytes. This number is still not identical to the number of array elements, since an integer array such as our Array% uses two bytes per array element. You'll remember that an integer can be a value between -32768 and +32767. The Amiga uses 16 bits (2 bytes) for storage.

Computing memory for graphics

How does the computation work for our example? The height of the section is 40 pixels, the width 100 pixels. We'll compute from there: (INT(100+16)/16)=INT(116/16)=7. Multiply 7*2=14. A screen line 100 pixels wide requires 14 bytes for storage. 14*40 (the height) equals 560. So, our little graphic requires 560 bytes of storage space.

Since the Workbench screen works with a standard of 2 bitplanes, we must double the number 560 to arrive at 1120. Add the 6 bytes for control information, and our graphic requires a total of 1126 bytes storage area.

When we dimension our array Array% for 1126 bytes, we must dimension the array to 1126/2, or 563 elements.

As you can see, graphics require a large amount of memory, much more than our statistical program needed for storing files.

If you're wondering where the 6 extra bytes go, you'll find them in the first three elements of Array%:

```
? Array%(0); Array%(1); Array%(2)
```

The first element of the array contains the width of the graphic object, the second element contains the height, and the third element contains the number of bitplanes. You shouldn't change the order of this data, since AmigaBASIC reads the internal graphic data in sequence.

PUT *and*
logical
operators

You can place a third parameter in the PUT command, following the array names: a logical comparison between the graphic from the data array and the screen background. Normally, AmigaBASIC compares the graphic and background with XOR. If no pixel is set in the background, a pixel in the graphic appears as normal. If a background pixel is already set, it will be inverted. Try this in direct mode and see for yourself:

```
CLS¶
LINE (100,120)-(199,139),1,bf¶
PUT (100,100),Array%¶
```

This inverts part of the face in which the selected block is located. An interesting effect occurs when you use the PUT command again:

```
put (100,100),Array%¶
```

Amazing, isn't it? The face is erased completely. The XOR operator will remove a graphic from the same area of the screen through a second PUT command without disturbing the background. This trick can be used for animation effects as well.

Let's try something else:

```
CLS
PUT (100,100),Array%,preset
```

PRESET

The PRESET comparison inverts the graphic parameters and displays reverse-video colors. The four standard colors of the Workbench are reversed from their normal state: blue is orange; white is black; black is white; and orange is blue.

You see the same effect when you activate an icon in the Workbench. The text label is also displayed in reverse video.

```
COLOR 0,1¶
CLS¶
PUT (100,100),Array%,pset¶
```

PSET

The PSET comparison displays the graphic on the screen as it was saved, without affecting the background.

```
CLS¶
LINE (100,120)-(199,139),1,bf¶
PUT (100,100),Array%,and¶
```

This example will combine the points with the background AND relational operator. Now wherever there is already a set point, a point of the graphic appears.

What's true for AND also applies to OR. Run the program again, and type in the following in direct mode:

```
CLS¶
LINE (100,120)-(199,139),1,bf¶
PUT (100,100),Array%,or¶
```

The OR operator copies the graphic in the screen without inverting the foreground points. Now we've put a funny nose on our little faces.

Now we know all the relational operators between graphic and background. We can use these to produce special effects.

Saving graphic data: One method

You know how you can copy a graphic area and put it anywhere on the screen. However, we haven't covered all the bases—we still need a method of storing graphic data to diskette. Here's an idea: Save the elements of the array to diskette. Try this demonstration program out:

```
DIM Array%(563) ¶
   ¶
CIRCLE (50,20),40¶
CIRCLE (35,12),5¶
CIRCLE (65,12),5¶
CIRCLE (50,20),8¶
CIRLCE (50,18),30,,3.5,5.8¶
PAINT (50,20),3,1¶
GET (0,0)-(99,39),Array%¶
   ¶
OPEN "Face" FOR OUTPUT AS 1¶
   FOR x=0 TO 563¶
     PRINT#1,MKI$(Array%(x));¶
   NEXT x¶
CLOSE 1¶
```

Save this version under a distinctive name.

MKI$

One element you may not recognize is the MKI$ function. You'll be using this function quite frequently. It is a big help in saving numbers to diskette. The essential ruling is that when a number like -32768 is saved to diskette in this form, it takes up 7 bytes: one byte for the minus sign, five bytes for the digits, and at least 1 byte as a divider for the next number. You also know that the number -32768 can be represented as a 16-bit number. That is 2 times 8 bits, or 2 bytes. We could use just a third of the memory—you could reduce reading and writing times and save a lot of diskette space.

You can use the MKI$ function (MaKe Integer $tring) to convert a 16-bit integer into 2 bytes. It creates a two-character-long string which you can save to diskette. Note: the CHR$ function performs a similar service on 8-bit numbers, allowing you to create a number up to 255 into one character (CHR$(255)).

ASC

When you want to read back that value, you need another function to convert the two bytes from MKI$ (or the single byte from CHR$) into a number again. The reverse of CHR$ is ASC, which returns the ASCII code number of a character. Try this:

```
a$=chr$(10) :  ? asc(a$)¶
```

If a$ is longer than one character, ASC will only look for the first character of the string. The ASC function is also helpful when you need a quick-n-dirty way of finding out the ASCII code of a character:

```
? asc("H")¶
```

This returns 72, the ASCII code for an uppercase H.

CVI

The opposite of MKI$ is called CVI (ConVert to Integer). CVI converts a string to an integer:

```
a$=mki$(32000)  :  ? cvi(a$)¶
```

The specified string must be at least two characters long. Longer strings will only have their first two characters converted, and the rest of the string is ignored.

Let's compare two commands that seem to have similar functions. You learned about the CINT function in **Chapter 1**. CINT rounds off a normal number, making the number an integer:

```
?CINT (3.9)¶
```

The VAL command converts a written number in a string to an actual number:

```
?VAL ("32768")¶
```

CVI combines two bytes containing a string into a 16-bit number and returns the result:

```
a$=chr$(0)+chr$(254) :  ? cvi(a$)¶
```

The two bytes are produced by the two CHR$ commands. The result is 254, since the most significant 8 bits all have the value 0.

This may seem a little complicated, but stick with it as we go deeper into BASIC programming. And all this numerical artistry is an integral part of BASIC. When you understand the subtle differences between these commands and functions, you can proceed to load your graphic data from diskette.

Now we'll save you some typing time. Load in the original demonstration program and make the changes printed below:

```
DIM Array% (563) ¶
¶
OPEN "Face" FOR INPUT AS 1¶
   FOR x=0 TO 563¶
      Array%(x)=CVI(INPUT$(2,1))¶
   NEXT x¶
CLOSE 1¶
¶
¶
CLS¶
FOR x=0 TO 5¶
   FOR y=0 TO 4¶
      PUT (x*100,y*40), Array%¶
   NEXT y¶
NEXT x¶
```

When you double-checked this program, you may have noticed that the little men are displayed on the screen without benefit of the CIRCLE command. We've loaded the array Array% from diskette.

INPUT$

CVI has already been described, but maybe you noticed a few branches from INPUT$. The INPUT$ command has been used often in this book, but without any explanation. You use INPUT$ when you want to read a specific number of characters from a disk file. INPUT$(2,1) produces a string that consists of the next two characters in the file numbered 1. The syntax is:

INPUT$(*no.chars, filenumber*)

If you've already determined how many characters you want to read, INPUT$ should have no commas in it. CVI requires two bytes, so we should read two items of data.

You must make sure that you read no more characters from the file than are available. Otherwise AmigaBASIC displays an Input past end error message—you tried to read in more data than was available. There are two ways of avoiding this problem.

LOF

The first solution is the LOF (x) function, which stands for Length of File. The number in parentheses indicates the file number. As long as a file is open, LOF gives the file length in bytes. You can read as many characters as LOF states. To read a graphic object, the syntax would look like this:

```
INPUT$(LOF(1),1)
```

All the characters from file number 1 will be packed into one string. When you read single characters you will need a loop:

```
FOR x=1 TO LOF(1)
```

EOF

The second item is the EOF (x) function. You already know about this one. It returns a value of -1 when the end of file is reached. Otherwise it returns a value of 0. You can also use a loop for this: WHILE EOF (1) =0, or (more elegantly, and in plainer English) WHILE NOT EOF (1) .

You shouldn't have any problems because we already know how many characters are written to the file.

More about **INPUT$**

INPUT$ has an interesting side-effect: If you don't provide a file number, INPUT$ reads the desired characters from the keyboard. Try this:

```
? INPUT$(10) ¶
```

After you press <RETURN> the BASIC cursor reappears on the screen. Type in a couple of characters. The characters are not displayed, but the Amiga reserves them. After the tenth character has been typed, the entire string is displayed on the screen.

INPUT$ is also handy for data transfer between other peripherals, and for telecommunications. It is one of the most important AmigaBASIC utility commands for reading data.

You've now learned a method of storing graphic data on diskette. This method isn't a bad one at all for screen blocks. However, when we try this method on entire screens we run into limitations. It would require 300*200 pixels and 5 bitplanes to store a graphic from our drawing program, giving us an array of 21,000 elements. AmigaBASIC can't handle an array this large—you'd need to read the screen section by section with GET, then save it.

But wait—there's a better way to store the graphic on diskette.

4.2

Data in the fast lane:
Interchange File Format (IFF)

As soon as you buy a few commercial graphic programs like DeluxeVideo™ or Aegis Animator™, one thing you'll notice immediately is they produce files which are compatible with each other. For example, a drawing made on Graphicraft™ can be read by DeluxePaint™, and this can be used as the background or foreground in an animation program. And so on.

IFF and what it means

This is no accident. In 1985, the software company Electronic Arts invented a concept of setting up data in a standard, universal format, so that any program could read and work with the files. This brainchild is named IFF (Interchange File Format). Many other software firms have taken the cue from the designers of IFF, and enjoy the format's advantages. There is a good reason for this: It improves the image of companies who sell software using this format. Plus, the usefulness of a program increases with file compatibility: $100 for a paint program that can only draw is a steep price. But $100 for a program which lets you draw, create video titles, animation and other graphics, and lets you move them to other graphic programs, is a better deal all around.

The IFF standard makes it possible to switch applications without worrying about compatibility. Without IFF, the old files would be useless anywhere else. The IFF data is recognized by virtually any program, and whatever isn't recognized is simply ignored.

Most other computer owners have not been so lucky. Many paint programs for popular home computers cannot interchange files, so a file created with Program A cannot be used by Program B. The Commodore 64 is a victim of this sort of incompatibility.

What else can IFF do?

IFF isn't just for graphics. This format can also save musical note code, text, fonts, etc., although we want to concentrate on graphic data here. Because you write graphic programs with IFF compatibility on the Amiga, it's possible to load the graphics into commercial paint programs from AmigaBASIC. It is also possible to read professionally produced graphics into the AmigaBASIC paint program you wrote. For example, you could load one of your "homegrown" graphics into a commercial program to take advantage of the hardcopy and cut and paste features. Also, you can exchange graphics and data files with anybody else who owns an IFF-compatible paint program.

Before we jump into programming, let's take a look at the fundamentals and functions of IFF.

Chunks and forms

IFF combines all data that has the same function into one group under IFF. This group of data is referred to as a *Chunk*.

An IFF file is comprised of several chunks. All chunks of similar types are in a common *form*. An Amiga program tests the type of every chunk by checking the identifier in each form, which contains information about file type and length.

Bitmap

An IFF graphic file contains a minimum of three chunks. The first chunk contains control data, like the width and height of the graphic and the number of bitplanes. A second chunk contains the RGB values for the colors. The third chunk contains the graphic itself—or more accurately, the bits from which the graphic is constructed are stored here. A collection of bits that make up a graphic is called a *bitmap*. This name works well for bitplanes, since they make up the bitmap. The bitmap can use more chunks: perhaps the data from a palette animation (you've probably seen one of these cyclic color changes that create the illusion of movement), or video hardware operating modes, or the coordinates at which a graphic segment is displayed on the screen.

Identifiers

A chunk identifier and form identifier each consist of four bytes. The four bytes make a code word that the IFF read routine can recognize, followed by four more bytes that reserve the amount of data in the graphic. This figure shows the design of a typical IFF graphic file:

FORM	40156

ILBM

BMHD	20

320, 200, 0, 0, 3, 0, 0, 0, 0, 10, 11, 320,320

CMAP	96

32, 48, 160, 240, 240, 0, 0, 0, 240, 128, ...

Figure 14: IFF file format

BODY	40000

124, 142, 42, 213, 140, 0,...

FORM and ILBM

The first four characters in the file get the word FORM. The next four bytes contain the length of the form (40156 bytes) as a 32-bit number. The reader program now knows that the beginning of a form has been read, and totals 40156 bytes. Following this is a marker that indicates the filetype. The example calls this ILBM, an abbreviation for InterLeaved BitMap—the bitmap is combined with other data in one form. The reader program knows that the remaining data of this form are in chunks, and all of them have something to do with the graphic.

BMHD and CMAP

Following this information is the first chunk: Four bytes containing the marker BMHD (BitMap HeaDer, which contains the control data). The next four bytes give the number 20: The BMHD chunk consists of 20 bytes. The reader program can now branch to the subroutine to read and interpret the control data. Then the four bytes from CMAP are read. A Color MAP is exactly 96 bytes long. This chunk contains the data for the RGB setting of colors. Red, Green and Blue each use up one byte. Multiplied by 32 colors this gives us a total here of 96 bytes. Therefore, the colors can be read from a standing subroutine.

BODY

96 bytes later, we read from the BODY file, which is 40,000 bytes long. The BODY chunk is the bitmap of the graphic. The data is arranged here according to IFF standards: The lines of different bitplanes are sequentially stacked in the file (the first line of the first bitplane, the the first line of the second bitplane, etc). Following these rows are the second line of the first bitplane, second line of the second bitplane, and so on.

When the reader program has read the last byte of the last line of the last bitplane, then a total of 40156 bytes have been read. The IFF file is completed.

Theoretically the BMHD comes first, followed by BODY and CMAP. BMHD must be the first chunk found in the file, since its data is important to the size of the bitmap in the BODY chunk. First the program gets the control data, then reads the colors. There is no preset order for the rest of the chunks, though.

NOTE:

A chunk must consist of an even number of bytes. If the CMAP chunk only contains color values for 7 color registers (21 bytes), a fillbyte must "pad" the odd number from 21 to 22. This fillbyte is usually a 0. The fillbyte will not be involved with the length information of the chunk; it is just there as padding. Any odd numbers must be incremented by 1 to the next even number. Figure 15 depicts the fillbyte's function:

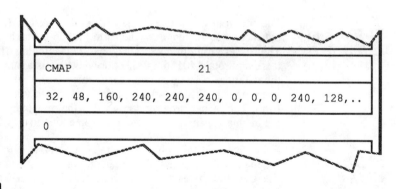

**Figure 15:
All odd-
numbered
chunks are
padded with
fillbytes**

4.3   American ingenuity at work: IFF reader routine

Now let's put our theory into practice so that we can read IFF data—one of the recent masterworks of good ol' American programming.

Before we do, one remark: Commodore has released a version of the Extras diskette (1.2 and 1.3) which has three additional programs in the BASICDemos drawer. These programs let you read and save IFF graphics. These routines are described under the Libraries category (see **Appendix D**). They run somewhat faster than the routines you'll find in this chapter. However, the programs on the Extras diskette are considerably harder to understand and use. For this reason, included are your own AmigaBASIC IFF programs, which can be used without accessing the libraries. But first we need to discuss all the AmigaBASIC commands.

The following programs won't teach you everything you need to know about programming disk input and output in AmigaBASIC. The goal here is to learn IFF file techniques. You'll find everything you need to know about the AmigaBASIC programs LoadACBM, LoadILBM-SaveACBM and SaveILBM that you'll find in **Appendix D**.

```
INPUT "Filename";Nam$¶
OPEN Nam$ FOR INPUT AS 1¶
   Form$=INPUT$(4,1)¶
   Length=CVL(INPUT$(4,1))¶
   IF INPUT$(4,1)<>"ILBM" THEN¶
     PRINT "ERROR IN DATA!"¶
     END¶
   END IF¶
¶
ReadData:¶
     IF EOF(1) THEN END¶
     Chunk$=INPUT$(4,1)¶
     Length=CVL(INPUT$(4,1))¶
     IF INT(Length/2)<>(Length/2) THEN Length=Length+1¶
     IF Chunk$="BMHD" THEN BMHeader¶
     IF Chunk$="CMAP" THEN ColorMap¶
     IF Chunk$="BODY" THEN BodyMap¶
     Dummy$=INPUT$(Length,1)¶
   GOTO ReadData¶
¶
```

```
BMHeader:   ¶
    xd=CVI(INPUT$(2,1))¶
    yd=CVI(INPUT$(2,1))¶
    Dummy$=INPUT$(4,1)¶
    BitPlane=ASC(INPUT$(1,1))¶
    Dummy$=INPUT$(11,1)¶
    IF xd=320 THEN Typ=1¶
    IF xd=640 THEN Typ=2¶
    IF yd>200 THEN Typ=Typ+2¶
    SCREEN 1,xd,yd,BitPlane,Typ¶
    WINDOW 2,Nam$,,0,1¶
    Addr=PEEKL(WINDOW(8)+4)+8¶
    FOR x=0 TO BitPlane-1¶
       PlaneAddr(x)=PEEKL(Addr+4*x) ¶
    NEXT x¶
    Dummy$=INPUT$(Length-20,1)¶
  GOTO ReadData¶
    ¶
ColorMap:¶
    FOR x=1 TO Length/3¶
       r=(ASC(INPUT$(1,1)) AND 240)/16¶
       g=(ASC(INPUT$(1,1)) AND 240)/16¶
       b=(ASC(INPUT$(1,1)) AND 240)/16¶
       PALETTE (x-1),r/16,g/16,b/16¶
    NEXT x¶
    IF INT(Length/3)<>(Length/3) THEN Dummy$=INPUT$(1,1) ¶
  GOTO ReadData¶
    ¶
BodyMap:¶
  ByteLine=xd/8¶
  FOR y1=0 TO yd-1¶
    FOR b=0 TO BitPlane-1¶
      FOR x1=0 TO ByteLine/4-1¶
        POKEL
PlaneAddr(b)+4*x1+ByteLine*y1,CVL(INPUT$(4,1))¶
      NEXT x1¶
    NEXT b¶
  NEXT y1¶
GOTO ReadData          ¶
```

This program can read IFF graphics in AmigaBASIC. Try this out in your spare time. Save the program as you type it in, since there are a few critical places where a typing error could cause a system crash. If it hasn't been previously saved, the entire program will be lost.

Using the program

Start the program, input the name of the file from your graphic diskette, insert the appropriate diskette in the disk drive, and off we go. If you don't have a graphics diskette, just type in the following: `Extras1.2:BasicDemos/Heart.ILBM`.

The program determines the screen's resolution, reads the colors (note that the pointer color is changed) and sets the graphic up line for line. Notice what happens to the window borders: They will be overwritten by the graphic data. When you first press the left mouse button, the border will reappear. Also note that no pulldown menus can be accessed while the top half of the graphic is being loaded. This is to prevent the graphic data being loaded from overwriting the menu and its items—the section on the graphic screen where the menus appear is skipped.

The graphic is loaded..

Now you have a **BASIC** window in which an IFF graphic is displayed. This gives you a thousand choices: You can put text over the graphic, copy segments of the graphic with GET and PUT, move graphic objects in front of the graphic, and more. But before you start experimenting, more explanation of the program:

INPUT takes on the filename given for the file to be loaded. The first INPUT$(4,1) reads the FORM identifier, and takes the form length into the variable length. We won't be working with this data any longer.

CVL

The CVL command (ConVert Long) in the fourth line is not a typo. In the same way that the CVI command converts 2 bytes into a 16-bit number, CVL converts 4 bytes into a 32-bit number.

MKL$

CVL's corresponding command for writing is called MKL$. We don't know why it's necessary for the length of a form to be 32 bits, but in any case, the IFF standard assigns file lengths of up to 4,294,967,295 bytes. In other words, up to 4 gigabytes can be filled with graphic data.

The next four bytes of the file should contain the identifier ILBM. If this isn't the case, we aren't reading an ILBM file, and the program terminates.

The variable Chunk$ reads the chunk identifier, and length reads the chunk length.

Testing for odd numbered chunks

The program line IF INT(Length/2)<>(Length/2) tests for whether an even number exists there: length is divided by 2, and any decimal value is removed. If both values are equal, then no decimal point is added, and it is assumed that the value is divisible by 2. The <> characters mean "not equal to". Odd numbers will be incremented by 1 to make the number even.

Storing the leftovers

The program branches to the next program section, depending on the contents of Chunk$. If the chunk is unrecognizable, the entire contents are read into Dummy$. "Dummy" is a nickname for a placeholder. Dummy$ contains the excess data, that is, the data which the program cannot interpret or understand.

The loop ReadData: repeats until no more data exists in the file.

269

The routine BMHD : reads the chunk of the same name. It usually has 20 bytes. The first two bytes contain 16-bit numbers for the width of the graphic, and the next two bytes contain the height. We assign these values to the variables xd and yd.

The next four bytes go into our Dummy$. In IFF standard, these stand for the X- and Y-coordinates of the upper left corner of those graphics that don't use the entire screen. Since we only want to work with full-screen graphics, these bytes don't interest us.

The next byte contains the number of bitplanes, and this value is assigned to the variable BitPlane.

The next 11 bytes will hold the data used by the IFF format save routine, and do not concern us at the moment.

xd can have a value of 320 or 640. yd can have a value of 200 or 400 (400 for interlace mode graphics). A value assigned for Typ is the variable controlling the resolution.

Once the SCREEN is created, a window is constructed in which the name of the file being read will be displayed.

Memory management

Now comes the tricky part. Like any computer, the Amiga must constantly monitor its memory. No bitmaps or data can be placed in memory areas being used for the other programs (e.g., Workbench routines or AmigaBASIC). The multitasking ability of the Amiga does not allow for simple memory divisions. In other words, you can't say "Here's where AmigaBASIC should go." The Amiga puts these programs in different areas of memory.

Every memory cell can store 1 byte, and the Amiga's RAM consists of about 262,000 or 524,000 memory cells that can be used for reading or writing. In addition to read/write memory (RAM), the Amiga 500 and 2000 have 256K of established *ROM* (Read Only Memory), where the Kickstart data resides. The Amiga 1000 has 256K of RAM into which the contents of the Kickstart diskette are loaded. After loading, the RAM is electronically moved, so that it behaves as if it were in ROM.

Each memory cell has a number assigned to it. This number is called an *address*. The absolute first memory address in the Amiga has the number 0, the second number 1, and so on.

Intuition

The Amiga operating system has a program that checks which memory range is allocated for a particular program. This memory management program is called Intuition. And Intuition itself is a part of the operating system. It knows, for example, that the addresses 0 through 40,000 are needed for the Workbench, addresses 40,001 to 72,000 are needed for screen display, addresses 72001 to 160,000 are needed to store AmigaBASIC, etc. (These numbers aren't real, they're just examples).

270

PEEK
POKE

Normally you wouldn't directly change the contents of memory locations, since most changes could result in conflicts of interest. Instead, AmigaBASIC gives you a series of commands to do this: PEEK lets you view the contents of a memory location, and POKE lets you write a value to a memory location. These commands are extremely important for most computers, since they allowed the user to replace routines for "missing" BASIC commands. For example, the Commodore 64 has so many useful PEEKs and POKEs that people have written books on the subject. AmigaBASIC uses PEEKs and POKEs much less, since virtually every command is available in AmigaBASIC. However, AmigaBASIC has no routines for saving or loading graphics, so we have to use PEEK and POKE to create them.

Type the following line into the **BASIC** window:

? PEEK (30000) ¶

This returns a number between 0 and 255. This is the value of the byte stored at the memory address 30000. To put it another way: You get a letter which contains an 8-bit number from the address 30000. The resident of address 30000 has informed you which number he has.

POKE 30000, (value) ¶

This line writes a value to memory address 30000. Type a value which can be read by PEEKing. Now you have sent a letter to the address 30000, which tells the resident of that address his new number.

PEEKW
POKEW

If you want to write to 16 bits rather than 8 bits, then you use the commands PEEKW and POKEW. The W stands for Word, the expression for a 16-bit value. The PEEKW and POKEW commands work with two bytes which reside next to one another in memory. The residents of both memory addresses handle a total of 16 bits. Each contains 8 bits. Our correspondent "resides" in the even-numbered memory address. Type this:

POKEW 30001, (value) ¶

The error message "Illegal function call" appears.

PEEKL
POKEL

The entire game applies to 32-bit numbers as well. The commands here are called PEEKL and POKEL (L=Longword). The address must also be an even number. Four memory locations reside next to one another in memory. This returns four addresses, each composed of 8 bits, for a total of 32 bits.

This was the first battle. Now for the second, for which we use the function WINDOW (8) .

WINDOW(x)

You should remember WINDOW(0). It returns the number of currently active windows. But there are more WINDOW functions with different capabilities. WINDOW(8) returns the address of a list (C programmers and the computer industry call this *structure*), which Intuition notes as data for the current windows. It's not as simple as it sounds: The second four bytes of the list, indicated by WINDOW(8), contain the address at which the other list begins. There are several 32-bit values in this 8th bit of the list. These are the starting addresses of the individual bitplanes. If you are not intimately acquainted with the memory layout of the Amiga, you may not understand this completely—you may not understand at all! However, you should understand that we have put the addresses into the array PlaneAddr(x), where our individual bitplanes of the graphic window lie in memory. More about this later.

Lastly, Dummy$ reads the extra bytes.

Reading the CMAP chunk

There is less involved in reading the CMAP chunk. Three bytes are read for every color: One for R, one for G and one for B. We have already mentioned that the IFF standard allows for this. The same applies to resolution. The Amiga can understand 16 levels of R, G and B. IFF is capable of giving 256 shades of color.

To utilize graphics from computers with more graphic ability than the Amiga, the IFF developers thought up a neat trick: The topmost 4 bytes are used to store the color intensities from 0 to 15. This means that between every color step, the Amiga has 15 numbers free to be used for later refinements in color resolution. The percentages of red, green and blue will still be in the correct proportions.

Reading the bytes, we isolate the top 4 bits with AND 240, and divide the result by 16. Then we get the correct value for the PALETTE command. Any fillbytes above and beyond that are taken by Dummy$.

Reading the BODY chunk

The last program section reads the BODY chunk, or the bitmap. The variable ByteLine calculates the number of bytes per screen line from xd. The last section told you that the lines are stored in the sequence of bitplane per screen line. We read that in the same way. Now we get to see our PlaneAddr in action. We recognize the starting address of the individual bitplanes, and put it in the proper place in memory line for line. We then use the POKEL command since we need to get the fastest result: Every execution of the loop reads 32 bits into memory.

The variable y1 counts up the lines of the graphic, b the bitplanes, and x1 the number of individual 32-bit numbers in the line. Once all the bitmap data has been transferred to memory, the system returns to the ReadData: routine.

If there are more chunks in the file, they will be read, even though our program may not comprehend these other chunks.

Compressed form

There is still a problem to be solved, which you may have run into in the last chapter, especially if you own DeluxePaint. This package and most other graphic programs have one disadvantage: The bitmap of the BODY chunk is saved in *compressed form*. What's that?

Graphics are stored in more or less equally colored form. Quite often, many areas of the screen are filled with the background color, which means most other screen details cannot be seen. It doesn't make sense to save the same value 2000 times to diskette. To save space on diskette, programmers have developed a key system by which a set of identical bytes can be combined. A graphic that takes up 40K in RAM can be compressed this way so that it only takes up about 25K on diskette. But compressed graphics can pose problems when you try to load them in AmigaBASIC. A compensating routine would be extremely difficult to write and extremely slow. So what does all this mean? This: a graphic that was saved in DeluxePaint format is not read directly into memory, the graphic will look nothing like the original. Try it—if you have the time.

Graphics in low (320 x 200) resolution aren't so disastrous if you have Graphicraft, for instance. Graphicraft doesn't compress when it saves. You can load a compressed graphic into Graphicraft and save it. Then the graphic can be read from AmigaBASIC. However, Graphicraft cannot read graphics in higher resolutions, such as 640 x 400. All the current graphic programs that use high resolution save compressed graphics, which can't be used in AmigaBASIC.

One other point: The IFF standard will allow any BASIC graphic to go into any degree of resolution. More on this later.

4.4

Passing the buck:
loading and saving paint program graphics

Back to the big issue: We still have yet to load DeluxePaint graphics in our paint program, or load our paint program graphics into Graphicraft, etc.

After the groundwork we've laid in the last few sections, it shouldn't be all that difficult to write a routine that loads and saves IFF files to and from our paint program. Save the program from the last section, if you haven't already, and then load the paint program.

We'll guide you step by step through the necessary stages. First type the following lines into the Project: section of the program:

```
IF MenChoice=4 THEN GOSUB ColorDone : GOSUB PatternDone :
GOSUB DrawLoad¶
IF MenChoice=5 THEN GOSUB ColorDone : GOSUB PatternDone :
GOSUB DrawSave¶
```

Now scroll through the listing to the PatternDone: section. Then type in the following section:

```
DrawLoad:¶
  MENU 2,0,0 : MENU 1,0,0¶
  MENU OFF : MOUSE OFF¶
  GOSUB EnterName¶
  WINDOW CLOSE 5¶
  WINDOW 2¶
  IF Nam$="" THEN EndLoad ¶
  OPEN Nam$ FOR INPUT AS 1¶
    Form$=INPUT$(4,1)¶
    Length=CVL(INPUT$(4,1))¶
    IF INPUT$(4,1)<>"ILBM" THEN BEEP : GOTO EndLoad¶
  ¶
ReadData:¶
    IF EOF(1) THEN EndLoad¶
    Chunk$=INPUT$(4,1)¶
    Length=CVL(INPUT$(4,1))¶
    IF INT(Length/2)<>(Length/2) THEN Length=Length+1¶
    IF Chunk$="BMHD" THEN BMHeader¶
    IF Chunk$="CMAP" THEN ColorMap¶
    IF Chunk$="BODY" THEN BodyMap¶
    Dummy$=INPUT$(Length,1)¶
  GOTO ReadData¶
  ¶
```

```
BMHeader:    ¶
     xd=CVI(INPUT$(2,1))¶
     IF xd>320 THEN EndLoad¶
     yd=CVI(INPUT$(2,1))¶
     IF yd>200 THEN EndLoad¶
     Dummy$=INPUT$(4,1)¶
     BitPlane=ASC(INPUT$(1,1))¶
     Dummy$=INPUT$(11,1)¶
     Addr=PEEKL(WINDOW(8)+4)+8¶
     FOR x=0 TO BitPlane-1¶
        PlaneAddr(x)=PEEKL(Addr+4*x)¶
     NEXT x¶
   GOTO ReadData¶
     ¶
ColorMap:¶
     FOR x=0 TO (Length/3)-1¶
        r=(ASC(INPUT$(1,1)) AND 240)/16¶
        g=(ASC(INPUT$(1,1)) AND 240)/16¶
        b=(ASC(INPUT$(1,1)) AND 240)/16¶
        PALETTE x,r/16,g/16,b/16¶
        Colors%(x,0)=r : Colors%(x,1)=g : Colors%(x,2)=b¶
     NEXT x¶
     IF INT(Length/3)<>(Length/3) THEN Dummy$=INPUT$(1,1)¶
   GOTO ReadData¶
     ¶
BodyMap:¶
     FOR y1=0 TO 199¶
        FOR b=0 TO BitPlane-1¶
           IF b<Colors THEN¶
              FOR x1=0 TO 9¶
                 POKEL
PlaneAddr(b)+4*x1+40*y1,CVL(INPUT$(4,1))¶
              NEXT x1¶
           ELSE¶
              Dummy$=INPUT$(40,1)¶
           END IF¶
        NEXT b¶
     NEXT y1¶
   GOTO ReadData          ¶
¶
EndLoad:¶
   CLOSE 1¶
   MENU ON : MOUSE ON¶
   MENU 1,0,1 : MENU 2,0,1¶
RETURN¶
¶
DrawSave:¶
   MENU 2,0,0 : MENU 1,0,0¶
   MENU OFF : MOUSE OFF¶
   GOSUB EnterName¶
   WINDOW CLOSE 5¶
   WINDOW 2¶
   IF Nam$="" THEN EndSave¶
```

```
    OPEN Nam$ FOR OUTPUT AS 1 LEN=FRE(0)-500¶
      PRINT #1,"FORM";¶
      PRINT #1,MKL$(156+8000*Colors);¶
      PRINT #1,"ILBM";¶
      PRINT #1,"BMHD";MKL$(20);¶
      PRINT #1,MKI$(320);MKI$(200);¶
      PRINT #1,MKL$(0);¶
      PRINT #1,CHR$(Colors);¶
      PRINT #1,CHR$(0);MKI$(0);MKI$(0);¶
      PRINT #1,CHR$(10);CHR$(11);¶
      PRINT #1,MKI$(320);MKI$(200);¶
      ¶
      PRINT #1,"CMAP";MKL$(96); ¶
      FOR x=0 TO 31¶
        PRINT #1,CHR$(Colors%(x,0)*16);¶
        PRINT #1,CHR$(Colors%(x,1)*16);¶
        PRINT #1,CHR$(Colors%(x,2)*16);¶
      NEXT x¶
      ¶
      PRINT #1,"BODY";MKL$(8000*Colors);¶
      Addr=PEEKL(WINDOW(8)+4)+8¶
      FOR x=0 TO Colors-1¶
        PlaneAddr(x)=PEEKL(Addr+4*x)¶
      NEXT x¶
      FOR y1=0 TO 199¶
        FOR b=0 TO Colors-1¶
          FOR x1=0 TO 9 ¶
            PRINT#1,MKL$(PEEKL(PlaneAddr(b)+4*x1+40*y1));¶
          NEXT x1¶
        NEXT b¶
        PAddr=PlaneAddr(0)+40*y1¶
        POKE PAddr,PEEK(PAddr) AND 63¶
        POKE PAddr+39,PEEK(PAddr+39) AND 252¶
      NEXT y1¶
      ¶
      PRINT #1,"CAMG";MKL$(4);¶
      PRINT #1,MKL$(16384);¶
    CLOSE 1¶
      ¶
EndSave:¶
  MENU ON : MOUSE ON¶
  MENU 1,0,1 : MENU 2,0,1¶
RETURN¶
```

How the routine works

You'll notice that this routine is only slightly different from the regular load routine in the paint program. The BMHeader: routine, which reads the BMHD chunk, tests the size of the graphic: If the graphic being read is wider than 320 pixels or taller than 200 pixels, the load routine jumps out, since the graphic won't fit on the screen.

The RGB values read from ColorMap: are put into the array Colors%, so that the paint program can use color normally.

The loops in the BodyMap: section set the values for a 320 x 200 graphic; the program will not read other formats.

Adapting bitplanes

Next we must adapt the number of bitplanes. When the graphic being read has a screen of numerous bitplanes used in the paint program, the data will be packed and taken up by Dummy$. The program only loads in the number of bitplanes determined in the Colors variables. Consequently, different colors can be specified at any time.

File buffers

There is more new material in the DrawSave subroutine, which writes the graphic to diskette in IFF format. It starts off just like DrawLoad:, the pulldown menus are disabled and a filename read, then the program opens a file for writing. But what does the LEN=FRE(0)-500 mean? As you know, AmigaBASIC sets up a buffer for every file where the bytes are first collected, before they are written to diskette. This saves a lot of time, since saving to diskette is the slowest computer operation. Normally the buffer is 128 bytes long. The more memory in the buffer, the faster the data transfer. Accordingly, the desired buffer length is specified in the OPEN command. This occurs by appending the LEN=(buffer size) to the OPEN command. For example:

OPEN Nam$ FOR OUTPUT AS 1 LEN=1000

This assigns file 1 a buffer of 1000 bytes.

The disadvantage of this method is that you don't have unlimited memory—the memory range in AmigaBASIC in which the variables, file buffer and arrays are located is only 25K in a 512K Amiga. The starting message in AmigaBASIC tells the Amiga how many free bytes are available.

FRE(0)

AmigaBASIC also has a function that determines the number of bytes free: FRE(x). Input the following into the **BASIC** window:

?FRE(0) ¶

FRE(-1)

The number returned tells you the number of free bytes in BASIC memory. The loaded paint program and 512K RAM will return a number of about 9000. If there is a 0 in parentheses after the FRE, the bytes free in BASIC memory are given. Replacing the 0 with -1 returns the entire system memory:

?FRE(-1) ¶

About system memory

The number returned is larger than the result of FRE(0). We can only make a guess at its actual size—it all depends on what is happening in the background, how many windows are open, and what programs are loaded in memory at the time. You may have guessed that memory can be found for the graphic bitmap in system memory. If you want more memory in AmigaBASIC, we'll discuss this later.

Now the expression LEN=FRE(0)-500 makes sense. The rest of BASIC memory is used as buffer memory, with 500 bytes reserved for variables. If you overfill BASIC memory by even one byte, AmigaBASIC displays an Out of memory error message.

How the save routine works

We save at the highest speed possible in our save routine. Then the buffer memory is freed up after the file is closed. The file opens, and we send the data to its destination.

First we write the FORM type indicator into the file, followed by the form length. This depends on the number of bitplanes. Every bitplane uses 8000 bytes. 156 bytes take the color and control data. The total memory requirement is 156+8000 x (no. of bitplanes).

The ILBM (interleaved bitmap) identifier follows.

Then the BMHD chunk is sent. It is usually 20 bytes long. The BMHD chunk is followed by the number 320 (width) and the number 200 (height), each as 16-bit numbers. Then four nullbytes follow (the starting coordinates for the graphic). The next byte contains the number of bitplanes, followed by another nullbyte.

The following two bytes identify whether the graphic data in the BODY chunk is stored in compressed form or not. The value 0 means no compression. (Programs which have a compression compensation routine use this information). Then two more nullbytes follow. These aren't used in current versions of IFF; they are reserved for later developments. Next come the two values 10 and 11. These values indicate the degree of a pixel's width in proportion to its height, so that the IFF graphic can be displayed on other computers. The screen proportion can be radically different from computer to computer. The Amiga uses 10:11 — MKI$(10);MKI$(11).

Next come the numbers 320 and 200. These determine the selected resolution, rather than the graphic size. Another 20 bytes and the BMHD chunk is full.

Now we come to the colors. We save 32 color values, which is the maximum number of colors we can display on a screen. We write a total of 96 (32 x 3) RGB values into the CMAP chunk from the Colors% array. You figure out the values as follows: IFF developers give the files a finer color resolution than the Amiga can display. Therefore, every color value must be multiplied by 16.

Computing bitplane addresses

Now comes the main routine, the BODY chunk: Its length depends on the number of bitplanes (each bitplane uses 8000 bytes). We compute the addresses of the bitplanes in both DrawLoad: and DrawSave:. It doesn't matter which routine is used first, but in any case we need the current data for the array PlaneAddr.

The loop itself first reads from memory with PEEKL and then writes the data to the file. To show what is being saved, we added the next three program lines.

The variable PlaneAddr computes the first byte in the current graphic line from the first bitplane for every execution. This byte is POKEd into the address after the most significant bits are cleared (with AND 63). Then the last byte of the graphic line is read into the least significant bits, after they have been cleared with AND 252. The result: The window borders disappear from top to bottom, and the line height is saved. That's how you know when the program is finished saving. The border then reappears when the menu button is clicked.

Saving the "spare" chunk

Last but not least, we save a chunk that our program won't read, but is necessary to Graphicraft and other commercial programs: The CMAG (Commodore AMiGa) chunk is only four bytes in size, and contains a 32-bit number which conveys information to Intuition about the graphic operating mode. Once the last chunk is sent to diskette, the file is closed.

That's it. Now your paint program is IFF-compatible. You can load graphics and save them, and use these graphics in other graphic programs. Commercial paint programs allow you to cut and paste sections of graphics, enlarge areas, or print hardcopies of your artwork, among other things. Your paint program has a fill pattern editor which you can put to good use with Graphicraft.

As you see, the Amiga has more compatibilities than incompatibilities. With this motto in mind, we'll make our video title program IFF compatible.

Intermission 4

Compatibility's the key: improving your video title program

How does this sound: You take a graphic created in Graphicraft, insert some patterns you designed in your paint program, and then use this graphic as the background for the animated video title program. To accomplish this, we need to alter the video title program so that it's able to read IFF files.

A matter of resolution

This presents one problem: the resolution mode. All Graphicraft graphics and most popular IFF graphic systems are 320 x 200 pixels (low res). Even your own paint program works only in this resolution. But the video title program is displayed in standard BASIC resolution (640 x 200 pixels). So IFF graphics are too small. What can we do about it?

The simplest and most sensible solution is to convert the video title program so that it will run in low resolution. Not many changes need to be made, since its first line sets the text display on the screen. The other changes involve displaying larger, easier-to-read characters.

Load your video title program (located in the `video` drawer on the `BASICdisk`).

If you save the program as you're typing the changes in, use a new name so that you have two versions of the video title program.

Changes

Here are the program lines that must be changed:

In the `Setup:` section, delete the `IF...THEN` before the `SCREEN` command. Line the old program, we only open one new screen when more than two bitplanes are being read. Now we want to open one in the new program everytime this occurs. The parameters for the `SCREEN` command will be rewritten into 320 x 200 pixels. After the alterations, the fifth line of `Setup:` should look like this:

[before]

```
If Colors>2 THEN SCREEN 2,640,200,Colors,2:WINDOW
2,"Videotitle",,28,2¶
```

[after]

```
SCREEN 2,320,200,Colors,1:WINDOW 2,"Videotitle",,28,2¶
```

A line below this contains a series of DIM statements. The Colormatrix should be limited to the highest possible color number. Change the parameter Colormatrix (d, 3) to Colormatrix (31, 3):

[before]

DIM Text$(d),Colormatrix(d,3),Move(d),Speed(d) ¶

[after]

DIM Text$(d),Colormatrix(31,3),Move(d),Speed(d) ¶

After these changes, we are done changing our Setup: routine. Now we come to the Beginning:

[before]

PRINT "Videotitle-Program ";¶

[after]

PRINT "Videotitle-Program "¶

The semicolon has been removed. This way we force a carriage return between Videotitle-Program and the name. Otherwise, part of the single line would read off the right edge of the screen.

Now we come to a longer, change-free section. Scroll to the ReadObject: section to make a few small alterations:

[before]

PRINT"Enter the name of the object you want to load."¶

[after]

PRINT"Enter the name of the":PRINT"object you want to load."¶

Now scroll to the Mover: section:

[before]

PRINT"Move the object to its starting point"¶
PRINT"using the cursor keys."¶

[after]

PRINT"Move the object to its"¶
PRINT"starting point using"¶
PRINT"the cursor keys."¶

Now for a much larger section. The screen display in `Colors:` must be changed and the color numbers increased:

[before]

```
Colors:¶
  FOR x=0 TO Colors¶
    COLOR -(x=0),x¶
    LOCATE 5,(X*4) + 1¶
    PRINT x;CHR$(32);CHR$(32) ¶
  NEXT x¶
```

[after]

```
Colors:¶
  FOR x=0 TO Colors¶
    IF (x/8)=INT(x/8) THEN PRINT ¶
    COLOR -(x=0),x¶
    PRINT x;¶
    IF x<10 THEN PRINT CHR$(32);¶
  NEXT x¶
```

This routine is fairly simple. `IF (x/8)=INT(8)`... means: If x is a multiple of 8 (8,16 or 24), then a linefeed should follow, especially when the color array is printed. And `IF x<10 THEN`... prints a blank for the arrays with the numbers 0 to 9, since these are only one digit numbers. From 10 on, the numbers are two-digit.

Alter the next `ColorChange:` section:

[before]

```
PRINT"Enter the number of the color you want to change."¶
```

[after]

```
PRINT"Enter the number of the color": PRINT "you want to
change."¶
```

The changes in the `RGBRegulator:` section also compensate for the smaller screen. The R, G and B sliders must be divided into two lines:

[before]

```
LOCATE 10,1:PRINT"Red: <7>=- <8>=+";Filler$
LOCATE 10,20+r:PRINT CHR$(124);
LOCATE 11,1:PRINT"Green: <4>=- <5>=+";Filler$
LOCATE 11,20+g:PRINT CHR$(124);
LOCATE 12,1:PRINT"Blue: <1>=- <2>=+";Filler$
LOCATE 12,20+b:PRINT CHR$(124);
LOCATE 13,1:PRINT"      <0>=Color o.k."¶
```

[after]

```
LOCATE 11,1: PRINT "Red: <7>=- <8>=+ ":PRINT Filler$¶
LOCATE 12,r+1 : PRINT CHR$(124);¶
LOCATE 13,1: PRINT "Green: <4>=- <5>=+ ":PRINT Filler$¶
LOCATE 14,g+1 : PRINT CHR$(124);¶
LOCATE 15,1: PRINT "Blue:  <1>=- <2>=+ ":PRINT  Filler$¶
LOCATE 16,b+1 : PRINT CHR$(124);¶
LOCATE 17,1: PRINT "          <0>=Color o.k."¶
```

Did you find the differences? The LOCATE lines are incremented by 1, and the LOCATE columns with 20+r are changed to 1+r. Then the Filler$ is preceded by a PRINT statement each time.

The next change to the LOCATE statement in EnterColor: and Loop3: is minor:

[before]

```
LOCATE 14,1¶
```

[after]

```
LOCATE 19,1¶
```

The last correction must also be made in two other places.

Alter Countdown: within the line of a column number:

[before]

```
LOCATE 10,39:PRINT c¶
```

[after]

```
LOCATE 10,20:PRINT c¶
```

Change the line width returned from the WIDTH command in StartDisplay: from 80 to 40.

[before]

```
WIDTH 80¶
```

[after]

```
WIDTH 40¶
```

The computations for line width should also be changed. Change the value 60 to 32 in the sixth and seventh lines of StartDisplay::

[before]

```
Text$=LEFT$(Text$(x),80)¶
h=INT((80-LEN(Text$))/2)+2¶
```

[after]

```
Text$=LEFT$(Text$(x),40)¶
h=INT((40-LEN(Text$))/2)+2¶
```

All finished. The changes you made allow the program to run in low (320 x 200) resolution. Experiment with the program until you find your typing errors, if any.

Don't forget to save the program under the new name. When you're ready , read on to discover how to load your IFF files.

4.5

Lights, Camera, *Action*:
loading graphics in the video title program

The video title program will also need an IFF load routine. Rather than making you type in the same program a third time, we'll use a few tricks we've picked up while working with the peripheral devices. Save and exit the video title program, change the current directory with CHDIR and then load your paint program.

Merging routines into programs

Your paint program contains a routine that reads 320 x 200 pixel graphics. We can move this routine over to the video title program with a minimum of effort. Type the following lines in the **BASIC** window:

```
list DrawLoad-EndLoad,"ram:iff.Load"
```

This command line saves the read routine of the paint program to the RAM disk as an ASCII file. All of the program lines between the labels DrawLoad: and EndLoad: will be saved as the file IFF.Load.

Now delete the paint program from memory with NEW and load up the new version of the video title program. Merge the IFF read routine by typing the following command:

```
merge"ram:iff.Load"
```

Refinements

Now we have the rough draft completed. Let's do some fine-tuning to integrate the new routine into the program. First we need to add a menu item for that routine. Go to Select: and type this in under line 5:

```
PRINT "6 Load Background Picture"
```

We have to compensate for this new menu item. Make the following changes to the Query: section:

[before]

```
IF a$<"1" OR a$>"5" THEN BEEP: GOTO Query
```

[after]

```
IF a$<"1" OR a$>"6" THEN BEEP: GOTO Query
```

The maximum input number is 6, not 5. A few lines later, in the series of IF...THEN statements, we insert a call for the new routine:

```
IF a$="6" THEN SetupScreen
```

285

You must set the input line 1 higher to accomodate the new line. Change the line parameter of the LOCATE instruction in the Query: section:

[before]

LOCATE 10,1

[after]

LOCATE 11,1

Type in the new routine SetupScreen: after the routine VelocityCalc:.

```
SetupScreen:¶
  CLS¶
  PRINT "Want to load a graphic"¶
  PRINT "background? (Y/N)"¶
¶
Loop5:¶
  LOCATE 2,19 : INPUT Answ$¶
  IF UCASE$(Answ$)="N" THEN IFF=0 : CLS : GOTO Begin¶
  IF UCASE$(Answ$)="Y" THEN IFF=1 : GOTO EnterName ¶
GOTO Loop5¶
¶
EnterName:¶
  PRINT¶
  PRINT "Enter name:"¶
  INPUT Nam$¶
  PRINT ¶
  PRINT "Use the color table for:"¶
  PRINT Nam$¶
  PRINT "Enter (Y/N)";¶
Loop6:¶
  LOCATE 9,12 : INPUT Answ$¶
  IF UCASE$(Answ$)="N" THEN IFFTab=0 : CLS : GOTO Begin¶
  IF UCASE$(Answ$)="Y" THEN IFFTab=1 : CLS : GOTO Begin¶
GOTO Loop6¶
```

The SetupScreen: routine first asks whether you want to load a background graphic or not. You can answer the prompt with either <y> or <n>. Any other input returns you to the input loop. The IFF variable later states whether an IFF graphic is being loaded (IFF=1) or not (IFF=0).

The EnterName: routine asks for the name of the graphic. This entry will be placed in Nam$. Then it asks whether or not it should load the color table for the desired graphic (from the CMAP chunk).

NOTE: The text and the graphic must be the same colors. If you have put different values in the text and background colors than those in the color map of the graphic, then answer <n>. Then the program uses the color table which was set up in the video title program. The variable IFFTab helps the program to make the distinction.

Now we have to alter the ReadData: subroutine. We want to add a few options to the current program. But we encounter a problem when we add GOTO or GOSUB commands pointing to the new routine.

Same variables, different uses?

Our IFF load routine uses a lot of variables that are needed in the main program. We can work around these variables, even Form$, Length or Chunk$, but what do we do with x and y? x and y are used as a sort of mathematical dimensioning. x has a value of 3000 in our program. After we load the new background graphic, the program returns to the load section. The variable x will then be used as the counting variable in ColorMap:, and returns the value 31. You've just lost 2969 pixels in one shot. That's no big deal, but which x is the most important one?

You see, using the same variable in both a main program and a subroutine can have unpredictable results. One solution is to use exotic variable names in your subroutines, but this is no guarantee of variable security.

The subprogram

The command SUB...STATIC was created to help. This lets you set up a special type of subroutine called a *subprogram*. Subprograms are different from subroutines in the sense of variable handling: Subprograms use *local variables*. This means that all the variables within the section have their own values apart from the variables in the main program. If you use x in a subprogram and x in the main program, the values are handled distinctly from one another.

SUB... STATIC

You can change the x in the main program to another value, and the x in the subprogram will remain unchanged. It's possible to assign the SUB variable its own memory register. If AmigaBASIC jumps to the main program from a subprogram, then back to the subprogram again, you'll find the same value contents as before. STATIC follows the SUB command. The name of the routine goes between SUB and STATIC. For example:

```
SUB converter STATIC
```

END SUB

This line has nothing to do with the video title program—it is simply used as an example. The command END SUB must be at the end of the subprogram. You can put a subprogram anywhere in a program. Because of the enclosure of SUB...STATIC and END SUB, AmigaBASIC knows that this section doesn't belong to the main program. The routine will not run itself, when you put it in the middle of the program. For example, the following program would only execute the first and last lines:

```
x-=100

SUB conversion STATIC
x=40
x=x*100+3
PRINT"Hi there!"
END SUB

PRINT x
```

Again, these lines are only used as an example.

Subprogram errors
There are some rules you should remember when programming subprograms. For example, no subprograms should be defined within a SUB/END delineator. The following structure is also prohibited:

```
SUB test STATIC
    SUB test2 STATIC
            PRINT "Test 2"
    END SUB
    PRINT"Test"
END SUB
```

The above lines display a Tried to declare SUB within a SUB error message.

If two identically named subprograms exist, the Amiga displays a SUB already defined error message.

If you forget the STATIC after the SUB, the Amiga displays a Missing STATIC in SUB statement error message.

The END SUB is also required. If you forget it, the Amiga displays a SUB without END SUB error message.

CALL
You use the CALL command to call a subroutine. For example:

```
CALL converter
```

You can even omit the CALL under certain conditions, and just give the name of the subprogram:

```
converter
```

Abbreviated
CALL

Following are a few examples of proper and improper situations to use the abbreviated CALL. (None of these have any bearing on the video title program, but soon we'll be able to apply this knowledge to reading graphics):

```
FOR x=1 TO 10: converter: NEXT x
```

This line is self-explanatory. The subprogram converter: is called within the FOR...NEXT loop. The next case is a little harder to see:

```
converter: PRINT x
```

Is converter: a SUB call followed by a colon, or is it a label belonging to the PRINT command? In this case, it is a label. CALL would be necessary in this instance. Therefore:

```
CALL converter: PRINT x
```

Here is a similar example:

```
IF x=10 THEN converter
```

Is converter a label to which the program should branch, or is it a subprogram? Here again, CALL is needed:

```
IF x=10 THEN CALL converter
```

Now that your burning questions about subprograms are answered, let's get back to the video title program. We'll make the DrawLoad: routine a subprogram. Now we can easily add changes to the IFF read routine.

Add this to the DrawLoad: label:

```
SUB DrawLoad STATIC
```

And now we'll go back to the program. Now delete the program section up to this line:

```
IF Nam$="" THEN EndLoad
```

You should have just deleted the first five lines of the DrawLoad: subprogram. We'll type in something new in place of these lines. Maybe you've already wondered: When the subprogram uses its own variables, and the variables in the main program are not affected, what do you do when you want to use values from the main program?

For example, you want to pass the number of bitplanes from the variable `Colors` to the array `Colormatrix` when we load the IFF graphic. Then you want to save the color values at `IFFTab`, from which we can get the read routine with the color table, and the filename `Nam$`.

What do you do?

SHARED

Luckily, the developers of AmigaBASIC dreamed up a command for this purpose: `SHARED`. Type the following line right after the SUB...STATIC line:

```
SHARED Colors,Colormatrix(),IFFTab,Nam$¶
```

The main program and the subprogram share the given variables. That means that they are now common variables. You can specify both variables and arrays in the `SHARED` command, if both groups use the same values. As you've seen above, you must type a pair of empty parentheses after an array name. This is how you distinguish between array names and variable names. Already our problems are solved.

The next program change is in `ColorMap:`. Here is the original:

```
ColorMap:¶
    FOR x=0 TO (Length/3)-1¶
      r=(ASC(INPUT$(1,1)) AND 240)/16¶
      g=(ASC(INPUT$(1,1)) AND 240)/16¶
      b=(ASC(INPUT$(1,1)) AND 240)/16¶
      PALETTE x,r/16,g/16,b/16¶
      Colors%(x,0)=r : Colors%(x,1)=g : Colors%(x,2)=b¶
    NEXT x¶
    IF INT(Length/3)<>(Length/3) THEN Dummy$=INPUT$(1,1) ¶
    GOTO ReadData¶
```

And here is the modified version:

```
ColorMap:¶
    FOR x=0 TO (Length/3)-1¶
      r=(ASC(INPUT$(1,1)) AND 240)/16¶
      g=(ASC(INPUT$(1,1)) AND 240)/16¶
      b=(ASC(INPUT$(1,1)) AND 240)/16¶
      IF IFFTab=1 THEN¶
        PALETTE x,r/16,g/16,b/16¶
        Colormatrix(x,1)=r : Colormatrix(x,2)=g :
Colormatrix(x,3)=b¶
      END IF¶
    NEXT x¶
    IF INT(Length/3)<>(Length/3) THEN Dummy$=INPUT$(1,1) ¶
    GOTO ReadData¶
```

First, an IF...THEN must be inserted. The colors being read will only be passed when IFFTab has a value of 1. Second, the array Colors% from our paint program is converted into the array Colormatrix in our video title program. The second dimension of the array will be incremented by one. The red value of color x is contained not in Colors%(x,0), but in Colors%(x,1). The same goes for green (changed from 1 to 2) and blue (changed from 2 to 3).

Next you alter to the EndLoad: routine :

```
EndLoad:¶
CLOSE 1¶
END SUB¶
```

We're almost done. The IFF routine is converted for the video title program. We have to get a call to the subroutine. Move the cursor to the program section StartDisplay: and insert a CALL command:

```
StartDisplay:¶
  WIDTH 32 ¶
  COLOR TextColor,Background : CLS¶
  COLOR TextColor,TextBackground¶
  IF IFF=1 THEN CALL DrawLoad¶
  FOR x=1 TO NoofLines¶
```

Now the background graphic reading is built in, and we're done with the program revision.

Don't forget to save the program to diskette!

Using the routine

The effect of the program alterations isn't difficult to follow. You click menu item six when you want to use a background graphic, or click it off when you don't. You can input a filename, and determine whether the current colors or the colors in the IFF file should be used. After the countdown, and before the text and animated objects are displayed, the background graphic parameters are loaded.

NOTE:

Loading clears the window borders. This does not affect the video titles. However, if you want the old border back, click the menu button on the mouse.

If you want a second, fully movable graphic object on your video title, redefine the pointer with Preferences. Then you can use the pointer as the second object, controlling its movement with the mouse.

We hope you have lots of fun with your video title program. One last treat for the video title fans is on the way. You'll see what it is in the next chapter.

4.6   Another idea: loading and saving title sequences

After you've designed a title, you may have been frustrated because you couldn't save the parameters. Why can't the program save a title set and call it back later? You'll find out in this section. You'll also find out a solution to this problem.

Type in the following routine at the end of the current version:

```
StoreTitle:¶
  CLS : PRINT "Save as what name:"¶
  INPUT DatName$¶
  OPEN DatName$ FOR OUTPUT AS 1¶
    PRINT #1,NoofLines      : REM Number of text lines¶
    FOR x=1 TO NoofLines¶
      WRITE #1,Text$(x) ¶
    NEXT x¶
    ¶
    PRINT #1,ObjFlag       ' Object loaded?¶
    WRITE #1,Objname$      ' file name¶
    ¶
    PRINT #1,Move(0)      ' Number of movements¶
    FOR x=1 TO Move(0) ¶
      PRINT #1,Move(x) ¶
    NEXT x¶
    ¶
    PRINT #1,Colors       ' Number of Bitplanes¶
    FOR x=0 TO 31        ' 32 Colors in IFF-Storage¶
      PRINT #1,CHR$(Colormatrix(x,1)*16);¶
      PRINT #1,CHR$(Colormatrix(x,2)*16);¶
      PRINT #1,CHR$(Colormatrix(x,3)*16);¶
    NEXT x       ¶
    PRINT #1,Background      ' Text color etc.¶
    PRINT #1,TextColor¶
    PRINT #1,TextBackground¶
    ¶
    PRINT #1,IFF        ' Screen background?¶
    PRINT #1,IFFTab      ' Change colors?¶
    WRITE #1,Nam$       ' file name¶
  CLOSE 1¶
  CLS¶
GOTO Begin¶
¶
ReadTitle:¶
  CLS : PRINT "Name of file to load:"¶
  INPUT DatName$¶
  OPEN DatName$ FOR INPUT AS 1¶
    INPUT #1,NoofLines¶
    FOR x=1 TO NoofLines¶
      INPUT #1,Text$(x) ¶
```

```
       NEXT x¶
       ¶
       INPUT #1,ObjFlag¶
       INPUT #1,Objname$¶
       ¶
       IF ObjFlag=1 THEN¶
         OPEN Objname$ FOR INPUT AS 2¶
           OBJECT.SHAPE 1,INPUT$(LOF(2),2)¶
         CLOSE 2¶
       END IF¶
       ¶
       INPUT #1,Move(0)¶
       FOR x=1 TO Move(0)¶
         INPUT #1,Move(x)¶
       NEXT x¶
       ¶
       INPUT #1,Color1¶
       IF Color1<=Colors THEN Colors=Color1¶
       MaxColors=(2^Colors)-1¶
       FOR x=0 TO 31¶
         r=(ASC(INPUT$(1,1)) AND 240)/16¶
         g=(ASC(INPUT$(1,1)) AND 240)/16¶
         b=(ASC(INPUT$(1,1)) AND 240)/16¶
         PALETTE x,r/16,g/16,b/16¶
         Colormatrix(x,1)=r : Colormatrix(x,2)=g :
Colormatrix(x,3)=b¶
       NEXT x¶
       INPUT #1,Background¶
       INPUT #1,TextColor¶
       INPUT #1,TextBackground¶
       ¶
       INPUT #1,IFF¶
       INPUT #1,IFFTab¶
       INPUT #1,Nam$¶
     CLOSE 1¶
     CLS¶
GOTO Begin ¶
```

You already have an idea of how the load and save routines work, so we won't go through that again. Here are some notes on the areas of the program which may not be clear to you:

We use the same syntax for saving colors as for IFF format, because this syntax saves memory. But the file created is not IFF compatible.

The WRITE command avoids problems with commas in strings.

The data of a graphic object will be read directly into memory, as long as the filename exists. OBJECT.SHAPE is defined as object number 1.

If the title file has more bitplanes than are allowed in the program, the video title program will only use the allowed number of planes. The variable `Color1` reads the value from the file. If `Color1` is less than or equal to the value in `Colors`, then the read routine places the new number into `Colors`.

REM
'

Everything clear so far? Let's talk about REM. This is a REMark used to write comments meant for the user or programmer—sort of like a Post-It Note within the program. A REM has nothing to do with the program's execution. Look at the `OPEN DatName$` line in `StoreTitle`:

```
OPEN DatName$ FOR OUTPUT AS 1¶
PRINT #1,NoofLines : REM Number of text lines¶
```

This tells us what is happening in the program. Any text following a REM statement is ignored by the program. Try typing this in the **BASIC** window:

```
FOR x=1 TO 10:REM remark:NEXT x
```

This loop will not run correctly, since AmigaBASIC ignores the `NEXT x` and displays a `FOR without NEXT` error message. To get the full effect of the REM, you can also use an apostrophe instead of REM. Look at a line in the `StoreTitle:` routine:

```
PRINT #1,ObjFlag       ' Object loaded?¶
```

The remark after `'` explains the purpose of the variable `ObjFlag`. REM and `'` are useful for explaining certain program sections, or offering suggestions to the user. We used them in `StoreTitle:` to explain the meanings of the variables.

The REM text is not executed by AmigaBASIC, but it must be read and handled, which requires processing time. It's best to leave REMs out of programs that require crucial timing. Although processing a REM only takes a tiny fraction of a second, a FOR...NEXT loop that has to handle a REM over 8000 times can eat up a half minute and more.

Adding to
the menu

Still missing are the new items to be used in `Select:`. Insert the following lines after item 6:

```
PRINT "7  Read title sequence"¶
PRINT "8  Store title sequence"¶
```

The `Query:` section must compensate for the new items. Add the following lines to this section:

```
Query:¶
  LOCATE 13,1¶
  PRINT "Enter number:";¶
  INPUT a$¶
  a$=LEFT$(a$,1)¶
  IF a$<"1" OR a$>"8" THEN BEEP: GOTO Query¶
  IF a$="1" THEN EnterText¶
  IF a$="2" THEN ReadObject¶
  IF a$="3" THEN DefineMoveObject¶
  IF a$="4" THEN DefineColor¶
  IF a$="5" THEN ShowTitle¶
  IF a$="6" THEN SetupScreen¶
  IF a$="7" THEN ReadTitle¶
  IF a$="8" THEN StoreTitle¶
  GOTO Query¶
```

The effect is fairly simple: When you have completed a title and want to save it, you select item 8. The subroutine asks for the desired filename. The data is then written into the given file. When you want to call up the title later, you select option 7 and enter the filename. After it loads the file, the program will recognize all data, and you select ShowTitle:.

The "short" title program

Another word about the title sequences. When you merge Setup:, ShowTitle:, VelocityCalc:, ReadTitle: and the DrawLoad: subprograms into one program, and omit the rest of the video title program, you'll have a short title routine that you can merge into other programs.

Save this program under a different name, so that you don't delete the video title program. When you need a program to load and execute another program, you can use the CHAIN command. You can then create a title with the video title program for opening a screen of a game, or even for your financial programs.

4.7 AmigaBASIC's little extra: adding your own commands

Now you know how the IFF load routine in a commercial program works. It would have been much simpler if Microsoft had included its own AmigaBASIC commands for loading and saving graphics. Although AmigaBASIC is an extremely good BASIC, there are times when you might want a specific, specialized command that just doesn't exist in AmigaBASIC.

User-defined BASIC commands

The developers of AmigaBASIC were prepared for this demand. They gave the language the ability to respond to user-defined commands just like BASIC commands. You've already seen one way to do this: with subprograms. Maybe you didn't realize that we can program new commands in with the SUB commands. For an example, remember the DATE$ function from Section 1.17?

```
date$
```

Modifying DATE$

This command furnishes AmigaDOS with the date for date stamping. If the date is unknown, no stamp is given. This is why you enter the correct date in Preferences. AmigaBASIC syntax for DATE$ puts the month first, then the day, then the year. Maybe you'd prefer to have your dates in European syntax (day,month,year). The following subprogram will do just that:

```
SUB Dates STATIC¶
     PRINT MID$(DATE$,4,2)"."LEFT$(DATE$,2)"."RIGHT$
(DATE$,4) ¶
END SUB¶
```

Thanks to this subprogram, you can now call DATES instead of PRINT DATE$ to see your new syntax. Or use CALL DATES. Where DATE$ returned 10-28-1986, the subprogram returns 28.10.1986. You can even call this subprogram in direct mode. Type this in the **BASIC** window:

```
DATES¶
```

When a subprogram is in a program currently in memory, you can call it in direct mode.

Now you understand why AmigaBASIC displays the error message Unidentified subprogram when it doesn't understand input. Most of the time, this error is the result of a typing error. For example, if you typed:

```
pint a$
```

instead of

```
print a$
```

AmigaBASIC branches out, looking for a subprogram called `pint`. Since it didn't find the program, it gives an error message instead. Try it once.

MID$

Do you recognize the `MID$` command? Unlike the `LEFT$` and `RIGHT$` commands, it locates the middle of a string. You give the string name, the position inside the string, and the length of the section you want located:

```
PRINT MID$(string name, position, length)¶
```

When you want to isolate two characters of the string `a$` starting at the fourth character, you would use `MID$(a$,4,2)`. Our subprogram uses `MID$` to get the two characters of the day (e.g., 28). The `LEFT$` takes the month (10) and the `RIGHT$` handles the four characters of the year (1986).

Multiple parameters

Most commands are followed by a set of parameters. You can specify parameters in a subprogram as well. A simple example:

Say you want to write a program that will convert the exchange rate for the American dollar into German Deutschmarks (DM). Or maybe you have a friend coming from Germany, and you want to convert the DM values to American dollars. Let's write a subprogram to do this. Picking up today's *Wall Street Journal*, we find out that the American dollar is worth 2.25 DM:

```
SUB Dollar (value) STATIC¶
    PRINT"$"value " = "value*2.25"DM"¶
END SUB¶
```

The parameters specified for a subprogram are enclosed in the parentheses following the name of the subprogram itself. In this case, the parameter has the name `value`. We can eliminate the parentheses after the initial call. Try typing this in the **BASIC** window:

```
Dollar 34.00¶
```

Input this last line as if you just wanted to print it. The Amiga replies:

```
$ 34 = 76.5 DM
```

Local
variables

Our example takes on the dollar value of 34.00. The subprogram assigns the given value to the variable `value`, and computes the DM value from it. `value` is a *local variable*. You cannot access this variable from the main program, nor from direct mode. This is unnecessary in our program, since we just want the subprogram to figure out the value to be computed.

But what do you do when you convert a value with a subprogram, and you don't need the calculation immediately? No problem. This time we'll compute the DM into dollars. The routine looks like this:

```
SUB Dollar(value) STATIC¶
     value = value *1/2.25¶
END SUB¶
```

Type this in the **BASIC** window:

```
value=13.50:Dollar value:?value¶
```

So 13.5 DM is equal to $6.00. How did this work? The variable `value` is assigned a value of 13.50. That is the DM value. Then the subprogram `Dollar` was called with the parameter `value`. As you displayed the variable, the contents were converted to 6. It is important that the variable `value` in direct mode and the variable `value` in the subroutine do not coincide. You could call the conversion with any other variable. Try this:

```
DM=13.50:Dollar DM: ?DM¶
```

There's no magic here, just a connection with the syntax of the subprogram. The local variable `value` in the `Dollar` subprogram functions only as a marker for the value, and prepares the value for computation. The value of DM is transferred to `value`. The computation is then made on `value`. Once completed, the contents of `value` are transferred back to DM and the subprogram is exited.

If you're not sure what we're talking about, here's another example. We've written a simple subprogram that doubles the given number.

```
SUB doubled (numr) STATIC¶
    numr=numr*2¶
END SUB¶
```

Call the subprogram in the **BASIC** window as follows:

```
a=2:doubled a:print a¶
```

`doubled` calls the subprogram and gives the variable a as the parameter. `numr` is computed within the routine. Then the routine passes the contents of its variable `numr` to the parameter a. That's how the main program processes the result. Nothing is previously known about the variable `numr`.

Naturally, there are situations where you don't want your variable to change. Instead, you want to be able to pass variables between subprograms and the main program. The parentheses act as a "safety zone" for the parameters where their contents can't be changed.

If you call the doubled routine repeatedly, a will not change:

```
a=2:doubled (a):print a¶
```

The variable a has the value 2 before and after the SUB call. The subprogram can be run as normal, but the result cannot be repeatedly given as a, since a is protected by the parentheses. The routine seems pretty useless. But when we go back to an earlier program, we see the logic behind it:

```
SUB Dollar (value) STATIC¶
    PRINT value "DM are";¶
    value=value*1/2.25¶
    PRINT"$" value¶
END SUB¶
```

When you call this subprogram as before,

```
DM=21.60:Dollar DM¶
```

converts 21.60 DM to $9.60. But now check out the value of DM:

```
? DM¶
```

The dollar has replaced the Deutschmark. The value of DM was placed in value, value was changed, and has been transferred back to DM. Result: DM has also been changed. Inside a program, the old value of DM no longer exists.

Consequently, you should avoid:

```
DM=21.60:Dollar (DM) ¶
```

The result is the same, but DM retains its original value.

It's quite possible that you are beginning to lose interest in foreign currency exchange rates. So now we'll move on to some big fun. The main reason we've spent so much time talking about subprograms is because we're going to develop a routine that saves IFF graphics. If you merge this program into your program, you'll be able to save any graphic to diskette with one simple command.

But we have one more Intermission before we tackle that.

Intermission 5

Amiga number systems

This Intermission is going to be a little rough: it deals with number systems and a lot of math. But both topics are very important to understanding subprograms, and we've done our best to make a difficult subject easily understood. Once you get to the end of this section, the rest of the book is easy to follow. Everything clear so far? Let's go.

Decimal numbers

Most people can see the need for programming their own commands. First we have to look at the internal functions of the Amiga. The different examples with dollars, dates, Deutschmarks and doubled numbers all used amounts notated as decimal numbers:

```
Dollar 34.00
```

We should be able to write just 34. That is the same as 34.00—or is it?

Call the original version of the `Dollar` subprogram into the **LIST** window:

```
SUB Dollar (value) STATIC
     PRINT "$"value "are "value*2.25" DM"
END SUB
```

Call this subprogram from the **BASIC** window with:

```
Dollar 34
```

Your Amiga will display a `Type mismatch` error. The number type is mismatched, and it isn't accepting the value of `Dollar`. It took a while to find out just why the Amiga reacts this way. As we said before, we're going to look at its innermost functions.

Floating-point numbers

The problem is this: The number 34 is a whole number to the Amiga. Logical, yes, but `value` is not a whole number: `value` is a *floating-point variable*.

Let's look at how the Amiga handles numbers. We've learned about different types of numbers: integers, 16-bit numbers, and 32-bit numbers. All of these use one small system.

You will deal with floating-point variables most frequently. Floating-point variables are variables that have no ending character. For example, `Hello`, `a`, and `Colors` are all floating-point variables. The term *floating-point* means that the decimal point is not in a fixed position.

Here are a few examples of floating-point numbers:

```
100.23
3.141593
1.3
.143
4.1165
```

The decimal point is not in a strictly-defined position. All the numbers above can be used in floating-point variables. These values can have up to seven places; more than seven places decrease accuracy. Try this:

```
a=0.2435475776443:?a
```

The result is .2435476. The digit after the seventh decimal place will be truncated and rounded off. But this a small number. What does AmigaBASIC do with larger numbers?

```
a=3426478236487367489:? a
```

The result is not the same number that you typed in. It has been "abbreviated." The result of the first input will be:

```
3.426478E+18
```

Scientific notation

You may already be familiar with *scientific notation*, or exponential notation. Its first name comes from the fact that scientists, especially physicists and mathematicians, work with very large and very small numbers. Consequently they developed an alternate method of notation:

```
3.426478E+18 = 3.426478*10^18 (^ means to the power of)
```

Back to binary

You learned in Intermission 3 how the binary system is based on the number 2. Every exponent of 2 increases the number by one digit: $2^0=1$ (binary 1), $2^1=2$ (bin. 10), $2^2=4$ (bin. 100), etc. The decimal system, our resident number system, works the same way, except it works in exponents of 10 to get to the next digit: $10^0=1$, $10^1=10$, $10^2=100$, $10^3=1000$. And so on. Every exponent of 10 increases the number's size. For your information: The number 10^{18} is equal to one trillion—that's 1 with 18 zeros after it. The number of the exponent states the number of zeros after the number.

```
1.0E+3  is 1.0*10^3, or 1000 (three zeros)
3.4E+2  is 3.4*10^2, or 3.4*100 (two zeros), or 340
```

AmigaBASIC can also use exponential notation for small numbers:

```
a=1/202 : ?a
```

The result 4.950495E-03 means 4.950495 *10^(-3). 10^(-3) is 1/10^3. In normal notation, the number would read 0.004950495.

For those of you with math anxiety, bear with us: If you normally don't work much with numbers and notations, you probably won't write any programs involving them.

Computers and floating-point numbers

The result of the above example couldn't be handled properly by the Amiga. All computers have difficulties with floating-point numbers. You've seen how whole numbers are handled in Intermission 3. Floating-point means that the computer has to start from scratch to figure these numbers out. If you really want to know you can look in Appendix D of the AmigaBASIC manual that came with your Amiga— but don't say we didn't warn you. This stuff is hard to follow.

Since the Amiga has to convert floating-point numbers into bits, some math errors can crop up. Most computers handle them as rounding errors. Try typing this:

```
? 100.1-100¶
```

Instead of the traditional (and correct) 0.1, AmigaBASIC gives an answer of 9.999847E-02. That's 0.099. It's close, but it still is incorrect.

Precision

Let's talk about precision. The example above would go under the category of *single precision*. When a number is given in single precision, it should be given with accurate numbers.

The precision depends on the internal number handling: Single precision numbers can have up to 7 decimal places. The values lie in the range between 10^{-38} and 10^{+37}. The opposite is *double precision*. You then have 16 decimal places, and values between 10^{-308} and 10^{+307}. Normally, AmigaBASIC uses single precision in its floating-point numbers. The double precision identifier is the # character following the variable name. Compare these:

```
a=1/202 : ?a (result: 4.950495E-03)
```

```
a#=1/202 : ? a# (result: 4.950494971126318D-03)
```

The second number has more decimal places, and consequently is more accurate. The D that replaces the E means it has been handled as a double precision number. 10E+3 and 10D+3 mean the same thing: 10^3, or 1000.

Why so precise?

You may be wondering why so many decimal places are needed. The degree of precision you want depends on the calculations you perform. When possible, you should avoid double precision numbers, since they have a major disadvantage: calculations take longer, and the numbers require much more memory.

You might want to take a break from all this now. It can be a strain trying to absorb these concepts. But you now have an idea of the essentials. The intermission won't get any more technical than what you've just been through.

To recap what you've just learned. You know about floating-points, single and double precision. Single precision is used on normal variables used by AmigaBASIC. Double precision is used when a # character is placed after a variable name.

Integers

You've probably noticed that the Amiga doesn't take floating-point numbers very well. You should avoid them when possible. You can safely use numbers without decimal points; *integer* values are much more acceptable. You know about integers: Variables like `Hello%`, `a%`, and `Colors%` can be values between -32768 and +32767—in other words, 16-bit numbers with a leading character bit. This range is more than adequate for most values (coordinates, colors, speeds, etc.). And when the number must be larger or smaller than the allowable range, AmigaBASIC uses 32-bit numbers. Then you can use integers between -2147483648 and +2147483647. (However, you will rarely use this full range when you program in BASIC).

When a variable should be a 32-bit integer, you must specify this by typing an & after the variable name. Look at these two examples:

`a%=100000`

This returns an `Overflow error` message—the number's too large. Now try it this way:

`a&=100000`

No more problem.

You've probably already noticed that AmigaBASIC displays 32-bit numbers in the `LIST` window appended with a & character. For example, your paint program uses the number 65535. This number won't fit into 15 bits (there is also the bit reserved for the leading character). The Amiga uses 32-bit representation instead.

Strings

You're almost home. The last variable type that we will discuss here is not difficult to understand: *string variables*. These variables contain strings of characters with a maximum length of 32767 (the Amiga likes that number), and are identified by the $ character.

Here's an overview of what we have learned:

Variable type	Identifier	Memory required	Sample variable
Floating-point, (single precision)	none or !	4 bytes	.3245643, 2.43E+09
Floating-point, (double precision)	#	8 bytes	4.901960957795, 382D-03
Short integer	%	2 bytes=16-bit	32767, -17
Long integer	&	4 bytes=32-bit	-2147483648,65535
String	$	5 bytes + string length	"Richard", "Ruby"

Table 9: Variable types in AmigaBASIC

The identifiers allow you to use the same variable names for completely independent variables. a and a$ are not related to each other. Similarly, a#, a% and a& are also independent variables. One thing to remember: Normally, floating-point variables have no identifier for single precision (they are the default variables for AmigaBASIC). If you add a !, it is merely a formality: Hello and Hello! <u>are</u> the same variable.

The bottom line

After all this, we still haven't explained why the Amiga won't accept 34 in the SUB call. It was expecting a floating-point number, and there was no decimal point or decimal places after 34.

value=34 would solve this. When AmigaBASIC finds a whole number in any input, it stores this number as an integer. This integer number <u>should</u> be a floating-point number in the subprogram. But it isn't. Therefore you get a Type mismatch error. AmigaBASIC uses internal number handling, so one solution is to "trick" your Amiga. Add a decimal point to the number, without zeros:

Dollar 34.

Solving the problem

The Amiga treats the blank space following the decimal point as zeros, and stores the value as a floating-point number. That solves the problem. You can also set up a number as a specific-precision by appending an identifier:

Dollar 34!

AmigaBASIC then recognizes the number as a floating-point number in single precision.

A few more examples: 3.4% is equal to 3 (this has nothing to do with percentages). The number, which would normally be stored as a floating-point number, is saved as a 16-bit integer. The decimal point is discarded. 0.4& is equal to 0 (the same, but with 32-bit handling). 3# is equal to 3. You see, the number doesn't change visually when you switch to double precision, but it does change internally. So you should know the difference between:

```
? 1/3
```

and

```
?1#/3
```

Let's use our integers in a subprogram:

```
SUB Pause (Sec%) STATIC¶
PauseIt:¶
     TIM=INT(TIMER)¶
     WHILE INT(TIMER)=TIM : WEND¶
     Sec%=Sec%-1
     IF Sec%>0 THEN PauseIt¶
END SUB¶
```

This subprogram is lifted from the parameter section of the video title program. It waits for a specified number of seconds. The variable Sec% waits for the input of an integer. So, calling the subprogram by typing:

```
Pause 10
```

results in a 10-second wait. When this subprogram is called, you should only use integers, or you'll get a Type mismatch error.

Now you know a little bit about the internal workings of the AmigaBASIC interpreter. Let's move on to the next project without further ado: We're going to write a subroutine for saving IFF pictures.

4.8

Save that picture:
the PICSAVE command routine

Here's a reward for your patience. The following subprogram creates a single command for saving graphic data.

```
SUB PicSave (Nam$,WindowNr%,ArrayYN%) STATIC¶
  IF ArrayYN%=1 THEN SHARED Colors%()¶
  IF ArrayYN%=0 THEN¶
    IF Colors%(0,0)<>2 THEN ERASE Colors% : DIM
Colors%(31,2)¶
    RESTORE ColorTable¶
    FOR x=0 TO 31¶
      READ Colors%(x,0),Colors%(x,1),Colors%(x,2)¶
    NEXT x¶
  ColorTable:   ¶
    DATA 2,3,10, 15,15,15, 0,0,0, 15,8,0¶
    DATA 0,0,15, 15,0,15, 0,15,15, 15,15,15¶
    DATA 6,1,1, 14,5,0, 8,15,0, 14,11,0¶
    DATA 5,5,15, 9,0,15, 0,15,9, 12,12,12¶
    DATA 0,0,0, 13,0,0, 0,0,0, 15,12,10¶
    DATA 4,4,4, 5,5,5, 6,6,6, 7,7,7¶
    DATA 8,8,8, 9,9,9, 10,10,10, 11,11,11¶
    DATA 12,12,12, 13,13,13, 14,14,14, 15,15,15¶
  END IF¶
  IF Nam$="" THEN EXIT SUB¶
  AltWindowNr=WINDOW(1)¶
  WINDOW WindowNr%¶
  Wide=WINDOW(2)¶
    IF Wide>320 THEN¶
      Wide=640¶
      Resolution=2¶
      Planes=16000¶
    ELSE¶
      Wide=320¶
      Resolution=1¶
      Planes=8000¶
    END IF¶
  Height=WINDOW(3)¶
    IF Height>200 THEN¶
      Height=400¶
      Planes=Planes*2¶
      Resolution=Resolution+2¶
    ELSE¶
      Height=200¶
    END IF¶
  Colors=LOG(WINDOW(6)+1)/LOG(2)¶
    ¶
```

```
OPEN Nam$ FOR OUTPUT AS 1 LEN=FRE(0)-500¶
   PRINT #1,"FORM";¶
   PRINT #1,MKL$(156+Planes*Colors);¶
   PRINT #1,"ILBM";¶
   PRINT #1,"BMHD";MKL$(20);¶
   PRINT #1,MKI$(Wide);MKI$(Height);¶
   PRINT #1,MKL$(0);¶
   PRINT #1,CHR$(Colors);¶
   PRINT #1,CHR$(0);MKI$(0);MKI$(0);¶
   PRINT #1,CHR$(10);CHR$(11);¶
   PRINT #1,MKI$(Wide);MKI$(Height);¶
   ¶
   PRINT #1,"CMAP";MKL$(96);  ¶
   FOR x=0 TO 31¶
      PRINT #1,CHR$(Colors%(x,0)*16);¶
      PRINT #1,CHR$(Colors%(x,1)*16);¶
      PRINT #1,CHR$(Colors%(x,2)*16);¶
   NEXT x¶
   ¶
   PRINT #1,"BODY";MKL$(Planes*Colors);¶
   Addr=PEEKL(WINDOW(8)+4)+8¶
   FOR x=0 TO Colors-1¶
      PlaneAddr(x)=PEEKL(Addr+4*x)¶
   NEXT x¶
   FOR y1=0 TO Height-1¶
      FOR b=0 TO Colors-1¶
         FOR x1=0 TO (Wide/32)-1 ¶
PRINT#1,MKL$(PEEKL(PlaneAddr(b)+4*x1+(Wide/8)*y1));¶
         NEXT x1¶
      NEXT b¶
      PAddr=PlaneAddr(0)+(Wide/8)*y1¶
      POKE PAddr,PEEK(PAddr) AND 63¶
      POKE PAddr+Wide/8-1,PEEK(PAddr+Wide/8-1) AND 252¶
   NEXT y1¶
   ¶
   PRINT #1,"CAMG";MKL$(4);¶
   PRINT #1,MKL$(16384);¶
   CLOSE 1¶
   WINDOW AltWindowNr  ¶
END SUB¶
```

When you save this program, save it in ASCII format:

```
save "PicSave",a
```

Use the MERGE command to include the PICSAVE routine with any program. And make sure that the program you're merging it to is also an ASCII file.

There are a few aspects of this program that you may not understand. Let's go through the individual steps of the program.

*Following
the program*

The name of our routine is in the SUB...STATIC line. We call it PICSAVE, short for PICture SAVE. The parameters follow the name, enclosed in parentheses. As you can see, you can have several values at once. The variable types must be given. The parameters for calling PICSAVE look like this:

```
PICSAVE "(filename)", (window_number),
(color_array_parameters) ¶
```

The filename needs no explanation. You can input any name, along with the drive number and the path to the subdirectory.

The second parameter is the window where the contents are stored.

The last parameter can be either a 0 or a 1. A value of 1 means that you have set up an array in the subprogram itself called Colors% which contains the dimension (31,2), and has all the RGB color values from 0 to 15 built in. We have already set up this type of array in the paint program. The value 0 means that the default Workbench colors should be used. This allows you to save graphics without much extra effort from BASIC (try doing this with your sine graph).

The last of the three values, ArrayYN%, is used the same way in the next two lines. If you enter a 1, the subprogram makes the Colors% array common. If the main program does not have an array named Colors%, AmigaBASIC returns an Undefined array error.

If ArrayYN% is 0, then there is a little more to do: First, the subprogram checks to see what value is in the array element Colors%(0,0). If the contents is a 2, the array doesn't need to be reDIMensioned.

*Self-
generating
arrays*

But what if the array hasn't been dimensioned yet? When you use a set data array without previously dimensioning it, AmigaBASIC automatically dimensions it for you, with a standard size of 10 elements. For example, type this in the **BASIC** window:

```
? Testarray(1) ¶
```

AmigaBASIC realizes that there is no array called Testarray, and so it inserts a command DIM Testarray(10). Now you can use elements from Testarray(0) to Testarray(10). Try using Testarray(11):

```
Testarray(11) ¶
```

You'll get a Subscript out of range error message (the element is past the allowable range area). Testarray is only dimensioned to 10. The same goes for two- and multi-dimensional arrays:

```
? Anothertestarray(1,1) ¶
```

automatically creates the array `Anothertestarray(10,10)`. The same happens with `Colors%(0,0)`: If no such array exists, AmigaBASIC will create the array `Colors%(10,10)`. Your color values are determined by the dimensioning `Colors%(31,2)`. So if no array exists, this is cleared, and the correct values are dimensioned.

ERASE

The `ERASE` command clears arrays. You simply type the array name after the command. The array and its contents are deleted, and can be redimensioned later with `DIM`. For example: `DIM Colors%(31,2)`.

As mentioned before, there are no commands to read the color values at this time. But we can pull other color values from the CMAP chunk. To solve this problem, we put a series of `DATA` statements in the `PICSAVE` subprogram that contain the default color values for RGB. These are the colors used by the `PALETTE` command in BASIC. When you change colors in your own programs and want to save the graphic, you have no other option than what is already in `Colors%` itself.

RESTORE

After reading the data array, we use a new command: `RESTORE`. `RESTORE` adjusts the pointer to the next `DATA` statement to be read, set at a specific label (in our case, `ColorTable:`). It is sure that the subprogram reads its own data and not the `DATA` lines in the main program. We get data protection and color protection all in one: First, you don't lose any of your data in the CMAP chunk of an IFF file, and second, no IFF reader program can produce colors from a string like "Grand Rapids."

The `FOR...NEXT` loop that follows reads the RGB values into the array `Colors%`. Also, if you ask how we came up with using the Workbench color data, the answer is: trial and error. We have compared every color with the originals, and these just won.

EXIT SUB

If `Nam$` is a null string, the routine should be stopped. `EXIT SUB` enables the return from a subprogram. `AltWindowNr` is marked as the current output window. This number is transferred with `WINDOW(1)`. After you return to the main program, you want to return everything to its original state. To call up some important data, we must make the window in the variable `WindowNr%` the current window.

Now we come to a pair of new window commands: for example, `WINDOW(2)` returns the width of the current window. This value is received by the variable `Wide`. We want windows to be saved according to the full size of the screen. The `IF/THEN/ELSE/END IF` structure determines whether the height is 320 pixels or 640 pixels. This is dependent upon the resolution (1 for 320 pixels, 2 for 640 pixels) and the memory requirements for bitplanes (8000 bytes for 320 pixels, 16000 bytes for 640 pixels). Then we proceed to `WINDOW(3)` for the height of the current window, either 200 or 400 pixels. 400 pixels (interlace mode) doubles the memory requirements for bitplanes, and the value for `Resolution` is raised by 21 (returns 3 for interlace pictures and 4 for high-res).

LOG

Finally, we come to the number of bitplanes. As computed before, it's all set up: `WINDOW(6)` returns the number of allowed colors in the current output window. 3 bitplanes would make the number 7. We've used the formula `Color=(2^bitplanes)-1` to compute the number of allowed colors. We know the number, then go looking for the bitplanes. We must also use the reverse of this formula. When you know that $2^x=8$, you can find the value of x with the formula `LOG(8)/LOG(2)`. LOG stands for logarithm. (Here's a little tip for the mathematicians: The LOG function computes the natural logarithm of e=2.718282).

The preparations are completed. We now write the IFF data to the given file. A few remarks: The `FORM` chunk needs are taken from `156+Planes*Colors`. 156 is the file length without BODY, and BODY has the length `(bytes per plane) * (number of planes)`.

After the `CLOSE`, we again make the window `AltWindowNr` the current window (we've made memory provisions for this) once the subprogram ends.

Calling
PICSAVE

That's all there is to it. Now you have your own IFF save command which can be attached to any program with MERGE. The degree of resolution, the height and width, and the number of bitplanes are set in the routine. For example, if you want to save the contents of the **BASIC** window, call the subprogram like this:

```
PICSAVE "BASICwindow",1,0
```

The resulting IFF file can be read with the IFF reader program in **Section 4.3**. To work with IFF from outside of AmigaBASIC, use a high-res program such as DeluxePaint. You can then make hardcopies from a program like this. When you want to edit BASIC graphics like your sine curve, you must create the graphic in a 320*200 resolution window.

You can also use this subprogram/command with your bar/pie chart program. Here's how:

√√   LOAD THE BAR CHART/PIE CHART PROGRAM

√√   MERGE THE PICSAVE ROUTINE

√√   DISPLAY THE SETUP: SUBROUTINE, AND ADD THE FOLLOWING TO THE MENU DEFINITION:

```
MENU 2,3,1,"Save Pic"
```

√√   INSERT UNDER THE MENUCONTROL: ROUTINE LINE:

```
IF Men=2 THEN
```

THE FOLLOWING:

```
IF MenuPoint=3 THEN¶
  MENU 1,0,0: MENU 2,0,0¶
  MENU OFF¶
    GOSUB EnterName¶
  WINDOW 99¶
    PicSave Nam$,99,0¶
  WINDOW 1¶
  MENU ON¶
  MENU 1,0,1 : MENU 2,0,1¶
END IF¶
```

√√   SAVE THE PROGRAM.

You'll see the new option Save Pic in the pulldown menu. When you select it, the current contents of the **Graphics** window are saved to diskette. (Make sure you created a graphic, or else you'll have saved an empty window). Remember that you can't use the graphic in Graphicraft, which goes for all 640*200 graphics. Because you have your own program, you can edit and print any graphics at any time.

Now that we've completed these IFF routines, we're in a position to move on to the next theme: We are going to cover some of the more interesting aspects of saving and loading non-graphic data.

311

All about data

5

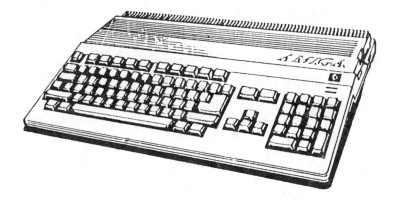

5

Getting it organized:
All about data

You won't learn <u>everything</u> you need to know about data in this chapter. You already know a number of BASIC commands used for file handling, more specifically, sequential files. But we still haven't touched on the topic of random access files. And random access files are the focus of the following pages.

After you've read this section and typed in the program lines, you'll be the proud owner of a versatile database program.

5.1

It's all relative: using random files

At this point you should be very familiar with sequential files. But in case you've forgotten, sequential means in sequence—that is, the data elements are stored one after the other. Sequential files work best at several specific programming tasks. However, they are not suitable for some more advanced applications.

About sequential files

All files sent to a printer are sequential. That makes sense, since a printer prints characters one after another. Files input from the keyboard or output to the screen are also sequential. And IFF files are sequential files too.

Sequential files are the logical choice for these programming task examples. However, when you want to read and write an address list, record collection or other information, the sequential file's major disadvantage is that they store their data in sequence on diskette. And that's how we have to read the files—one after another. That's fine if you need the address of Mrs. Andover from your telephone directory file that contains 1000 listings. But in order to get to Ms. Tiemstra's phone number, you have to go through the entire file each time—through the addresses of Mr. Fischer, Mrs. Lloyd, Dr. Taber, and so on. You'd be waiting for a long time for the system to read through the file.

About random files

Consequently, AmigaBASIC offers you a second type of file management—the *random file*, also called the *random access file*. Random access means that the individual file elements can be accessed quickly and easily. Another definition of a random file would be a file whose individual entries can be accessed relative to the first entry. This is why a random access file is sometimes referred to as a relative file.

A name, street, city, state and zip are known as the *fields* of a record— in this case, make up an address. We have an address for Mr. Fischer, Mrs. Lloyd, Ms. Tiemstra, the Doctor, etc. Data *records* are a collection of connected data fields.

A random access file assigns a number to each record. This lets you quickly and easily access any record by its number when you want to read or write to it. You can access the file no matter where the file is located on the disk, or how large the file.

Creating a random access file requires only a few more commands than creating a comparable sequential file. It's really quite easy.

Let's start with a simple example. Type in the following address book program:

```
OPEN "r",#1,"AddressFile.rel",92¶
FIELD #1,30 AS Nam$,30 AS Address$,20 AS City$,12 AS
Phone$¶
¶
Entry:¶
  PRINT ¶
  INPUT "Name";NamEntry$¶
  INPUT "Address";AddressEntry$¶
  INPUT "City";CityEntry$¶
  INPUT "Phone";PhoneEntry$¶
  LSET Nam$=NamEntry$¶
  LSET Address$=AddressEntry$¶
  LSET City$=CityEntry$¶
  LSET Phone$=PhoneEntry$¶
  x=x+1¶
  PUT #1,x¶
  PRINT "Record "x" ("Nam$") stored."¶
  PRINT "Add more records?"¶
  INPUT "Y/N:";Ans$¶
  IF UCASE$(Ans$)="Y" THEN Entry¶
  ¶
CLOSE 1¶
PRINT "File closed. Program ended."¶
```

Save this program before you run it.

Random file OPEN

Now let's take a closer look at the program. We used the same syntax for the OPEN command as we used earlier. OPEN has a second syntax, used for random access files. It has one mode for all file operations (no separate syntaxes for input, output or appending). The lower-case r stands for random. Then the file number and filename follow. The last parameter gives the random access file record length in bytes. The number in the above program assigns a total address record length of 92 bytes.

Sequential files allow you to give the length of the file buffer. You don't need to do anything like that with random access files; AmigaBASIC sets up the buffer according to the length of the file record.

FIELD

The FIELD command is the first new command we've seen in this program. It allows you to divide the data record buffer into individual fields. Each of these fields is assigned a parameter variable.

```
FIELD [#](file number),(number of bytes) AS (variable
name),...
```

Your example uses the variable Nam$ to represent the 30 bytes available. The contents of Nam$ will need no more than 30 bytes per record in the file. It could be shorter, though. With the values in the FIELD command, you set the maximum length of a variable outside the file.

317

This also goes for the other variables: Address$ should be up to 30 characters in length, City$ up to 20, and Phone$ up to 12 characters in length. Any extra charcters that are typed in will be lost.

We read in the address with the Entry: routine that follows. Here is where we use other variables for input: variables NamEntry$, AddressEntry$, CityEntry$ and PhoneEntry$. As you can see, you can use entire names, but with one condition: You must use names other than those placed in the FIELD command line so that the next command (LSET) can function properly.

LSET

The FIELD variables are parameter variables. Nam$ is the name for a 30-byte-long area in the data buffer. The LSET command stores data to this buffer area. In your case, the data is the variable NamEntry$. The range with the name Street$ is assigned the contents of the variable StreetEntry$. City$ and Phone$ work the same way.

If the assigned variable is longer than the corresponding buffer range, the excess is truncated. If it is shorter than the buffer range, the rest of the range is filled with blanks.

The FIELD command variables have an additional function: You can assign a quantity that will go in the data buffer with LSET. If you read the contents of a parameter variable, you would get the buffer contents for the area defined by FIELD. Look at the following line:

```
PRINT "Storing record"x" :"Nam$
```

Nam$ contains the first 30 bytes of the buffer contents. The moment you assign a value to Nam$ without using the LSET command (also when using INPUT or Nam$=), the buffer assignment is changed. The 30 buffer bytes are then no longer available. Therefore, the data input is transferred from the variable NamEntry$.

The entire statement above also applies to the other parameter variables of the data record buffer. The syntax of LSET is very simple:

```
LSET (parameter variable) = (variable)
```

Random file
PUT

The data is now in buffer memory. We need a PUT command to place the data on diskette. You've already used this command in your graphic projects in **Chapter 4**, but these used the *screen PUT*, which is one of two forms of the PUT command. The second PUT command is called the random file PUT.

You type the file number following the random file PUT, and following that the record number to which the current buffer data will be written. Since writing will increment the record numbers by 1, no record will remain unused. Theoretically you can use record numbers between 1 and 16777215. But before you try this number, there is one small stipulation: 16777215 is theoretically the highest number that AmigaBASIC can handle. The highest <u>actual</u> number depends on the available memory and the size of the record. In either case, that puts us way below 16777215—in fact, a file this large would nearly fill a 20-megabyte hard disk. An empty 3 1/2" Amiga diskette will hold 10000 records for your address file.

That's all the new commands on the file writing section. The rest of this program is nothing new to you.

Reading the file

Save about 10 addresses for your family and friends in the address file program. Then type in the following program to learn a little bit about reading random files:

```
OPEN "r",#1,"AddressFile.rel",92¶
FIELD #1,30 AS Nam$,30 AS Address$,20 AS City$,12 AS
Phone$¶
¶
ReadData:¶
  INPUT "Address Number";Nmbr¶
  GET #1,Nmbr¶
  IF EOF(1) THEN PRINT "Record out of range." :GOTO
ReadData¶
  PRINT Nam$¶
  PRINT Address$¶
  PRINT City$¶
  PRINT Phone$¶
  INPUT "Read another record (Y/N)";ans$¶
  IF UCASE$(ans$)<>"N" THEN ReadData¶
CLOSE 1¶
PRINT "File closed. Program ended."¶
```

The OPEN and FIELD program lines are the same as in the random file writing program. The file is opened and the matching buffer is set up. The buffer number and the record length used for reading must be identical to the values used when you wrote the file.

Large file programs use sequential files as well as random access files. The sequential file reads the necessary information about record length into the program for use by the random file.

Since you give no read or write mode when opening random access files, you can exchange reading and writing in any sequence you desire. This is another advantage to random access files.

Running the program

Your address reading program will first prompt you for the address number (the record number). Since you've written 10 addresses into your file, you can type any number between 1 and 10. Writing fewer addresses means you can read fewer addresses—that is, the number must be correspondingly lower.

Random file GET

Now for the partner to the PUT command: GET. This command also has two forms—the random file GET and the screen GET.

The random file GET command reads a given data record from diskette, and writes the data into the buffer. You supply the file number and the desired record number. After the GET command the record is read, then transferred from diskette to the buffer. You can then read the buffer's contents from the parameter variables. Now we come to the address data.

EOF

The function EOF works for random access files as it does for sequential files. If you try to read a higher record number than actually exists, EOF(1) returns the value -1. This gives you an idea of how many records exist. If you don't include this command in your program, you'll get strange data in your buffer: Either fragments and random combinations of different records, or assortments of random characters, mostly control characters.

Displaying the data

The PRINT statement brings the address to the screen. As already explained, you can read individual data fields from the parameter variables with the GET command: Nam$, Address$, City$ and Phone$ supply the assigned buffer contents.

Your program then asks whether you want to read more data or not. When you press <n>, the file is closed and the program terminates. If you press any other key the program will read a new data record.

A little experimentation with this program will demonstrate you the advantages of random access files. Try reading address number 1, address 10, then address 8 and address 2. The Amiga finds your data almost immediately.

Once you've thoroughly explored this program, we'll learn something new, and at the same time create a useful program based on random access files. You'll be able to file and organize anything from your stamp collection to your financial portfolio.

5.2

Store it:
a database program

We've actually written one database program already: The statistical analysis program collects data at the first line of the program. This sequential approach makes more sense when you're working with pie charts or bar charts than it does with addresses or a record collection. Besides, your statistical program isn't capable of handling two or more sets of data. So now we'll write a more effective database program.

"Effective" means that you'll have the option of saving and altering your data quickly and easily, at any time. You can use your database for archiving your classical record collection, cataloging your CDs, putting your recipes on disk, and so on.

Here's the program. It's the preparatory routines for your next project. (You might want to make a trip to the refrigerator first to help this project along).

```
Setup:¶
  PALETTE 0,0,.1,.4¶
  PALETTE 2,0,1,0¶
  ¶
Begin:¶
  CLS : LOCATE 1,1 : PRINT   "Select"¶
  LOCATE 1,32 : COLOR 3,0 : PRINT "Filename:"; : COLOR
1,0¶
  IF Altname$<>"" THEN PRINT Altname$ ELSE PRINT "(no
file)"¶
  PRINT¶
  COLOR 0,3 :PRINT SPACE$(31)"AmigaBASIC
DataBase"SPACE$(31)¶
  LOCATE 5,32 : COLOR 3,0¶
  PRINT "Please Choose:"¶
  LOCATE 7,32¶
  COLOR 0,1 :PRINT " 1 "; : COLOR 1,0 : PRINT " Create
file"¶
  LOCATE 9,32¶
  COLOR 0,1 :PRINT " 2 "; : COLOR 1,0 : PRINT " Enter
data"¶
  LOCATE 11,32¶
  COLOR 0,1 :PRINT " 3 "; : COLOR 1,0 : PRINT " Read
file"¶
  LOCATE 13,32¶
  COLOR 0,1 :PRINT " 4 "; : COLOR 1,0 : PRINT " Search
file"¶
  LOCATE 15,32¶
  COLOR 0,1 :PRINT " 5 "; : COLOR 1,0 : PRINT " End"¶
  ¶
```

```
Select:¶
  LOCATE 18,1 : PRINT SPACE$(80)¶
  LOCATE 18,32 :   COLOR 3,0 : PRINT   "Enter number:";¶
  COLOR 1,0 :   LINE INPUT number$¶
  number$=LEFT$(number$,1)¶
  IF number$<"1" OR number$>"5" THEN Select¶
  IF number$="1" THEN CreateFile¶
  IF number$="2" THEN EnterData¶
  IF number$="3" THEN DataSearch=0 : GOTO ReadData¶
  IF number$="4" THEN DataSearch=1 : GOTO ReadData¶
  PRINT  "Program ended."¶
END¶
```

Setting up
the program

There's not much new in Setup:. We call two PALETTE commands, for cosmetic purposes. These commands make the blue background a little darker, giving the program a more professional look. Don't laugh—the screen is easier to read if you don't use the normal Workbench colors. Also, the altered colors make the program look less like it was written in AmigaBASIC. The second PALETTE command changes the Workbench black to green. This color contrasts better with the background.

The Begin: routine clears the screen and displays the word Select in the upper left corner of the screen. We'll write the current mode in this corner in the database program. This way, the user always knows where this prompt will be displayed.

The middle of the first line will list the current file. We have no file the first time we start the program, so the word None is displayed.

SPACE$(x)

Now we print the headline list. Here's a new command: SPACE$(x). This refers to the spacebar (which we'll call <SPACE>). SPACE$ creates x number of spaces. You can print colorful bars with this, like in the title bar; simply make a text color the same as the background color, e.g., COLOR 0, 3. We used dark blue on orange in the title bar. SPACE$ also can erase text, but we'll talk more about that later.

Next comes a menu from which we select individual items.

Create file is called to create a new file. This program section lets us give a filename, and the lengths of individual fields.

Enter data is where you type in your data.

Read file makes it possible to page through an entire file and change individual data records.

Search file helps you to look for specific criteria in a data record.

End ends the program.

Next follow the program lines used for the selection. Here is where SPACE$ acts as a delete function: Any time the user types something into a selection, the old selection is erased and replaced by the new.

The individual routines of the program are called depending on the input. Readfile: and Searchfile: both use ReadData:. The variable DataSearch tells the program whether to read all data records or just look for one.

```
CreateFile:¶
   CLS : LOCATE 1,1 : COLOR 1,0 : PRINT  "Create File"¶
   LOCATE 1,32 : COLOR 3,0 : PRINT "Filename:";¶
   COLOR 1,0 : PRINT "(no file)" ¶
   COLOR 3,0 : LOCATE 3,1¶
   PRINT "Enter field name and field length."¶
   COLOR 1,0¶
   FOR x=0 TO 9¶
      Fieldname$="" : Length(x)=0¶
   NEXT x¶
   LOCATE 4,1 : PRINT "Name" : LOCATE 4,26 : PRINT "Length
(<40)"¶
   FOR x=0 TO 9¶
      NoOfFields=x¶
      LOCATE x+6,1 : LINE INPUT Fieldname$(x)¶
      IF Fieldname$(x)="" THEN x=10 :
NoOfFields=NoOfFields-1¶
      Fieldname$(x)=LEFT$(Fieldname$(x),25)¶
      LOCATE x+6,26 : PRINT SPACE$(40);¶
      LOCATE x+6,26 : LINE INPUT Length$¶
      IF Length$="" OR ABS(VAL(Length$))>40 THEN
Length$="40"¶
      Length(x)=INT(ABS(VAL(Length$)))¶
      IF Length(x)=0 THEN Length(x)=40¶
   NEXT x¶
¶
Corrections:¶
   GOSUB EntryOK¶
   IF Corr=0 THEN OpenFile¶
   IF Corr=1 THEN ErrorCorrection¶
GOTO Corrections¶
¶
ErrorCorrection:¶
   FOR x=0 TO NoOfFields¶
      LOCATE x+6,1 : PRINT SPACE$(80)¶
      LOCATE x+6,25 : PRINT  Length(x)¶
      LOCATE x+6,1 : PRINT  Fieldname$(x)¶
   NEXT x¶
   FOR x=0 TO NoOfFields¶
      LOCATE x+6,1 : LINE INPUT Fieldname$¶
      IF Fieldname$<>"" THEN¶
Fieldname$(x)=LEFT$(Fieldname$,25)¶
      LOCATE x+6,26 : LINE INPUT Length$¶
      IF ABS(VAL(Length$))>40 THEN Length$="40"¶
      IF Length$<>"" THEN Length(x)=INT(ABS(VAL(Length$)))¶
      IF Length(x)=0 THEN Length(x)=40¶
```

```
          NEXT x¶
          GOTO Corrections¶
     ¶
     OpenFile:¶
       LOCATE 19,1 : PRINT  SPACE$(80);¶
       LOCATE 19,1 : COLOR 3,0 : PRINT  "Enter Filename:";¶
       COLOR 1,0 : LINE INPUT Nam$¶
       RecordLength=0¶
       FOR x=0 TO NoOfFields¶
          RecordLength=RecordLength+Length(x)¶
       NEXT x¶
       IF Nam$="" OR RecordLength=0 THEN BEEP : GOTO Begin¶
       OPEN "R",#1,Nam$,RecordLength¶
          FIELD #1,Length(0) AS Dat$(0),Length(1) AS
     Dat$(1),Length(2) AS Dat$(2),Length(3) AS
     Dat$(3),Length(4) AS Dat$(4),Length(5) AS
     Dat$(5),Length(6) AS Dat$(6), Length(7) AS
     Dat$(7),Length(8) AS Dat$(8),Length(9) AS Dat$(9)¶
```

**About line
length**

We should discuss the line length acceptable to AmigaBASIC. Program lines can be up to 255 characters in length, but good programming style doesn't allow this. In this case, however, it's unavoidable—you must completely define the range within one line with FIELD. If you start a new FIELD line, you erase the old contents of the buffer. If you want to use 10 variables, we have to construct this line. Type in the entire FIELD line above. But press <RETURN> <u>only when you've typed in the entire passage</u> (ended with the printed paragraph mark).

The next section is typed in as usual:

```
          FOR x=1 TO NoOfFields¶
             LSET Dat$(x)=" " ¶
          NEXT x¶
        CLOSE 1¶
        OPEN Nam$+".Flds" FOR OUTPUT AS 2¶
          PRINT #2,NoOfFields¶
          PRINT #2,RecordLength¶
          PRINT #2,0¶
          FOR x=0 TO NoOfFields¶
             WRITE #2,Fieldname$(x)¶
             PRINT #2,Length(x)¶
          NEXT x¶
        CLOSE 2¶
        Altname$=Nam$¶
     GOTO Begin¶
```

You create your file with this routine. First we print Create file in the upper left corner of the screen while in the current mode. The file currently being edited is named (no file), because no file is being edited, so there is no filename.

About color usage

Perhaps you were wondering about the elaborate use of COLOR in the listing. We're trying to display a text color that's easy on the eyes: Notes, warnings and explanations appear in orange. The data, title bar and user input appear on the screen in white. The field names in the data records are green. COLOR 3, 0 specifies orange, COLOR 2, 0 specifies green and COLOR 1, 0 specifies white text.

CreateFile: is where the user states the name and length of the data fields. These entries go in as mentioned earlier.

Every data record can contain up to 10 single elements (from the loop FOR x=0 TO 9).

The program marks the number of fields per data record in the variable NoOfFields. This value increments by 1 for each new field input.

Field names

First we enter the field names. These are identifiers like Name, Street, City, Title, etc. The maximum length of a field name is 25 characters. Then we need to allocate some space for the data itself.

If you enter a blank in this mode, the program recognizes that all fields have been input. If you enter ten fields, then the loop will end on the next NEXT.

If the field name is input, the field length is still missing. The maximum length of a data field is 40 characters.

First a deleting SPACE$(40) wipes out the current field name input— 25 characters are trimmed off. Now you input a value for the variable Length$. If you don't type anything in, or type more than 40 characters, the field length will be limited to 40 characters. The nested functions INT(ABS(VAL(Length$))) filters all intentional or unintentional user errors out of the input. VAL converts the string to a number. If they are letters or control characters, they are discarded. ABS converts the number into a positive number; in other words, input beginning with a minus sign is converted to positive. INT converts numbers to integers. The field length must be a whole number. If the user inputs 0, the default value of 40 is used. Hopefully this anticipates all erroneous input.

The loop executes 10 times. Then we have 10 field names, the highest allowable number.

Making corrections

The Corrections: routine calls the EntryOK: subroutine. It's used to ask you if your input has an error. If you answer <yes>, the variable Corr accepts the corrected input. Then the ErrorCorrection: routine is called.

Here is where your previously entered data is printed on the screen, in columns and underneath the field names and field lengths. A FOR...NEXT loop counts from 1 to NoOfFields. Any field input can be corrected.

325

The cursor is displayed at each field and asks for new input through a LINE INPUT. If the answer is a null string, then the previously input remains unchanged. Any other input replaces the old input. The reading limitations of the field lengths are identical to the program lines performing the same function in CreateFile:.

After all corrections are made, the program jumps back to the label Corrections:, in case you want to make further revisions to your fields. The routine runs as many times as you want to make corrections.

Opening a file

Next comes the OpenFile: routine, which asks for the name that the file should find. A FOR...NEXT loop calculates the usable record length from the array contents of Length(x). If this record length equals zero, then no fields have been defined for the record, and the Amiga will BEEP and return to Begin:.

Otherwise, the random access file opens with the name given in Nam$. Now we come to the abovementioned FIELD line. You must type this in carefully as one single line.

As you can see, you can use field variables like Dat$(x) as parameter variables. The solution is different from your use of the amount of data per record, as long as the names and their lengths are variable. Every element of the data field Dat$(x) is set into the buffer with the length Length(x). If this length is made null by unused array elements, then the overnumbered variables lose no buffer memory.

Finally, the data field in the buffer is filled with spaces, which erases any current data.

That's the end of the database preliminary routines for the random access file.

We created a sequential file in which we saved the number of fields (NoOfFields), the length (RecordLength), the number of data records from time 0, the field name and its length. The sequential file has the name of the random access file with the extension .Flds. The address file is called Addresses.Flds.

If this file is written, it uses Altname$ as the last-used filename and the program returns to Begin:.

Now that we have a nice, open random access file begging for input, lets fill it with data:

```
EnterData:¶
  CLS : LOCATE 1,1 : PRINT "Enter data"¶
  IF Nam$="" THEN¶
    LOCATE 3,1 : COLOR 3,0 : PRINT "Enter Filename:"¶
    COLOR 1,0 : LINE INPUT Nam$¶
    IF Nam$="=" OR Nam$="*" THEN Nam$=Altname$¶
```

```
    Altname$=Nam$¶
END IF¶
GOSUB FieldFileExistYN¶
IF FileExist=0 THEN¶
    COLOR 3,0 : PRINT ¶
    PRINT "Press any key."¶
    WHILE INKEY$="" : WEND : COLOR 1,0¶
    GOTO Begin¶
END IF¶
GOSUB ReadFileField¶
RecordNumber=NoOfRecords+1¶
    OPEN "R",#1,Nam$,RecordLength  ¶
```

(Here's the long `FIELD` line again. You could use `Copy` and `Paste`
to duplicate it above and paste it here):

```
    FIELD #1,Length(0) AS Dat$(0),Length(1) AS Dat$(1),
Length(2) AS Dat$(2),Length(3) AS Dat$(3),Length(4) AS
Dat$(4),Length(5) AS Dat$(5),Length(6) AS
Dat$(6),Length(7) AS Dat$(7),Length(8) AS
Dat$(8),Length(9) AS Dat$(9)¶
```

Now for some more program lines:

```
InputLoop:¶
    CLS : LOCATE 1,1 : COLOR 1,0 : PRINT "Enter new
data"¶
    LOCATE 1,32 : COLOR 3,0 : PRINT "File:";¶
    COLOR 1,0 : PRINT  Nam$¶
    Inpt=0¶
    LOCATE 1,65 : PRINT "Record:";RecordNumber¶
    PRINT : COLOR 3,0¶
    PRINT  "Enter new data:" : COLOR 1,0¶
  FOR x=0 TO NoOfFields¶
    LOCATE 5+x,1 : COLOR 2,0 : PRINT Fieldname$(x)": "¶
  NEXT x : COLOR 1,0¶
  FOR x=0 TO NoOfFields¶
    LOCATE 5+x,LEN(Fieldname$(x))+3¶
    LINE INPUT Entry$¶
    IF Entry$<>"" THEN Inpt=1¶
    Entry$(x)=LEFT$(Entry$,Length(x))¶
    LSET Dat$(x) = Entry$(x)¶
  NEXT x¶
 Corrections2:¶
  GOSUB EntryOK¶
  IF Corr=0 THEN WriteRecord¶
  IF Corr=1 THEN EnterCorrection¶
 GOTO Corrections2¶
¶
 EnterCorrection:¶
  CLS : LOCATE 1,1 : COLOR 1,0 : PRINT  "Add Data"¶
  LOCATE 1,32 : COLOR 3,0 : PRINT "File:";¶
  COLOR 1,0 : PRINT  Nam$¶
¶
    LOCATE 1,65 : PRINT "Record:";RecordNumber¶
```

```
             PRINT : PRINT ¶
           FOR x=0 TO NoOfFields¶
             LOCATE 5+x,1 : COLOR 2,0 : PRINT Fieldname$(x)":
    ";¶
             COLOR 1,0 : PRINT Entry$(x)¶
           ¶
         NEXT x¶
         FOR x=0 TO NoOfFields¶
           LOCATE 5+x,LEN(Fieldname$(x))+2¶
           LINE INPUT Entry$¶
           IF Entry$<>"" THEN¶
             Inpt=1¶
             Entry$(x)=LEFT$(Entry$,Length(x))¶
             LSET Dat$(x) = Entry$(x)¶
           END IF¶
         NEXT x¶
         GOTO Corrections2¶
         ¶
    WriteRecord:¶
       IF Inpt=1 THEN¶
         PUT #1,RecordNumber¶
         IF DataFlag=1 THEN DataFlag=0 : GOTO ReadLoop¶
         RecordNumber=RecordNumber+1¶
       END IF¶
       IF DataFlag=1 THEN DataFlag=0 : GOTO ReadLoop¶
    NextYN:¶
       LOCATE 19,1 : PRINT SPACE$(80) : COLOR 3,0¶
       LOCATE 19,1 : PRINT "Next Record (Y/N)";¶
       COLOR 1,0 : LINE INPUT a$¶
       IF UCASE$(a$)="Y" OR a$="" THEN InputLoop¶
       IF UCASE$(a$)="N" THEN CloseFile¶
    GOTO NextYN¶
    ¶
    CloseFile:¶
       CLOSE 1¶
       OPEN Nam$+".Flds" FOR OUTPUT AS 2¶
         PRINT #2,NoOfFields¶
         PRINT #2,RecordLength¶
         PRINT #2,RecordNumber-1¶
         FOR x=0 TO NoOfFields¶
           WRITE #2,Fieldname$(x)¶
           PRINT #2,Length(x)¶
         NEXT x¶
       CLOSE 2¶
       Nam$=""¶
    GOTO Begin¶
```

Entering data

The EnterData: routine displays its name in the upper left corner of the screen. If Nam$ has no contents, a new filename should be entered. You can also use an equal sign (=) or an asterisk (*) to signify that you wish to use the last filename used.

After this the following occurs: Normally the single program section with Nam$ is cleared, followed by the file access. CreateFile: alone is the exception to this. When you switch from the file preparation to data input, the data is automatically placed in the file. You can normally get newly created files from this value. That is why the function is automatic.

The next call is the subroutine FieldFileExistYN:. It determines whether there is a field file in existence with the same name. FieldFileExistYN: puts its result into the variable FileExist. If the value is 0, then the file is not read. If the value is 1, the file is read. If the .Flds file exists, then a corresponding random access file is read as well. We want to determine whether a specific file already exists, without generating a File not found error. The trick to this is in the subroutine.

If the file doesn't exist, the system returns to Begin: when you press any key.

The subroutine ReadFileField: reads the .Flds file that corresponds to the selected random file. Consequently, the values for the variables NoOfFields, RecordLength and NoOfRecords are read in addition to the field names and lengths.

Adding data

If you want to append new data to your record, type the new RecordNumber from NoOfRecords+1. The data will open the random access file, as well as the FIELD line.

InputLoop:, the actual input routine, displays Enter new data and prints the current filename in the center of the first screen line. These formalitites set a variable named Inpt to zero. This variable stands for Input, and will later convey whether input is found or not.

Input to records

The right corner of the screen displays the current record number with which the user is working. Now the new data should be entered. The program assists with a corresponding prompt. From 0 to NoOfFields, the field names appear on the screen. The cursor moves behind the first name and waits for input with LINE INPUT. The first non-null input (anything other than a <SPACE>) sets the variable Inpt to 1. This signals that correct input will be found there. The input Entry$ is set into the appropriate field length and then written to the file buffer by LSET. The array Entry$(x) marks all current data record input, regardless of the status of the file buffer.

Correcting
errors

If the loop is running, the user receives more opportunities to correct errors. EntryOK: asks the question and divides the duties with Corr. Setting Corr to 1 activates the EnterCorrection: routine. This routine first displays the text Change Data in the upper left screen line. The file and record numbers are also displayed. The next FOR...NEXT loop displays field names and field contents on the screen. This is followed by the input loop, which should look familiar. After all corrections are made, the record is written to diskette by the WriteRecord: routine (but only if Inpt=1).

If DataFlag=1, the end of the input jumps to ReadLoop:. If not, then RecordNumber is incremented by 1 and a new input can be made. NextYN: asks the user if he wants another record. If yes, then the file is set for input. If not, the file is closed and a new .Flds file with the current values is written. Note that this time Nam$ is cleared before the jump back to Begin: before it is executed. A new filename must be input before the next file access.

```
ReadData:¶
    CLS : LOCATE 1,1 : PRINT "Read Data"¶
    IF DataSearch=1 THEN LOCATE 1,1 : PRINT "Search
Data"¶
    LOCATE 3,1 : COLOR 3,0 : PRINT "Enter filename:"¶
    COLOR 1,0 : LINE INPUT Nam$¶
    IF Nam$="=" OR Nam$="*" THEN Nam$=Altname$¶
    IF Nam$="" THEN Begin¶
    Altname$=Nam$¶
¶
    GOSUB FieldFileExistYN¶
    IF FileExist=0 THEN¶
      PRINT : COLOR 3,0¶
      PRINT "Press any key."¶
      COLOR 1,0¶
      WHILE INKEY$="" : WEND¶
      GOTO Begin¶
    END IF¶
    GOSUB ReadFileField¶
    IF NoOfRecords=0 THEN¶
      PRINT : BEEP¶
      COLOR 1,0¶
      PRINT "No records in file!"¶
      PRINT : COLOR 3,0¶
      PRINT "Press any key."¶
      COLOR 1,0¶
      WHILE INKEY$="" : WEND¶
      GOTO Begin¶
    END IF¶
   IF DataSearch=1 THEN GOSUB SearchData¶
   OPEN "R",#1,Nam$,RecordLength   ¶
        FIELD #1,Length(0) AS Dat$(0),Length(1) AS Dat$(1),
Length(2) AS Dat$(2),Length(3) AS Dat$(3),Length(4) AS
Dat$(4),Length(5) AS Dat$(5),Length(6) AS
Dat$(6),Length(7) AS Dat$(7),Length(8) AS
Dat$(8),Length(9) AS Dat$(9)¶
```

```
          RecordNumber=1¶
```

You should be able to handle everything here. On to the next routine:

```
ReadLoop:¶
     CLS : LOCATE 1,1 : COLOR 1,0 : PRINT  "Read Data"¶
     LOCATE 1,32 : COLOR 3,0 : PRINT "File:";¶
     COLOR 1,0 : PRINT Nam$¶
     COLOR 3,0¶
     LOCATE 17,1 : PRINT  "[Cursor UP]   = Previous
Record"¶
     LOCATE 17,37 : PRINT "[F1]       = First Record"¶
     PRINT "[Cursor Down] = Next Record"¶
     LOCATE 18,37 : PRINT "[F2]       = Last Record"¶
     PRINT "[CTRL]-[P]    = Print Record"¶
     LOCATE 19,37 : PRINT "[HELP]     = Alter Record"¶
     PRINT "[F10]         = Main Menu";¶
¶
  ReadRecord:¶
     COLOR 1,0¶
     IF RecordNumber>NoOfRecords THEN BEEP :
RecordNumber=NoOfRecords¶
     IF RecordNumber<1 THEN BEEP : RecordNumber=1¶
     LOCATE 1,65 : PRINT "Record:";RecordNumber¶
     GET #1,RecordNumber¶
     IF DataSearch=1 THEN LOCATE 1,1 : PRINT "Search Data"
: GOSUB ExamSearchData¶
     IF DataSearch=1 AND Found=0 THEN¶
         IF RecordNumber=NoOfRecords THEN Direction=-1¶
         IF RecordNumber=NoOfRecords AND FindRecord=0 THEN¶
           CLS¶
           LOCATE 5,10 : PRINT "No record found!"¶
           LOCATE 7,10 : COLOR 3,0¶
           PRINT  "Press any key."¶
           COLOR 1,0 : BEEP¶
           WHILE INKEY$="" : WEND : CLOSE 1 : GOTO Begin¶
         END IF¶
         IF RecordNumber=1 THEN Direction=1¶
         RecordNumber=RecordNumber+Direction¶
        GOTO ReadRecord¶
     END IF¶
     FindRecord=1¶
     FOR x=0 TO NoOfFields¶
        LOCATE 5+x,1 : COLOR 2,0 : PRINT Fieldname$(x)":
"¶
     NEXT x : COLOR 1,0¶
     FOR x=0 TO NoOfFields¶
        LOCATE 5+x,LEN(Fieldname$(x))+3¶
        PRINT  Dat$(x)¶
        Entry$(x)=Dat$(x)¶
     NEXT x¶
     Key$=""¶
     WHILE Key$="" : Key$=INKEY$ : WEND¶
     IF Key$=CHR$(28) THEN RecordNumber=RecordNumber-1 :
Direction=-1¶
     IF Key$=CHR$(29) THEN RecordNumber RecordNumber+1 :
```

```
Direction=1¶
    IF Key$=CHR$(129) THEN RecordNumber=1¶
    IF Key$=CHR$(130) THEN RecordNumber=NoOfRecords¶
    IF Key$=CHR$(138) THEN EndLoad¶
    IF Key$=CHR$(16)  THEN¶
        FOR x=0 TO NoOfFields¶
          LPRINT Fieldname$(x)":"Dat$(x) ¶
        NEXT x¶
        LPRINT¶
    END IF¶
    IF Key$=CHR$(139) THEN DataFlag=1 : GOTO
EnterCorrection¶
GOTO ReadLoop¶

EndLoad: ¶
    CLOSE 1¶
    Nam$=""¶
GOTO Begin¶
```
Before you continue, save the program.

Reading and searching

ReadData: writes mode Read Data at position 1,1. The Select: section should look familiar. The ReadData: subprogram has two modes: Read data and Search data. In search mode, only the record containing the previously input search key is displayed on the screen. The variable DataSearch determines which mode is used. If DataSearch has a value of 1, then search mode is active, otherwise read mode is active. The first consequence of DataSearch=1 is that another identifier is displayed on the screen—Search Data.

Both modes are identical in the next section. A filename is input. The last-used filename can be abbreviated with = or *.

The subroutine FieldFileExistYN: is called to determine whether a file with the given name already exists on diskette. If not (FileExist=0), then the subroutine prints a corresponding message. After the message, the user presses a key and the subroutine exits. If the file already exists, then ReadFileField: reads the file.

It's possible that no data records will be found, which results in a No records in file! message. After the user presses a key, the program returns to Begin:. Data must be written into the given file through menu item 2 (Enter data) before it can be read.

If the search mode is active (DataSearch=1), the subroutine SearchData: is called, where the user types in a word for the system. Finally, the random access file may be opened. You've seen the FIELD command before. Again, you might want to copy this section as you did with Copy and Paste.

Data display

The program displays the records beginning with record 1. Accordingly, we set the starting value of RecordNumber with this value.

Now the ReadLoop: begins. This routine reads and displays the data. The program section begins with a mode identifier, stating the current file being read. Then the screen setup begins. Beneath the area where the data fields are displayed, the user gets an overview of the available keys and their functions within the program. Let's look at which keys do what.

Flipping through the records

The <cursor up> key lets you page back through the records, while the <cursor down> key lets you page forward. <F1> goes directly to the first record, and <F2> to the last record. Note that while in search mode, only the records involved in the search are affected by these keys. Jumps would be made to the next or previous record containing the search string. <CTRL><P> prints the current record to the printer, and the <HELP> key allows you to change the represented record, either for correction or for updating. <F10> closes the file and returns you to Begin:.

You can access your data with ReadRecord:. So that you can page through records with the cursor keys, the program must test whether the desired record number is too large or too small. In this case, it determines the allowed values. The record number is displayed in the upper right corner of the screen. The GET command loads the given record from diskette into the data buffer.

Now we come to the data search routines. If the search mode is active, the mode identifier will first be shown (Search Data rather than Read Data). The program routine called ExamSearchData: checks to see whether the record read fits the pattern of the search key. If so, then Found is assigned the value of 1. If not found, it is assigned a value of 0. The IF/END IF block follows this, and decides what action is taken if the record does not have the search phrase. If the upper limits of the record numbers are reached, the direction reverses and the value becomes -1. The search is executed from back to front, and will continue until the last record is found.

NOTE:

There is a problem with the search routines. If the current file doesn't have the search string within any of the records, the program will continue searching back and forth indefinately. Another problem is that if the current record is the last record of the file, and no more records could possibly be searched (FindRecord=0), then the search is stopped and the No record found!—Press any key message appears on the screen. Pressing a key returns us to the main menu.

But if the program finds at least one matching record, we can continue. At the lower limit of the file (RecordNumber=1), the search moves forward again (Direction=1) and looks toward the top of the file for a search string. Direction is added to RecordNumber and new records is read. After the END IF, FindRecord can be set to 1,

333

assuming that at least one matching record is found. From this we come to two operating modes: The field name, then the contents of the field, are displayed on the screen. The current record contents are marked at the same time as the array Entry$(x), so this data can be corrected.

The WHILE...WEND loop that follows waits for a keypress, and sends the pressed key to Key$. If Key$ gets the value CHR$(28), then you've pressed the <cursor up> key; the record number is decremented by one. If the search mode is active, we search from back to front. CHR$(29), the code for <cursor down>, switches the search forward. <F1> sends a CHR$(129). This tells the computer you want to jump to the beginning of the file and sets RecordNumber to 1.

CHR$(130) corresponds to <F2>, and sends the program to the end of the file. The variable NoOfRecords will contain the last record number. CHR$(138) corresponds to the <F10> key. This key returns you to the main menu, but first closes the file in EndLoad:.

Getting a printout

When you want to print out the current record on a printer, press <CTRL><P>. This key combination sends the code CHR$(16). The field names and field contents are sent to the printer by an LPRINT command. The blank LPRINTs place the necessary space between individual data records on paper.

The <HELP> key (CHR$(139)) lets you perform corrections or input new data. DataFlag is set to 1 then EnterCorrection: is called. These variables let the program know what routine to go to for correction. Then the ReadLoop: is ended by calling it again.

EndLoad: returns the system to the main menu. The random access file is closed, Nam$ is deleted, and the computer jumps back to Begin:.

You still need routines to search your data, check whether the field file you want to search is on the disk, and then read the field file. Go to the end of the program you've typed so far, and type in the following lines:

```
SearchData:¶
  CLS : LOCATE 1,1 : COLOR 1,0 : PRINT "Search Data"¶
  LOCATE 1,32 : COLOR 3,0 : PRINT "File:";¶
  COLOR 1,0 : PRINT Nam$¶
  FOR x=0 TO NoOfFields¶
    LOCATE 5+x,1 : PRINT Fieldname$(x)":"¶
  NEXT x¶
  COLOR 3,0 : LOCATE 4,1  ¶
  PRINT  "Enter search string."¶
¶
```

```
     COLOR 1,0¶
       FOR x=0 TO NoOfFields¶
         LOCATE 5+x,LEN(Fieldname$(x))+2¶
         LINE INPUT Entry$¶
         IF Entry$<>"" THEN¶
           Search$=LEFT$(Entry$,Length(x))¶
           SearchNo=x : x=10¶
         ELSE¶
           Search$=""¶
         END IF¶
       NEXT x¶
     Corrections3:¶
        GOSUB EntryOK¶
       IF Corr=0 THEN EndSearch¶
       IF Corr=1 THEN SearchCorr¶
     GOTO Corrections3¶
¶
   SearchCorr:¶
     LOCATE 5+SearchNo,1 : PRINT
Fieldname$(SearchNo)":"Search$¶
     LOCATE 5+SearchNo,LEN(Fieldname$(SearchNo))+2¶
     LINE INPUT Entry$¶
     IF Entry$<>"" THEN
Search$=LEFT$(Entry$,Length(SearchNo))¶
   GOTO Corrections3¶
    ¶
EndSearch:¶
   IF Search$="" THEN SearchNo=0 : DataSearch=0¶
   FindRecord=0¶
RETURN¶
¶
ExamSearchData:¶
     x=0¶
SearchLoop:¶
     x=x+1¶
     IF x>LEN(Dat$(SearchNo))-LEN(Search$) THEN Found=0 :
RETURN¶
     IF MID$(Dat$(SearchNo),x,LEN(Search$))=Search$ THEN
Found=1 : RETURN  ¶
GOTO SearchLoop  ¶
¶
EntryOK:¶
   LOCATE 19,1 : COLOR 3,0¶
   PRINT "Entry Okay? (Y/N)";¶
   COLOR 1,0 : INPUT "",a$¶
   IF UCASE$(a$)="Y" OR a$="" THEN Corr=0 : RETURN¶
   IF UCASE$(a$)="N" THEN Corr=1 : RETURN¶
GOTO EntryOK¶
¶
FieldFileExistYN:¶
   OPEN Nam$+".Flds" FOR APPEND AS 1¶
     IF LOF(1)<=0 THEN FileExist=0 ELSE FileExist=1¶
   CLOSE 1¶
   IF FileExist=0 THEN¶
     LOCATE 3,1 : PRINT  SPACE$(80) : BEEP¶
     LOCATE 3,1 : COLOR 1,0 : PRINT "File ";Nam$¶
```

```
      PRINT "not found!"¶
      KILL Nam$+".Flds"¶
      Nam$="" : COLOR 3,0¶
   END IF¶
RETURN¶
¶
ReadFileField:¶
   FOR x=1 TO 10¶
      Fieldname$(x)="" : Length(x)=0¶
   NEXT x¶
   OPEN Nam$+".Flds" FOR INPUT AS 2¶
      INPUT #2,NoOfFields¶
      INPUT #2,RecordLength¶
      INPUT #2,NoOfRecords¶
      FOR x=0 TO NoOfFields¶
         INPUT #2,Fieldname$(x)¶
         INPUT #2,Length(x)¶
      NEXT x¶
   CLOSE 2¶
RETURN¶
```

SearchData: contains all setups for the search mode. It identifies the program section and determines the current filename. It displays the field names on the screen, followed by Enter search string. You have the option of inputting a string that tests all the fields in every record.

Hints for data searching

If you want to look for every record in your collection by Elton John, you'd enter the string Elton John in the Artist field. The program then looks for the records in which the Artist field contains Elton John. If you had entered the search text Elton John in the Title field, for example, the Amiga would look for any references to Elton John in the Title fields, where it might find Elton John's Greatest Hits. This lets you see what follows the found search strings, as well as the search strings themselves. It would be sufficient to type John in the Artist field, although this would also give you references to Olivia Newton-John and Robert John. You'd probably get better results by using Elton as your search string.

NOTE:

Uppercase and lowercase lettering are matched exactly in the search. If you had input john, you would not find Elton John. You can use this search technique in an address list by searching by zipcode or telephone number exchange. When you press the <SPACE> bar or single character such as <e>, the computer will find as many listings which contain the search pattern.

And how did we program all this?

How the
search
routines
work

The SearchData: section runs through the input loop. You can move through all the fields by simply pressing <RETURN>, until you reach the area into which you wish to input a search string. This input is stored in the variable Search$. SearchNo contains the number of fields that are compared. Corrections3: offers a correction option. You can still only change the contents of Search$, and the selected field is already taken.

EndSearch: jumps back to the line from which the subroutine was first called. If Search$ has no contents, the search is aborted: SearchNo and DataSearch each get the value 0. If 0 is in the variable FindRecord, it can later be determined whether a record was really found according to the last used search criteria.

ExamSearchData: is the section where the current record is tested for the search string. The loop SearchLoop: runs until all possible positions are compared between Dat$ and Search$. We get a partial string from Dat$ by taking a section of the string the same length as Search$. When x becomes greater than the length of Dat$ minus the length of Search$, Search$ is assumed as not found in this data record. Found is set to 0, and the subroutine returns. If the partial string is found, Found is set to 1. The computer will jump back with RETURN.

Corrections

The next program section, EntryOK:, is called several times. This determines whether the user wants to correct any input. The question Entry Okay? (Y/N) appears on the screen, and INPUT waits for a response. INPUT "",a$ suppresses the question mark. Pressing either <n> or <SPACE> sets Corr equal to 0; no correction. We'll accept any blank string, in order to make work with selection as fast as possible, ended with <RETURN>. If you press <y>, Corr is set to 1. The program then continues execution at the next routine.

The subroutine FieldFileExist: has already been mentioned here: The .Flds file is checked to see if the given file actually exists. If you want to open a reading file that isn't available, you get a File not found error. The program ends, and the old contents are erased—that's not a good solution. We can solve this problem with the APPEND mode. When you open a sequential file FOR APPEND, then new records are appended to the old entries without deleting them. If no file exists, a new file is created.

Thus, we open the .Flds file FOR APPEND, and check it with the LOF(1) for file length: If it is 0 or -1, there is no data in the file. You must use APPEND for initially opening a file, since it doesn't yet exist. Therefore, FileExist=0 ELSE FileExist=1. If FileExist has a value of 0, the message indicating that this file was not found is displayed.

Last but not least, is the subroutine `ReadFileField:`. When the
`.Flds` file is read, this subroutine examines its contents. First a
`FOR...NEXT` loop deletes the contents of `FieldName$(x)` and
`Length(x)`. Since these read files have used fewer fields than the last
used, the old field name will remain stored, for a reason you'll see later.
Then the values for the number of fields per record (`NoOfFields`), the
total record length (`RecordLength`) and the past number of records in
the file (`NoOfRecords`) is loaded. The program can then use these to
open and access the file.

If you haven't saved this program yet, do it now! When that electrical
storm hits, or when someone trips over the power cord, you'll thank us
for reminding you.

5.3   A database is what you put into it: using the database

All the important information you need to use this database program is found in the previous program explanations. This section offers a few helpful tips for using your AmigaBASIC database.

The most common use for a computer is data processing. But data processing can be used for more than business—it could be used for fun as well. You can store recipes, poems, videotapes, books, care instructions for your houseplants, unsavory data about fellow employees, football scores, stamp collections, your Amiga programs, notes about newspaper articles, favorite restaurants—whatever you can dream up, you can store it in your new database.

The first step is to create a new file with menu item 1. You can specify up to 10 field names, as well as the length for each field. The maximum field length is 40 characters. This value is the default if you don't provide field length parameters—for example, if you simply press <RETURN> in response to Name. Figure 16 shows typical input in this mode:

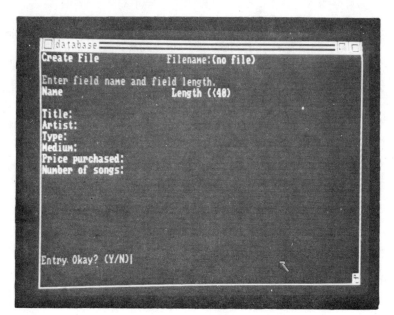

Figure 16: Database program in Create File mode

Press <RETURN> twice to signal the database that you are through creating your file field. Now you have the option of correcting any typing errors. If you have made a mistake, then press <n><RETURN> to answer the question Entry Okay? (Y/N). The cursor will be displayed in the first data field. Either type in the new input or press <RETURN>. When everything looks right, and you've pressed <RETURN> to get through the rest of the fields, the program will ask you Entry Okay? (Y/N) again. Answer <y><RETURN>. The program will then ask you to Enter Filename:. Type the name you want to call the file and press <RETURN>. The program opens the two disk files and returns to the main menu.

You'll go directly to input mode when you choose item 2 (Enter Data). If you have not created a file immediately before going to this option, you must type a filename. The last filename used can be abbreviated to = or *. This is especially practical when you want to change between reading data and searching data in input mode.

A *mask* that includes your field names appears on the screen. The cursor is in the first data field of the current record. Type in the data, and remember that you'll get to correct your mistakes later. A completely empty record will not be saved; instead, the input procedure is repeated. When you answer the question Next Record (Y/N) with <y> or <RETURN>, you'll go on to the next input. Answering <n> closes the file and returns you to the main menu.

Menu item 3 displays the contents of a file. Input the filename or the abbreviation = or *. If you don't provide a filename, or if no records exist, the program will ask for input again. Beneath the data area, you'll see the available keys and options printed in orange. You can flip through the records either forward or backward, jump directly to the first or last record, print the contents of a record, or alter the screen. The <F10> key returns you to the main menu.

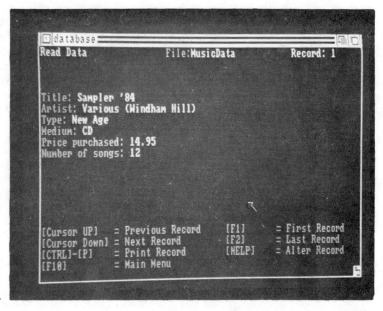

Figure 17:
Database
program in
Read Data
mode

Menu item 4, the Data Search mode, allows you to search all records for your specified search criterion. Only the records in which the criterion is found are displayed.

After selecting Search file, you type the filename to be searched. The program displays the field names on screen, and asks you to input a search string in one of the fields. This search string is searched for in all the data records. After any input corrections, the program opens the file and begins searching. When at least one record is found containing the search string, the program displays the found record. Otherwise the No record found message is displayed. The record found can be handled as you would in Read Data mode. The program will only exit the routine when the final record is displayed.

In closing... Your data should be handled with the same caution that you use in handling your money. It's possible that your data might get mixed up or destroyed, and many personal things that you were keeping in the database may be lost.

What next? Well, we're not quite finished with data processing. Quite the contrary. You may wonder what data has to do with computer speech, or even computer music, but the next section will tell you all about it.

Speech in BASIC

6

6 AmigaSpeak: Speech in BASIC

Conversations with your Amiga have been one-sided—until now. You'll soon see that just because the Amiga speaks only when spoken to doesn't mean that it has nothing to say.

The Amiga has all of the hardware and software necessary to generate computer speech that's amazingly understandable. Perhaps you have already heard it talk. The Workbench demos have speech programs, and you will also find examples of Amiga's eloquence in the BASICDemos drawer from the Extras diskette.

For the rest of this section, we assume that you have hooked your Amiga to an auxiliary speaker of some sort. The monitor's built-in speaker will do nicely, but there's nothing wrong with running the Amiga's sound channel through a 200-watt stereo system. Whatever you use, set the volume to a comfortable level, out of consideration for the neighbors. We will be trying out noises and special effects later, and not many people would be amused by an "attack imminent" siren.

6.1

The third teaser:
the Amiga speaks

You'll recall we had no short samples in the chapters on file management. There's a reason for this: It's almost impossible to give a simple but meaningful demonstration of the Amiga's file handling. We had to explain in detail before we could do anything at all with files. Now for some fun with your Amiga. Type in this simple program:

```
Text$="Amiga"¶
    Begin:¶
      Speech%(0)=90+180*RND¶
      Speech%(1)=RND¶
      Speech%(2)=50+200*RND¶
      Speech%(3)=RND¶
      Speech%(4)=17000+10000*RND¶
      Speech%(5)=40+24*RND¶
      Speech%(6)=11*RND¶
      Speech%(7)=0¶
      Speech%(8)=0¶
¶
      SAY TRANSLATE$(Text$),Speech%¶
    GOTO Begin¶
```

You can use your Speech drawer for the first time when you save this program. Type the command CHDIR ": Speech" first to save the program in this drawer.

When you run the program, AmigaBASIC calls up the Workbench. If you only have one disk drive, or if the Workbench is not presently in one of your drives, a requester will ask for the Workbench disk. After a short pause for loading, your Amiga begins to say its own name in many different voices, speeds, tone frequencies, and loudnesses.

Your Amiga already has a split personality, doesn't it? If you don't want it to talk about itself all the time, you can substitute other values for Text$.

Do you want to learn to make your Amiga a veritable William Safire among computers? Then read the next section.

6.2

Say it with phonemes:
SAY and TRANSLATE$

In the last sample, you already used the two most important commands of speech synthesis: SAY and TRANSLATE$. The SAY command creates artificial speech. However, it cannot function on its own. If you try to get your Amiga to speak by typing a command like this in the **BASIC** window:

```
SAY "Amiga"¶
```

you will get an Illegal function call error message. The SAY command does not directly pronounce the contents of a string.

Translating text for the Amiga

First the text has to be translated into a form the Amiga can understand. This is where the TRANSLATE$ command comes in:

```
Text$=TRANSLATE$("Amiga")¶
SAY Text$¶
```

It translates the text into a form which SAY can handle—a form called a *phoneme code*, which we will discuss later. We will now attempt to make the Amiga speak an entire sentence. It would be wise to enlarge the display area on the screen first:

```
width 60
```

Otherwise, some of the sentence would disappear behind the right edge of the display. Once this is done, we get back to work:

```
Text$="This is your Amiga speaking. I feel good. How are
you?"¶
Text$=TRANSLATE$(Text$)¶
SAY Text$¶
```

If you don't know the text ahead of time, you have to concentrate a little to understand the Amiga, but it gets easier the more you work with it.

Making a bilingual Amiga

Say you want to make the Amiga speak another language, German for example. This is a problem, since the Amiga is a native-born American and doesn't know any foreign languages particularly well. To demonstrate, let's try a version of the above program which tries to say roughly the same thing, only in German:

347

```
Text$="Hallo, hier spricht Ihr Amiga. Wie geht es
Ihnen?"¶
Text$=TRANSLATE$(Text$)¶
SAY Text$
```

The first sentence sounds okay to a German ear, but the Amiga mispronounces the second sentence badly, saying "Wy jate ess innen" instead of "Vee kait ess eenen."

Phoneme codes

As we already mentioned, the SAY command only understands text formatted in a special code. This code is called phoneme code. To see what the foreign sentence "Wie geht es Ihnen?" looks like in phoneme code, type this in:

```
Text$="Wie geht es Ihnen?"¶
Text$=TRANSLATE$(Text$)¶
SAY Text$¶
? Text$¶
```

The following then appears on the screen:

```
WAY4 JEH4T EH4Z IH4NEHN.
```

This is what a phoneme string looks like. It is the translation of "Wie geht es Ihnen?" using the TRANSLATE$ function. You can now see that the SAY function is not to blame for the mispronunciation of the German. The blame lies with TRANSLATE$, which assumes that all text given it is in English.

Rewriting the language

There are two ways that the existing AmigaBASIC can produce reasonably correct German. The first would be to rewrite TRANSLATE$ to work with other languages. Whether Commodore or Microsoft are planning to do this, we don't know. The second method would be to create our own German phonemes. The third is to trick the TRANSLATE$ routine; we could rewrite the sentence in American sound spellings, somewhat like a basic book phrase, so that the result sounds more or less German. An example:

```
Text$=TRANSLATE$("Vee kaiht ass eenan")¶
SAY Text$
```

However, to do this correctly, you have to be very familiar with both English and the language with which you're working, or else subject yourself to a lot of trial and error.

Let's look at the phoneme code translation:

```
? Text$¶
```

Response:

```
VIY4 KEY3T AE4S IY4NAEN.
```

Spelling doesn't count here

The phoneme is an idea from linguistics, and means "sound." The phoneme code is a form of phonetic writing which has very little to do with the correct spelling of a word, but is concerned with how the word is pronounced. IY is the phoneme for a long "e", like in "bee" or "eat." Thus, two sets of letters can be represented by the same phoneme. The number 4 is a *stress mark*. It can be any number from 0 to 9, and determines how strongly a syllable is stressed.

But capitals do

One very important thing about creating your own phonemes: They must be typed in using capital letters. One lowercase letter will give you an Illegal function call error message.

Let's try our own phoneme string. Type in the following:

```
Text$="VIY9 GEY3T AE1S IY6NAEN?"¶
SAY Text$¶
```

This version of "Wie geht es Ihnen?" is strongly stressed in the first word, less so in the second and third, with a bit of an accent on the last word. If you do not speak German, try and find someone who does, and see what he thinks.

The format of phoneme code follows strict rules. You can't just substitute letters for sounds when you feel like it. If you want to work with phonemes in more detail, and have the ambition, we recommend you read Appendix H of the AmigaBASIC manual. It thoroughly explains how to build phoneme codes.

narrator device

AmigaBASIC's SAY and TRANSLATE$ routines are stored under the name narrator.device in the Workbench. These routines are loaded on the first use in AmigaBASIC of SAY or TRANSLATE$. When you restart the translation program, the Amiga goes immediately to the Workbench. This is so the Amiga can jump to these routines as quickly as possible when they are called. They consistently take up 30K in RAM. Every NEW and RUN command deletes narrator.device from memory, and then must be reloaded every time the speech commands are used.

NOTE:

There are occasions when the translation routine is supposed to be deleted, but the Amiga doesn't cooperate—it stays in memory. The partnership between AmigaBASIC and the Workbench is not as friendly as you might think. That's when TRANSLATE$ is dropped and every SAY command gives an Illegal function call error. We have no cure for this problem, aside from reloading the Workbench. Don't forget to save everything before reloading.

The problem occurs most frequently when you use the speech commands in direct mode immediately after deleting a speech program. It won't affect your speech program, so don't panic.

And now, let's get back to the Amiga and the spoken word.

349

6.3

All talk, no music:
options with the SAY command

The really interesting thing about the example in **Section 6.1** was the amount of variation possible in the Amiga's voice. It can speak high or low, fast or slow, accented or monotone, male or female. If you were patient and sat through the entire program, you probably heard some impressive examples, as well as some funny ones. The next question is, how can you program these examples yourself? It's not difficult, as you will soon see. The number of options and the extent of the Amiga's abilities are really all that may be confusing you. Before we start, please clear the program from the **LIST** window. We are going to write a test program section by section.

Defining an array for SAY

First, a basic principle: You can specify an integer array of up to nine elements after the text in the SAY command. More than nine elements would accomplish nothing—SAY uses the first nine and ignores the extra elements. So the first thing you type in the **LIST** window should be:

```
DIM speech%(8)
```

You already know that DIM speech%(8) allows <u>nine</u> elements, because the first element is zero, not one. It is really no great loss if you leave the DIM statement out of a speech program. Default dimensioning is 10, so only two bytes are wasted.

Each of the nine elements is a number that represents a certain property or mode of the resulting voice. In this program, we want to read these numbers from DATA statements:

```
FOR x=0 TO 8¶
  READ Speech%(x) ¶
NEXT x¶
```

Now we need some way to input the text to be spoken:

```
speechinput:¶
  LINE INPUT "Text: ", typein$¶
  If typein$<>"=" THEN text$=typein$¶
  speech$=TRANSLATE$(text$)¶
  CLS : PRINT text$¶
  SAY speech$, speech%: 'Note the two different
speech variables¶
GOTO speechinput¶
```

We have constructed the program in such a way that you can repeat the last sentence you entered by typing <=><RETURN>.

Here we go! With the following line, the Amiga will have a new voice:

DATA 140,0,160,0,22000,64,11,1,0¶

Voice
parameters

Now try the program out. You'll notice that Amiga's voice has really changed. It sounds a little higher and softer than the original voice. The change is caused by the DATA statements, so let's look at what these numbers do.

Base
frequency

The first value in the integer field specifies the *base frequency* of the voice. This value essentially decides the pitch of the voice, its most important quality. The allowed values for the base frequency are 65 (very, very deep) through 320 (a real squeaky voice). The default base frequency value is 110. We have chosen 140, which is a bit higher. You can specify any base frequency that suits you. Experiment with any number within the allowed range, and listen for yourself.

Change the listing for a moment, and set the base frequency to 80. Quite resonant, don't you think? Try the extremes, 65, which sounds a little morbid, and 320, which sounds unnaturally high. Now find a frequency that you prefer, and use it.

Inflection

The second value in the integer field can be 0 or 1. This value regulates *inflection*. 0 means inflection as found in normal speech. 1 yields a completely monotone ("computer") voice. Naturally, the human voice sounds nicer, but if you want to intentionally make your Amiga sound like a robot, or to show off how much better the natural Amiga sounds than a simple monotone, you know how to do it. The AmigaBASIC default for this value is 0 (inflected speech).

Rate

The third value is really fun to play with. It represents the *rate* (number of words per minute). The AmigaBASIC default rate is 150. We had the Amiga speak a little faster with a value of 160. Change the speed to 350 and type "The big black bug bled black blood" or "Unique New York." Try to say the phrase yourself at the same speed. Allowed values for rate of speech are 40 through 400. At the faster rates, there is the danger that Amiga will overtake itself and swallow syllables. Conversely, very slow speeds (below 70) will put you to sleep.

Voice

The fourth value chooses the gender (sex) of the voice. The female voice often sounds very similar to the computer onboard a certain starship in a certain TV series. 0 (the default) creates a male voice, and 1 selects a female voice. To produce a true female vocal sound, you must use a higher base frequency (try 240).

Tuning

This next value should also be modified for a female voice. Try setting it to 23000. This value sets the *tuning*, or sampling frequency. Those words may not mean anything to you–we'll talk some more about it in **Chapter 7: Sound and Music**. For now, let's just say that it affects both the tone of the voice and the base frequency. The value may be any number between 5000 and 28000. The Amiga's default value is 22200, and ours is only a little higher. You should be careful when you try variations at first, because even the smallest changes make a big difference in the voice quality.

Volume

The sixth value is much simpler. Here, we choose a *volume* between 0 and 64. We are using the highest volume, just like AmigaBASIC. This value is useful for programming conversations or multiple voices, where different volumes are desired. Remember that the volume control on your monitor or stereo is also working, and that both the volume control and the sixth field value will determine the total loudness.

Channel

The seventh value sets the output *channel* to one or more sound channels. You need to pay attention to this only when you can hook up your Amiga to some kind of stereo device. The monitor's speaker only has monoraul output, and sends everything to one speaker. However, the Amiga is fully equipped for stereo. A total of four channels are assigned to the left and right speakers. Channels number 0 and 3 (the highest and lowest) represent Amiga's left outputs. The middle values, 1 and 2, represent the right outputs. You can achieve neat stereo effects by changing the channels correctly, or a conversation between right and left, at the very least.

There are a few limitations to the Amiga's true "stereo" capabilities. An echo effect exists in a true stereo system, where, even when just a single voice is being transmitted, a slightly different signal is sent to each speaker, instead of the exact same signal. The Amiga does not have this capability. In addition, a normal stereo will have at least a trace of every signal sent to each speaker. The Amiga has no such effect. This sounds unnatural, especially when you're wearing headphones. If a sound is sent to the left channel only, the right speaker is completely dead. This sounds better on free-standing speakers, where the echo effect is stimulated by the room acoustics.

There are twelve possible channel combinations, as listed in Table 10:

7th value in integer array	channel/channels	remarks
0	channel 0	left
1	channel 1	right
2	channel 2	right
3	channel 3	left
4	channels 0 and 1	stereo
5	channels 0 and 2	stereo
6	channels 3 and 1	stereo
7	channels 3 and 2	stereo
8	all free left channels	0 and/or 3
9	all free right channels	1 and/or 2
10	any free pair	default value
11	any free channel	

Table 10: channel setups for the SAY command

About "free channels"

A channel can already be occupied by a previous program or BASIC command. This only happens if a sound is already being created. A channel is free if no sound is being sent on it.

You can use the given value to send your speech on any combination of channels. When other SAY commands or sound commands are running, you can choose one of the options that uses free channels.

AmigaBASIC uses the value 10 (any free left-right pair) as its standard value. You used the value 11 (any free channel) in our DATA statements. Remember: These experiments work only when a stereo system is connected to the Amiga.

The last two values in the integer array decide how the Amiga should behave when other commands follow a SAY command.

Mode

The eighth value is the *synchronizaiton mode*. If this value is 0, AmigaBASIC performs *synchronous speech output*. That is, it waits until the output of the SAY command is completely executed before it executes any of the commands following it. 1 generates *asynchronous speech output*. This works in a manner similar to OBJECT commands, in that it simply starts the speech and executes the next commands at the same time the speech is being output. The speech can run in the background while AmigaBASIC performs other tasks. AmigaBASIC's default synchronization mode is 0.

Control

The ninth value is *control* (narrator.device control) is in effect only when the eighth value is set at 1 (asynchronous output speech output) for background execution. It determines how the Amiga should behave when it encounters a SAY command while it is executing speech. 0 starts each SAY command only after the previous one has been executed. 2 interrupts the current output, and the new SAY command is executed immediately.

The 1 was left until last for a good reason. It has nothing to do with the 0 and 2 values. A 1 deactivates the SAY command and makes it completely independent of all else that goes on. It can be used in larger programs. The SAY command is toggled on or off through a variable which contains a 0 for speech or a 1 for silence.

There we have it. There were a lot of options, weren't there? Experience should tell you that a lot of experimentation will let you find the most pleasant voice. To save you a lot of needless work and waiting time (every time the program starts, a new narrator.device file is created), we'll write a speech utility program in the next section.

6.4   When all is said and done: the speech utility

This next utility helps you experiment with the different voice options. When you find a voice that you want to use later, you can store it and add it to your programs with MERGE.

NOTE: First, remember to set the Amiga to 60-character screen mode. As we've said before, you can set this mode using Preferences.

```
BuildScreen:¶
  CLS¶
  PALETTE 0,.1,.1,.4¶
  LOCATE 2,2 : PRINT "Text:"¶
  LINE (60,7)-(612,18),1,b¶
  LOCATE 22,6¶
¶
PRINT "Freq.    Speed       Tuning      Volume"¶
  LINE (40,30)-(65,160),1,b¶
  LINE (120,30)-(145,160),1,b¶
  LINE (205,30)-(230,160),1,b¶
  LINE (285,30)-(310,160),1,b¶
  LOCATE 6,56 : PRINT "Male         Female"¶
  LINE (420,30)-(495,48),1,b¶
  LINE (510,30)-(585,48),1,b¶
  LOCATE 9,56 : PRINT  "Human        Comp."¶
  LINE (420,57)-(495,75),1,b¶
  LINE (510,57)-(585,75),1,b¶
  LOCATE 12,61 : PRINT "Speak"¶
  LINE (450,84)-(555,102),1,b¶
  LOCATE 17,61 : PRINT "Store"¶
  LINE (450,120)-(555,138),1,b¶
```

Setting up the screen

The BuildScreen: routine constructs a system of labels and gadgets. As you have seen in previous examples where we played with screen color, we have darkened the blue Workbench to make it look better. The top line accepts the input for the text to be spoken. Beneath this are the four sliders for adjusting the base frequency, the speech rate, the tuning, and the volume. All of these values can be adjusted within their full ranges.

Next to these are a pair of gadgets to select a male or female voice, and one used to determine inflected (human) or unaccented (computer) voice output. Below these, one gadget executes the speech with the presently displayed values. You click the last gadget when you want to store the present values for later use. Figure 18 shows how the screen should look, so you can tell if you typed in the program correctly:

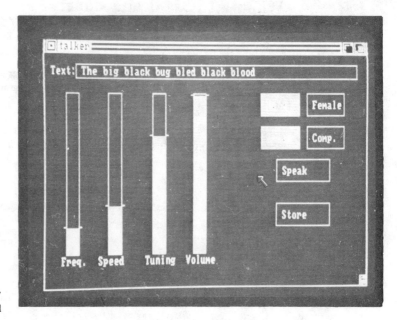

**Figure 18:
Speech
utility
program—
main menu**

```
StartingValue:¶
   FOR x=0 TO 8¶
      READ Speech%(x)¶
   NEXT x¶
   DATA 110,0,150,0,22200,64,10,0,0¶
   GOSUB ShowValue¶
¶
MainLoop:¶
   ON MOUSE GOSUB ReadMouse¶
   MOUSE ON¶
   WHILE 1 : WEND¶
```

StartingValue: places the AmigaBASIC default values for the
SAY command into the integer array Speech%. You can change any of
these values as the program runs, but we have to start somewhere; this
is why we provided these values for the DATA. If you would rather start
with different values, you can change the DATA statements without
causing any problems. However, it's important that you include a
DATA line. Toward the end of this section we call the ShowValue:
routine, which redisplays the sliders and gadgets to match the current
values in the integer array.

MainLoop: should tip you off that this program runs with event
trapping as well. The mouse and the keyboard are used only for our user
input, because pulldown menus are really not needed in this program.

```
ReadMouse:¶
  Test=MOUSE(0)¶
  x=MOUSE(3)  :  y=MOUSE(4)¶
  IF x>39 AND x<311 AND y>29 AND y<161 THEN¶
    IF x<66 THEN¶
      Frequency:¶
      Speech%(0)=(255-(y-30)*(255/130))+65¶
      FreqValue=((320-Speech%(0))/255)*130¶
      LINE (41,31)-(64,31+FreqValue),0,bf¶
      LINE (41,32+FreqValue)-(64,159),3,bf¶
      y=MOUSE(6)¶
      IF y<31 THEN y=31¶
      IF y>159 THEN y=159¶
      IF MOUSE(0)<=-1 THEN Frequency¶
    END IF¶
```

You should copy the last program lines (following `IF x<66`) using Copy from the **Edit** menu and then paste it in three times with Paste. These program lines will be used four times, with minor alterations. The three copies follow immediately after the original, then the program executes normally.

```
    IF x>119 AND x<146 THEN¶
      Speed:¶
      Speech%(2)=(360-(y-30)*(360/130))+40¶
      SpeedValue=((400-Speech%(2))/360)*130¶
      LINE (121,31)-(144,31+SpeedValue),0,bf¶
      LINE (121,32+SpeedValue)-(144,159),3,bf¶
      y=MOUSE(6)¶
      IF y<31 THEN y=31¶
      IF y>159 THEN y=159¶
      IF MOUSE(0)<=-1 THEN Speed¶
    END IF¶
    IF x>204 AND x<231 THEN¶
      Tuning:¶
      Speech%(4)=(23000-(y-30)*(23000/130))+5000¶
      TuningValue=((28000-Speech%(4))/23000)*130¶
      LINE (206,31)-(229,31+TuningValue),0,bf¶
      LINE (206,32+TuningValue)-(229,159),3,bf¶
      y=MOUSE(6)¶
      IF y<31 THEN y=31¶
      IF y>159 THEN y=159¶
      IF MOUSE(0)<=-1 THEN Tuning¶
    END IF¶
    IF x>284 AND x<311 THEN¶
      Volume:¶
      Speech%(5)=(64-(y-30)*(64/130))¶
      VolumeValue=((64-Speech%(5))/64)*130¶
      LINE (286,31)-(309,31+VolumeValue),0,bf¶
      LINE (286,32+VolumeValue)-(309,159),3,bf¶
      y=MOUSE(6)¶
      IF y<31 THEN y=31¶
      IF y>159 THEN y=159¶
      IF MOUSE(0)<=-1 THEN Volume¶
    END IF¶
```

357

```
END IF¶
IF x>419 AND x<496 AND y>29 AND y<49 THEN¶
  Speech%(3)=0¶
  PAINT (422,32),3,1 : PAINT (512,32),0,1¶
END IF¶
IF x>509 AND x<586 AND y>29 AND y<49 THEN¶
  Speech%(3)=1¶
  PAINT (422,32),0,1 : PAINT (512,32),3,1¶
END IF¶
IF x>419 AND x<496 AND y>56 AND y<76 THEN¶
  Speech%(1)=0¶
  PAINT (422,59),3,1 : PAINT (512,59),0,1¶
END IF¶
IF x>509 AND x<586 AND y>56 AND y<76 THEN¶
  Speech%(1)=1¶
  PAINT (422,59),0,1 : PAINT (512,59),3,1¶
END IF¶
IF x>59 AND x<613 AND y>6 AND y<19 THEN¶
  LOCATE 2,9 : PRINT  SPACE$(54)¶
  LOCATE 2,9 : LINE INPUT Text$¶
END IF¶
IF x>449 AND x<556 AND y>83 AND y<103 THEN¶
  PAINT (452,85),3,1¶
  SAY TRANSLATE$(Text$),Speech%¶
  PAINT (452,85),0,1¶
END IF¶
IF x>449 AND x<556 AND y>119 AND y<139 THEN¶
  PAINT (452,121),3,1¶
  LOCATE 2,9 : PRINT  SPACE$(54)¶
  LOCATE 2,9 : COLOR 0,3 : PRINT "Filename:";¶
  COLOR 1,0 : LINE INPUT Nam$¶
  IF Nam$<>"" THEN¶
    IF Nam$="=" OR Nam$="*" AND Altname$<>"" THEN
Nam$=Altname$¶
    OPEN Nam$ FOR OUTPUT AS 1¶
      PRINT #1, "REM DATAs made with AmigaBASIC-
Talker"¶
      PRINT #1, "DATA ";¶
      FOR x=0 TO 7¶
        PRINT #1,Speech%(x)",";¶
      NEXT x¶
      PRINT #1,Speech%(8)¶
    CLOSE 1¶
    Altname$=Nam$¶
  END IF¶
  LOCATE 2,9 : PRINT SPACE$(54)¶
  LOCATE 2,9 : COLOR 1,0 : PRINT  Text$¶
  PAINT (452,121),0,1¶
END IF¶
¶
RETURN¶
```

Reading the mouse

The program spends most of its time in the `ReadMouse:` routine. First, we call `MOUSE(0)` and assign the result to a dummy variable called `Test`. We want only the most up-to-date values for the mouse position.

We use the functions `MOUSE(3)` and `MOUSE(4)` to determine the X- and Y-coordinates of the mouse position. (If you don't remember the mouse functions very well, look back to **Section 2.9** or **Appendix B.4**). `MOUSE(3)` and `MOUSE(4)` return the coordinates when the mouse button is pressed, calling a subprogram. These values are used because we are only interested in the position of the mouse when the mouse is clicked.

Then the pointer position is checked relative to the fields on the screen. Where did the click occur? If the mouse was clicked somewhere in the slider area, the program jumps to an independent program routine for each slider (`Freq`, `Speed`, `Tuning`, and `Volume`). These four routines are the same except for the numbers, data, and names.

We will go through the first slider `Freq`. (frequency) as an exercise. Since the rest of the slider routines work exactly the same way, we will spare you the tedium of explaining each one of them.

Sliders

If the mouse pointer is located in the `Freq`. slider, we first determine a new frequency and write it into the field `Speech%(0)`. The variable `FreqValue` contains the calculated value of the coordinates that correspond to this frequency. The first of the two `LINE` commands uses the blockfill option to fill the area above the mouse position blue. The second `LINE` command colors the area below the mouse position orange. We end up with a bar graph that rises with increasing frequency, like the mercury in a thermometer.

`y` is the current position of the mouse at the click. If `y` is outside the allowed values for the graph (31 to 159), the adopted value will be the minimum or maximum value, depending on the pointer's position. If `MOUSE(0)` is less than or equal to -1, this means that the mouse button is still pressed. In this case, the indicator will be repositioned again, because program control will loop back to the label.

Gadgets

The other slider routines manipulate their values in the same way using the appropriate data. Next we check the gadget marked `Male`. If you have clicked there, the variable `Speech%(3)` is assigned the corresponding value (0). The `Male` gadget changes color, and the `Female` gadget is filled with the normal background color. The next block checks to see if the click was in the `Female` gadget or not. If so, `Speech%(3)` is set to 1, the `Male` gadget is filled with the normal background color, and the `Female` gadget changes color.

The third Human gadget produces inflected speech when clicked. Speech% (1) is set to zero, and the gadgets change color accordingly: Human on, Comp. off. The fourth Comp. gadget accomplishes exactly the opposite of the Human gadget when clicked. Inflected speech is toggled to the monotone voice. Speech% (1) is set to 1, the Human gadget is filled with the background color, and the Comp. gadget changes color.

The next routine accepts the input of the string to be spoken. Note that this input must be ended with <RETURN> before normal event trapping can resume. If the coordinates of the mouse click are within the Speak gadget, a SAY command uses all of the present data, and presents you with the desired (or undesired) speech.

Saving the data

The next program routine controls the storage of the DATA file. We use the text window for filename input. We clear space with SPACE$ and read the name in (= and * can be used as abbreviations for the last-used name). If the name is not a null string, the file opens.

We're doing something tricky here, since the computer cannot tell the difference between a sequential file and a BASIC program in ASCII format. We are writing a series of commands into a file that we can later add to another program using MERGE.

The REM line simply gives credit where credit is due—it tells where the data came from. The next line contains the DATA statement, followed by eight single numbers from Speech% (x) separated by commas. The ninth value is written by itself following the loop, because the last value after a DATA statement cannot be followed by a comma. This completes the routine, and the file can be closed.

Altname$ stores the present filename so that we can use the abbreviations = and * next time. Now we have to pay for all of this user-friendliness and put everything back the way it was before we started. A SPACE$ removes the filename and the old Text$ is put back in its place. PAINT fills the Store gadget blue (it was orange during the save operation).

The RETURN at the end of the ReadMouse: routine returns control to the MainLoop: section, where the infinite WHILE...WEND loop does what it does best.

We are still missing the subroutine that positions the gadgets and field choices at the beginning of the program:

```
ShowValue:¶
  LOCATE 2,9 : PRINT  SPACE$(54)¶
  LOCATE 2,9 : PRINT  Text$¶
  IF Speech%(3)=0 THEN¶
    PAINT (422,32),3,1 : PAINT (512,32),0,1¶
  ELSE¶
    PAINT (422,32),0,1 : PAINT (512,32),3,1¶
  END IF¶
  IF Speech%(1)=0 THEN¶
    PAINT (422,59),3,1 : PAINT (512,59),0,1¶
  ELSE¶
    PAINT (422,59),0,1 : PAINT (512,59),3,1¶
  END IF¶
¶
  FreqValue=((320-Speech%(0))/255)*130¶
  LINE (35,31+FreqValue)-(70,31+FreqValue)¶
  LINE (41,31)-(64,31+FreqValue),0,bf¶
  LINE (41,32+FreqValue)-(64,159),3,bf¶
  ¶
  SpeedValue=((400-Speech%(2))/360)*130¶
  LINE (115,31+SpeedValue)-(150,31+SpeedValue)¶
  LINE (121,31)-(144,31+SpeedValue),0,bf¶
  LINE (121,32+SpeedValue)-(144,159),3,bf¶
  ¶
  TuningValue=((28000-Speech%(4))/23000)*130¶
  LINE (200,31+TuningValue)-(235,31+TuningValue)¶
  LINE (206,31)-(229,31+TuningValue),0,bf¶
  LINE (206,32+TuningValue)-(229,159),3,bf¶
  ¶
  VolumeValue=((64-Speech%(5))/64)*130¶
  LINE (280,31+VolumeValue)-(315,31+VolumeValue)¶
  LINE (286,31)-(309,31+VolumeValue),0,bf¶
  LINE (286,32+VolumeValue)-(309,159),3,bf¶
  ¶
RETURN¶
```

Some sections of this routine should look familiar to you. They are already in the ReadMouse: section in the same or a similar form. Even so, you should not neglect to write them again in a single subprogram, because this is necessary to complete the screen construction. If we left the ShowValue: subroutine out of the program, the individual sliders would not appear on the screen until they were used for the first time. Every slider also has a "notch" in its original position. This makes it easier to find the standard values later.

If you use your own values in the DATA line in the StartingValues: routine, the notches will correspond to these values. The program considers values in the DATA line to be defaults.

Problem?

If your Amiga displays an Out of memory error, save the program, reload Workbench, restart AmigaBASIC and close all open windows (the **BASICDisk** window, other **Workbench** windows, and the **LIST** window). After this, there should certainly be enough free memory to run the program without worry.

Using the
program

The speech utility is very simple to use. Use the mouse to push the sliders up and down. After you click in the Text field, you can type in the text to be spoken. Remember to press <RETURN> before you use the mouse again. Event trapping notices the mouse clicks, but cannot do anything about it while an INPUT statement is active.

You can use the designated gadgets to choose whether the voice sounds male or female, and inflected or monotone. A click in the Speak gadget tells the Amiga to speak the current text using the current speech parameters. The program must access Workbench before the Amiga can speak.

If you like the resulting voice, you can save the current values using a click in the Store gadget. This produces an ASCII file that can be added to another program with MERGE.

Save the speech utility with its final corrections. Now for a demonstration: Create a pleasant voice and save it on the diskette. Call your file speechdata. Then clear the LIST window (type NEW) and type in this small example program:

```
FOR x=0 TO 8¶
   READ a%(x)    ¶
NEXT x¶
SAY TRANSLATE$("Hello Amiga."),a%¶
```

Now we type the MERGE command in the **BASIC** window:

```
MERGE "speechdata"¶
```

This will add two new lines to your program:

```
REM DATAs made with AmigaBASIC-Talker¶
DATA ...¶
```

The DATA line contains all the values for the voice that you selected.

One final tip: if you are using the speech utility to develop a larger program, just use the RAM disk. Use a name with the format RAM:speechdata and MERGE from the RAM disk later. This works much more quickly and does not use up space on your diskette. However, if you want to keep your little DATA programs, you still have to save them on a diskette. You can assemble your own collection of voices on the diskette. Soon you'll have a rich selection of voices from which to choose when your Amiga has something to say.

Sound and music

7

7

From special F/X to symphonies: Sound and music

Now that we have covered one of the speech capabilities of the Amiga, let's discuss musical possibilities. The Amiga hardware that generates the speech is so powerful that you can use it to easily make very complex special effects and music. However, there is one small problem which needs attention. The full capabilities of the hardware are not supported 100% by AmigaBASIC. While virtually all of the Amiga's abilities discussed so far have been accessible through complex and powerful BASIC commands, music and sound output is produced by two seemingly limited commands.

7.1 The fourth teaser: the music of Star Wars

All the information in the following sections focus on tone production in AmigaBASIC. You shouldn't expect to produce the sort of music you see in a professional music program or in Workbench demos, but this next program shows what you can do in AmigaBASIC without a lot of hard work:

```
GetInfo:¶
    READ freq,dur¶
    IF freq=-1 THEN SOUND RESUME : END¶
    SOUND WAIT¶
    SOUND freq,dur,21,0¶
    SOUND freq/2,dur,127,1¶
    SOUND freq*2,dur,21,2¶
    GOTO GetInfo¶
¶
    DATA 523.25,15,784,15,698.48,6¶
    DATA 659.28,6,587.28,6,1046.52,15¶
    DATA 784,17,-1,-1¶
```

Sounds familiar
We've programmed the music from one of our favorite films. This program performs the first few measures of the theme from Star Wars™. If by chance the music doesn't sound as smooth and melodic as you remember it from your last visit to the theater, take another look at the DATA statements. You may have made an error typing them in.

7.2

Let's play some music: the SOUND command

The SOUND command plays a critical role in producing all types of sounds and notes. You've already seen SOUND at work in previous programs. For example, the SOUND command was used to create a warning beep in the paint program. This sort of task is pretty boring for an artist like SOUND. But like most artists, SOUND is a freelancer, and has to accept whatever work comes along.

BEEP

There is also a BEEP command for producing warning tones. This command produces the familiar Amiga beep and screen flash that lets the user know something is wrong. BEEP produces a note with a fixed frequency (pitch) and duration.

SOUND

The SOUND command, on the other hand, is extremely flexible when it comes to both frequency and duration. SOUND can do even more than that, but we will talk about that soon.

Music-it's all physics

Physical science says that music and sound are nothing more than vibrations in the air which are received and processed by the human ear. The *frequency* of a tone is the number of cycles (vibrations) that the tone makes in one second. The more cycles per second, the higher the tone. The unit for cycles per second is *hertz*, named after Heinrich Rudolf Hertz, the German physicist who discovered electromagnetic waves. If that discovery doesn't mean much to you, remember that his work helped to make radio and television possible.

A radio, cassette recorder, or any stereo component handles the music as a series of electrical signals, which are then sent to one or more speakers. A magnet in the speaker causes a paper or plastic cone to vibrate. This causes the air around the cone to vibrate, and we hear these vibrations as music.

The sound synthesis on your Amiga works in exactly the same way. The chip responsible for tone production creates an electrical signal of corresponding frequency and sends it to one or both sound outputs. Like with a stereo component, this signal must be amplified before it can be sent to the speakers. The Amiga monitor has a small amplifier and speaker built into it.

Controlling the frequency

Enough theory for now. Let's get back to the Amiga. You can use SOUND to input the frequency of a tone directly. The Amiga can produce tones from 20 to 1500 hertz. Any moderately good stereo system can handle notes in this range.

Controlling duration

The other important value is the duration of the tone. Allowed values are 0 through 77. A 0 produces no tone at all; a 1 produces a very short tone; a 77 produces a tone of approximately four seconds' length. It's possible to control the duration of the tone more precisely, but that is not important to us right now. The following command:

```
SOUND 440,18¶
```

produces a 440-hertz tone that lasts for about one second. This frequency is the international standard for "A", for those of you who are accomplished musicians. For those of you who aren't, the international standard "A" is the note to which every musician (supposedly) tunes.

The following command:

```
SOUND 500,10¶
```

produces a tone that's a little higher-pitched and shorter. If you want to find out the values responsible for the infamous Amiga BEEP, try this:

```
SOUND 880, 3¶
```

If you're interested, 880 hertz is the "A" one octave above the "A" you heard before. Do you want to hear your Amiga through its entire range? No problem—just type in:

```
FOR x=20 TO 1500 STEP 10 : SOUND x,1 : NEXT X¶
```

Do yourself and your ears a favor and turn the volume down a bit before you press <RETURN>. It is an interesting acoustical phenomenon that the human ear hears the medium frequency tones as louder than the extremely high and low frequency tones. Also, very high tones played at high volume can be very unpleasant to hear.

STEP

We used STEP 10 in the FOR line to avoid having to wait several minutes for the computer to finish. If you're curious, you can delete that statement and see how long it takes.

With what you know so far, you can already produce all kinds of beeps and tones. The only way you know to find the right tone is by trial and error—but that will change soon.

Perhaps you think it's inconvenient to have to change your volume control all the time. It's easy enough on your monitor, but maybe your stereo is on the other side of the room. Then you have to keep walking back and forth to change the volume control.

Volume

AmigaBASIC has the solution: The third value of the SOUND command. You can enter a value for *volume* just as you did with SAY. This time, the allowed values are 0 (no sound) through 255 (maximum loudness). If you do not enter a value for volume, AmigaBASIC uses the default value 127—right in the middle.

Compare this command:

SOUND 880,10,48

with this command:

SOUND 880, 10, 255

Yes, the Amiga is quite a screamer. Let's listen to the same tone with increasing volume:

FOR x=0 TO 255 : SOUND 880,1,x : NEXT x

This volume control is also quite helpful for warning beeps. You can use it to make tones more or less noticeable. For music, it is indispensible because *dynamics* (the relative loudness of musical passages to one another) are an important aspect of music.

Voice

The fourth and last value that you can include with a SOUND command is the *voice*. It determines which of the four stereo channels your signal will use. Unlike the SAY command, SOUND can use only one channel at a time (0, 1, 2, or 3). It's easy to remember: 0 and 3 are left channels, 1 and 2 are right channels. Channel 0 is the default value.

You need a stereo to actually hear output come from the left or right, but the four channels have their uses in mono as well. You can use the channels to play four different notes at the same time. For example, the demonstration program used three tones at the same time. You have to learn two more commands to make sure that all of the notes play simultaneously. Please be patient a little longer.

In stereo

When you combine volume control and channel assignment, interesting things can happen. A tone that gets softer in the left channel and louder in the right seems to travel from left to right. Let's try it. Type this short program in the **LIST** window:

```
FOR x=0 TO 255¶
        SOUND 440,1,x,0¶
        SOUND 440,1,255-x,1¶
NEXT x¶
```

Add the same code written "in reverse" to create an acoustical tennis match.

Now we're familiar with the SOUND command, but our examples so far have been less than melodic. You need information about frequencies to play notes. Our system is based on A-440 (440 hertz). Let's look at the *octave* in which this note falls. (An octave is the interval from one "C" to the next.) Table 11 has all the information you really need to make music:

Table 11: Frequencies in one octave

Note name	Frequency (in hertz)	Note name	Frequency (in hertz)
C	261.63	G	392.00
D	293.66	A	440.00
E	329.63	B	493.88
F	349.23	C	523.25

The principle behind calculating frequencies is fairly simple. The frequency doubles with every octave. In the next higher octave, the "A" is 880 hertz, the "F" 698.46 hertz, and so on. Divide the values by two, and you go an octave lower. For example, the "A" in the next lower octave is 220 hertz. Notes lower than the "C" (130.82 hertz) in this octave are almost worthless for music, because notes begin to sound like low rumblings from about 100 hertz on down. Table 12 contains the most usable musical frequencies, to save you the trouble of calculating the notes everytime.

Table 12: SOUND command notes and frequencies

Note name, octave no.	Frequency (in hertz)	Note name, octave no.	Frequency (in hertz)
c,1	130.82	c,3	523.28
d,1	146.83	d,3	587.28
e,1	164.82	e,3	659.28
f,1	174.62	f,3	698.48
g,1	196.00	g,3	784.00
a,1	220.00	a,3	880.00
b,1	246.94	b,3	987.76
c,2	261.63	c,4	1046.52
d,2	293.66	d,4	1174.52
e,2	329.63	e,4	1318.52
f,2	349.23	f,4	1396.92
g,2	392.00	g,4	1568.00
a,2	440.00	a,4	1760.00
b,2	493.88	b,4	1975.52
c,5	2093.00		

The 2093 hertz "C" is already a bit high. Higher frequencies will hardly sound musical.

Now you can find out which notes were used in our Star Wars sample by looking up the values from the DATA line in the table. When you compose music, it will be the other way around. You will know the notes first, and will have to look up the frequencies in the table.

Now all you need is information about tone duration. This is not measured in seconds, but in smaller units, so that 18.2 duration units equal one second. Table 13 contains more accurate values:

Table 13: Tone lengths in seconds and equivalents for SOUND

Duration in seconds	SOUND duration units	Duration in seconds	SOUND duration units
0.1	1.8	0.8	14.6
0.2	3.6	1.0	18.2
0.4	7.3	2.0	36.4
0.5	9.1	3.0	54.6
0.6	10.9	4.0	72.8

You can use this table to compute any duration. If you need 3.5 seconds, just add the value for 3.0 seconds with the value for 0.5—that is, $54.6 + 9.1 = 63.7$. Therefore, a tone duration value of 63.7 produces a three & one half second tone.

We just played it by ear when we assigned tone durations in the demonstration program. Try experimenting with the tempo in this latest program to see how it sounds.

Now you are prepared to program your own songs if you want to. Try a folk tune or, if you're feeling really ambitious, something classical like Beethoven's Symphony #5.

7.3

Hurry up and wait:
SOUND WAIT and SOUND RESUME

The SOUND command plays notes in sequence, one after the other. A SOUND command does not normally start until the tones from any preceding SOUND commands are finished. The rest of the program can usually run in the background. While the Amiga is making music, AmigaBASIC can devote itself to other problems. This means that all you have to do to keep music playing constantly is stick a note here and there in the program. Don't overdo it, though. Every note takes some memory space, and if you try to encode an entire symphony, you will probably get an Out of memory error message.

SOUND WAIT

We've already said that it's possible to play up to four notes at once. How is this done? You need a command that prevents the notes from being played immediately: SOUND WAIT.

SOUND RESUME

All SOUND commands following SOUND WAIT are stored in sequence without being played, until a SOUND RESUME command is encountered. SOUND RESUME plays all of the notes stored since the previous SOUND WAIT according to the following rule: Tones that are assigned to the same channel are played one at a time in sequence. Tones assigned to different channels are played simultaneously.

First, let's try this:

```
SOUND WAIT¶
SOUND 440,10¶
SOUND 880,10¶
SOUND RESUME¶
```

The notes are played one after the other because they are both assigned to the default channel, 0. Now try this:

```
SOUND WAIT¶
SOUND 261.63,36,,0¶
SOUND 329.63,36,,1¶
SOUND 392,36,,2¶
SOUND RESUME¶
```

The notes of this musical triad are played simultneously, because they use different channels. If you want to compose musical pieces where notes in different channels are played for different durations, you have to fill unused channels with zero-volumes so that the right notes stay together. A short table should make this more clear:

**Table 14:
Sounds and
channels**

Tones→ channels ↓	1st tone	2nd tone	3rd tone	4th tone	5th tone	6th tone	7th tone
0	523.25	784	698.48	659.28	587.28	1046.52	784
1	659.28	987.76	0	0	0	1318.52	987.76
2	784.00	1174.52	0	0	0	1568	1174.52
3	-	-	-	-	-	-	-

If channels 1 and 2 are not filled with "null" notes between the third and
fifth notes, the sixth notes of these channels would be played with the
third note of channel 0. Look at the table closely, and the last sentence
should become clear.

Would you like to hear the results? Type the following program into
your **LIST** window:

```
SOUND WAIT¶
¶
GetInfo:¶
   READ freq,dur,vol,chl¶
   IF freq=-1 THEN Play¶
   SOUND freq,dur,vol,chl¶
GOTO GetInfo:¶
¶
Play:¶
   SOUND RESUME¶
¶
DATA 523.23,15,127,0,  659.28,15,96,1,  784,15,96,2¶
DATA 784.15,15,222,0,  987.76,15,180,1,  1174.52,15,180,2¶
DATA 698.48,6,127,0,  0,6,0,1,  0,6,0,2¶
DATA 659.28,6,127,0,  0,6,0,1,  0,6,0,2¶
DATA 587.28,6,127,0,  0,6,0,1,  0,6,0,2¶
DATA 1046.52,15,225,0,  1318.52,15,180,1,  1568,15,180,2¶
DATA 784,24,180,0,  987.76,24,160,1,  1174.52,24,160,2¶
DATA -1,-1,-1,-1¶
```

Sounds good, doesn't it? The DATA lines correspond exactly with the
above table. The GetInfo: loop reads in all of the values for the
SOUND command, and SOUND writes all of the values into a line where
they wait to be played. When the value -1 is read in as a frequency, then
the program knows that there is no more DATA, and exits.

If the melody is too high for your tastes, just divide the frequency by
two after it is read in:

```
SOUND freq/2,time,volume,chl
```

Now, the song plays an octave lower. But don't use frequencies much
higher or lower than these two octaves.

These commands give you a lot to play with when you compose
music. But stay tuned—it gets better.

7.4   Listen up: a bit of acoustical theory

Before we explore any more of AmigaBASIC's musical talents, let's cover some more theory and fundamentals so that you can better understand what is being explained.

You already know that a tone is a vibration in the air. Every device that produces any kind of music must therefore produce the right vibrations.

Vibrations

A musical instrument starts the vibration from a string (guitar, violin, piano), a membrane or hard object (percussion instruments) or a column of air (organ, brasses or woodwinds). Stereo equipment, electronic musical instruments and computers use an *oscillator* to produce electronic vibrations. An amplifier sends the speaker an electrical signal, stronger or weaker depending on the vibration, based on the signal from the attached equipment. The characteristics of the tone depend on the qualities of the vibration.

To better comprehend the characteristics of these air vibrations, they can be compared to the ripples made in a body of water when you drop a stone into the water. The change in air density follows a similar pattern to the ripples on the surface.

A typical sound *waveform* is the sine wave, similar to the one we worked on in Chapter 2.

Sine waves

If you talk about a sine wave in reference to tones, it means that the vibration moves up and down according to the SIN function. For audible sound, this is generally pretty fast—440 times per second for our "A", for example.

Take a look at Figure 19. This sine curve stands for a complete vibration. The curve begins at the level of the middle line, climbs up, falls back to the level of the middle line, keeps falling, and then climbs back up. When the curve gets back to the middle line, one cycle has been completed. This vibration must take place 440 times per second for us to hear an "A" in our basic octave. The more vibrations per second, the higher the tone.

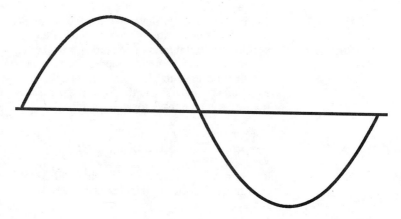

**Figure 19:
A sine wave**

Vibrations below a certain frequency, in the neighborhood of 20 hertz, are no longer heard as tones. We still hear low-frequency vibrations when they are very large, as when someone slams a door. To repeat, the pitch of a tone depends on the frequency of the vibration.

Amplitude

The volume also depends on the vibration. The higher the wave, the louder we hear it. The height of a wave—that is, the distance from the highest point of the wave to the middle line—is called the *amplitude*. The amplitude of the wave is responsible for the loudness of the tone.

Timbre

Other properties of the wave influence the tone produced. The waveform also determines the *timbre* (pronounced either "timber" or "tamber", depending on the musician you ask) or *tone color* of a particular musical instrument or sound. We will cover this in more detail in the next section.

Analog and digital music

Until recently only the "analog" method was used to store and replay sound. When you play a record, the phonograph needle vibrates, and the amplifier changes these vibrations into electrical signals that are output to the speakers. Tapes and cassettes work similarly, except that tapes have a variable magnetic signal which the tape head can read.

In recent years, a computer concept has found its way into the home in the form of CDs (compact disks) and synthesizers: *digital recording*. "Digital" involves bits and computers. Small wonder that this concept is used in the Amiga. How does it work? The Amiga is made to store and process numbers, and does that best. Digital recording, storage, and replay is achieved by representing analog vibrations as digital values.

Basics of digital recording

The principle is simple. Let's look at how tones are digitally recorded and stored on CDs. Several thousand times per second, the present position of the vibration is recorded and converted to a number. If the position of the vibration is recorded often enough, the resulting series of numbers quite accurately represents the actual wave. These numbers can then be used to play the sound back. The frequency (tone), the amplitude (loudness) and the form of the wave can thus be divided into fragments and put back together again.

The process of representing vibrations using numbers is called *sampling*. The realism of a sampled sound depends mainly on the *sampling frequency*, or number of amplitude readings made at a time. The sampling frequency can run up to 30,000 values per second on the Amiga. A CD player samples disk data more than 40,000 times per second.

Paula

Playback, or synthesis, of music simply reverses the recording process. The chip inside the Amiga which is responsible for sound synthesis (we call it *Paula*) converts designated digital values in memory into analog electrical signals. For this purpose, Paula is equipped with a *digital/analog* (D/A) *converter*. These are electronic circuits that read in a digital number (a byte, for example), and create an electrical signal with an intensity corresponding to the number. This electrical signal then needs only to be sent to Amiga's sound output port and sent to the speaker(s). A digital sound is born. Because Paula has four of these D/A converters, we have four stereo channels to work with.

7.5 Splish, splash: waveforms

You already know which characteristics of a sound wave are responsible for volume and pitch: the frequency dictates the pitch, and the amplitude dictates the volume. The *waveform* is sometimes even more important. It determines the tonal characteristics of a note. If you sampled sound from a musical instrument or any other specific tone generator and turned the sample into a graphic representation, you would see a characteristic waveform for every instrument chosen. A sine wave sounds very soft and harmonic. Pure sine waves do not occur in nature, however. Percussion instruments like the drum produce irregular, sharp-edged waveforms.

The higher the sampling rate, the better the original wave can be reproduced. Perhaps you have already seen and heard programs that play short musical passages with amazingly good fidelity. These programs use a very high sampling rate and play only a short passage of a digitized piece of music. Usually, the memory is used up in just a few seconds. In these cases, 512K is not much memory at all. A compact disk, which can play about 70 minutes of acoustically high-quality music, has a storage capacity of 550 megabytes.

WAVE

Despite these limitations, the music reproducing capabilities of the Amiga should not be ignored. AmigaBASIC itself remains pretty quiet about what these capabilities are. There are only two commands for producing tones: SOUND and WAVE. You already know about the SOUND command. WAVE allows you to vary the waveform.

AmigaBASIC normally uses the sine wave. This is all we have heard in our examples so far. If you want to use another waveform, start by dimensioning an integer array with at least 256 elements. The numbers in the array can range between -128 and 127. Each element represents an analog/digital conversion of 8 bits. The digital values resulting from the conversion are 8-bit numbers.

For comparison, a CD player reads digital values of 16 bits. This does not mean that the CD player delivers sound twice as good as the Amiga's. Various hardware and software tricks allow the Amiga to produce tones that sound considerably better than you might expect.

Now, back to WAVE. In the WAVE array, the value -128 means that the wave has the lowest possible value below the middle line. Likewise, 127 is the largest value above the middle line for the vibration. You can write a program to calculate the values used to produce a waveform for Amiga tone reproduction. But what should the waveforms look like?

Triangle wave

There are other waveforms besides the sine wave, and they all yield different tonal results. First, we have the *trianglewave*. This runs similarly to the sine wave, but sounds "sharper" because the vibration changes values abruptly, rather than gradually as in the sine curve. There is a drawing of a triangular wave in Figure 20.

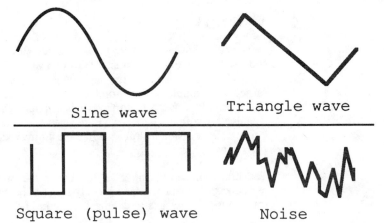

Sine wave   Triangle wave

**Figure 20:
Different
waveforms**

Square (pulse) wave   Noise

Let's try this new waveform with our three-voice Star Wars program. Add the following segment to the beginning of the program:

```
DIM triangle%(255) ¶
    FOR x=0 TO 62¶
      a=a+2¶
      triangle%(x)=a¶
    NEXT x¶
    FOR x=63 TO 188¶
      a=a-2¶
      triangle%(x)=a¶
    NEXT x¶
    FOR x=189 TO 255¶
      a=a+2¶
      triangle%(x)=a¶
    NEXT x¶
    WAVE 0,triangle%¶
    WAVE 1,triangle%¶
    WAVE 2,triangle%¶
    ERASE triangle%¶
```

First, we need to define the integer array triangle%. The first FOR...NEXT loop calculates the array elements for the segment of the triangular wave that goes from the starting point to the high extreme value. The next loop produces the values for the descent to the lowest extreme. Finally, the third loop takes care of the climb back to the starting point. Take a quick look at Figure 20 and compare the lines drawn in the graphic to the corresponding program commands.

Changing
waveforms

The WAVE commands converts the three voices we use to correspond with the array triangle%. If you wanted to, you could use a different waveform for each of the Amiga's four voices. Each WAVE statement assigns its voice a section of memory, for storage of sampling values. Once this memory has been allocated, we no longer need the array triangle% unless we are going to use it later. Since we're not going to use it later in the Star Wars theme program, clear out the array with ERASE. If you have a lot of these waveforms or are writing a large program, it's a good idea to ERASE them once they are assigned to voices. Otherwise you waste a lot of memory.

When you run the program, you'll notice that the tones sound a little different. This new waveform also stays in effect when you return to direct mode. This allows you to try some quick and easy experiments right in the **BASIC** window. For example, you'll notice that the BEEP sounds different than before. This is because the BEEP is sent through channel 0.

If you want to go back to the old familiar BEEP, just type in:

```
WAVE 0, SIN¶
```

This command sets the waveform for channel 0 back to a sine wave. SIN is not an integer array, but an option of the WAVE command that allows you to quickly restore the default sine wave.

Square
waves

The next waveform we'll look at is the square wave. This waveform consists only of jumps from one amplitude to another. This produces a wooden sound. Look at Figure 20 for a graph of this waveform. If you want to hear a square wave, store the triangular version of the Star Wars program and edit the beginning routine so that it looks like this:

```
DIM rectangle%(256) ¶
FOR x=0 TO 127¶
   rectangle%(x)=127¶
NEXT x¶
FOR x=128 TO 256¶
   rectangle%(x)=-128¶
NEXT x¶
¶
WAVE 0,rectangle%¶
WAVE 1,rectangle%¶
WAVE 2,rectangle%¶
¶
ERASE rectangle%¶
```

The rest of the program needs no changes. A square wave is very easy to construct. In the first half of the data field, you read in the maximum value 127, and in the second half read the lowest possible value -128. If you want to store this program, remember to give it a new name like square.

White noise

The fourth waveform is *white noise*. This wave doesn't follow any hard and fast rules—it's actually a random sound. The result often sounds like an electric bell or an alarm clock buzzer. With lower frequencies, you can also imitate explosions and other sound effects. Figure 20 shows a typical white noise waveform.

```
DIM noise%(255)¶
FOR x=0 TO 255¶
  noise%(x)=RND*255-128¶
NEXT x¶
WAVE 0,noise%¶
WAVE 1,noise%¶
WAVE 2,noise%¶
ERASE noise%¶
```

If you save the new routine, don't forget to assign it a new name.

The formula RND*255-128 chooses a random number between -128 and 127. This is the range allowed for sampling values.

Now you are familiar with three different computer-produced waveforms. The triangular wave sounds somewhat sharper and clearer than the sine wave. The square wave sounds wooden but clear. The white noise usually sounds pretty bad.

It's interesting to note that lower notes sound better in the square and white noise waveforms than the same notes with the sine wave or the triangular wave.

If you are the curious type, you'll want to try out several other waveforms. Next you'll write a utility to make this testing easier. This is also the last utility program that we'll write together in this book— but the book isn't over yet....

7.6

Grand Finale:
the synthesizer utility

This synthesizer program is certainly no substitute for commercial music programs like Musicraft™, Instant Music™ or the Deluxe Music Construction Set™. Using AmigaBASIC alone, is impossible to produce music comparable with what these packages can do.

This program is designed to produce various waveforms for you to try out. If you find a sound that you like, you can save the WAVE data array and then use it later in your own programs. Type in the program now:

```
Setup:¶
  DIM Waveform%(256)¶
  DEF FNYWaveform(a)=ABS(Waveform%(a)-128)¶
  ¶
  SCREEN 1,320,200,2,1¶
  WINDOW 2,"Waveform",(0,0)-(256,63),22,1¶
  FOR x=0 TO 256¶
    Waveform%(x)=127*SIN(x/20)¶
  NEXT x¶
¶
¶
  WINDOW 3,"Function",(195,80)-(310,175),22,1¶
  WINDOW OUTPUT 3¶
  LINE (5,5)-(55,30),1,b¶
  PSET (5,17)¶
  FOR x=0 TO 48¶
    LINE -((x+5),17-10*SIN(x/3.8))¶
  NEXT x¶
  LINE (59,5)-(110,30),1,b¶
  LINE (59,18)-(67,7) : LINE -(83,27)¶
  LINE -(99,7) : LINE -(107,18)¶
  LINE (5,35)-(55,60),1,b¶
  LINE (7,47)-(7,37)¶
  LINE -(18,37) : LINE -(18,57)¶
  LINE -(30,57) : LINE -(30,37)¶
  LINE -(41,37) : LINE -(41,57)¶
  LINE -(53,57) : LINE -(53,47)¶
  LINE (59,35)-(110,60),1,b¶
  LOCATE 6,7 : PRINT "Clear"¶
  LINE (5,65)-(55,90),1,b¶
  LOCATE 9,2 : PRINT "Save"¶
  LINE (59,65)-(110,90),1,b¶
  LOCATE 9,7 : PRINT "Load"¶
  ¶
  WINDOW OUTPUT 2¶
  GOSUB ShowWave¶
¶
¶
  ON MOUSE GOSUB MouseControl¶
```

```
    MOUSE ON¶
  ¶
    WINDOW 3¶
  ¶
KeyInput:¶
  a$=INKEY$¶
  F=0¶
  IF a$="" THEN F=0 : GOTO KeyInput¶
  IF a$=CHR$(9) THEN F=261.63¶
  IF a$="1" THEN F=277.18¶
  IF a$="q" THEN F=293.66¶
  IF a$="2" THEN F=311.13¶
  IF a$="w" THEN F=329.63¶
  IF a$="e" THEN F=349.23¶
  IF a$="4" THEN F=369.99¶
  IF a$="r" THEN F=392!¶
  IF a$="5" THEN F=415.3¶
  IF a$="t" THEN F=440!¶
  IF a$="6" THEN F=466.16¶
  IF a$="y" THEN F=493.88¶
  IF a$="u" THEN F=523.25¶
  IF a$="8" THEN F=554.37¶
  IF a$="i" THEN F=587.58¶
  IF a$="9" THEN F=622.25¶
  IF a$="o" THEN F=659.28¶
  IF a$="p" THEN F=698.48¶
  IF a$="-" THEN F=739.99¶
  IF a$="[" THEN F=784!¶
  IF a$="=" THEN F=830.61¶
  IF a$="]" THEN F=880¶
  IF a$=CHR$(93) THEN F=932.33¶
  IF a$=CHR$(13) THEN F=987.76¶
  IF a$=CHR$(139) THEN F=1046.52¶
  IF F=0 THEN KeyInput¶
¶
Play:¶
  Vol=127 : IF F=0 THEN 1=0¶
  SOUND WAIT¶
  SOUND F,3,Vol,0¶
  SOUND F,3,Vol,1¶
  SOUND RESUME¶
GOTO KeyInput¶
¶
MouseControl:¶
  IF WINDOW(0)=2 THEN AlterWaveform¶
  IF WINDOW(0)=3 THEN AlterFunction¶
RETURN¶
¶
AlterWaveform:¶
  WINDOW 2¶
  WHILE MOUSE(0)<0¶
    x=MOUSE(5) ¶
  IF x>256 THEN GOSUB ShowWave : RETURN¶
  IF x<1 THEN x=1¶
  y=MOUSE(6) ¶
  IF y> 63 THEN GOSUB ShowWave :RETURN¶
```

```
      LINE (x-1,FNYWaveform(x-1)/4) - (x,FNYWaveform(x)/4),0¶
      LINE (x-1,FNYWaveform(x-1)/4)-(x,y),1¶
      Waveform%(x)=127-(y*4)¶
WEND¶
   GOSUB ShowWave¶
RETURN¶
¶
AlterFunction:¶
   Test=MOUSE(0)¶
   x=MOUSE(3)¶
   y=MOUSE(4)¶
   IF x>4 AND x<56 AND y>4 AND y<31 THEN¶
      WINDOW 3 : PAINT (7,6),3,1¶
      FOR x=0 TO 256¶
         Waveform%(x)=127*SIN(x/20)¶
      NEXT x¶
      GOSUB ShowWave¶
      WINDOW 3 : PAINT (6,6),0,1¶
   END IF¶
   IF x>58 AND x<111 AND y>4 AND y<31 THEN¶
      WINDOW 3 : PAINT (60,6),3,1¶
      FOR x=0 TO 256¶
         IF x<41 THEN Waveform%(x)=x*3 : a=x*3¶
         IF (x>=41 AND x<126) OR (x>=210) THEN a=a-2.57 :
Waveform%(x)=a¶
         IF x>=126 AND x<210 THEN a=a+2.57 : Waveform%(x)=a¶
      NEXT x¶
      GOSUB ShowWave¶
      WINDOW 3 : PAINT (60,6),0,1¶
   END IF¶
   IF x>4 AND x<61 AND y>34 AND y<61 THEN¶
      WINDOW 3 : PAINT (6,36),3,1¶
      FOR x=0 TO 256¶
         IF x<64 OR (x>=128 AND x<191) THEN
Waveform%(x)=127¶
         IF (x>=64 AND x<128) OR x>192 THEN Waveform%(x)=-
128¶
      NEXT x¶
      GOSUB ShowWave¶
      WINDOW 3 : PAINT (6,36),0,1  ¶
   END IF¶
   IF x>58 AND x<111 AND y>34 AND y<61 THEN¶
      WINDOW 3¶
      PAINT (60,36),3,1¶
      FOR x=0 TO 256¶
         Waveform%(x)=0¶
      NEXT x¶
      GOSUB ShowWave¶
      WINDOW 3 : PAINT (60,36),0,1¶
   END IF¶
   IF x>4 AND x<61 AND y>64 AND y<91 THEN¶
      WINDOW 3¶
      PAINT (6,66),3,1¶
      GOSUB EnterName¶
         IF Nam$="" THEN PAINT (6,66),0,1 : RETURN¶
         OPEN Nam$ FOR OUTPUT AS 1¶
```

```
        FOR x=0 TO 256¶
            PRINT #1,CHR$(127-Waveform%(x));¶
        NEXT x¶
      CLOSE 1¶
      WINDOW 3 : PAINT (6,66),0,1¶
    END IF¶
    IF x>58 AND x<111 AND y>64 AND y<91 THEN¶
      WINDOW 3¶
      PAINT (62,66),3,1¶
      GOSUB EnterName¶
      IF Nam$="" THEN PAINT (62,66),0,1 : RETURN¶
      OPEN Nam$ FOR INPUT AS 1¶
        FOR x=0 TO 256¶
          Waveform%(x)=127-ASC(INPUT$(1,1))¶
        NEXT x¶
      CLOSE 1¶
      WINDOW 3 : PAINT (62,66),0,1¶
      GOSUB ShowWave¶
    END IF¶
RETURN¶
¶
ShowWave:¶
  WINDOW 2 : CLS¶
    FOR x=1 TO 256¶
      LINE (x-1,FNYWaveform(x-1)/4)-
(x,FNYWaveform(x)/4),1¶
    NEXT x¶
  WINDOW 3¶
  WAVE 0,Waveform%¶
  WAVE 1,Waveform%¶
RETURN¶
¶
EnterName:¶
  WINDOW 4,"Enter Filename:",(5,100)-(300,110),0,1¶
  CLS : LINE INPUT Nam$ ¶
  IF Nam$="=" OR Nam$="*" THEN Nam$=Altname$¶
  IF Nam$<>"" THEN Altname$=Nam$¶
  WINDOW CLOSE 4 : WINDOW 3¶
RETURN¶
```

Save the program immediately.

In the Setup: segment, we start out by dimensioning the integer array Waveform%. We can use 257 individual values for our waveform.

DEF FN

The next command, DEF FN, is one you haven't used or really needed yet. This command is helpful in programs that have to perform a lot of calculations. DEF FN stands for DEFine FunctioN. It allows you to define your own BASIC functions.

y=SIN(x) is a function that's built into AmigaBASIC. If, for example, you wanted to use the   following function repeatedly throughout a program:

y=SIN(x)*COS(x)+0.5*(SIN(x)-COS(x))

then it would be unnecessary to type in the entire line every time you use it. You could save a lot of effort and make your program much easier to read if you type a line like this:

DEF FNhello(x)=SIN(x)*COS(x)+ 0.5*(SIN(x)-COS(x))

at the beginning of the program. From then on, you could specify the function FNhello instead of that long formula. The name of the function is hello; the prefix FN distinguishes it from normal variables. If you type PRINT FNhello(1), AmigaBASIC looks up the function definition and calculates the result for x=1.

One or more variables can follow the function name. Then comes the formula expressed in terms of these parameters. You can use the variable names in the definition line quite normally in the rest of the program. The function definition does not process them in any way, but uses them only as a method of expressing the procedure to be performed.

Let's look at another example, this time a simple one: DEF FNdouble(x)=2*x. Whenever the line FNdouble(2) appears in the program, AmigaBASIC looks for the definition of FNdouble and then knows that it must do to the 2 in the command line what the definition line tells it to do with the x. If you call a function that is not defined with DEF FN, you'll get an Undefined user function error message.

DEF FN *in our program*
We use the function FNYWaveform to convert the values we used for field definition into integers between 0 and 255. If you remember, WAVE fields have to be composed of values between -128 and +127. If you subtract 128 from one of these values and remove the minus sign, we get a number between 0 and 255. In BASIC, all this translates to DEF FNYWaveform(a)=ABS(Waveform%(a)-128).

Our program runs in a low-res screen (320 by 200 points). Next to this, we display a second window which shows us the waveform type.

The synthesizer uses a sine wave as an initial waveform. This wave is a bit different from the default wave that AmigaBASIC normally uses. The FOR...NEXT loop in the Setup: section of the program calculates these initial values.

Waveform gadgets

The window contains the gadgets that you click to specify options. One gadget chooses the sine wave, one a triangular wave, and one for a square wave. We used LINE commands to construct the gadgets. The first gadget has a sine wave drawn inside it, the second gadget has a triangular wave, and third a square wave, using a total of nine lines. Besides these gadgets, there is a gadget for erasing the current wave, one for storing the WAVE array, and one for reading in wave data.

If window 3 is closed, we call ShowWave: to display the present waveform (a sine wave at the beginning of the program) in window 2. The output window for all other functions is window 3. This window must be activated when you play tones (click window 3 after you alter the waveform). AmigaBASIC can receive input from only one window, so we chose window 3 for this. The other windows merely perform event trapping with the mouse.

The keyboard

KeyInput: checks the keyboard input and assigns it to a$. You have simulated the upper and lower rows of a piano keyboard. The keys <TAB>, <Q>, <W>, <E>... <HELP> represent the white keys of the piano. The row of keys above these represents the black keys. We assign a frequency to F depending on the value of a$. You already know the frequencies of the white keys from Table 12. We have calculated the rest; you can see them in the program listing.

Play: plays the tone specified by the keypress. You send one tone to a left channel and one to a right channel. Both tones start at the same time with SOUND RESUME. This means that the music will play off both speakers if you are listening to your Amiga in stereo.

MouseControl: uses the function WINDOW(0) to determine the window in which the mouse was clicked. Depending on the result, the subprogram AlterWaveform: or AlterFunction: is called.

AlterWaveform: makes window 2 an output window. You can use the mouse in this window to input a waveform as you would in the paint program. The present waveform is erased.

Combined waveforms

If you move the mouse out of the window (IF x>256 or IF y>63), then the subprogram ShowWave: properly combines the new part of the curve with the part of the old curve which has not been erased yet, removing lines from the screen which are no longer relevant. The program returns to AlterWaveform: with RETURN.

The LINE commands erase the old wave segments (color 0) and draw in the new ones (color 1). Finally, the position in Waveform% corresponding to the X-coordinate of the mouse click is given its value. The variable y (the Y-coordinate of the mouse click) lies between 0 and 63, which is the height of the window. To get values between -128 and +127, we use the formula 127-(y*4).

Finally, the subroutine ShowWave: is called at the end of AlterWaveform:. Parts of the old wave which are no longer a part of the array Waveform% will often remain on screen after the new lines are drawn, especially if you move the mouse quickly. For this reason, we always clear the screen and draw the present wave after every change. Besides this, ShowWave: serves to assign the array to the two channels with WAVE.

Changing functions

Next comes the program segment AlterFunction:. This function detects and acts upon clicks in window 3 (titled **Function**). The variables x and y contain the position of the mouse when it was last clicked. The position of the mouse at other times is not important and is not recorded.

The first IF/END IF block checks to see if the click took place in the sine gadget. If so, we store the values for the sine wave in Waveform%, call ShowWave:, and jump back. Whenever a gadget is clicked, it is filled with color before the work begins and then returned to its original color when the work is completed. The next routine for the triangle gadget works exactly the same way. The variable a is counted up and then back down to get the values for the triangular wave. The gadget for the square wave also works this way. The values in Waveform% are 127 for a while, then -128, then 127 again, etc.

The Clear gadget erases the present waveform by simply setting all of the values in Waveform% to zero.

Saving and loading

That leaves the Save and Load gadgets. If the Save gadget is clicked, a sequential file is opened for writing. If the Load gadget is clicked, the file is opened for reading. EnterName: is an old friend from previous programs; it takes care of finding a filename.

That finishes off AlterWaveform:. This just leaves two short subprograms to go.

ShowWave: displays the current waveform in window 2. Once again, FNYWaveform is used to calculate the screen coordinates (we used it before in AlterWaveform:). You calculate the Y-coordinate by dividing the values ranging from 0 to 256 by four. The WAVE commands at the end of the subroutine ensure that the waveforms are used to play the notes.

EnterName: asks for the input of a filename. You can use = or * as an abbreviation for the last name used. We use a fourth window for a short time for this filename input.

Well, that was easy. It's pretty simple to use the program, too.

Using the program

Take the mouse and draw a waveform in the **Waveform** window. If you keep experimenting, you will soon know how different waveforms sound.

You can play notes on the upper two rows of the keyboard. Unfortunately, you can only play one note at a time because the computer can only input one keystroke at a time.

If you want to call up one of the standard waveforms so that you can alter it, just click the corresponding gadget in the Function window. You can also start from scratch by clicking the Clear gadget. Once you do that, you can't make any music until you enter something.

If you like a particular waveform, you can save it by clicking the Save gadget. All you have to do then is supply a filename. A click on Load lets you read in values which have already been saved.

You can read values stored into your own programs with a routine like this:

```
OPEN filename FOR INPUT AS 1¶
     FOR x=0 TO 256¶
          Waveform%(x)=127-ASC(INPUT$(1,1))¶
     NEXT x¶
CLOSE 1¶
```

All you have to do then is assign the waveform array to the voices you want that waveform to have. Remember, you can assign different waveforms to different voices. Every SOUND command uses the waveform of the voice that it chooses.

All that's left to do is wish you the best of luck and lots of fun with your music. As we have said, there's really no more music in AmigaBASIC. But there's more music in the Amiga itself, as anyone who has listened to a professional music program can attest.

Appendices

A   Error and
help messages

This chapter contains an alphabetical listing of all the error messages
that you can run into while working with AmigaBASIC. If you come
across an error number while working with this book or programming,
look in this Appendix to find possible causes and hints to get rid of the
problem.

AmigaBASIC will find some errors before the program runs. Others it
will find only while the program is running. In both cases, the error
will be displayed in the LIST window and an error requester will
appear. You must click the OK gadget in the requester before you can
fix the error. The error numbers included here are used with the ON
ERROR command and the ERR system variable. Appendix B.4
(Program control commands) contains more information about this.

Normal errors are printed here in all uppercase lettering, and include the
error number. The errors found before a program is executed are
displayed in both uppercase and lowercase characters, and have a hyphen
(-) instead of an error number.

ADVANCED FEATURE   Error number: 73

This error will only appear if you use a command that isn't in this
book. This message appears when AmigaBASIC recognizes a command
as legitimate but realizes that it hasn't been implemented in the current
version of AmigaBASIC. We don't know of any such commands. This
error is a holdover from earlier Microsoft BASIC versions.

ARGUMENT COUNT MISMATCH   Error number: 37

This message occurs when you call a subprogram with too many or too
few arguments/values/text. Look at the first line of the subprogram to
find out how many and what sort of arguments are needed. Pass exactly
that many parameters when you call the subprogram.

BAD FILE MODE   Error number: 54

You'll get this error message if you try to use commands that can't be
used with that sort of file. Here are possible reasons for this error:

You tried to use MERGE to append a program that wasn't stored in
ASCII format. You need to load the program and resave the program
using SAVE "program name", A to be able to merge the files.

391

You tried to load a random file with the LOAD command.

You used random file commands in a sequential file (for example, GET or PUT).

You entered a mode other than "I", "O", "A", or "R" for the OPEN command.

BAD FILE NAME   Error number: 64

You gave a filename in an incorrect format (either too long or in a form unacceptable to AmigaBASIC). Section 3.2 describes filename formats. The basic format is:

```
"(device name or drive):(directory)/(directory)/.../
(file name)"¶
```

BAD FILE NUMBER   Error number: 52

This usually means that you gave a file number that wasn't opened yet to a command like PRINT# or INPUT#. Look at the OPEN commands in your program to find the file numbers.

BAD RECORD NUMBER   Error number: 63

You tried to access an illegal record with a GET or PUT command. Legal record numbers range from 0 to 16777215.

BLOCK ELSE/END IF must be the first statement on the line

Error number: −

These two commands must be the first and only command on a line. Otherwise AmigaBASIC can't recognize an IF/ELSE/END IF structure. This problem can usually be avoided by writing structured code. This error is recognized before the program is run.

CAN'T CONTINUE   Error number: 17

This message appears after CONT is input, or when Continue is chosen from the Run pulldown menu. Continuation is possible only if no errors have occurred, and if the program has not been modified since the break. You need to restart the program with the RUN command.

DEADLOCK   Error number: 77

We're not sure about this one: The error message exists, but we can't find any documentation on it. It's probably an operating system message, and not from AmigaBASIC. It could be some sort of internal error.

DEVICE I/O ERROR   Error number: 57

AmigaDOS could not complete an input/output operation. The cause could be a technical problem—with a disk, for example. Usually you need to reload the Workbench when this problem occurs.

DEVICE UNAVAILABLE   Error number: 68

The device is either not connected or not turned on. AmigaBASIC can't access the device. You may need to reload the Workbench.

DISK FULL   Error number: 61

This error usually occurs when you are saving programs or writing data. There isn't enough room on the disk to store your file. Either delete a few programs that you don't want (or copy them to another disk before deleting them) or use a newly formatted disk.

If you come across this error for the first time while working with the Extras diskette in **Chapter 1** of this book, please take a look at **Section 3.1**.

DIVISION BY ZERO   Error number: 11

It is illegal to divide by 0. This error will show up when you do something like PRINT 1/0. It could occur through a variable that hasn't been assigned a value, or from an error in your formula. It is also possible that you mistyped a variable name.

DUPLICATE DEFINITION   Error number: 10

You'll get this error if you try to redimension an array that has already been dimensioned. The array could not be redimensioned because you used a DIM command for this variable name, or because you used the array before using the DIM statement. In this case you can delete the array with the ERASE command. You can find the array's upper and lower limits with UBOUND and LBOUND. If you use the OPTION BASE command after the first DIM in the program, you will get this error message.

DUPLICATE LABEL   Error number: 33

Two different program sections have been assigned the same label. You need to rename one program section. It might be that AmigaBASIC read something as a label that you didn't intend to be a label; delete the colon at the end of a piece of text. It may be that you have mistaken a subprogram for a subroutine, or the other way around. You're allowed to give a subprogram a name that has already been used as a label (that's a bad idea, because it makes the code more difficult to follow), but then the CALL command is needed to avoid confusing the program.

ELSE/ELSE IF/END IF without IF   Error number: -

One of these commands was found even though there isn't an IF to start a legal IF/END IF block. Perhaps you put a command after the THEN in the IF line. You may not do that in an IF/END IF block, or the program won't be able to distinguish the two uses of the IF command. AmigaBASIC finds this error before the program starts.

EXIT SUB outside of a subprogram   Error number: -

The command EXIT SUB may only appear in a block of code that is started with SUB and ended with the END SUB command. You may have put the END SUB too early in the program, or you might have interchanged the END SUB and EXIT SUB commands. AmigaBASIC finds this error before the program starts.

FIELD OVERFLOW   Error number: 50

This error means that in a random file, more buffer bytes should have been assigned in FIELD than were stated in the OPEN command as the file length. Your file structure should be carefully planned in advance so that you'll always know how many bytes will be needed.

FILE ALREADY EXISTS   Error number: 58

You entered a name that already exists with the SAVE or NAME command. Use another name. If you insist on using that name, use CHDIR to move the system into another directory.

FILE ALREADY OPEN   Error number: 55

This message appears when you try to open a file that is already open. AmigaBASIC also displays this message when you try to KILL a file that is presently open. You need to close the file before you can KILL it.

FILE NOT FOUND   Error number: 53

The file you are looking for cannot be found. You may have mistyped the filename. It is also possible that you are in the wrong directory (use FILES to view directories, and CHDIR to change directories).

FOR WITHOUT NEXT   Error number: 26

AmigaBASIC found a FOR that doesn't have a corresponding NEXT. You either forgot the NEXT, or made an error when you typed the counting variable. It works best if you make sure your FOR...NEXT loops match up and avoid putting a variable name behind NEXT.

IF without END IF   Error number: –

If you use an IF/END IF block, you need to put an END IF at the end. You may have forgotten the END IF command. Perhaps you didn't want an IF/END IF block but didn't put anything after the THEN in the IF line. In this case, AmigaBASIC thinks that this is an IF/END IF block. If you don't want to put a command after the THEN, use a REM statement.

Since this error is found before the program starts, it may occur while you are developing a program because you haven't finished programming a line.

ILLEGAL DIRECT   Error number: 12

Some commands may only be used in programs, and cannot be used in direct mode. You'll get this error message when you type program mode commands in the **BASIC** window. The commands DEF FN, COMMON, and SUB are typical examples.

ILLEGAL FUNCTION CALL   Error number: 5

This error occurs when you pass illegal values to a BASIC command. You'll get this error if you use negative values for array elements, or if you use them with the GET and PUT commands.

This error also happens when you attempt to pass parameters to a BASIC command that are too large, too small, or of the wrong type. If this error message appears after LIST, the program was saved in protected form (SAVE "filename", P).

INPUT PAST END   Error number: 62

This message appears when you try to read past the end of a file, or try to read a file that was opened FOR OUTPUT only. Use the EOF and LOF commands to avoid this error.

INTERNAL ERROR   Error number: 51

You can't do anything about this: AmigaBASIC found an internal error. You must reload the AmigaBASIC program.

LINE BUFFER OVERFLOW   Error number: 23

You'll get this message when the screen editor in the LIST window has problems. You may have tried to put too many characters on a line—255 is the maximum number of characters per line.

The cause can also be an error in the screen editor. Try using Cut and Paste from the Edit menu a few times. The error will often disappear.

MISSING OPERAND   Error number: 22

This message appears when you omit a value after a command (like AND, OR, XOR, etc.) or a calculation sign (like +, −, etc.).

Missing STATIC in SUB statement   Error number: −

Every SUB needs a STATIC command. You must enter a STATIC, and if you don't, AmigaBASIC will give you this error message before the program starts.

NEXT WITHOUT FOR   Error number: 1

AmigaBASIC found a NEXT statement that wasn't paired with a FOR statement. This is the logical complement of the "FOR WITHOUT NEXT" error message (see that message for more information).

NO RESUME   Error number: 19

AmigaBASIC can't find a RESUME command inside an ON ERROR routine. RESUME is needed to close the subprogram and jump back to the error's location.

OUT OF DATA   Error number: 4

You reached the end of the DATA statements while READing DATA values. There are no more DATA available. Your program should be able to recognize this on its own. You can, for example, use -1 as the last DATA value and compare the data read with this number. Don't forget that you can change the DATA pointer with the RESTORE command.

OUT OF HEAP SPACE   Error number: 14

This message is pretty frightening the first time it appears. It shows up in red on the screen. This message occurs if there isn't enough system memory to perform your task. Click with the left mouse button to continue. Using the CLEAR command might help; if it doesn't, save your program, restart the Workbench, and click AmigaBASIC. Close extra programs and windows. When there are not any other memory users in the Amiga, you'll have a bit more space.

OUT OF MEMORY   Error number: 7

This message means that the BASIC memory area is out of space. It doesn't necessarily mean that the whole system is out of memory. It only means that your program and your BASIC files together take up too much space. The CLEAR command will often help here (also, see "OUT OF HEAP SPACE" above).

OVERFLOW   Error number: 6

This means that a number is too big to be represented in the numeric format desired (see Intermission 5 for an explanation of number formats). You can usually avoid this error by using double precision variables.

PERMISSION DENIED   Error number: 70

This error usually occurs when you are trying to write to a write-protected disk. If you are sure you want to write on it, take the disk out of the drive when the red light is off and move the write-protect slider. Then put the diskette back in the drive.

RENAME ACROSS DISKS   Error number: 74

You tried to enter a new diskette name for the NAME command in a filename. You may not change the diskette name, however, because the result would be a copying process and not a renaming process.

RESUME WITHOUT ERROR   Error number: 20

AmigaBASIC found a command even though an error hasn't occurred. The program probably got into an ERROR loop accidentally. You should end the main program before ERROR loops and subroutines, or make sure to put jumps before ON ERROR/RESUME blocks. Neither subroutines nor ON ERROR/RESUME blocks are automatically jumped over.

RETURN WITHOUT GOSUB   Error number: 3

AmigaBASIC found a RETURN command, but there was no GOSUB performed beforehand. This usually happens when a program accidently gets into a subroutine. Remember that subroutines aren't automatically executed, even though subprograms are. Your program should jump to another area in the last line before the subroutine.

SHARED outside of a subprogram   Error number: -

You may only use the SHARED command within a subprogram. The END SUB statement could be a few lines too early. Perhaps you interchanged the EXIT SUB and END SUB commands.

Statement illegal within subprogram
                                           Error number: -

Some commands may not be used in a subprogram. You may not use the DEF FN, the COMMON, or the CLEAR commands there. Do not use them between the SUB and END SUB commands.

STRING FORMULA TOO COMPLEX   Error number: 16

You'll get this error if your string commands (MID$, LEFT$, RIGHT$, etc...) are nested too deeply. Divide your formulas into several lines.

STRING TOO LONG   Error number: 15

Strings may be up to 32767 characters long in AmigaBASIC. You'll get this error if a string is any longer than this. Just divide the string into several smaller strings.

SUB already defined   Error number: -

You get this error when you have two subprograms with the same name. You need to rename one of them.

SUBPROGRAM ALREADY IN USE   Error number: 36

A subprogram may call other subprograms, but it may not call itself. This error occurs if a subprogram calls itself.

You'll also get this error if you abort a subprogram, then call it again. In this case, end the old subprogram with CONT, or restart the program with the RUN command.

SUBSCRIPT OUT OF RANGE   Error number: 9

This error happens when you try to access an array element which lies out of the range set by automatic dimensioning. It can also occur when you enter more dimensions than you declared in the DIM statement.

This error is often the result of mistyping an array name. It may be that you are accessing array elements using a variable that has the wrong value.

SUB without END SUB   Error number: -

The SUB and END SUB commands belong together. You'll get this error if you have a SUB command without a corresponding END SUB command. Structured programming helps avoid this problem.

SYNTAX ERROR   Error number: 2

AmigaBASIC understood part of the command, but another part is incorrect—things are in the wrong order, or are being used in the wrong context. There may be an unequal number of left and right parentheses. You'll also get a "Syntax error" if you try to READ a string from a DATA line into a normal variable. See Appendix B if you aren't sure how a particular command should be used.

TOO MANY FILES   Error number: 67

In other BASIC versions created by Microsoft, this means that there are too many files on a disk. That can't happen on the Amiga, since the disk is organized differently here than on other computers. If there isn't any more room on the diskette, the "Disk full" error message is displayed.

You are allowed a maximum of 256 files open simultaneously in AmigaBASIC. Since you'll rarely need that many files, you may never see this error message.

Tried to declare SUB within a SUB   Error number: –

You are not allowed to declare a subprogram inside another subprogram. You may define them one after the other, though.

TYPE MISMATCH   Error number: 13

You'll get this error if you try to assign something in one numeric format to something in another format without converting it first (see Intermission 5 [Amiga number systems] for a detailed description). Variables must be of the same type for the SWAP command as well.

UNDEFINED ARRAY   Error number: 38

You entered the name of a array that doesn't exist in the program behind the SHARED command. Perhaps you didn't intend to use an array name. If not, you need to erase the parentheses behind the variable name.

UNDEFINED LABEL   Error number: 8

You used a label that doesn't exist in the program (probably behind a GOTO or GOSUB statement). See if you mistyped the name. It is common to forget the colon behind labels. However, colons are needed if the label names a line or a program section.

UNDEFINED SUBPROGRAM   Error number: 35

You'll get this message if you call a nonexistent subprogram. You may not realize that you called a subprogram because AmigaBASIC doesn't recognize a command that you mistyped, it will look for a subprogram with the same name. If it doesn't find one, this message will appear. You'll probably see this fairly often.

UNDEFINED USER FUNCTION   Error number: 18

You'll get this if you try to use a function (FN...) that you didn't define with the DEF FN command. Maybe you mistyped the function name. Perhaps you started a variable name with FN (which is not allowed). Remember that CLEAR deletes function definitions.

UNKNOWN VOLUME   Error number: 49

You'll get this error if you enter a diskette name that AmigaBASIC can't find. It could be a typing error. If you enter a diskette name that AmigaBASIC can't find, AmigaDOS asks about the diskette in a requester. If you click Cancel in this requester, AmigaBASIC will know that the diskette name was a mistake.

UNPRINTABLE ERROR   Error numbers: 21, 24, 25, 27, 28, 31, 32, 39-48, 56, 59, 60, 65, 69, 71, 72, 75, 76, 78-255

An error has occurred for which AmigaBASIC has no error text. This usually happens when you define your own error routines with the ON ERROR and ERROR commands. If you define your own error numbers, these must be requested from ON ERROR as well.

WEND WITHOUT WHILE   Error number: 30

You need a WHILE for every WEND command. If you get this error, AmigaBASIC has found at least one WEND too many. If you write a structured code, you are less likely to forget something. Since WHILE and WEND always go together, pair up the WHILEs and WENDs to find where the missing one is.

WHILE WITHOUT WEND   Error number: 29

This is the reverse of "WEND without WHILE"—AmigaBASIC has found at least one WHILE too many. See the WEND without WHILE message.

B   AmigaBASIC reference section

This Appendix contains a description of AmigaBASIC's commands. We arranged them by type, and put them in alphabetical order according to their type. You can find out about unfamiliar commands here, as well as learn more about ones you know something about.

You'll have to do more experimenting yourself with the unfamiliar commands, since they often have lots of options. We explain the options completely, but due to space constraints not as thoroughly as before.

The following information is given about each command:

Command: [This is the command name]   Section [This lists the section that first mentions the command]

Syntax: This area lists all command options. [parameters in brackets are optional].

Here is where you'll find descriptions of each command, and a few examples of program code using the command.

B.1

Screen input and output

BEEP

Section 1.6

Syntax: BEEP

This command outputs a tone and a short flash on the screen. You can use this to get the user's attention. The beep can't be heard unless at least one sound channel (channel 0) is connected to a loudspeaker.

You can use PRINT CHR$ (7) instead of BEEP—they do exactly the same thing.

CLS

Section 1.3

Syntax: CLS

CLS erases the screen in the current output window. The output cursor will be placed in the upper left corner. That means that the next output made with the PRINT or some similar command will appear in this position.

COLOR

Section 1.16

Syntax: COLOR [Foreground-color] [,Background-color]

The COLOR command sets the foreground color (text and graphics color) and the background color (screen background). A number is entered for each color. The size of the number depends on the number of bits per pixel being used by the screen.

Using the PALETTE command and the settings in Preferences, you can set which color corresponds to which number. If you leave off one or both values, AmigaBASIC immediately defaults to color number 1 (usually white) as Foreground-color and number 0 (usually blue) as Background-color.

If you change Background-color value right before displaying text, the text appears on a colored bar.

The background is usually unchanged in most graphic commands.

CSRLIN

Syntax: CSRLIN

CSRLIN is a system variable. Like DATE$ and FRE(0), it is a variable assigned to a value by AmigaBASIC. The user can't modify these variables.

The variable CSRLIN contains the current line that the cursor is in. It is used to make calculations for LOCATE. Compare this with the POS command.

INKEY$ Section 1.13

Syntax: INKEY$

This command reads a character from the keyboard buffer and passes it as a string one character long. If a key wasn't hit (the buffer is empty), INKEY$ passes an empty string.

The INKEY$ command does not display a character on the screen—it only passes the character.

INPUT   Section 1.6

Syntax: INPUT ["(Explanatory text)"] [, or ;] Variable [,
           Variable, Variable,...]

INPUT allows the user to enter values from the keyboard during a program run. The values are then assigned to the variables.

If you want, you can have the INPUT command print explanatory text on the screen so the user will know what to type. If the text is followed by a semicolon (;), AmigaBASIC displays a question mark after the text. If you put a comma (,) after the text, a question mark will not be printed.

You can have several variables assigned values. The individual values must be separated from each other by commas. If the number of inputs expected and the number received are different, the error message "?Redo from start" will appear. That means that the input must be typed in over again.

If you put a semicolon before the explanatory text, the cursor will stay behind the last character INPUT to the program. The next output from the computer will be displayed starting there.

LINE INPUT   Section 1.7

Syntax: LINE INPUT ["(Explanatory text)"] [, or ;] String
                   variable

The LINE INPUT command reads a string variable from the keyboard.
The string may include any character, including commas, semicolons,
etc. <RETURN> must end the input.

You can give explanatory text here, too. Unlike INPUT, LINE INPUT
can have only one variable. This variable must be a string variable; any
other types will give you a "Type mismatch" error.

LINE INPUT doesn't put a question mark after the explanatory text; it
makes no difference whether you put a comma or a semicolon between
the text and the variable.

If you put a semicolon between LINE INPUT and the explanatory text,
the next output to the screen will start at the location right after the
user input.

LOCATE   Section 1.7

Syntax: LOCATE [Row] [,Column]

This command puts the output cursor at a particular position on the
screen. You need to give positive values for Row and Column, since the
(1,1) position is the upper left corner of the screen. In 60-character
mode, the largest possible value for Row is 21, and 62 is the largest
value for Column. In 80-character mode, Row can be a maximum of 23,
and Column a maximum of 77.

POS

Syntax: POS(x)

You may enter anything for x. It is just a dummy variable. (Many
BASIC functions require that you give an *argument*, a value in
parenthesis.) POS(x) returns the number of the column where the
cursor is presently located (the output cursor, the position on the screen
where the next output will be printed). If you need to know the current
cursor position, you can do the following:

Row=CSRLIN : Column=POS(0)

PRINT   Section 1.3

Syntax: PRINT [Variable or Value] [Separator] [Variable or
                   Value]...

You can abbreviate the PRINT command to ?. PRINT is used to output
variables and values, including string variables and text, to the screen.
Text must be in quotation marks.

If you don't write any variables or values down, a blank line will be
printed.

Several characters can be used as separators. A semicolon (;) has the
outputs printed right after each other. A comma (,) will print the next
output at the next tab position (normally the tabs are set at every 15th
column, but you can change that with the WIDTH command).

You can also use #, &, and % to separate variable names. They work just
like the semicolon.

If there is a semicolon at the end, the next output will directly follow
the last item printed by this line. Otherwise a linefeed will be executed.

PRINT USING

Syntax: PRINT USING [format string]; [Variable or Value] [;]

You can use PRINT USING to format your output. It is useful for
printing numbers in tables. You can also use it for string variables.
You use format string to enter the desired format. There are a
number of options possible: A number sign (#) stands for a digit. The
numbers after the decimal point that aren't printed are rounded.

```
print using "###.##";32.4  produces        32.40
print using "###.##";17                     17.00
print using "###.##";324.124               324.12
print using "###.##";128.489                28.49
print using "###.##";129.9984              130.00
```

If the number has more places in front of the decimal point than there
are number signs in front of the decimal point in the format string, a %
will be printed as an identifier.

```
print using "####.###";43259.3253   %43259.325
```

Putting a + in front of the string guarantees that a plus sign or minus
sign (leading character) will be printed in front of the value. The + can
also be at the end; then the plus/minus sign will appear after the value.
You may also put a − at the end of the format string. Then a minus
sign will be printed behind negative values.

```
print using "+###.##";324.234       +324.23
print using "+###.##";-518.284      -518.28
print using "###.##+";-518.294      518.28-
print using "###.##-";324.234       324.23
print using "###.##-";-518.294      518.27-
```

If you put two asterisks (**) in front of the number signs (#), the blank spaces will be filled with asterisks. The two asterisks count as digit positions as well.

```
print using "**##.##";42.2          **42.20
print using "**#####.##";43.1       *****43.10
print using "**###.##";-523.456     *-523.46
```

Two dollar signs ($ $) cause a single dollar sign ($) to be printed. The first dollar sign is the signal for the character to be printed later; the second dollar sign marks a digit position. If you want to have a + printed in every case, it must be behind the number.

```
print using "$$###.##";43.54        $43.54
print using "$$###.##";-43.54       -$43.54
print using "$$###.##";-53245.345   %-$53245.35
print using "$$###.##+';45.3        $45.30+
print using "$$+##.##";45.3         %$45+
```

The last example above shows the sort of error that occurs when you try to use + and $$ together. The PRINT USING command will not print the digits that come after the decimal point, since the $$+ confuse the computer. But you can combine the effects of the ** and $$ combinations. Type "**$". This represents three character positions— one for the dollar sign, and two for digits or asterisks. It works like this:

```
print using "**$##.##";45.3         **$45.30
print using "**$##.##";345.3        *$345.30
```

If you put a comma to the left of the decimal point, you can get neater formatting for large numbers.

```
print using "########,.##";3444233.50
                        3,444,233.50
```

The commas count as character positions. Does this remind you of Intermission 5, especially the exponential notation of numbers? If you want, PRINT USING can work in exponential form. To do so put four carets (exponent signs,^^^^) at the end of the format string.

```
print using "##.##^^^^";34.53       3.45E+01
print using "###.##^^^^";.009       9.00E-03
```

The underline character (_), causes the next character to be printed, instead of being treated as a formatting character.

```
print using "_####.##";34.95        # 34.95
```

You may also put text in the format strings. The text may be of any length. However, you may not define more than 24 digits in a string. If you try, for instance, to use more than 24 numbers, you will get an "Illegal function call" error.

```
print using "Here is the number: ##.##";3.3   Here is the
number:  3.3
```

If the PRINT USING command does not understand your text formatting, just type a _ in front of the formats.

Now we're ready for the next topic. We can format strings as well as numbers. An exclamation point (!) tells the computer to print the first character of a string only:

```
print using "!";"Amiga"                           A
```

If you want to set a maximum size of more than one character, put blank spaces between two backslashes (\). You can find this key to the left of the <BACKSPACE> key. The number of spaces between the two backslashes plus two is the total length of the string.

```
print using "\  \";"Hello"                         He
```

There are two spaces between the backslashes in the example. If the string is longer, it will be shortened. If it is shorter than the given length, spaces will be added. Finally, there is the & format symbol. It lets you print strings of any length.

```
print using "\\";"Amiga"   Am
print using "&";"Amiga"   Amiga
```

Of course, you could get that result without using the PRINT USING command.

PRINT USING isn't a very simple command to use. However, if you use the most important options, it makes creating formatted lists and tables much easier. It works much better than using LOCATE and the string functions.

Experiment with the PRINT USING command; it will pay off.

SPC

Syntax: SPC(x)

This command prints x number of blank spaces. x must be between 0 and 255. The SPC command is often useful for constructing screen masks.

TAB   Section 3.4

Syntax :   TAB(x);

This command is used to format printer output. AmigaBASIC fills the space between the current print position and column x with blanks. Print output begins at column x. If the current print position is past column x, the next line will be printed starting at column x.

You can only use TAB with the PRINT, PRINT#, and LPRINT commands.

WIDTH   Section 1.16

Syntax :   WIDTH [Width] [,Tab width]
                      WIDTH [LPRINT] [,Width] [,Tab width]
                      WIDTH #File number [,Width] [,Tab width]
                      WIDTH Device name [,Width] [,Tab width]

The WIDTH command has four valid syntaxes, some of which are used for data handling. We'll go through them one by one.

The basic WIDTH function sets the line width for output. Since the Amiga is quite willing to write to the right of the screen border (it has no automatic linefeed), the screen width needs to be set in your BASIC programs. You do this using the syntax: Use WIDTH 61 for 60 characters per line; Use WIDTH 76 for 80 characters per line.

The second value behind WIDTH gives the distance for positioning by commas in PRINT statements. You can also set line width and tab distance for the printer. You can do it with the LPRINT option, or by using the third syntax. Open a printer file and set the file number. The value set with WIDTH is only used in the file that it is specified for. Printer output using LPRINT is not affected.

The fourth syntax lets you write values directly to a device (SCRN, LPT1, COM1). The line width and tab distance, will be used after the next file is OPENed. If a file is already open, it won't be affected. The printer's default value is 80 characters per line.

WRITE   Section 3.4

Syntax :   WRITE [Variable or Value] [Separator] [Variable or
                      Value]...

The WRITE command prints characters starting at the current print position like the PRINT command. Only commas (,) and semicolons (;) may be used as separators. The difference between the two commands is that WRITE puts commas between the individual values and puts quotation marks on strings. This makes WRITE especially good for outputting values to files.

B.2   Object animation

COLLISION

Syntax: Value=COLLISION(Object number)

Here COLLISION is a function. The word can be used in several ways to deal with collisions. Every collision is written in a delay area so that you can ask about and work with each collision. AmigaBASIC cannot handle more than 16 collisions at the same time.

The number of the object involved in the collision is placed in parentheses. The result is the number of the object that collided with the object you asked about. It is also possible to collide with the window borders. That gives results between -1 and -4:

-1 =   upper border
-2 =   left border
-3 =   lower border
-4 =   right border

You can also write 0 or -1 for Object number.

The function COLLISION(0) returns the number of the object that was involved in the most recent collision without removing it from the waiting area. This is useful for finding out which collisions have occurred without having to work with them right away.

COLLISION(−1) tells you in which window the collision occurred. This can be useful if you have objects moving in several windows.

COLLISION ON
COLLISION OFF
COLLISION STOP

Syntax: COLLISION ON
                COLLISION OFF
                COLLISION STOP

These commands are used for event trapping of object collisions. The COLLISION ON command makes the computer start looking for collisions. The COLLISION OFF command tells it to quit looking, while COLLISION STOP tells it to stop looking until another COLLISION ON command is sent.

You can use ON COLLISION GOSUB to branch to the appropriate subroutine when collisions occur. You can then use the COLLISION function to find out more about which objects were involved.

OBJECT.AX
OBJECT.AY   Section 1.15

Syntax :   OBJECT.AX Object number, Acceleration
                      OBJECT.AY Object number, Acceleration

You set the acceleration for an object with these commands. The horizontal acceleration is set with the OBJECT.AX command. Positive numbers move the object from left to right, negative numbers from right to left.

OBJECT.AY sets the vertical acceleration. Positive values move the object downward, negative values upward. Look at Figure 4 in Section 1.15 to find out more.

The acceleration is entered in pixels per second. The movement does not actually start until you give the OBJECT.START command.

OBJECT.CLIP

Syntax: OBJECT CLIP (x1,y1)-(x2,y2)

You declare a rectangle with the OBJECT.CLIP command. AmigaBASIC will only move objects within this rectangle. In other words, the object is only visible when its coordinates are within the clip area.

AmigaBASIC takes the window size as the default value. If the window is enlarged or reduced, however, the rectangle will have to be changed as well. It isn't automatic!

OBJECT.CLOSE

Syntax :   OBJECT.CLOSE [Object number] [,Object number...]

An object uses up space as long as it is in memory. If it is no longer needed, you should use OBJECT.CLOSE to free up that space.

If you don't enter an object number, all the objects that belong to the current output window will be erased, and their memory spaces freed up.

OBJECT.HIT

Syntax: OBJECT.HIT Object number, [Value1] [,Value2]

This command is used to set which objects (or screen boundaries) can collide with which objects. You can keep certain objects from colliding (for instance, it might not matter if objects go past the screen boundaries, or you might not want a space ship to collide with a star in a program).

If a collision is possible and it does occur, it can be checked with collision event trapping. You can find more about this in the description of ON COLLISION GOSUB and COLLISION.

The default setting is that any object can collide with any other object and with the screen boundries. You can enter 16-bit decimal numbers for Value1 and Value2. If the low bit in Value2 is set (if Value2 is a odd number), the object can collide with the screen boundary. If it isn't set, it can fly out of the visible area.

The rest of the bits are used as follows. Value1 stands for the object itself. Value2 stands for other objects that our object can run into. If there is a collision, AmigaBASIC ANDs Value2 of the strange object with Value1 of our object. If none of the set bits match up (if we get a zero ANDing), then a collision has not occurred. If any bits match, a collision has happened. For example:

Object	Value1:	Value2:
Space ship	00000000 00000010	00000000 00000011
Rocket	00000000 00000010	00000000 00000010
Star	00000000 00000100	00000000 00000100

We wrote the numbers in binary to make comparing them easier. You need to give the value as a decimal number when you call the OBJECT.HIT command. For example, the command for the space ship is:

OBJECT.HIT 1,2,3

Now we'll look at the bits. The low bit in the space ship's Value2 is set. The space ship cannot leave the boundaries of the screen. The rocket and the star may leave the screen in any direction.

Value1 of the space ship and Value2 of the rocket are set so those two can collide—that is, if the rocket meets up with the space ship, a collision occurs.

We set the second bit in Value2 of the space ship and in Value1 of the rocket so that a collision will occur if the reverse happens. Only the third bit is set for the star so it can't get into collisions.

OBJECT.ON   Section 1.15
OBJECT.OFF

Syntax: OBJECT.ON [Object number] [,Object number,...]
                  OBJECT.OFF [Object number] [,Object number, ...]

OBJECT.ON makes the object whose number is given, visible. The
OBJECT.OFF command makes it invisible. If you don't give a number,
the command applies to all the objects in the current output window.

OBJECT.OFF also stops moving objects so that you can't get into
collisions with invisible objects.

OBJECT.PLANES

Syntax: OBJECT.PLANES Object number [,Bitplane] [,Planevalue]

You probably won't use this command very often, because it deals
mostly with the inner workings of the Amiga. Bitplane is an 8-bit
value which is written as a decimal number. The set bits determine in
which bitplanes the object will appear. For example, if you have four
bitplanes available and want to have the object show up in the first and
third plane (levels 0 and 2), you need to enter $2^0 + 2^2 = 1 + 4 = 5$.

The other value, Planevalue (also an 8-bit number), tells what
should be put in the other bitplanes.

OBJECT.PRIORITY

Syntax: OBJECT.PRIORITY Object number, Priority number

You can set the priority of individual objects using the
OBJECT.PRIORITY command. You can use it to determine which
object will be visible when several objects occupy the same screen
location.

Priority number is a number between -32768 and +32767. When
two objects are at the same spot, the one with higher priority will be
displayed in front. If they have the same value, either could be in the
foreground.

OBJECT.SHAPE   Section 1.13

Syntax: OBJECT.SHAPE Object number, Definition string
                  OBJECT.SHAPE Object number, other Object number

This command sets the shape, size, and color of an object. All of this information is in a definition string that you can read from a sequential file.

```
OPEN "(Object file)" FOR INPUT AS 1
OBJECT.SHAPE Object number, INPUT$(LOF(1),1)
CLOSE 1
```

You can create the data items in the sequential object file with the ObjectEditor from the BASICDemos drawer of the Extras diskette. You can find out more about this in Section 1.11 (the object editor).

The second syntax lets you copy the definition of an object already in memory to another object. Then you can have several identical objects in memory.

OBJECT.START   Section 1.15
OBJECT.STOP

Syntax: OBJECT.START [Object number] [,Object number, ...]
                 OBJECT.STOP [Object number] [,Object number, ...]

The OBJECT.START command starts an object's movement. The OBJECT.STOP command makes it stop moving. You can make several objects start or stop moving at the same time.

OBJECT.VX and .VY set the object's speed and/or acceleration. You can use OBJECT.X and OBJECT.Y to set where the object should be put initially, then start the movement using the OBJECT.START command. Now the object will move on its own and your program can worry about other things.

AmigaBASIC automatically executes OBJECT.STOP for objects involved in collisions.

OBJECT.VX   Section 1.15
OBJECT.VY

Syntax: OBJECT.VX Object number, Speed
                 OBJECT.VY Object number, Speed

These two commands set the speed of moving objects. You set the horizontal speed with OBJECT.VX and the vertical speed with the OBJECT.VY command. Positive values move the object toward the left or downward.To move right or upward use negative numbers.

Look at Figure 4 on page 70 for more information. The speed is entered in pixels per second. The object starts moving from the place specified with the OBJECT.START command.

OBJECT.VX   Section 1.15
OBJECT.VY

Syntax: Value = OBJECT.VX (Object number)
                 Value = OBJECT.VY (Object number)

This function tells you the present speed of an object. You can use this
information in calculations, for instance, to vary the speed from time to
time.

OBJECT.X   Section 1.15
OBJECT.Y

Syntax: OBJECT.X Object number, X-coordinate
                 OBJECT.X Object number, Y-coordinate

You use OBJECT.X and OBJECT.Y to set the position and/or the starting
point of an object's movement. X-coordinate and Y-coordinate
give the location of the upper left corner of the object. The values that
make the object visible on the screen depends on the resolution of the
current window.

Objects don't have to be in the visible region, but the coordinates must
be between –32768 and +32767. Remember that objects won't be
visible until you use the OBJECT . ON command.

OBJECT.X   Section 1.15
OBJECT.Y

Syntax: Value = OBJECT.X (Object number)
                 Value = OBJECT.Y (Object number)

Here OBJECT.X and OBJECT.Y function as BASIC functions. You can
find the present location of an object using these commands. Using this
information, you can decide what to do with the object. In this way,
your program need only look at an object as needed. Value is set to the
screen coordinates of the upper left corner of the object.

ON COLLISION GOSUB

Syntax: ON COLLISION GOSUB Label

You can use this command to deal with collisions. You determine which subroutine to branch to when a collision occurs. Just give the label for the routine that is in charge at the parameter Label.

If you enter a 0 instead of a label or line number, event trapping for collisions will be turned off. This happens even if "0" is also a label or a line number in your program. To turn on collision event trapping, use the COLLISION ON command.

B.3   Graphic commands

AREA   Section 2.6

Syntax: AREA [STEP] (x,y)

You use AREA to enter a point on a polygon. The AREAFILL command draws the polygon on the screen (see AREAFILL for more information). If you add STEP to AREA, the x and y will be added to the last coordinates used.

AREAFILL   Section 2.6

Syntax: AREAFILL [mode]

You can give up to twenty corner points with the AREA command; AmigaBASIC can't handle any more. If you use the AREAFILL command, the polygon specified using the AREA command will be put on the screen. This goes very quickly because of the blitter chip.

There are two values for mode. If you enter a 0, the polygon will be filled with the pattern you set with the PATTERN command. If you enter a 1, the polygon will be inverted. If your colors are set normally, this means that:

> BLUE WILL BECOME ORANGE
> WHITE WILL BECOME BLACK
> BLACK WILL BECOME WHITE
> ORANGE WILL BECOME BLUE

CIRCLE   Section 2.6

Syntax: CIRCLE [STEP] (x,y),Radius [,Color] [,Start angle]
               [,End angle] [,x/y relationship]

This command draws a circle or an ellipse with the center located at (x,y). Radius is the x-direction of the radius in pixels. If you have a STEP preceding (x,y), AmigaBASIC adds the values x and y to the last graphic coordinates used.

Color is the number of the color to be used. The value allowed for the number depends on how many bitplanes are being used by that screen.

Start angle and End angle make it easier to draw sections of a circle. Enter the angles (a multiple of π) of the start and end points in radians. Negative angles cause the start and end points to be connected to the middle point. Figure 6 on page 116 will help you determine the angle.

x/y relationship determines the relationship between the x-radius and the y-radius. By changing this value, you can draw all sorts of ellipses. Values of less than 0.44 yield a small y-radius. Values over 0.44 yield an ellipse with the y-radius bigger than the x-radius. The value 0.44 will usually (depending on the monitor) draw a perfect circle.

GET (*screen GET*)   Section 4.1

Syntax: GET (x1,y1)-(x2,y2),array name [(index,...)]

You can use this command to store the contents of a section of the screen in a data array. The array must be a number. You can use an integer, a floating-point array, or a double precision floating-point array. Use the following formula to calculate the size of the array in bytes:

6 + Bitplanes * Height * 2 * INT((Width + 16) / 16)

You can then divide this number by the number of bytes per array element.

2 bytes for an integer array (Anarray%(x))
4 bytes for a floating-point array (Anarray(x))
8 bytes for a double precision floating-point array (Anarray#(x))

Array element 0 contains the width, element 1 the height, and element 2 the number of bitplanes in the screen segment that was saved.

If you have a multi-dimensional array, you can store several segments in the array. You can also store different views of the same figure so that you can change them quickly.

To display the segment on the screen again, use the PUT command.

LINE   Section 2.5

Syntax: LINE [[STEP] (x1,y1)] - [STEP] (x2,y2) [,Color] [,B or ,BF]

This command can be used to draw a line, a box, or a filled in box. The simplest use is to give a starting and ending point (LINE (x1,y1) - (x2,y2)), which gives you a straight line.

If you leave off the first point (LINE – (x2,y2)), AmigaBASIC draws
a line from the last graphic point used to the point (x2,y2). You can
use both possibilities in connection with STEP. Then the x and y
values will be added to the previous graphic point. You can enter a
color number to set the color this should be drawn in. You can put a , B
at the end; then a box will be drawn. The coordinates (x1,y1) and
(x2,y2) are two opposite corners of the box. If you use , BF, a box
filled in with the drawing color will be drawn on the screen.

PAINT   Section 2.6

Syntax: PAINT [STEP] (x,y) [,Paint color] [,Boundary color]

This command paints an enclosed surface in the Paint color. If you
didn't enter a Boundary color, Paint color will be used as
Boundary color. If neither color is stated, AmigaBASIC uses the
current drawing color. To use PAINT, you must be in a window whose
type is between 16 and 31 (the window contents must be buffered in
memory).

PALETTE   Section 1.16

Syntax: PALETTE Color-id, Red, Green, Blue

You can produce colors using the PALETTE command. The number of
possible colors depends on the number of bitplanes on the screen. Every
color has a Color-id number assigned to it. This number (that can
range from 0 to 31 at best) is assigned to a particular color.

Enter a number between 0 (0%) and 1 (100%) for the Red, Green, and
Blue components. The new color settings replace the old ones. The
four Workbench colors (colors 0 to 3 are used by Workbench, and can
be changed in Preferences) will be returned by the Amiga when a
program starts and ends.

PATTERN   Section 2.10

Syntax: PATTERN [16-bit value for line] [,array for surface]

You can use this command to set the fill pattern for lines and surfaces.
If you're using PATTERN with lines, you can give a 16-bit value. This
defines a 16-pixel-wide pattern. Every set bit in the number corresponds
to a point on the screen. The 16-bit number can be entered in decimal
(e.g., 65535), hex (&HFFFF), or octal (&O177777) format.

For areas, enter an integer array. The numbers in the array define a pattern that can be used for fill and paint activities (PAINT, AREAFILL, or LINE..., BF). The set bits correspond to visible points on the screen here as well.

The number of elements in the array must be a power of 2 (e.g., 1, 2, 4, 8, 16, or 32).

POINT

Syntax: POINT(x,y)

This BASIC function gets the number of the color at POINT (x,y) in the current output window. If the point is outside the window, the value returned will be -1.

PRESET
PSET

Section 2.5

Syntax: PRESET [STEP] (x,y) [color-id]
                   PSET [STEP] (x,y) [,Color]

These commands draw a point in the current output window. x and y are the point's coordinates. You can use STEP to draw additional points relative to the last point drawn. The point color is set by entering the color-id. There is only one difference between PRESET and PSET; when the color is not specified, PRESET draws using the background color, while PSET draws the current drawing color.

PTAB

Syntax: PRINT PTAB(x)

This function works just like TAB except that the position is given here in pixels instead of characters. Using this, you can position text accurately within the current line. For example:

```
FOR x=0 TO 100
PRINT PTAB(x);"Hello!"
NEXT x
```

PUT (*screen PUT*)

Section 4.1

Syntax: PUT [STEP] (x,y), array name [(index,...)] [,action-verb]

You need this command to PUT the screen sections that you placed in an array with the GET command back onto the screen. The parameters are the same as for the GET command, so please look there if you need more information.

Only action-verb is new here. You can choose several different ways to put the object onto the screen:

PSET: The data will overwrite the screen area. It will look exactly the same after being writtten to the screen as it did when it was read.

PRESET: The picture is inverted.

AND: Only the points that remain after ANDing the segment being read in with the background will be put on the screen.

OR: The array contents and the background are ORed together. The segment will be completely copied onto the background.

XOR: This is the default for action-verb. The segment is copied to the screen. The picture underneath will be displayed inverted.

SCREEN   Section 2.3

Syntax :   SCREEN screen-id, width, height, depth, mode

You can use this command to create a new screen. AmigaBASIC allows four screens in addition to the Workbench screen (numbers 1 - 4).

width and height are in pixels. depth sets the number of bitplanes used on the screen.

depth (number of bitplanes)	total number of colors available
1	2
2	4
3	8
4	16
5	32

mode states the degree of resolution and whether or not interlace mode is operating. mode is a number between 1 and 4.

Mode:	Description:	Memory needed per bitplane:
1	320*200 pixels	8000 bytes
2	640*200 pixels	16000 bytes
3	320*400 pixels (interlace)	16000 bytes
4	640*400 pixels (interlace)	32000 bytes

SCREEN CLOSE

Syntax: SCREEN CLOSE screen-id

Since screens use quite a bit of memory, you should close them when you no longer need them. The SCREEN CLOSE command is used for this. It clears the screen whether there are windows on it or not, and frees up the memory that was being used by the screen.

SCROLL   Section 1.17

Syntax: SCROLL (x1,y1)-(x2-y2),delta-x,delta-y

Using this command, you can move a screen segment in any direction. (x1,y1)-(x2,y2) is the format for a rectangle. The rectangle's contents are moved. delta-x determines how many points the contents should be moved in a horizontal direction. Positive values move the screen segment to the right, and negative values move it to the left. delta-y does the same for the vertical direction. Positive values move the segment downward, negative values upward.

WINDOW   Section 2.4

Syntax: WINDOW window-id [,title] [, (x1,y1)-(x2,y2)]
                 [,type] [,screen-id]

You can use this to create and use new windows. Every window has a window-id, a number that allows you to easily access windows. The **BASIC** window has a window-id of 1, user created windows have window-id numbers from 2 on up.

When you create a window, you can give it a title and declare a rectangle sized (x1,y1)-(x2,y2) that states the upper left and lower right corners of the window. If you don't set a size, AmigaBASIC uses the entire screen for the window.

type is a number formed by one or a combination of the following numbers added together:

1   You can enlarge and shrink the window with the size gadget and your mouse.

2   You can move the window using the title bar and the mouse.

4   The window has a back gadget so that you can click it to the background on the screen.

8   The window has a close gadget.

16   The window contents are reconstructed after being moved, or covered by another window. You need to use this option if you want to use the PAINT command in the window.

You can also say which screen the window should be placed on. If you omit all the options and use the WINDOW command as follows:

WINDOW window-id

the window will be put in the foreground and used as the output window.

WINDOW   Section 2.4

Syntax: WINDOW(x)

This version of WINDOW is a BASIC function. You can find out things about the current output window using it. x is a value between 0 and 8.

WINDOW(0) gives you the window-id of the selected output window. It does not have to be the current output window; it can also be the window that was last clicked with the mouse (the window whose title isn't printed in ghost print).

WINDOW(1) gives the window-id of the current output window (the window to which AmigaBASIC sends all screen output).

WINDOW(2) gives the width of the current output window in pixels.

WINDOW(4) gives the X-coordinate in pixels of the location in the current output window where the next character will appear. It gives you the current location of the output cursor.

WINDOW(5) gives the Y-coordinate in pixels of the location in the current output window where the next character will appear.

WINDOW(6) tells you the maximum color number allowed in the current output window.

WINDOW(7) is a pointer to the record of the Intuition window corresponding to the current output window.

WINDOW(8) gives the address of the Intuition data area of the RASTPORT structure (see the manual entitled *Intuition: The Amiga User Interface*, available from your Amiga dealer). You'll only use this value if you know the Amiga operating system very well.

WINDOW CLOSE   Section 2.4

Syntax: WINDOW CLOSE window-id

This command removes the window from the screen without erasing the
window. You can still send output to the window even though it is
invisible.

WINDOW OUTPUT   Section 2.4

Syntax: WINDOW OUTPUT window-id

The window stated in this function will be turned into the output
window, but it won't be brought to the foreground. That is its only
difference from the WINDOW window-id command. In this way, you
can send output to invisible windows.

B.4   Program control commands

BREAK ON
BREAK OFF
BREAK STOP

Syntax: BREAK ON
                 BREAK OFF
                 BREAK STOP

This command takes care of event trapping for program breaks. Normally you can break by hitting <CTRL><C>, or by choosing Stop from the Run pulldown menu. If you want to stop users from stopping a program, or even just one section of a program, you can use these commands. You set the corresponding subroutine responsible with the ON BREAK GOSUB command. The BREAK ON command turns on event trapping, while BREAK OFF deactivates it until the program finds another BREAK ON command. The BREAK STOP command turns off BREAK event trapping.

CALL   Section 4.5

Syntax: [CALL] name [(argument-list, ...)]
                 [CALL] Variable [(Value, ...)]

The first form is for CALLing a subprogram. You can find more about these programs under the SUB...STATIC command. Usually you can leave off the CALL; you only need it if confusion might occur otherwise (for instance, if you have a normal label with the same name).

You can also CALL machine language subroutines. As you may know, BASIC isn't the Amiga's native language; it uses an interpreter. If you want to communicate with the Amiga in its native language, you need to know 68000 assembly language. If you don't, you can skip the next several paragraphs.

You need to get the machine language program in memory. You can load it from the diskette or READ it into a DATA array. You can find the machine language routine's starting address with the VARPTR or SADD function.

An example:

```
DIM MachineProgram% (20)
FOR x=0 TO 20
 READ MachineProgram% (x)
NEXT x
StartAddress&=VARPTR (MachineProgram% (0))
CALL StartAddress& (10,20)
DATA …
```

The whole program is stored in the `MachineProgram%` array. You can find the address this array starts at using

```
VARPTR (MachineProgram% (0))
```

You can pass parameters to the routine with the CALL command (in our example, we passed 10 and 20). You can also put a machine language program in a string.

```
Ma$=""
FOR x=0 TO 20
 READ Value
 Ma$=Ma$+MKI$ (Value)
NEXT x
StartAddress&=SADD (Ma$)
CALL StartAddress& (10,20)
DATA …
```

The SADD function gives you the starting address of a string. Using MKI$, you put together a string using the single values that you find on the DATA line.

You can also CALL machine language routines from a library. Look under the LIBRARY command for more information.

CHAIN

Syntax: CHAIN [MERGE] filename [,expression] [,ALL]
               [,DELETE range]

This command makes it possible for one BASIC program to load and pass control to another BASIC program. The difference between this command and the MERGE command is that the calling program is partially or completely erased in CHAIN. The word MERGE is just one of several options for the CHAIN command. If you use it, the calling program will be overwritten starting at the line number stated in expression. The program that you load must be stored as an ASCII file on the diskette.

If you don't use the MERGE command, expression states the line number in the loaded program from which the program should run. You may not use a label instead of a line number. Here, a line number must be used in AmigaBASIC. The ALL option passes all the variables in the current program to the program that is loaded. If you just want to pass some of them, you can use the COMMON command to say which ones should be passed. If you use the COMMON command, you may not use the ALL option.

The DELETE option deletes a range of lines in the loaded program. You can declare a range using either line numbers or labels.

The CHAIN command resets the DATA element pointer to the beginning. It works like the RESTORE command. All open files remain open after executing the CHAIN command, as do settings like OPTION BASE. However, CHAIN turns off event trapping. You must reactivate event trapping in the new program if it is needed. The type declarations made with DEFINT, DEFLNG, etc., are also dropped. If the DEF FN command isn't in the newly created program, AmigaBASIC will forget the function definition.

CLEAR

Syntax: CLEAR [,basicData] [,stack]

You can use CLEAR to erase all variables, strings, and arrays. This command also shuts all open files and more.

The CLEAR command lets you change the amount of memory used by AmigaBASIC. You can enlarge or reduce the memory allocation for BASIC programs and data. The minimum BASIC memory size is 1024 bytes (1K). The upper limit is the amount of system memory. The Amiga needs lots of space for graphics in graphic programs, so leave enough space available. If the Amiga runs out of space, you'll get a system crash (see Section 1.6 [more BASIC functions] for our discussion of Guru Meditations).

If a program works mostly with data and doesn't need much graphic memory, you can make the BASIC memory area fairly large. The default setting for basicData is 25000 bytes on the 512K Amiga. For example:

CLEAR, 40000

This makes 40000 bytes available for the BASIC system.

The stack is the memory area that AmigaBASIC uses for internal things. For instance, it keeps track of the counters in a FOR...NEXT loop here. It also keeps track of the line to RETURN to. Its normal setting is 4789 bytes. It cannot be smaller than 1024 bytes. Take a look at the FRE(x) command, which will tell you about determining current memory sizes.

COMMON

Syntax: COMMON Variable-list

This command passes individual variables to a program that you load with the CHAIN command. If you want to pass arrays, you need to identify them with empty parentheses:

```
CHAIN "(Program name)"
COMMON a,B$,Hello%, Colors(), Texts$()
```

You may use several COMMON commands but each variable may appear only once.

CONT

Syntax: CONT

With CONT, you can have a program continue from the point where it was stopped by a <CTRL><C>, Stop from the **Run** pulldown menu, or a STOP or END command in the program. The program couldn't have been altered since the break, or you'll get a "Can't continue" error.

DATA   Section 2.9

Syntax: DATA constant-list

You can put values (numbers or strings) on a DATA line. You can then READ them. The values are separated by commas. If a string has commas or semicolons, these must be put in quotation marks.

You may put DATA lines any place in the program. The DATA values will be read one after the other.

DECLARE FUNCTION...LIBRARY

Syntax: DECLARE FUNCTION-id[param-list] LIBRARY

If you want to use a machine language program that is a function (i.e., which produces a value), and this function is contained in a library, you need to declare the function with the D E C L A R E FUNCTION...LIBRARY command (see also CALL and LIBRARY). If the value produced is a certain type, just put the type designator on the end of the function's name:

```
DECLARE FUNCTION Test%(Test_value) LIBRARY
```

The machine language function Test% (Test_value) produces a 16-bit integer as its value. Inputting the variables that the machine language program expects is unnecessary since AmigaBASIC doesn't get involved in that. If you write them though, you'll know which values later need to be passed to the function when you call it.

DEF FN   Section 7.6

Syntax :   DEF FN name [(parameter-list)] = function-definition

Using DEF FN, you can create your own BASIC functions. You write the function name right after FN. If you want to use the function in a program, you do something like PRINT FNa (100) or Test=FNText (1,2,4). The optional values in parentheses are used in the formula the same way as the values in parentheses in the definition (DEF FNa (x) = 2*x). The program can also use variables that aren't in parentheses to calculate the value of the function:

```
DEF FNTest (x)  = 2*x*a
a=100 : PRINT FNTest (25)
a=12 : PRINT FNTest (25)
```

These examples return the values 5000 and 600. You can also define functions using string functions:

```
DEF FNFirst$ (a$)  = LEFT$ (a$,1)
PRINT FNFirst$ ("Amiga")
```

This example prints an A.

DEFDBL
DEFINT
DEFLNG
DEFSNG
DEFSTR

Syntax :   DEFDBL letter-range
                    DEFINT letter-range
                    DEFLNG letter-range
                    DEFSNG letter-range
                    DEFSTR letter-range

You can use these commands to set certain variable names to certain variable types. Give the first letter of each variable name in the letter-range. For example, DEFINT a-c means that from this time on, all variables that start with a, b, or c (i.e., Amiga, alpha, Beta, Charlie, ...) become 16-bit integers. You don't need to use % any more. This holds true for arrays as well. However, if you use a type designator, the designator gets top priority. For instance, Answer$ will be treated as a string, although Answer will be treated as a 16-bit integer. The following settings are possible:

Command:	Variable type:	Sample variable :
DEFINT	16-bit integer (short INTeger)	Hello%
DEFLNG	32-bit integer (LoNG integer)	Hello&
DEFSNG	SiNGle-precision floating-point	Hello, Hello!
DEFDBL	DouBLe-precision floating point	Hello#
DEFSTR	STRing	Hello$

You need to set the variable type before you use the variables.

DELETE

Syntax :　　　　DELETE [Label or Line number] [-] [Label or Line number]

You can use DELETE in both program and direct modes to delete lines. Enter the range of lines to be deleted:

DELETE Beginning - ColorDef deletes all the lines between the two labels.

DELETE Beginning - deletes all the lines from the label Beginning to the end of the program.

DELETE - ColorDef deletes all the lines from the beginning of the program to the ColorDef label.

DIM　　　　　　　　　　　　　　　　　　　　　　　　　Section 1.7

Syntax :　　　　DIM [SHARED] Array (Value [,Value, …]) [,Array (…), …]

You use DIM to dimension arrays used in your program. If you don't dimension the array, AmigaBASIC automatically sets the array size to 10 elements. Dimensioning is intended to keep an array from taking up any more memory than is necessary.

If you use the SHARED option, the array can be used by subprograms as well as the main program. You may only put the DIM SHARED command in the main program, though. If you want to use a number of normal variables in all subprograms, you can use the DIM SHARED command:

DIM SHARED Colors%(31,2), Colors

The variable Colors is a global variable, in contrast to the local variables that subprograms use.

Using the OPTION BASE command, you can set whether the smallest array element in all arrays is a zero or a one.

You can set up multi-dimensional arrays (for example, DIM Array(2,2,2)). You may have up to 255 dimensions. The highest number of a array element is 32767. You'll never reach either maximum number, since you would run out of memory long before that.

END   Section 2.10

Syntax: END

This command ends a BASIC program. All open files are closed.

END SUB   Section 4.5

Syntax: END SUB

This ends a subprogram. See the SUB command explanation for more information.

ERASE

Syntax: ERASE Array [, Array ...]

The ERASE command erases an array. The memory the array occupies is freed up, and the contents are erased. You can redimension an array with DIM after erasing it.

ERL

Syntax: ERL

This system variable contains the number of the last line executed before an error occurs when you are doing error trapping (event trapping for errors). It is impossible to find the label name that comes before the error. See ON ERROR GOSUB for more information.

ERR

Syntax: ERR

This and ERL are system variables for error trapping. This gives you the number of the error. You can find out which number goes with which error by looking in Appendix A (Error and help messages). See ON ERROR GOSUB in this Appendix for more information.

ERROR

Syntax :   ERROR error-number

Here is a third command used in connection with errors. Using ON
ERROR GOSUB to do error trapping, you can create your own error
messages. Just take an error number that isn't in use, and use the
ERROR command to create this error. Error trapping branches to the
corresponding subroutine. There you can use ERR to find out the error
number. AmigaBASIC's **error** window cannot display your error
messages. However, you can create your own **error** window and have
it displayed by your subroutine.

If you enter an error number that AmigaBASIC uses and don't use error
trapping, you create an error that really hasn't occurred. You can use
that to protect your program against unauthorized users. Try this:

ERROR 2

A "Syntax error" will occur.

EXIT SUB   Section 4.8

Syntax :   EXIT SUB

This command makes it possible to leave a subprogram before it is
done executing. You can find more in the SUB...STATIC command
description.

FOR...NEXT   Section 1.7

Syntax :   FOR variable=x TO y [STEP z] NEXT [variable] [,variable
                  ...]

This command is used for loops. Everything between the FOR and NEXT
command will be performed several times. The first time through the
loop, the counter variable has the value x. The next time through,
the variable is incremented by z (if STEP z is omitted then x is
incremented by 1 each time the loop is executed). This continues until
variable is greater than y.

The variable after the next command is optional. If it is omitted, it
increments the most recent FOR command. It is possible to match
several FOR...NEXT loops with a single NEXT command.

```
FOR x=1 TO 100
 FOR y=1 TO 20
  FOR z=1 TO 30
NEXT z,y,x
```

As you can see in the example, you can also nest your FOR...NEXT loops. The inner loops must be closed before the outer ones can be closed.

FRE(x)   Section 4.4

Syntax: FRE(x)

These system variables give information about the size of individual memory ranges. You enter a value for x to specify the memory range.

FRE(0) tells you how much free memory there is in BASIC memory; that is, the number of bytes that aren't presently being used by the program and its variables.

FRE(-1) tells you how much space is left in system memory.

FRE(-2) tells you how many bytes on the stack are not being used by AmigaBASIC.

GOSUB...RETURN   Section 1.16

Syntax: GOSUB line
                 RETURN [line]

You can call a subroutine with GOSUB. AmigaBASIC notes where the GOSUB is located and then branches to the line. If it finds a RETURN command in this subroutine, it returns to the line following the GOSUB command and continues.

You can also put the line number line following the RETURN command. Then AmigaBASIC branches to the label following the RETURN command. You need to make sure that the GOSUB command isn't inside of a loop (i.e., FOR...NEXT, WHILE...WEND), or inside of another subroutine. Otherwise the loop or subroutine will be ended incorrectly, if it ends at all. This can lead to error messages like "FOR WITHOUT NEXT" or "WHILE WITHOUT WEND".

GOTO   Section 1.6

Syntax: GOTO line

This command causes the program to jump to the line that follows the GOTO; the program continues working there. line can be either a line number or a label.

433

IF...THEN...ELSE   Section 1.6

Syntax :   IF expression THEN then-clause [ELSE else-clause]
                  IF expression GOTO line [ELSE else-clause]
                  IF expression THEN statementBlock
                  [ELSEIF expression THEN statementBlock]
                  [ELSE statementBlock]
                  END IF

The IF...THEN statement makes it possible to check conditions and then execute commands or make jumps based on the results.

There are many different syntaxes. The simplest IF...THEN command looks like this:

```
IF expression THEN then-clause
```

The condition is always a comparison that has a logical value (for example IF a<10 or IF Hello=0...). If the condition is met, AmigaBASIC returns the value -1 (true). If the condition is not met, the result is 0 (false). In the example above, the then-clause that follows the THEN will be executed if its condition is met. You can also expand the command with an ELSE. Here you can tell the program what to do if the conditions aren't met.

```
IF a<10 THEN PRINT "a is smaller than 10"
 ELSE PRINT "a isn't smaller than 10"
```

You can put a GOTO and a label or line number behind the condition instead of a THEN and a command.

If several program lines should be executed if the condition is met, you should use the IF/ELSE IF/ELSE/ENDIF structure.The IF...THEN line sets the condition. There may not be any other commands behind the THEN command. The commands that are below this line and before the next END IF, ELSE, or ELSE IF command will be executed if the conditions are met. The optional ELSE IF...THEN line gives a second condition to be checked if the first condition isn't met. There may not be a command behind the THEN here, either. The commands that should be executed if the second condition is met begin on the next line.

The optional ELSE line tells what to do if none of the previous conditions were met.

The END IF command ends the whole IF ELSE IF/ELSE structure. You can nest these structures inside each other. For example:

```
IF...THEN
 IF...THEN

 ...

 ELSE

 ...

 END IF
ELSE IF...THEN
 IF...THEN

 ...

 END IF
ELSE

 ...

END IF
```

Structured programming here is almost unavoidable.

LET   Section 1.3

Syntax :   LET variable=value

LET assigns value to variable. The LET can be omitted; a simple
assignment, like a=10, works.

LIBRARY

Syntax :   LIBRARY filename

If you want to use machine language subroutines in your program, you
don't necessarily have to write them yourself. You can use *libraries*.
These libraries contain a number of machine language programs or calls
that perform certain useful functions. You need information about
parameters and parameter types that the library routines expect. To find
this, you'll have to use the documentation that exists for machine
language programmers and software developers: the *Amiga ROM
Kernel Manual* and *Intuition: The Amiga User Interface*. All the
machine language routines in the operating system and in the libraries
are explained there.

You can't do anything without this information. For this reason, we
have not included an example of Library in this book. The program
Library in the BASICDemos drawer of the Extras diskette will explain
how it goes. You CALL the machine language routines. For instance, in
the subprogram Font: from the Library program, we CALL
CloseFont (pFont&). The CloseFont: routine is part of the
graphics.library that is accessed at the beginning of the program.
These libraries must be in .BMAP format. Read Appendix D to find an
explanation of the Library and ConvertFD programs. AmigaBASIC
can use up to five libraries simultaneouly.

You cannot only CALL programs, you can use machine language functions. These functions (which produce a result in contrast to CALL routines) must be accessed with the DECLARE FUNCTION...LIBRARY command. For example, the Library demo contains the AskSoftStyle&, OpenFont&, and Execute& functions.

LIST   Section 1.5

Syntax: LIST [line] [-] [line] [,"filename"]

This command lists the program in memory. You can list an entire program from the beginning to end by typing LIST without any options, or you can list starting from a certain line number or label in the program to another line number or label.

Enter the range of lines to be listed:

LIST lists the entire program from the beginning to end.

LIST line lists the line specified. line can be either a line number or label.

LIST Beginning - ColorDef lists all the lines from Beginning to ColorDef.

LIST Beginning - lists all the lines from the Beginning label to the end of the program.

LIST - ColorDef lists all the lines from the beginning of the program to the ColorDef label.

LIST normally lists the program in the **LIST** window. However, adding , filename to LIST will send the program listing to a file or a device:

LIST, "SCRN:" you list a program in the **BASIC** window.

LIST, "PRT:" sends your listing to the printer.

LIST, "DF0:Test" sends the program to diskette in ASCII format.

MENU   Section 2.8

Syntax: MENU menu-id, item-id, state [,title-string]

You can use MENU to create your own pulldown menus in AmigaBASIC. You can use event trapping to respond to menu choices.

menu-id is the number of the pulldown menu. The first pulldown menu is number 1, the last is number 10.

item-id is an item within the chosen pulldown menu. A pulldown menu may have up to 19 options. The value 0 sets the title of the pulldown menu.

There are three possible values for state:

0   turns off the menu item. The item will be printed in ghost print and will not be available. If you enter 0 for item-id, the whole menu will be turned off.

1   turns on a menu option (or the whole menu if you enter item-id 0).

2   activates a menu item and puts a small check next to it. You should put two spaces in your text so that the check doesn't overwrite your text. You can't have a check next to the title of the menu.

If you use the MENU command to turn menu items on and off, that's it. If you create a new menu, you must enter the text that goes with each menu option.

MENU   Section 2.8

Syntax: MENU(x)

This BASIC function gives information about the last menu option that was chosen.

MENU(0) lets you know the number of the menu that the item was in.

MENU(1) lets you know which item was chosen from the pulldown menu.

MENU ON
MENU OFF
MENU STOP

Syntax: MENU ON
                 MENU OFF
                 MENU STOP

These commands activate, deactivate or hold event trapping for menu control. The MENU ON command turns on menu trapping; MENU OFF turns it off; and MENU STOP turns it off until the next occurrence of MENU ON.

You can let the program know which subroutine is in charge of the menus with the ON MENU GOSUB command.

MOUSE   Section 2.8

Syntax :   MOUSE(x)

The MOUSE function gives information about the clicks and movement of the mouse.

The value in the parenthesis can range from 0 to 6. They have the following meanings: MOUSE(0) tells you the present state of the left mouse key. If MOUSE(0) is executed during the program, AmigaBASIC notes the present condition of the mouse. You should call MOUSE(0) before you use MOUSE(1) through MOUSE(6). If you don't need the value, assign it a dummy variable. MOUSE(0) can take on the following values:

0   The left mouse key is not being pressed.

1   The left mouse key is not being pressed right now, but it was pressed since the last time MOUSE(0) was called.

2,3   The left mouse key is not currently being pressed, but it has been pressed several times since the last time MOUSE(0) was called. 2 means that the left mouse key was pressed twice; 3 means that it was pressed three or more times.

-1   The left mouse key is now being held down after having been clicked once.

-2,-3   The left mouse key is now being held down after having been clicked two (-2) or three (-3) times.

MOUSE(1) gives the X-coordinate of the pointer the last time MOUSE(0) was called.

MOUSE(2) gives the Y-coordinate of the pointer the last time MOUSE(0) was called.

MOUSE(3) gives the starting X-coordinate of the pointer the last time the left button was pressed before calling MOUSE(0).

MOUSE(4) gives the starting Y-coordinate of the pointer the last time the left button was pressed before calling MOUSE(0).

MOUSE(5) gives the ending X-coordinate of the pointer the last time the left button was pressed before calling MOUSE(0).

MOUSE(6) gives the ending Y-coordinate of the pointer the last time the left button was pressed before calling MOUSE(0).

MOUSE ON   Section 2.8
MOUSE OFF
MOUSE STOP

Syntax :   MOUSE ON
                    MOUSE OFF
                    MOUSE STOP

These commands activate, pause or deactivate event trapping for the mouse. A mouse click is something that can be checked for event trapping. The MOUSE ON command makes it possible to do mouse trapping; MOUSE OFF turns it off; and MOUSE STOP turns it off until the next MOUSE ON command.

The subroutine that handles mouse clicks can be set with the ON MOUSE GOSUB command.

NEW   Section 1.9

Syntax :   NEW

The NEW command erases the program currently in memory. Before it does this, all the files are closed and the trace mode is turned off by the TROFF command.

If you haven't saved the program in its current form, a requester will advise you of that fact.

ON BREAK GOSUB

Syntax :   ON BREAK GOSUB label

You can use this command to tell AmigaBASIC which subroutine to branch to, if there is a program break and if event trapping is active for this event.

You can give a label or a line number. If you enter 0 as the label, program break event trapping will be turned off. You need to use BREAK ON to reactivate it.

The subroutine should let the user know that the program can't be broken and how he can end the program anyway (it would be nice to have a "Would you really like to quit" requester which has yes and no gadgets).

AmigaBASIC blocks break trapping while the subroutine is running so that a second event can't disturb taking care of the first.

The subroutine must be ended with the RETURN command.

ON ERROR GOSUB

Syntax :   ON ERROR GOSUB label

Using this command, you can let AmigaBASIC know which
subroutine to call if an error shows up and event trapping for errors is
active. You can enter a label or a line number. If you enter a 0, event
trapping for errors will be turned off.

You can use ERR to find out which error it was, and ERL to find out the
last line number before the incorrect line occurred. Using the ERROR
command, it is even possible to use your own error numbers in the
program. If another error occurs in the subroutine, AmigaBASIC
crashes the program. To return to the main program, you need a
RESUME command at the end of the subroutine (see RESUME for more
information).

ON...GOSUB   Section 2.9

Syntax :   ON x GOSUB label [, label] [, label]

Using this command, you can call various subroutines making your
choice based on the value of x. If x=1, the program jumps to the first
label, if x=2 it jumps to the second, etc. If x is a floating-point
number, the value will be rounded. If x is bigger than the number of
labels that follow the GOSUB, the program continues moving along, but
it doesn't jump. If x is negative, you'll get an "Illegal function
call" error.

ON...GOTO   Section 2.9

Syntax :   ON x GOTO label [, label] [, label]

Read the explanation of ON...GOSUB above, since ON...GOTO functions are
the same way. The only difference is that the program jumps to another
section instead of calling a subroutine.

ON MENU GOSUB   Section 2.8

Syntax :   ON MENU GOSUB label

You use this command to tell AmigaBASIC which subroutine to call
when the user chooses an item from a pulldown menu, and when event
trapping is active for this event. You can give a label or a line number
for label. If you enter 0 as the label, event trapping for pulldown
menus will be turned off. To reactivate it, you need to use the MENU ON
command. You can find which option was chosen with the MENU (x)

function. AmigaBASIC blocks menu trapping while the subroutine is running, so that a second event can't take over the first event. The subroutine must be ended with a RETURN command.

ON MOUSE GOSUB   Section 2.8

Syntax :   ON MOUSE GOSUB Label

You can use this command to tell AmigaBASIC which subroutine to call when the user clicks the left mouse key, and when event trapping is active for this event. You can use a label or a line number for label. If you enter 0 for label, event trapping for the mouse will be turned off. To activate it, you need to use the MOUSE ON command. You can get information about the mouse using the MOUSE(x) function. AmigaBASIC blocks mouse trapping while the subprogram is running, so that a second event can't interfere with processing the first event.

The subroutine must be ended with the RETURN command.

ON TIMER GOSUB

Syntax :   ON TIMER(x) GOSUB Label

This tells AmigaBASIC which subroutine to call if x seconds have gone by since the last timer event, and if event trapping is active. This version of event trapping makes it possible to call a subprogram at regular intervals. x must be between 1 (1 second) and 86400 (60*60*24 seconds = 24 hours). You can use a label or a line number. If you enter 0 for a label, timer event trapping will be turned off. To activate it, you need to use the TIMER ON command.

AmigaBASIC blocks timer trapping while the subroutine is running, so that a second event can't interfere with processing the first. The subroutine must end with a RETURN command.

OPTION BASE

Syntax :   OPTION BASE x

Arrays usually have a starting element number of 0 (such as Hello(0), Hue(0,0)). If you want your arrays to start with 1 (Hello(1), Hue(1,1)), use the OPTION BASE 1 command. This command must be executed before any DIM statements are executed and before array elements are accessed. Otherwise, you'll get a "Duplicate definition" error.

RANDOMIZE

Syntax :   RANDOMIZE [x]
                  RANDOMIZE TIMER

If you use random numbers (RND), you'll get the same values every time you run the program. The RANDOMIZE command gets around this problem by giving you a series of random numbers. If you give RANDOMIZE a number between - 32768 and 32767, the number will be used for random number computations. If you enter the same number, you'll get the same sequence of random numbers. If you don't enter a value, AmigaBASIC asks you for a value with:

Random Number Seed (-32768 to 32767)?

If you don't want to enter values manually, just use RANDOMIZE TIMER. AmigaBASIC uses the current time to make the calculations. In this way, you can get truly random numbers—your program will give different numbers each time it runs.

READ   Section 2.9

Syntax :   READ variable-list

This command reads a value from a DATA line, and puts the value in the variable that follows it. The variable must be of the same type as the value read (string to string, number to number). Each READ command increments an internal DATA pointer. If all the DATA statements are read before the pointer is done, you'll get an "Out of DATA" error.

REM   Section 4.6

Syntax :   REM [text]

You can use REM to put comments at the end of a BASIC line. You can also use it to produce a whole line of text. The REM command must be the last command on a line, or the only command on a line. Everything that comes after it in the line will be ignored by AmigaBASIC. You can use an apostrophe (') instead of the REM command if you wish.

RESTORE   Section 4.8

Syntax: RESTORE [line]

As you've read in the READ and DATA commands, READ increments a
pointer which points to the next DATA element to be read. You can use
RESTORE to move the pointer to a line or label you specify (backwards
or forwards). If you don't have a label behind RESTORE, the DATA
pointer will be reset to the beginning of the program.

RESUME

Syntax: RESUME [0]
                 RESUME NEXT
                 RESUME line

The RESUME command is used to end the subroutine that handles the
error caught with error trapping (see ON ERROR GOSUB). RESUME or
RESUME 0 executes the command that caused the error. RESUME NEXT
returns to the line following the one where the error occurred. In this
way, commands which contain errors can be ignored. RESUME line
lets you jump to any label, like one version of the RETURN command.

RUN

Syntax: RUN [label]
                 RUN filename [,R]

The RUN command starts the current BASIC program. The screen is
cleared, the **LIST** window is moved to the background, and any open
files are closed. You can use the RUN command in the **BASIC** window
and in the program. If you put label after RUN, the program starts at
the label entered. If you follow RUN with filename, the program
named will be loaded and started. If you put a ,R after filename, all
the open files stay open. This lets you load a program that will do more
file handling on these open files.

SHARED   Section 4.5

Syntax: SHARED variable-list

This command goes inside a subprogram. It says which variables from
the main program can be used in the subprogram as well. The variable
names are placed after the SHARED command. You identify arrays with a
pair of empty parentheses:

SUB Test STATIC
SHARED Testnumber, TestArray(), Test$

443

You can use several SHARED commands but only inside a subprogram. Compare this with the DIM command, which also has a SHARED option.

SLEEP

Syntax: SLEEP

This command is useful when you're doing event trapping. It stops the program until something happens that can be checked by event trapping. It isn't necessary that event trapping be activated for the event in this case. The following actions end SLEEP:

- Pressing a key on the keyboard

- Clicking the left mouse key

- Choosing a menu option in a pulldown menu

- Graphic object collision

- End of a TIMER execution

The SLEEP command is useful when you want to have the user press a key, any key. In contrast to INKEY$, SLEEP recognizes keys like <SHIFT>, <ALT>, <CTRL>, and <Amiga>.

STOP

Syntax: STOP

This command stops a running BASIC program. You can use CONT to continue the program. The STOP command does not close open files. You should keep that in mind when you return to direct mode.

SUB...STATIC

Syntax: SUB subprogram-name [(parameter-list, ...)] STATIC

You start a subprogram with this command. A subprogram is a subroutine that is independent from the rest of the program. It uses its own variables, but can use variables from the main program by using the SHARED command. Every subprogram has a name that can be used to call it. You can call it with the CALL command, but you can usually leave off that command. The name may be up to 40 characters in length. You can pass variables to the subprogram. You need to make sure that the type of variable that is passed agrees with the kind the SUB...STATIC line indicates. You identify arrays with parentheses:

```
SUB Hello (Test, Colors(), Alpha) STATIC
```

A subprogram is ended with the END SUB command. The lines of code between SUB and END SUB are only executed when the routine is called. If a subprogram is in the middle of the main program, AmigaBASIC jumps right over it.

The EXIT SUB command makes it possible to leave a subprogram before the END SUB command is reached.

SWAP

Syntax:
```
SWAP variable1,variable2
```

This command switches the values of two variables. After executing this command, variable1 has variable2's old value and vice versa. The two variables must be of the same variable type.

SYSTEM

Section 1.9

Syntax:
```
SYSTEM
```

This command ends AmigaBASIC. The Amiga returns to the Workbench or to the CLI, depending on where you called AmigaBASIC from.

If the current program wasn't saved yet, AmigaBASIC will alert you to that and offer you the chance to save the program.

TIMER ON
TIMER OFF
TIMER STOP

Syntax:
```
TIMER ON
TIMER OFF
TIMER STOP
```

These commands control timer event trapping. The TIMER ON command activates it; TIMER OFF turns it off; and TIMER STOP causes all timer events before the next TIMER ON command to be ignored.

Using the ON TIMER GOSUB command, you can declare which subprogram to jump to when there is a timer break.

TRON   Section 1.14
TROFF

Syntax: TRON
                 TROFF

These two commands control the Trace function. The TRON
command turns trace mode on; TROFF turns it off.

If the Trace function is activated, the current command will be
displayed in the **LIST** window in an orange rectangle. That can be
very useful when you are testing the program.

WHILE...WEND   Section 2.8

Syntax: WHILE expression
                 [statement] WEND

A WHILE...WEND loop is executed as long as the conditions are met.
When the conditions are no longer met, the program continues after the
WEND command.

A typical example is waiting for someone to input something from the
keyboard:

WHILE INKEY$="" : WEND

You can nest WHILE...WEND loops to any depth within each other.

B.5   Calculations and BASIC functions

ABS   Section 1.17

Syntax: ABS(Value)

The ABS function returns the absolute value of a number. The absolute value is the number without its positive or negative leading character. For example, ABS(-2) is 2; ABS(0) is 0.

AND   Intermission 3

Syntax: value = Value1 AND Value2

The logical operation AND produces value by combining the individual bits of Value1 and Value2 as follows:

```
0 AND 0 = 0
0 AND 1 = 0
1 AND 0 = 0
1 AND 1 = 1
```

ASC   Section 4.3

Syntax: Value=ASC(String)

The ASC function puts the ASCII (American Standard Code for Information Interchange) code of the first character of the string that is in parentheses into Value. If the string is empty, you'll get an "Illegal function call" error. You can find a table of ASCII codes in the description of CHR$.

ATN

Syntax: Value=ATN(Value)

The ATN command calculates the arctangent of the value in parentheses, with the answer in radians. The value lies between -1/2*π and +1/2*π. If you want to convert degrees into radians, use one of the following formulas:

```
Degrees = (180 * Radians)/π
Degrees = 57.296 * Radians
```

CDBL   Section 1.17
CINT
CLNG
CSNG

Syntax: CDBL (Value)
                 CINT (Value)
                 CLNG (Value)
                 CSNG (Value)

This series of commands convert a number into another format.

CDBL produces a double precision floating point number.

CINT produces a 16-bit integer. The number will be rounded in the usual fashion (i.e., CINT (3.4) =3 and CINT (3.5) =4). The Value in parentheses must be between -32768 and 32767.

CLNG produces a 32 bit integer. The number is rounded. The Value in parentheses must be between - 2147483648 and 2147483647.

CSNG produces a single precision floating point number.

If Value is too big to fit into a variable of the desired numeric type, you'll get an "Overflow" error. Read Intermission 5 to find out about the various numeric types.

CHR$ Section 1.15

Syntax: CHR$ (Value)

The CHR$ statement produces the character that corresponds to the ASCII (American Standard Code for Information Interchange) code number stated in parentheses as Value. Value must be in integer between 0 and 255. The ASCII code is a code which assigns every printable character and every control character a value between 0 and 255. The codes from 128 to 255 are non-standard, but the Amiga uses them for function keys and foreign characters. The characters with boxes next to them haven't been assigned values. Figure 21 is a table of ASCII codes.

0 [CTRL]-[@]		64 @	128 □		192 À
1 [CTRL]-[A]		65 A	129 □	(F1)	193 Á
2 [CTRL]-[B]		66 B	130 □	(F2)	194 Â
3 [CTRL]-[C]	(Break)	67 C	131 □	(F3)	195 Ã
4 [CTRL]-[D]		68 D	132 □	(F4)	196 Ä
5 [CTRL]-[E]		69 E	133 □	(F5)	197 Å
6 [CTRL]-[F]		70 F	134 □	(F6)	198 Æ
7 [CTRL]-[G]	(Beep)	71 G	135 □	(F7)	199 Ç
8 [CTRL]-[H]	(BACKSPACE)	72 H	136 □	(F8)	200 È
9 [CTRL]-[I]	(TAB)	73 I	137 □	(F9)	201 É
10 [CTRL]-[J]	(Line feed)	74 J	138 □	(F10)	202 Ê
11 [CTRL]-[K]		75 K	139 □	(HELP)	203 Ë
12 [CTRL]-[L]	(Delete)	76 L	140 □		204 Ì
13 [CTRL]-[M]	(Return)	77 M	141 □		205 Í
14 [CTRL]-[N]		78 N	142 □		206 Î
15 [CTRL]-[O]		79 O	143 □		207 Ï
16 [CTRL]-[P]		80 P	144 □		208 Ð
17 [CTRL]-[Q]		81 Q	145 □		209 Ñ
18 [CTRL]-[R]		82 R	146 □		210 Ò
19 [CTRL]-[S]		83 S	147 □		211 Ó
20 [CTRL]-[T]		84 T	148 □		212 Ô
21 [CTRL]-[U]		85 U	149 □		213 Õ
22 [CTRL]-[V]		86 V	150 □		214 Ö
23 [CTRL]-[W]		87 W	151 □		215 □
24 [CTRL]-[X]		88 X	152 □		216 Ø
25 [CTRL]-[Y]		89 Y	153 □		217 Ù
26 [CTRL]-[Z]		90 Z	154 □		218 Ú
27 [CTRL]-[[]	(ESC)	91 [	155 □		219 Û
28 [CTRL]-[\]	(up)	92 \	156 □		220 Ü
29 [CTRL]-[]]	(down)	93]	157 □		221 Ý
30 [CTRL]-[^]	(right)	94 ^	158 □		222 Þ
31 [CTRL]-[_]	(left)	95 _	159 □		223 ß
32		96 `	160		224 à

Figure 21a:
ASCII table

33	!	97	a	161	¡	225	á
34	"	98	b	162	¢	226	â
35	#	99	c	163	£	227	ã
36	$	100	d	164	¤	228	ä
37	%	101	e	165	¥	229	å
38	&	102	f	166	¦	230	æ
39	'	103	g	167	§	231	ç
40	(	104	h	168	¨	232	è
41	)	105	i	169	©	233	é
42	*	106	j	170	ª	234	ê
43	+	107	k	171	«	235	ë
44	,	108	l	172	¬	236	ì
45	-	109	m	173	-	237	í
46	.	110	n	174	®	238	î
47	/	111	o	175	¯	239	ï
48	0	112	p	176	°	240	ð
49	1	113	q	177	±	241	ñ
50	2	114	r	178	²	242	ò
51	3	115	s	179	³	243	ó
52	4	116	t	180	´	244	ô
53	5	117	u	181	µ	245	õ
54	6	118	v	182	¶	246	ö
55	7	119	w	183	·	247	÷
56	8	120	x	184		248	ø
57	9	121	y	185	¹	249	ù
58	:	122	z	186	º	250	ú
59	;	123	{	187	»	251	û
60	<	124	|	188	¼	252	ü
61	=	125	}	189	½	253	ý
62	>	126	~	190	¾	254	þ
63	?	127	⌂	191	¿	255	ÿ

Figure 21b:
ASCII table

COS   Section 2.5

Syntax: Value=COS(Value)

The COS function calculates the cosine of a value. The value in parentheses must be in radians. If you want to convert from degrees to radians, use one of the following formulas:

```
Radians = (π * Degrees)/180
Radians = 0.0175 * Degrees
```

CVD   Section 4.1
CVI
CVL
CVS

Syntax: `Value=CVD(8-byte-long string)`
                   `Value=CVI(2-byte-long string)`
                   `Value=CVL(4-byte-long string)`
                   `Value=CVS(4-byte-long string)`

It is quicker and consumes less memory to read numbers from and write numbers to files as strings. The `MK*$` functions help you do this. To convert these strings back to numbers when you read them, these four functions are available.

The `CVD` function converts an 8-byte-long string into a double precision floating-point number.

The `CVI` function converts a 2-byte-long string into a 16-bit integer.

The `CVL` function converts a 4-byte-long string into a 32-bit integer.

The `CVS` function converts a 4-byte-long string into a single precision floating-point number.

Read Intermission 5 to find out more about numeric types.

DATE$ Section 1.17

Syntax: `String=DATE$`

This function gives you the system date in the form of a string that is 10 characters long. The system date is the date that is set with `Preferences`. The date is in MM-DD-YYYY format.

EQV   Intermission 3

Syntax: `Value = Value1 EQV Value2`

The logical operation `EQV` combines the individual bits of `Value1` and `Value2` to produce `Value` in the following way:

```
0 EQV 0 = 1
0 EVV 1 = 0
1 EQV 0 = 0
1 EQV 1 = 1
```

EXP

Syntax: Value=EXP (Value)

The EXP function calculates the exponent of e (2.7182818284590). e is the base number for natural logarithms.

See LOG for more information.

FIX

Syntax: Value=FIX (Value)

This function removes the decimal places of a number. For example, FIX(3.235325) is 3 and FIX(-2.3532325) is -2. In contrast to INT and CINT, FIX does not round off numbers, merely returns the whole number left when the decimal places are removed.

HEX$

Syntax: HEX$ (Value)

This function produces a hexadecimal number from a decimal number. Value is a number between—32768 and 65535.

print HEX$ (60037) produces EA85.

You can find more about hexadecimal numbers in Intermission 3.

IMP   Intermission 3

Syntax: Value = Value1 IMP Value2

The logical operator IMP uses the individual bits of Value1 and Value2 to produce Value in the following ways:

```
0 IMP 0 = 1
0 IMP 1 = 1
1 IMP 0 = 0
1 IMP 1 = 1
```

INSTR

Syntax: Value=INSTR([Value,] string, search-string)

This function searches for search-string in the preceding String. If it finds search-string within string, it gives the position at which search-string starts in string.

INSTR will return 0 if search-string isn't found, if it is an empty string, or if it is longer than the string to be searched.

You have the option of including the position in the string from which the search should begin. If this position is bigger than the length of the string to be searched, you'll get a 0 as the result.

```
INSTR("Amiga","iga") gives a 3.
INSTR("Hello","iga") gives a 0.
INSTR(3,"Test","es") gives a 0.
```

INT   Section 1.17

Syntax: `Value=INT(Value)`

This function converts a floating-point number into an integer. This function has the following differences from CINT and FIX: It drops off the part behind the decimal point if the number is positive, but it rounds the number if it is negative; the INT command produces the nearest integer smaller than or equal to the input number.

```
INT(3.4) is 3.
INT(3.8) is 3.
INT(-2.2) is -3.
```

The INT function can work with numbers in any range.

LBOUND
UBOUND

Syntax: `Value=LBOUND(Array [,Dimension])`
                  `Value=UBOUND(Array [,Dimension])`

This function gives you the number of the first (Lower BOUNDary) array element and the last (Upper BOUNDary) array element. In this way, you can find the values which were set with DIM and OPTION BASE.

For example, using OPTION BASE 0 :DIM a(200) would make LBOUND(a) equal to 0, and UBOUND(a) equal to 200.

If you give a dimension value, you can find the upper and lower bounds of individual dimensions.

For example, from DIM a(3,4,56), UBOUND(a,1) gives you the size of the first array dimension, which is 3. UBOUND(a,2) gives 4; UBOUND(a,3) gives 56.

If you leave off the dimension value, you'll get the answer for the first array dimension.

LEFT$ Section 1.16

Syntax: `String= LEFT$ (String, Number)`

LEFT$ produces a string using the left part of the string that is entered. The number is the number of characters in the string on the left side of the equal sign (i.e., the one you are producing with this function). Since strings may not be longer than 32767 characters in AmigaBASIC, the number must be between 0 and 32767.

`LEFT$ ("Amiga is great!",5)` returns `"Amiga"`.

LEN   Section 1.17

Syntax: `Value=LEN (String)`

The LEN function tells you how many characters `String` contains. Blanks and control characters in the string are counted as well.

`LEN ("Amiga is great!")` returns 15.

LOG   Section 4.8

Syntax: `Value=LOG (Value)`

The LOG function calculates the natural logarithm of a number. The natural logarithm is the logarithm of e. e is 2.7182818284590.

The logarithm of a to base b is the number c where $b^c=a$. `LOG (a)` to the base b is c.

If you need logarithms for calculations in BASIC (like in our PICSAVE routine), then you may need another base. Here is the formula to find the logarithm of a number in another base:

`LOG (a)` to the base b = `LOG (a) /LOG (b)`

MID$ Section 4.7

Syntax: `String section=MID$ (String,Position [,Length])`

You can use MID$ to extract a piece of a string. Enter the `String` and the `Position` of the first character to be included in the new string. You can also enter the `Length` of `String`. If you don't enter a length, you'll get everything at and following the position specified.

`MID$ ("Amiga is great!",10,5)` produces `"great"`.

MID$

Syntax: MID$(String,Position [,Length])=Replace-string

This version of MID$ is used to overwrite part of String with Replace-string. Position is the position at which the overwriting starts. If you enter a Length, only that many characters will be overwritten.

```
a$="Amiga is super!" : MID$(a$,10)="great"
```
returns "Amiga is great!".

MKD$ Section 4.1
MKI$
MKL$
MKS$

Syntax: MKD$(double precision floating-point number)
                 MKI$(16-bit integer)
                 MKL$(32-bit integer)
                 MKS$(single precision floating-point number)

Time and memory can be saved by storing numbers as strings which contain as many characters as the number has bytes:

MKD$ converts a double precision floating-point number into an 8-byte-long string.

MKI$ converts a 16-bit integer into a 2-byte-long string.

MKL$ converts a 32-bit integer into a 4-byte-long string.

MKS$ converts a single precision floating-point number into a 4-byte-long string.

You can convert these numbers back to the original format using the CV* commands.

NOT   Intermission 3

Syntax: Value = NOT Value

The logical operation NOT converts a 0 to a -1 and a -1 to a 0. It reverses the value of a condition:

```
IF NOT (a<1) THEN...
```

The THEN will be executed when a is **not** less than 1, i.e., when a is greater than or equal to 1. This is done using the following formula:

```
NOT x = -(x+1)
```

This doesn't make much sense for values other than -1 and 0.

OCT$

Syntax: `String=OCT$(Value)`

This function produces a string containing the octal representation of a number. If you've forgotten what an octal number is, look at Intermission 3.

`OCT$(60037)` produces &O165205.

OR   Intermission 3

Syntax: `Value = Value1 OR Value2`

The logical operation OR produces `Value` by combining the individual bits of `Value1` and `Value2` as follows:

```
0 OR 0 = 0
0 OR 1 = 1
1 OR 0 = 1
1 OR 1 = 1
```

PEEK   Section 4.3

Syntax: `PEEK(Address)`

PEEK finds the contents of the address given to it. It returns a number between 0 and 255, a byte. The highest allowable number for `Address` on the Amiga is 16777215. Many of the addresses in this range will have nothing in them, unless you have a full 8 megabytes of RAM added on.

PEEKL   Section 4.3

Syntax: `PEEKL(Address)`

PEEKL returns the contents of four consecutive bytes starting at `Address`. `Address` must be an even number. It returns a number between -2147483648 and +2147483647, a 4-byte integer. You can find out more about addresses under the PEEK command.

PEEKW

Syntax: PEEKW(Address)

PEEKW returns the contents of the two bytes which start at Address. Address must be an even number. It returns a number between 32768 and +32767, a 2-byte integer. You can find more about addresses under the PEEK command.

POKE

Syntax: POKE Address, Value

POKE writes a one-byte value into the memory location you specify at Address. You can find out more about addresses under PEEK.

You should be careful when you write values to memory. If you don't plan correctly and don't know a fair amount about the Amiga operating system, you might do more harm than good.

POKEL

Syntax: POKEL Address, Value

The POKEL command writes a 4-byte value to the four-byte-long range starting at Address. Address must be an even number. You can find more about the command itself under the PEEKL and POKE commands.

POKEW

Syntax: POKEW Address, Value

POKEW writes a 2-byte value in the two-byte-long memory block starting at Address. Address must be an even number. You can find more about the legal addresses under the PEEK command. You'll also find more information concerning this command under the PEEKW and POKE commands.

RIGHT$

Syntax: String section=RIGHT$(String,Length)

This string function produces a string containing Length number of characters from the right end of String.

RIGHT$("Amiga is great!",6) produces "great!".

RND

Section 2.5

Syntax :

Value=RND[(x)]

The RND function produces a random number between 0 and 1.

If you enter a value in the brackets, you can control the production of the random number: 1 and all positive values produce a fixed sequence of random numbers. Everytime you execute the program, the same numbers will be used. The default is this mode.

0 gives you the last random number. If you just work with RND(0), you'll always get the same number. -1 and all negative values pass a new starting value that is used to produce random numbers. If you enter the same random numbers, you'll get the same random number sequence. You can find more by reading about the RANDOMIZE command.

You'll often need a random number within a certain range. Here is the formula.

Random = Start + ((End-Start)*RND)

If the numbers must be integers, use

Random = INT(Start +((End-Start+1)*RND))

SADD

Syntax

Value=SADD(String)

This function is especially good for machine language programs. It gives you the starting address in memory of String. If you use new strings in your program, you'll need to ask about the starting address again, because AmigaBASIC moves strings around a lot.

SGN

Syntax

Value=SGN(Value)

The SGN function finds the sign of a variable. It comes back

-1 for negative numbers
0 for the number 0
1 for positive numbers

SIN   Section 2.5

Syntax: `Value=SIN(Value)`

The `SIN` function calculates the sine of an angle entered in radians. If you would prefer to work in degrees, look under `COS` to find out how to calculate the radians that correspond to degree measurement.

SPACE$ Section 5.2

Syntax: `String=SPACE$(Length)`

This string function produces a string containing `Length` number of spaces. `Length` must be in integer between 0 and 32767. Strings like this are useful for formatting screen and printer output. They can also be used to erase single lines on the screen.

SQR

Syntax: `Value=SQR(Value)`

SQR calculates the square root of a number.

`SQR(4)` is 2, `SQR(2)` is 1.414214.

STR$ Section 3.4

Syntax: `String=STR$(Value)`

`STR$` converts a number into a string. It doesn't produce bytes for storage, but instead produces a string containing all the digits in the number.

`STR$(4095)` is "4095".

STRING$ Section 1.16

Syntax: `STRING$(Length, ASCII-code)`
                   `STRING$(Length,String)`

The `STRING$` function produces a string of the desired `Length` containing just the character that corresponds to `ASCII-code`, or to the first character of the string:

```
PRINT STRING$(100,191)
PRINT STRING$(100,"A")
```

TAN

Syntax: TAN (Value)

The TAN function calculates the tangent of an angle which is entered in radians. You can find out how to convert degrees into radians by the description of the COS function.

TIME$ Section 1.17

Syntax: TIME$

The TIME$ function gives the system time. You can set this time in Preferences; it is not automatically correct. An 8-character-long string is returned in the form HH:MM:SS (hours:minutes:seconds).

TIMER   Section 1.17

Syntax: TIMER

The function TIMER gives you the current system time in seconds. It tells you the number of seconds that have gone by since midnight (00:00:00). The value comes from the Amiga's inner clock, so it is not necessarily set to the current time. You need to set it with Preferences to be sure that it is correct.

UCASE$ Section 1.16

Syntax: UCASE$ (String)

The UCASE$ command converts all the lower-case letters in the input string into upper-case letters.

UCASE$ ("Amiga") is "AMIGA".

This is really useful for sorting text alphabetically and for checking user input.

VAL   Section 1.7

Syntax: VAL (String)

The VAL function is the converse of the STR$ function. A string that contains a number will be converted into a number. It will only read characters up to the point the first letter appears:

VAL ("1234Hello") is 1234.
VAL ("1234Hello4567") is 1234 as well.
VAL ("Hello1234") is 0.

VARPTR

Syntax: VARPTR(Variable)

This is similar to what SADD does for strings; VARPTR finds the
starting address of a variable in memory.

You'll need VARPTR a lot if you use machine language subroutines in
AmigaBASIC. You can find more information in the description of the
CALL command.

XOR   Intermission 3

Syntax: Value1 XOR Value2

The XOR operation produces Value by operating on the bits of Value1
and Value2 as follows:

```
0 XOR 0 = 0
0 XOR 1 = 1
1 XOR 0 = 1
1 XOR 1 = 0
```

B.6

File, disk, and input/output commands

CHDIR

Section 3.2

Syntax:

CHDIR " [Device or disk drive:] [Directory]
[/Directory...]"

The CHDIR command changes the current directory. You can either go deeper into the subdirectories, or you can choose a totally new path. Figure 13 on page 204 shows you how a system of subdirectories is constructed.

You can use CHDIR "/" to move up one level in the system of directories. If you are already at the highest level and try to move up, you'll get a "File not found" error. You'll get the same message if you enter a subdirectory that doesn't exist. You can get to the top level directory with CHDIR ":".

CLOSE

Section 3.3

Syntax:

CLOSE [[#] File number] [, [#] File number]

The CLOSE command can be used to close one or more files.

There are several reasons to close files.

First, AmigaBASIC has a temporary buffer for every file. The last buffer contents won't be written to disk until you use the CLOSE command. Second, AmigaDOS writes certain information to disk about the current status of the file (for example, the length of the file). Third, the file number will be freed up for use by another OPEN command.

You can find more about files under the description of the OPEN command.

EOF

Section 3.3

Syntax:

EOF (File number)

The EOF function checks if there are more data to be read from a file. EOF (File number) returns 0 when more data are read. It returns -1 when you've reached the end of the file.

You can use this function to see whether you may read in more data or not. If you try to read data and no more data is available, you'll get the "Input past end" error message.

FIELD   Section 5.1

Syntax: FIELD [#] File number, Length AS STRING [, Length AS STRING, ...]

This command is used for working with random files. You can use it to set up a data record buffer and to define different string variables as transfer variables for the buffer. Length is the number of characters in a field. STRING is a variable name. If you want to set up a record buffer with 10 bytes for the first name and 20 bytes for the last name, you can do as follows:

FIELD #1, 10 AS FirstName$, 20 AS LastName$

Only the commands LSET and RSET may be used to assign new values to these variables or the relationship between variable and buffer will be messed up. The total length of all the fields may not be longer than the record length declared for the file when you used the OPEN command. Otherwise you'll get a "Field overflow" error. If you enter a new FIELD line for the same file, the buffer will be completely redivided.

FILES   Section 3.2

Syntax: FILES [Directory]

FILES shows the current directory contents on the screen. You can use CHDIR to change the directory you are in. If you enter a directory after the FILES command, you can look at the directory's contents without making it into the current directory. This is useful when you are searching for a specific directory.

GET (*Random file GET*)   Section 5.1

Syntax: GET [#] File number [, Record number]

The GET command reads the record whose number is specified into the file buffer when you are working with random files. If you don't enter a record number, the next record number will be used. The record number must theoretically lie between 0 and 16777215. In practice, the storage capacity of the device (floppy disk, hard disk, RAM disk) governs the size of the biggest record number. In any case, the number is usually much less than 16777215.

After using the GET command, you can read the contents of the buffer. You can either use the transfer variables defined with the FIELD command or with the INPUT# and LINE INPUT# commands.

INPUT$ Section 4.1

Syntax: String=INPUT$(Length [, [#] File number])

This command is used for sequential files. It reads a string of the specified length from the file specified.

If you leave off the file number, INPUT$ reads the desired number of characters from the keyboard. The text cursor appears while this is being read, but your input won't be put on the screen while you type. You can't stop the reading from the keyboard with the <RETURN> key. The only way to stop it is by using <CTRL><C>. When you read bytes using INPUT$, you can convert them back to numbers using the CV* functions.

INPUT#   Section 3.3

Syntax: INPUT# File number, Variable [,Variable, ...]

This command works like the normal screen INPUT, but it reads variables or strings from a file instead. This file must have been OPENed beforehand. The data that INPUT# read was previously written into the file with PRINT# or WRITE#.

INPUT# reads a variable until it reaches the next separator in the file. This command recognizes spaces, commas, carriage returns (CHR$(10)), and linefeeds (CHR$(13)) as separators. Spaces aren't recognized as separators for strings. If you want to read strings which contain commas, you need to write the strings to the file in quotation marks.

KILL   Section 3.2

Syntax: KILL File name

You can use KILL to erase files from a floppy disk, hard disk, or RAM disk. Files that are currently open may not be erased. The current version of AmigaBASIC automatically erases the info file at the same time.

LINE INPUT#

Syntax: LINE INPUT# File number, Variable

This command works just like LINE INPUT, except that it reads characters from a file. It only recognizes carriage returns (CHR$(10)) and linefeeds (CHR$(13)) as separators. All other characters, including spaces and commas, will be included in the string.

LLIST   Section 3.5

Syntax: LLIST [Line number or label] [-] [Line number or label]

The LLIST command works like LIST, except that it sends the listing to a printer connected to the Amiga. You can tell the Amiga what kind of printer and interface you are using in the Preferences menu. See the LIST command description for more information.

LOAD   Section 1.13

Syntax: LOAD [Filename] [,R]

The LOAD command loads a program from a floppy disk, hard disk, or RAM disk. If you put ,R behind the program name, the program will be started right after loading. If you do not enter Filename, AmigaBASIC will use a requester to ask you for a name.

LOC

Syntax: Value=LOC(File number)

The LOC function gives the number of the data block on floppy disk, hard disk, or RAM disk that was last read or written. Even though this value is dependent only on the division of memory by AmigaDOS, it will give you the number of the last record that was read when you are working with random files. This is because a block in a buffer always corresponds to a record when you are working with random files.

It's more complicated for sequential files. Here, the LOC function gives the block number in a way that is dependent on the buffer size. The standard size for the buffer is 128 bytes, but you can change that when you use the OPEN command.

LOF   Section 4.1

Syntax: LOF (File number)

The LOF function finds the length of a file in bytes. You can use this to read in the information when you recognize the value or read in the whole file at once (e.g., for OBJECT.SHAPE).

LPOS

Syntax: LPOS (x)

This works like POS, but gives the value of the last character in the printer buffer that was output. You can use this to find how many characters in the current line have already been sent to the printer. The value x is just a formal parameter here too (compare this with POS).

LPRINT   Section 3.5

Syntax: LPRINT [Variable or Value] [separator] [Variable or Value ...]

This works like PRINT, except that the output is sent to a printer connected to the Amiga. The characters are buffered, and are printed when a carriage return code is found (CHR$ (10)). If you don't put a separator after the last variable, AmigaBASIC automatically sends a CHR$ (10) to the printer.

See the description of PRINT for more information.

LPRINT USING

Syntax: LPRINT USING (Format string) ; (Variable or Value) [;]

This works like the PRINT USING statement, except that the output goes to the printer. See the LPRINT and PRINT USING command descriptions for more information.

LSET   Section 5.1

Syntax: LSET Transfer-string=String

The LSET command is used for working with random files. It transfers data into the record buffer. Take Transfer-string that you defined in the FIELD command and assign it a string. This string will be transferred to the buffer. The L in LSET stands for Left-justified. If the data are shorter than the length specified in the FIELD command, it will be put in the data field in left-justified format (i.e., the text will be placed flush with the left margin, and spaces will be inserted to the right of the text). Compare this with the RSET command. To transfer numeric information to the buffer, you need to use conversion functions like MK*$ or STR$. To move data from the buffer to the diskette, use the PUT command.

MERGE   Intermission 2

Syntax: MERGE Filename

You can use MERGE to read a program or subprogram from diskette and append it to the current program. The program you read must be in ASCII format on the diskette (see SAVE).

You can execute MERGE during the program. However, after executing MERGE, AmigaBASIC returns to direct mode. The CHAIN command is better for chaining and loading programs. In contrast, the MERGE command is intended for use while developing your program.

NAME   Section 3.2

Syntax: NAME (Old filename) AS (New filename)

You can use NAME to rename a file on a floppy disk, hard disk, or RAM disk. Don't use a device or directory identifier in the new name that isn't in the old name, or you'll get a "Rename across disks" error.

The current version of AmigaBASIC automatically renames the info file at the same time.

OPEN   Section 3.3

Syntax: OPEN File name [FOR Mode] AS [#] File number
               [LEN=Length]
               OPEN Mode-symbol, [#] File number, File name
               [, Length]

The OPEN command opens a file. You can use either syntax version; both do the same thing. In the first syntax, you first enter the filename and then the mode. You can open a file FOR INPUT, FOR OUTPUT, or FOR APPEND. All of these modes are for working with sequential files. If you leave off FOR and the mode in the first syntax, AmigaBASIC opens a random file.

At the end of the OPEN line, you have the option of entering the length of the buffer in bytes. This is really important for random files. The number that you enter here is the sum of the field lengths from the FIELD command. The second version looks a bit different, but works exactly the same. mode-symbol is a letter that represents the file's mode: I stands for sequential input, O for sequential output, A for sequenial append mode, and R for a random file. The other things mean exactly the same thing as they did in the first version.

You can open sequential files for all input and output devices (SCRN:, KYBD:, PRT:, PAR:, SER:) and read data from them or send data to them. A sequential file may only be opened for reading or writing. You can't do both at the same time.

OPEN "COM1:"

Syntax: OPEN "COM1: [Baud] [,Parity] [,Wordlength]
                 [,Stopbits]" [FOR mode] AS [#] [File number]

You can use this variation of the OPEN command to open a file for an RS-232 interface, an interface for serial data transfer. If you do not intend to use one of these interfaces, the following information won't be of much use to you.

Baud is the rate of transfer (baudrate). It can be 110, 150, 300, 600, 1200, 1800, 2400, 4800, 9600, or 19200. The standard value is 9600. The value you use depends on the device you wish to exchange data with.

Parity sets the mode for checking the data when you send and receive it. The sender and receiver must use the same value. There are three options: E (even), O (odd), and N (none—no parity check). The standard setting is E.

Wordlength tells how many bits per byte contain information. The values 5, 6, 7, and 8 are possible; 7 is the standard value.

Stopbits sets the number of stop bits. This value must be controlled for serial transfer as well. The values available are 1 and 2. Normally 2 stop bits are used at 110 baud, and all the other baud rates use 1 stop bit. You may change this if you wish.

You can choose FOR INPUT or FOR OUTPUT as modes. If you leave off FOR mode, you'll be in a mode where you can both send and receive information.

PRINT#
PRINT# USING

Section 3.3

Syntax: PRINT# File number [USING (Format string);] [[Variable
            or value] [Separator] [Variable or Value ...]

These two commands work just like PRINT and PRINT USING, except
that they write their output to a file. You can find more information
under the descriptions of the PRINT, PRINT USING, and INPUT#
commands.

PUT (*random file PUT*)

Section 5.1

Syntax: PUT [#] File number [,Record-number]

The PUT command writes the data in the record buffer of a random file
to the disk. Only after using it is the data really in the file. You can
enter or leave off Record-number. It you don't enter it, AmigaBASIC
writes it to the record whose number is one larger than the current
record. The record number must be between 0 and 16777215. You can
find more information under the random file GET command.

RSET

Syntax: RSET Transfer string=String

The RSET and LSET commands are used for writing data in the record
buffer when you are working with random files. You use a transfer
variable that was defined by a FIELD command and assign it a string.
This string will be transferred to the buffer. The R in RSET stands for
Right-justified. That means that when the data is shorter than the field
that is reserved for it in the file, the data will be right-justified in the
data field. That means that all the blanks will be on the left, at the
beginning of the field, and the text will be moved so that its right edge
is flush with the right margin.

This is especially useful for numeric values that are printed out in a
standard format. To set up the data record buffer, you need the FIELD
command. To move the data from the buffer to the diskette, use the PUT
command. By the way, RSET and LSET can be used on normal strings
to produce strings that are right- or left-justified. Try it out.

```
Form$=SPACE$(20)
RSET Form$="Amiga"
WRITE Form$
```

SAVE   Section 1.8

Syntax: SAVE [(Filename)] [,A] [,B] [,P]

You can SAVE programs to floppy disk, hard disk, or RAM disk with
this command. If you don't enter Filename, AmigaBASIC will use a
requester to ask you for the name of the program. If you put an ,A after
Filename, it will be stored in ASCII format. You need this format if
you want to use MERGE to combine programs, or to edit an
AmigaBASIC program using a text editor.

If you put ,B after Filename, the program will be stored in binary
format. That is the default file form; the ,B can be left off if you wish.
The commands will be stored in tokenized form. You can store the
program in a protected form by using the ,P option. The program can
be loaded and run, but cannot be listed or changed.

STICK   Section 3.5

Syntax: STICK(x)

This command returns information from the joysticks that are connected
to the Amiga. The x tells what information you want:

Value:	Information:
0	x-movement of joystick 1
1	y-movement of joystick 1
2	x-movement of joystick 2
3	y-movement of joystick 2

STICK(x) returns 1 if the joystick was moved up or to the right.

STICK(x) returns 0 if the joystick asked about wasn't moved.

STICK(x) returns -1 if the joystick was moved down or left.

Be careful with joystick 1. If there's a mouse there instead of a joystick,
the mouse is blocked from registering, as soon as you use STICK(0)
or STICK(1).

STRIG   Section 3.5

Syntax: STRIG(x)

You can use STRIG to find whether the fire button on a joystick was
hit. The x tells which information you want to have.

STRIG(0) asks if the fire button on joystick 1 was hit since the last
STRIG(0). If yes, you'll get a -1, if no, you'll get a 0.

STRIG(1) asks if the fire button on joystick 1 is presently being pressed. A -1 = yes, while a 0 = no.

STRIG(2) asks if the fire button on joystick 2 was pressed since the last STRIG(2). A -1 = yes, while a 0 = no.

STRIG(3) asks if the fire button on joystick 2 is presently being pressed. A -1 = yes, while a 0 = no.

You can find more information in the description of the STICK command.

WRITE#   Section 3.4

Syntax: WRITE# File number, [Variable or Value] [Separator] [Variable or Value...]

This command works like WRITE, except that its output is sent to a file.

The command is especially good for writing strings to sequential files, since they'll be sent to the file within quotation marks. When you read them, you'll get the whole string, even if it contains separators. You may not have quotation marks in the string.

B.7   Speech and tone production

SAY   Section 6.2

Syntax: SAY Phoneme-string [, Array%(0), Array%(1), Array%(2),
                  Array%(3), Array%(4), Array%(5), Array%(6), Array%(7),
                  Array%(8)]

The SAY command says a string that is written using phoneme codes.
You can use the TRANSLATE$ command to convert normal text into
phoneme code. You can also enter the text in phonemes yourself.
Appendix H of the *Amiga BASIC* manual explains how to do this. You
can put the name of an integer array that has at least 9 elements behind
Phoneme string. The integers influence the way the Amiga will talk:

Array%(0) is the pitch of the speech. You can set how high the voice
should be here. Values range from 65 (deep) to 320 (high). The default
value (value that will be used if you don't put an array behind the
phoneme string) is 110.

Array%(1) determines whether the speech should be inflected (0) or
computer monotone (1). The default value is 0.

Array%(2) sets the rate of speed. This value is in words per minute.
Values can range from 40 (slow) to 400 (fast). The default value is 150.

Array%(3) determines whether the voice should sound male (0) or
female (1).

Array%(4) determines the tuning, or sampling frequency. This value
influences the voice deepness most of all. Values may range from 5000
(deep) to 28000 (high). The default value is 22200. Extreme values lead
to incomprehensible speech.

Array%(5) determines the volume level. The values may range from 0
(sound off) to 65 (loud). The default value is 65.

Array%(6) determines which channel the voice will go through (see
Table 10 in Section 6.3). The default value is 10 (any free pair of right
and left channels).

Array%(7) determines whether AmigaBASIC should halt the program
while the computer is talking (0) or if the speech should run in the
background while the program continues (1).

Array%(8) determines what should happen if two SAY commands follow each other (on condition that you have a 1 in Array%(7)). 0 means that the first SAY command will go to completion and then the new one will follow. 2 means that the new command will be executed immediately. The old speech output will be halted. 1 means that the current speech command won't be executed, regardless of the value in Array%(7). As long as this value is a 1, the SAY command cannot be executed.

SOUND   Section 7.2

Syntax :   SOUND frequency, duration[, volume] [, voice]

This command produces a tone. Enter the frequency in hertz. Values from 20 to 15000 hertz are allowed. Table 11 in Section 7.2 shows you which frequencies correspond to which musical notes. The duration of the tone is a value between 0 and 77. If you want the tone to play for about a second, you need to enter a value of about 18. Take a look at Table 12 on page 374. You can enter a volume level between 0 and 255. If you don't enter one, AmigaBASIC uses the default value 127. You can also control the voice channel the tone will use. There are four values available:

0 and 3 = left channel

1 and 2 = right channel

The default channel for both SOUND and BEEP is channel 0.

SOUND RESUME   Section 7.3
SOUND WAIT

Syntax :   SOUND RESUME
                  SOUND WAIT

To get several tones playing at the same time, or have a tune play in the background, put the tones into a wait loop. The SOUND WAIT command causes the SOUND commands to be stored instead of immediately executed. For multiple-voice music, unoccupied sound channels must be set; the best thing to do is use a tone with a volume level of 0.

The SOUND RESUME command causes the tone loop to start.

TRANSLATE$ Section 6.2

Syntax: Phoneme string=TRANSLATE$(String)

This string function translates String into Phoneme string. Phoneme string lets the SAY statement speak. Read the description of the SAY statement.

WAVE   Section 7.5

Syntax: WAVE Channel number, Integer array%
                    WAVE Channel number, SIN

You can use WAVE to change the waveform that will be used with the SOUND command. You can use SIN to have a sine wave. SIN is the default value, the one used when you don't state WAVE.

You can also use an integer array that contains at least 256 elements. The integer array contains a user-defined waveform. The array values lie between -128 and +127; they give the amplitude of the wave at the time of sampling. If you're confused, read Sections 7.4 (A bit of acoustical theory) and 7.5 (Waveforms).

The waveform will be assigned to one or more of the four tone channels (0 and 3 = left channel, 1 and 2 = right channel). After this assignment, you should ERASE the array to save memory.

C   "Error-free" listings

The following programs were directly transferred from the Amiga to our publishing equipment to ensure error-free programs. They are noticeably lengthy, and due to their size, your chances of making errors increase. If you would like to purchase a optional diskette containing the programs in this book (saving you the hassle of typing them in) there is ordering information in the back of this book.

The ¶ marker signifies the <Return> key. Formatting the programs to fit into this book caused some lines that must be typed in on one line to appear on more than one line. The ¶ symbol is used to show when the <Return> key should be pressed.

C.1

Video title program

```
Setup:¶
  Colors=4¶
  d=15 : MaxColors=(2^Colors)-1 ¶
  TextColor=1¶
  SCREEN CLOSE 2¶
  IF Colors>2 THEN SCREEN 2,640,200,Colors,2 : WINDOW
2,"Videotitle",,28,2¶
  DIM Text$(d),Colormatrix(d,3),Move(d),Speed(d)¶
  Filler$=STRING$(16,"-")¶
  Colormatrix(1,1)=15¶
  Colormatrix(1,2)=15¶
  Colormatrix(1,3)=15¶
¶
Begin:¶
  PRINT "Videotitle-Program ";¶
  PRINT "by Hannes R"CHR$(252)"gheimer"¶
  PRINT¶
¶
Select:¶
  PRINT "Select:"¶
  PRINT "1   Enter Text"¶
  PRINT "2   Read Object"¶
  PRINT "3   Move Object"¶
  PRINT "4   Define Color"¶
  PRINT "5   Show Title"¶
  PRINT¶
¶
Query:¶
  LOCATE 10,1¶
  PRINT "Enter number:";¶
  INPUT a$¶
  a$=LEFT$(a$,1)¶
  IF a$<"1" OR a$>"5" THEN BEEP: GOTO Query¶
  IF a$="1" THEN EnterText¶
  IF a$="2" THEN ReadObject¶
  IF a$="3" THEN DefineMoveObject¶
  IF a$="4" THEN DefineColor¶
  IF a$="5" THEN ShowTitle¶
  PRINT¶
  END¶
  ¶
EnterText:¶
  CLS:INPUT "How many lines of text (1-15)";NoofLines$¶
  IF NoofLines$="" THEN CLS: GOTO Begin¶
  NoofLines=VAL(NoofLines$)¶
  IF NoofLines<1 OR NoofLines>15 THEN BEEP: GOTO
EnterText¶
  FOR x=1 TO NoofLines¶
    LINE INPUT "Text:";Text$(x)¶
```

```
    NEXT x : CLS : GOTO Begin¶
¶
ReadObject:¶
  CLS¶
  PRINT "Enter the NAME of the object you want TO load."¶
  INPUT Objname$¶
  IF Objname$="" THEN CLS : GOTO Begin¶
  OPEN Objname$ FOR INPUT AS 1¶
    OBJECT.SHAPE 1,INPUT$(LOF(1),1)¶
  CLOSE 1¶
  ObjFlag=1 : CLS : GOTO Begin¶
¶
DefineMoveObject:¶
  CLS:IF ObjFlag=0 THEN BEEP ELSE Mover¶
  PRINT "No object currently in memory!"¶
  PRINT "Press any key."¶
Pause:¶
  a$=INKEY$¶
  IF a$="" THEN Pause¶
  CLS: GOTO Begin¶
¶
Mover:¶
  PRINT "Move the object to it's starting point"¶
  PRINT "using the cursor keys."¶
  PRINT "When located press <RETURN>"¶
  ox=100 : oy=100 : Destination=0¶
  OBJECT.HIT 1,0,0¶
  OBJECT.ON 1¶
  OBJECT.STOP 1¶
Loop:¶
  a$=INKEY$¶
  IF a$=CHR$(13) THEN DestDef¶
  IF a$=CHR$(28) THEN oy=oy-2¶
  IF a$=CHR$(31) THEN ox=ox-5¶
  IF a$=CHR$(30) THEN ox=ox+5¶
  IF a$=CHR$(29) THEN oy=oy+2¶
  OBJECT.X 1,ox : OBJECT.Y 1,oy¶
  GOTO Loop¶
¶
DestDef:¶
  CLS¶
  Move(Destination*2+1)=ox : Move(Destination*2+2)=oy¶
  Destination=Destination+1 : Move(0)=Destination¶
  IF Destination=7 THEN Enddef¶
  PRINT "Move the object to location"Destination¶
  PRINT "<RETURN> = Set another location"¶
  PRINT "<ESC> = End"¶
Loop2:¶
  a$=INKEY$¶
  IF a$=CHR$(13) THEN DestDef¶
  IF a$=CHR$(27) THEN Enddef¶
  IF a$=CHR$(28) THEN oy=oy-2¶
  IF a$=CHR$(31) THEN ox=ox-5¶
  IF a$=CHR$(30) THEN ox=ox+5¶
  IF a$=CHR$(29) THEN oy=oy+2¶
  OBJECT.X 1,ox : OBJECT.Y 1,oy¶
```

```
      GOTO Loop2¶
¶
Enddef:¶
  Move(0)=Destination¶
  OBJECT.OFF 1¶
  CLS : GOTO Begin¶
¶
DefineColor:¶
  CLS:PRINT "Color values:"¶
Colors:¶
  FOR x=0 TO MaxColors¶
    COLOR -(x=0),x¶
    LOCATE 5,(x*4) + 1¶
    PRINT x;CHR$(32);CHR$(32)¶
  NEXT x¶
¶
ColorChange:¶
  LOCATE 7,1:COLOR TextColor,Background¶
  PRINT "Enter the number of the color you want to
change."¶
  PRINT "(e = End)"; : BEEP¶
  INPUT Answer$¶
  IF UCASE$(Answer$)="E" THEN AssignColor¶
  Answer$=LEFT$(Answer$,2)¶
  ColorNumber=VAL(Answer$)¶
  IF ColorNumber<0 OR ColorNumber>MaxColors THEN BEEP:
GOTO ColorChange¶
¶
RGBRegulator:¶
  r=Colormatrix(ColorNumber,1)¶
  g=Colormatrix(ColorNumber,2)¶
  b=Colormatrix(ColorNumber,3)¶
  LOCATE 10,1: PRINT "Red:   <7>=- <8>=+ ";Filler$¶
  LOCATE 10,20+r : PRINT CHR$(124);¶
  LOCATE 11,1: PRINT "Green: <4>=- <5>=+ ";Filler$¶
  LOCATE 11,20+g : PRINT CHR$(124);¶
  LOCATE 12,1: PRINT "Blue:  <1>=- <2>=+ ";Filler$¶
  LOCATE 12,20+b : PRINT CHR$(124);¶
  LOCATE 13,1: PRINT "         <0>=Color o.k."¶
  PALETTE ColorNumber,r/15,g/15,b/15¶
¶
EnterKeys:¶
  Key$=INKEY$¶
  IF Key$="" THEN EnterKeys¶
  IF Key$="7" THEN r=r-1¶
  IF Key$="8" THEN r=r+1¶
  IF Key$="4" THEN g=g-1¶
  IF Key$="5" THEN g=g+1¶
  IF Key$="1" THEN b=b-1¶
  IF Key$="2" THEN b=b+1¶
  IF Key$="0" THEN ColorChange¶
  ¶
  IF r<0 THEN r=0¶
  IF r>15 THEN r=15¶
  IF g<0 THEN g=0¶
  IF g>15 THEN g=15¶
```

```
      IF b<0 THEN b=0¶
      IF b>15 THEN b=15¶
   ¶
     Colormatrix(ColorNumber,1)=r¶
     Colormatrix(ColorNumber,2)=g¶
     Colormatrix(ColorNumber,3)=b¶
     GOTO RGBRegulator¶
   ¶
AssignColor:¶
   a=Background : a$="Background"¶
   GOSUB EnterColor:Background=a¶
   ¶
   a=TextColor : a$="Text Color"¶
   GOSUB EnterColor:TextColor=a¶
   ¶
   a=TextBackground : a$="Text Background"¶
   GOSUB EnterColor:TextBackground=a¶
   ¶
   COLOR TextColor,Background¶
   CLS : GOTO Begin¶
¶
¶
EnterColor:¶
   LOCATE 14,1¶
   PRINT a$": ";a¶
Loop3:¶
   LOCATE 14,1¶
   PRINT a$; : INPUT Answer$¶
   Answer=VAL(Answer$)¶
   IF Answer$="" THEN Answer=.5¶
   IF Answer<0 OR Answer>MaxColors THEN BEEP : GOTO Loop3¶
   IF Answer<>.5 THEN a=Answer¶
   RETURN¶
¶
¶
ShowTitle:¶
   CLS¶
   PRINT "Press the <RETURN> key"¶
   PRINT "to begin showing the title."¶
WaitforKey:¶
   a$=INKEY$¶
   IF a$=CHR$(13) THEN CLS : c=10 :GOTO Countdown¶
   GOTO WaitforKey¶
¶
Countdown:¶
   LOCATE 10,39 : PRINT c¶
   c=c-1:IF c<0 THEN StartDisplay¶
   Tim=INT(TIMER)¶
Wait2:¶
   IF INT(TIMER)=Tim THEN Wait2¶
   GOTO Countdown¶
¶
StartDisplay:¶
   WIDTH 80 ¶
   COLOR TextColor,Background : CLS¶
   COLOR TextColor,TextBackground¶
```

```
      FOR x=1 TO NoofLines¶
         Text$=LEFT$(Text$(x),80)¶
         h=INT((80-LEN(Text$))/2)+2¶
         LOCATE x+17-NoofLines,h : PRINT Text$¶
      NEXT x¶
      COLOR TextColor,Background¶
      IF Move(0)=0 THEN MoveText¶
            ¶
      OBJECT.X 1,Move(1)¶
      OBJECT.Y 1,Move(2)¶
      OBJECT.ON 1¶
      FOR x=1 TO Move(0)-1¶
         OBJECT.STOP 1¶
         GOSUB VelocityCalc¶
         OBJECT.X 1,Move(x*2-1)¶
         OBJECT.Y 1,Move(x*2)¶
         OBJECT.VX 1,Speed(x*2-1)¶
         OBJECT.VY 1,Speed(x*2)¶
         OBJECT.HIT 1,0,0¶
         OBJECT.START 1¶
            ¶
         Tst=TIMER¶
   Loop4:¶
         px=ABS(Move(x*2+1)-OBJECT.X(1))¶
         py=ABS(Move(x*2+2)-OBJECT.Y(1))¶
         IF INT(TIMER-Tst)<18 AND (px>15 OR py>15) THEN Loop4¶
      NEXT x¶
      OBJECT.OFF 1¶
            ¶
MoveText:¶
   Tst=TIMER¶
   IF Move(0)<>0 THEN Finish¶
   Wait3:¶
      IF TIMER-Tst<(2*NoofLines+2) THEN Wait3¶
   Finish:¶
      FOR x=1 TO 30 ¶
         SCROLL (1,1)-(630,100),0,3¶
         SCROLL (1,100)-(630,180),0,-3 ¶
      NEXT x¶
      COLOR TextColor,Background¶
   CLS : GOTO Begin¶
¶
VelocityCalc:¶
   ox=OBJECT.X (1) : oy=OBJECT.Y (1)¶
   Move(x*2-1)=ox : Move(x*2)=oy¶
   zx=Move(x*2+1) : zy=Move(x*2+2)¶
      FOR xx=1 TO 64 STEP .2¶
         Speed(x*2-1)=CINT((zx-ox)/xx)¶
         Speed(x*2)=CINT((zy-oy)/xx)¶
         IF ABS(Speed(x*2-1))<40 AND ABS(Speed(x*2))<40 THEN
xx=64¶
      NEXT xx¶
   RETURN¶
¶
¶
```

480

C.2   Video title program (IFF format)

```
Setup:¶
  Colors=5¶
  d=15 : MaxColors=(2^Colors)-1 ¶
  TextColor=1¶
  SCREEN CLOSE 2¶
  SCREEN 2,320,200,Colors,1 : WINDOW
2,"Videotitle",,28,2¶
  DIM Text$(d),Colormatrix(31,3),Move(d),Speed(d)¶
  Filler$=STRING$(16,"-")¶
  Colormatrix(1,1)=15¶
  Colormatrix(1,2)=15¶
  Colormatrix(1,3)=15¶
¶
Begin:¶
  PRINT "Videotitle-Program"¶
  PRINT "by Hannes R"CHR$(252)"gheimer"¶
  PRINT¶
¶
Select:¶
  PRINT "Select:"¶
  PRINT "1  Enter Text"¶
  PRINT "2  Read Object"¶
  PRINT "3  Move Object"¶
  PRINT "4  Define Color"¶
  PRINT "5  Show Title"¶
  PRINT "6  Load Background Picture"¶
  PRINT "7  Read title sequence"¶
  PRINT "8  Store title sequence"¶
  PRINT ¶
¶
Query:¶
  LOCATE 13,1¶
  PRINT "Enter number:";¶
  INPUT a$¶
  a$=LEFT$(a$,1)¶
  IF a$<"1" OR a$>"8" THEN BEEP: GOTO Query¶
  IF a$="1" THEN EnterText¶
  IF a$="2" THEN ReadObject¶
  IF a$="3" THEN DefineMoveObject¶
  IF a$="4" THEN DefineColor¶
  IF a$="5" THEN ShowTitle¶
  IF a$="6" THEN SetupScreen¶
  IF a$="7" THEN ReadTitle¶
  IF a$="8" THEN StoreTitle¶
  GOTO Query¶
  ¶
  ¶
EnterText:¶
```

```
  CLS:PRINT "How many lines" : INPUT "of text (1-
15)";NoofLines$¶
  IF NoofLines$= "" THEN CLS: GOTO Begin¶
  NoofLines=VAL(NoofLines$)¶
  IF NoofLines<1 OR NoofLines>15 THEN BEEP: GOTO
EnterText¶
  FOR x=1 TO NoofLines¶
    LINE INPUT "Text:";Text$(x)¶
  NEXT x : CLS : GOTO Begin¶
¶
ReadObject:¶
  CLS¶
  PRINT "Enter the name of the" : PRINT "object you want
to load."¶
  INPUT Objname$¶
  IF Objname$="" THEN CLS : GOTO Begin¶
  OPEN Objname$ FOR INPUT AS 1¶
    OBJECT.SHAPE 1,INPUT$(LOF(1),1)¶
  CLOSE 1¶
  ObjFlag=1 : CLS : GOTO Begin¶
¶
DefineMoveObject:¶
  CLS:IF ObjFlag=0 THEN BEEP ELSE Mover¶
  PRINT "No object currently in memory!"¶
  PRINT "Press any key."¶
Pause:¶
  a$=INKEY$¶
  IF a$="" THEN Pause¶
  CLS: GOTO Begin¶
¶
Mover:¶
  PRINT "Move the object to it's"¶
  PRINT "starting point using"¶
  PRINT "the cursor keys."¶
  PRINT "When located press <RETURN>"¶
  ox=100 : oy=100 : Destination=0¶
  OBJECT.HIT 1,0,0¶
  OBJECT.ON 1¶
  OBJECT.STOP 1¶
Loop:¶
  a$=INKEY$¶
  IF a$=CHR$(13) THEN DestDef¶
  IF a$=CHR$(28) THEN oy=oy-2¶
  IF a$=CHR$(31) THEN ox=ox-5¶
  IF a$=CHR$(30) THEN ox=ox+5¶
  IF a$=CHR$(29) THEN oy=oy+2¶
  OBJECT.X 1,ox : OBJECT.Y 1,oy¶
  GOTO Loop¶
¶
DestDef:¶
  CLS¶
  Move(Destination*2+1)=ox : Move(Destination*2+2)=oy¶
  Destination=Destination+1 : Move(0)=Destination¶
  IF Destination=7 THEN Enddef¶
  PRINT "Move the object to location"Destination¶
  PRINT "<RETURN> = Set another location"¶
```

```
    PRINT "<ESC> = End"¶
Loop2:¶
  a$=INKEY$¶
  IF a$=CHR$(13)  THEN DestDef¶
  IF a$=CHR$(27)  THEN Enddef¶
  IF a$=CHR$(28)  THEN oy=oy-2¶
  IF a$=CHR$(31)  THEN ox=ox-5¶
  IF a$=CHR$(30)  THEN ox=ox+5¶
  IF a$=CHR$(29)  THEN oy=oy+2¶
  OBJECT.X 1,ox : OBJECT.Y 1,oy¶
  GOTO Loop2¶
¶
Enddef:¶
  Move(0)=Destination¶
  OBJECT.OFF 1¶
  CLS : GOTO Begin¶
¶
DefineColor:¶
  CLS:PRINT "Color values:"¶
¶
Colors:¶
    FOR x=0 TO MaxColors¶
    IF (x/8)=INT(x/8) THEN PRINT ¶
    COLOR -(x=0),x¶
    PRINT x;¶
    IF x<10 THEN PRINT CHR$(32);¶
    NEXT x¶
¶
ColorChange:¶
  LOCATE 7,1:COLOR TextColor,Background¶
  PRINT "Enter the number of the color"¶
  PRINT "you want to change."¶
  PRINT "(e = End)"; : BEEP¶
  INPUT Answer$¶
  IF UCASE$(Answer$)="E" THEN AssignColor¶
  Answer$=LEFT$(Answer$,2)¶
  ColorNumber=VAL(Answer$)¶
  IF ColorNumber<0 OR ColorNumber>MaxColors THEN BEEP:
GOTO ColorChange¶
¶
RGBRegulator:¶
  r=Colormatrix(ColorNumber,1)¶
  g=Colormatrix(ColorNumber,2)¶
  b=Colormatrix(ColorNumber,3)¶
  LOCATE 11,1: PRINT "Red:   <7>=- <8>=+ ":PRINT Filler$¶
  LOCATE 12,r+1 : PRINT CHR$(124);¶
  LOCATE 13,1: PRINT "Green: <4>=- <5>=+ ":PRINT Filler$¶
  LOCATE 14,g+1 : PRINT CHR$(124);¶
  LOCATE 15,1: PRINT "Blue:  <1>=- <2>=+ ":PRINT
Filler$¶
  LOCATE 16,b+1 : PRINT CHR$(124);¶
  LOCATE 17,1: PRINT "       <0>=Color o.k."¶
  PALETTE ColorNumber,r/16,g/16,b/16¶
¶
EnterKeys:¶
  Key0 INKEY$¶
```

```
      IF Key$="" THEN EnterKeys¶
      IF Key$="7" THEN r=r-1¶
      IF Key$="8" THEN r=r+1¶
      IF Key$="4" THEN g=g-1¶
      IF Key$="5" THEN g=g+1¶
      IF Key$="1" THEN b=b-1¶
      IF Key$="2" THEN b=b+1¶
      IF Key$="0" THEN ColorChange¶
      ¶
      IF r<0 THEN r=0¶
      IF r>15 THEN r=15¶
      IF g<0 THEN g=0¶
      IF g>15 THEN g=15¶
      IF b<0 THEN b=0¶
      IF b>15 THEN b=15¶
   ¶
      Colormatrix(ColorNumber,1)=r¶
      Colormatrix(ColorNumber,2)=g¶
      Colormatrix(ColorNumber,3)=b¶
      GOTO RGBRegulator¶
   ¶
AssignColor:¶
   a=Background : a$="Background"¶
   GOSUB EnterColor:Background=a¶
   ¶
   a=TextColor : a$="Text Color"¶
   GOSUB EnterColor:TextColor=a¶
   ¶
   a=TextBackground : a$="Text Background"¶
   GOSUB EnterColor:TextBackground=a¶
   ¶
   COLOR TextColor,Background¶
   CLS : GOTO Begin¶
   ¶
   ¶
EnterColor:¶
   LOCATE 19,1¶
   PRINT a$": ";a¶
Loop3:¶
   LOCATE 19,1¶
   PRINT a$; : INPUT Answer$¶
   Answer=VAL(Answer$)¶
   IF Answer$="" THEN Answer=.5¶
   IF Answer<0 OR Answer>MaxColors THEN BEEP : GOTO Loop3¶
   IF Answer<>.5 THEN a=Answer¶
   RETURN¶
   ¶
   ¶
ShowTitle:¶
   CLS¶
   PRINT "Press the <RETURN> key"¶
   PRINT "to begin showing the title."¶
WaitforKey:¶
   a$=INKEY$¶
   IF a$=CHR$(13) THEN CLS : c=10 :GOTO Countdown¶
   GOTO WaitforKey¶
```

```
¶
Countdown:¶
  LOCATE 10,20 : PRINT c¶
  c=c-1:IF c<0 THEN StartDisplay¶
  Tim=INT(TIMER)¶
Wait2:¶
  IF INT(TIMER)=Tim THEN Wait2¶
  GOTO Countdown¶
¶
StartDisplay:¶
  WIDTH 40 ¶
  COLOR TextColor,Background : CLS¶
  COLOR TextColor,TextBackground¶
  IF IFF=1 THEN CALL DrawLoad¶
  FOR x=1 TO NoofLines¶
    Text$=LEFT$(Text$(x),40)¶
    h=INT((40-LEN(Text$))/2)+2¶
    LOCATE x+17-NoofLines,h : PRINT Text$¶
  NEXT x¶
  COLOR TextColor,Background¶
  IF Move(0)=0 THEN MoveText¶
     ¶
  OBJECT.X 1,Move(1)¶
  OBJECT.Y 1,Move(2)¶
  OBJECT.ON 1¶
  FOR x=1 TO Move(0)-1¶
    OBJECT.STOP 1¶
    GOSUB VelocityCalc¶
    OBJECT.X 1,Move(x*2-1)¶
    OBJECT.Y 1,Move(x*2)¶
    OBJECT.VX 1,Speed(x*2-1)¶
    OBJECT.VY 1,Speed(x*2)¶
    OBJECT.HIT 1,0,0¶
    OBJECT.START 1¶
     ¶
    Tst=TIMER¶
  Loop4:¶
    px=ABS(Move(x*2+1)-OBJECT.X(1))¶
    py=ABS(Move(x*2+2)-OBJECT.Y(1))¶
    IF INT(TIMER-Tst)<18 AND (px>15 OR py>15) THEN Loop4¶
  NEXT x¶
  OBJECT.OFF 1¶
     ¶
MoveText:¶
  Tst=TIMER¶
  IF Move(0)<>0 THEN Finish¶
  Wait3:¶
    IF TIMER-Tst<(2*NoofLines+2) THEN Wait3¶
  Finish:¶
    FOR x=1 TO 30 ¶
      SCROLL (1,1)-(630,100),0,3¶
      SCROLL (1,100)-(630,180),0,-3 ¶
    NEXT x¶
    COLOR TextColor,Background¶
  CLS : GOTO Begin¶
  ¶
```

```
VelocityCalc:¶
  ox=OBJECT.X (1) : oy=OBJECT.Y (1)¶
  Move(x*2-1)=ox : Move(x*2)=oy¶
  zx=Move(x*2+1) : zy=Move(x*2+2)¶
    FOR xx=1 TO 64 STEP .2¶
      Speed(x*2-1)=CINT((zx-ox)/xx)¶
      Speed(x*2)=CINT((zy-oy)/xx)¶
      IF ABS(Speed(x*2-1))<40 AND ABS(Speed(x*2))<40 THEN
xx=64¶
    NEXT xx¶
  RETURN¶
¶
SetupScreen:¶
  CLS¶
  PRINT "Want to load a graphic"¶
  PRINT "background? (Y/N)"¶
¶
Loop5:¶
  LOCATE 2,19 : INPUT Answ$¶
  IF UCASE$(Answ$)="N" THEN IFF=0 : CLS : GOTO Begin¶
  IF UCASE$(Answ$)="Y" THEN IFF=1 : GOTO EnterName ¶
GOTO Loop5¶
¶
EnterName:¶
  PRINT¶
  PRINT "Enter name:"¶
  INPUT Nam$¶
  PRINT ¶
  PRINT "Use the color table for:"¶
  PRINT Nam$¶
  PRINT "Enter (Y/N)";¶
Loop6:¶
  LOCATE 9,12 : INPUT Answ$¶
  IF UCASE$(Answ$)="N" THEN IFFTab=0 : CLS : GOTO Begin¶
  IF UCASE$(Answ$)="Y" THEN IFFTab=1 : CLS : GOTO Begin¶
GOTO Loop6¶
  ¶
¶
SUB DrawLoad STATIC¶
SHARED Colors,Colormatrix(),IFFTab,Nam$¶
  IF Nam$="" THEN EndLoad ¶
  OPEN Nam$ FOR INPUT AS 1¶
    Form$=INPUT$(4,1)¶
    Length=CVL(INPUT$(4,1))¶
    IF INPUT$(4,1)<>"ILBM" THEN BEEP : GOTO EndLoad¶
¶
ReadData:¶
    IF EOF(1) THEN EndLoad¶
    Chunk$=INPUT$(4,1)¶
    Length=CVL(INPUT$(4,1))¶
    IF INT(Length/2)<>(Length/2) THEN Length=Length+1¶
    IF Chunk$="BMHD" THEN BMHeader¶
    IF Chunk$="CMAP" THEN ColorMap¶
    IF Chunk$="BODY" THEN BodyMap¶
    Dummy$=INPUT$(Length,1)¶
  GOTO ReadData¶
```

```
                            ¶
BMHeader:    ¶
     xd=CVI(INPUT$(2,1))¶
     IF xd>320 THEN EndLoad¶
     yd=CVI(INPUT$(2,1))¶
     IF yd>200 THEN EndLoad¶
     Dummy$=INPUT$(4,1)¶
     Bitplane=ASC(INPUT$(1,1))¶
     Dummy$=INPUT$(11,1)¶
     Addr=PEEKL(WINDOW(8)+4)+8¶
     FOR x=0 TO Bitplane-1¶
         PlaneAddr(x)=PEEKL(Addr+4*x)¶
     NEXT x¶
   GOTO ReadData¶
       ¶
ColorMap:¶
     FOR x=0 TO (Length/3)-1¶
       r=(ASC(INPUT$(1,1)) AND 240)/16¶
       g=(ASC(INPUT$(1,1)) AND 240)/16¶
       b=(ASC(INPUT$(1,1)) AND 240)/16¶
       IF IFFTab=1 THEN¶
          PALETTE x,r/16,g/16,b/16¶
          Colormatrix(x,1)=r : Colormatrix(x,2)=g :
Colormatrix(x,3)=b¶
       END IF¶
     NEXT x¶
     IF INT(Length/3)<>(Length/3) THEN Dummy$=INPUT$(1,1)¶
   GOTO ReadData¶
       ¶
BodyMap:¶
     FOR y1=0 TO 199¶
       FOR b=0 TO Bitplane-1¶
         IF b<Colors THEN¶
            FOR x1=0 TO 9¶
              POKEL
PlaneAddr(b)+4*x1+40*y1,CVL(INPUT$(4,1))¶
            NEXT x1¶
         ELSE¶
              Dummy$=INPUT$(40,1)¶
         END IF¶
       NEXT b¶
     NEXT y1¶
   GOTO ReadData       ¶
¶
EndLoad:¶
CLOSE 1¶
END SUB¶
¶
StoreTitle:¶
   CLS : PRINT "Save as what name:"¶
   INPUT DatName$¶
   OPEN DatName$ FOR OUTPUT AS 1¶
     PRINT #1,NoofLines     : REM Number of text lines¶
     FOR x=1 TO NoofLines¶
       WRITE #1,Text$(x)¶
     NEXT x¶
```

```
      ¶
      PRINT #1,ObjFlag       ' Object loaded?¶
      WRITE #1,Objname$      ' file name¶
      ¶
      PRINT #1,Move(0)       ' Number of movements¶
      FOR x=1 TO Move(0)¶
        PRINT #1,Move(x)¶
      NEXT x¶
      ¶
      PRINT #1,Colors        ' Number of Bitplanes¶
      FOR x=0 TO 31          ' 32 Colors in IFF-Storage¶
        PRINT #1,CHR$(Colormatrix(x,1)*16);¶
        PRINT #1,CHR$(Colormatrix(x,2)*16);¶
        PRINT #1,CHR$(Colormatrix(x,3)*16);¶
      NEXT x     ¶
      PRINT #1,Background       ' Text color etc.¶
      PRINT #1,TextColor¶
      PRINT #1,TextBackground¶
      ¶
      PRINT #1,IFF           ' Screen background?¶
      PRINT #1,IFFTab        ' Change colors?¶
      WRITE #1,Nam$          ' file name¶
    CLOSE 1¶
    CLS¶
GOTO Begin¶
¶
ReadTitle:¶
    CLS : PRINT "Name of file to load:"¶
    INPUT DatName$¶
    OPEN DatName$ FOR INPUT AS 1¶
      INPUT #1,NoofLines¶
      FOR x=1 TO NoofLines¶
        INPUT #1,Text$(x)¶
      NEXT x¶
      ¶
      INPUT #1,ObjFlag¶
      INPUT #1,Objname$¶
      ¶
      IF ObjFlag=1 THEN¶
        OPEN Objname$ FOR INPUT AS 2¶
          OBJECT.SHAPE 1,INPUT$(LOF(2),2)¶
        CLOSE 2¶
      END IF¶
      ¶
      INPUT #1,Move(0)¶
      FOR x=1 TO Move(0)¶
        INPUT #1,Move(x)¶
      NEXT x¶
      ¶
      INPUT #1,Color1¶
      IF Color1<=Colors THEN Colors=Color1¶
      MaxColors=(2^Colors)-1¶
      FOR x=0 TO 31¶
        r=(ASC(INPUT$(1,1)) AND 240)/16¶
        g=(ASC(INPUT$(1,1)) AND 240)/16¶
        b=(ASC(INPUT$(1,1)) AND 240)/16¶
```

```
        PALETTE x,r/16,g/16,b/16¶
        Colormatrix(x,1)=r : Colormatrix(x,2)=g :
Colormatrix(x,3)=b¶
    NEXT x¶
    INPUT #1,Background¶
    INPUT #1,TextColor¶
    INPUT #1,TextBackground¶
    ¶
    INPUT #1,IFF¶
    INPUT #1,IFFTab¶
    INPUT #1,Nam$¶
  CLOSE 1¶
  CLS¶
GOTO Begin     ¶
¶
```

C.3

Paint program

```
Setup:¶
  Colors=5 : MaxColors=2^Colors-1¶
  DIM Pointer(4,1),AltColor(4),Colors%(31,2)¶
  DIM FillPattern%(7),AllPatterns%(8,7),Solid%(1)¶
  DrawType=1 : DrawColor=1 : FillColor=2 : Mode=1¶
¶
  Solid%(0)=&HFFFF : Solid%(1)=&HFFFF¶
  FOR x=0 TO 7¶
    FillPattern%(x)=&HFFFF¶
    AllPatterns%(0,x)=&HFFFF¶
  NEXT x¶
  FOR x=1 TO 8¶
    FOR y=0 TO 7¶
      READ AllPatterns%(x,y)¶
    NEXT y¶
  NEXT x¶
¶
  DATA 24672,1542,24672,1542,24672,1542,24672,1542¶
  DATA -13108,13107,-13108,13107,-13108,13107,-
13108,13107¶
  DATA 26214,13107,-26215,-13108,26214,13107,-26215,-
13108¶
  DATA -13108,-26215,13107,26214,-13108,-
26215,13107,26214¶
  DATA -258,-258,-258,0,-4113,-4113,-4113,0¶
  DATA -8185,-8197,-18019,-20491,-20467,-8197,-8185,-1¶
  DATA 0,0,1632,4080,4080,2016,384,0¶
  DATA 960,1984,3520,6592,16320,25024,-3104,0¶
¶
  SCREEN 1,320,200,Colors,1¶
  WINDOW 2,"AmigaBASIC Draw Program",,16,1¶
  WINDOW CLOSE 3¶
  WINDOW CLOSE 4¶
  WINDOW 2¶
¶
  FOR x=0 TO 31¶
    READ r,g,b¶
    PALETTE x,r/16,g/16,b/16¶
    Colors%(x,0)=r : Colors%(x,1)=g : Colors%(x,2)=b¶
  NEXT x¶
¶
  DATA 0,0,3,  15,15,15,  0,3,12,  15,0,0¶
  DATA 0,14,15, 15,0,15,  3,10,1,  15,14,0¶
  DATA 15,8,0,  10,0,14 ,8,5,0,  11,8,3¶
  DATA 2,11,0,  15,10,15, 0,0,9,  7,15,0¶
  DATA 14,12,0, 15,2,3,  0,0,0,  15,11,10¶
  DATA 0,6,8,  3,3,3,  4,4,4,  5,5,5¶
  DATA 6,6,6,  7,7,7,  8,8,8,  9,9,9¶
  DATA 11,11,11, 13,13,13, 0,0,15, 12,15,12 ¶
```

```
¶
Pulldown:¶
  MENU 3,0,0,""¶
  MENU 4,0,0,""¶
  MENU 1,0,1,"Program"¶
  MENU 1,1,1,"Draw            "¶
  MENU 1,2,1,"Color Palette"¶
  MENU 1,3,1,"Fill Pattern  "¶
  MENU 1,4,1,"Load Screen   "¶
  MENU 1,5,1,"Save Screen   "¶
  MENU 1,6,1,"Clear Screen  "¶
  MENU 1,7,1,"End           "¶
  MENU 2,0,1,"Drawing tools"¶
  MENU 2,1,2,"  Draw freehand  "¶
  MENU 2,2,1,"  Draw thick     "¶
  MENU 2,3,1,"  Points         "¶
  MENU 2,4,1,"  Spray          "¶
  MENU 2,5,1,"  Lines          "¶
  MENU 2,6,1,"  Frame          "¶
  MENU 2,7,1,"  Box            "¶
  MENU 2,8,1,"  Connected lines"¶
  MENU 2,9,1,"  Oval           "¶
  MENU 2,10,1,"  Fill          "¶
  MENU 2,11,1,"  Eraser        "¶
  MENU 2,12,1,"  Text          "¶
¶
MainLoop:¶
  ON MENU GOSUB MenuSelect¶
  ON MOUSE GOSUB EvalMouse¶
  MENU ON¶
  MOUSE ON¶
¶
  WHILE -1¶
  WEND¶
¶
MenuSelect:¶
  Men=MENU(0)¶
  MenChoice=MENU(1)¶
  ON Men GOTO Project,DrawTools¶
¶
EvalMouse:¶
  IF Mode=1 THEN ON DrawType GOSUB
DrawThin,DrawThick,Points,Spray,DrawLines,Frame,Box,Conne
ctedLines,Oval,Fill,Eraser,Text¶
  IF Mode=2 THEN GOSUB ColorPalette : IF EndOK=1 THEN
GOSUB ColorDone¶
  IF Mode=3 THEN GOSUB DefinePattern : IF EndOK=2 THEN
GOSUB PatternDone¶
  IF Mode=4 THEN GOSUB RGBDef : IF EndOK=3 THEN Mode=2 :
GOSUB SelectColor¶
RETURN¶
¶
Project:¶
  IF MenChoice=1 THEN GOSUB ColorDone : GOSUB
PatternDone¶
```

```
    IF MenChoice=2 THEN GOSUB PatternDone : MENU 2,0,0 :
Mode=2 : GOSUB SelectColor¶
    IF MenChoice=3 THEN GOSUB ColorDone : MENU 2,0,0 :
Mode=3 : GOSUB PatternEditor¶
    IF MenChoice=4 THEN GOSUB ColorDone : GOSUB PatternDone
: GOSUB DrawLoad¶
    IF MenChoice=5 THEN GOSUB ColorDone : GOSUB PatternDone
: GOSUB DrawSave¶
    IF MenChoice=6 AND Mode=1 THEN OK=0 :GOSUB Query : IF
OK=1 THEN Adef=0 : AREAFILL: CLS¶
    IF MenChoice=7 THEN GOSUB ColorDone : GOSUB PatternDone
: OK=0 : GOSUB Query : IF OK=1 THEN EndIt ¶
RETURN¶
¶
DrawTools:¶
  MENU 2,DrawType,1¶
  DrawType = MENU (1)¶
  MENU 2,DrawType,2¶
RETURN¶
¶
DrawThin:¶
  Test= MOUSE(0) : x=MOUSE(1) : y=MOUSE(2)¶
  WHILE MOUSE(0)<>0¶
    LINE (x,y)-(MOUSE(1),MOUSE(2)),DrawColor ¶
    x=MOUSE(1) : y=MOUSE(2)¶
  WEND¶
RETURN¶
¶
DrawThick:¶
  Test=MOUSE(0)¶
  WHILE MOUSE(0)<>0¶
    x=MOUSE(1) : y=MOUSE(2)¶
    LINE (x,y)-(x+5,y+5),DrawColor,bf¶
  WEND¶
RETURN¶
¶
Points:¶
  Test=MOUSE(0)¶
  WHILE MOUSE(0)<>0¶
    PSET (MOUSE(1),MOUSE(2)),DrawColor¶
  WEND¶
RETURN¶
¶
Spray:¶
  Test=MOUSE(0)¶
  WHILE MOUSE(0)<>0¶
    x=MOUSE(1)+14*RND : y=MOUSE(2)+7*RND¶
    LINE (x,y)-(x,y),DrawColor,bf¶
  WEND¶
RETURN¶
¶
DrawLines:¶
  Test=MOUSE(0)¶
  x1=MOUSE(3) : y1=MOUSE(4)¶
  PSET (x1,y1),DrawColor¶
  WHILE MOUSE(0)<>0¶
```

```
    WEND¶
    LINE (x1,y1)-(MOUSE(5),MOUSE(6)),DrawColor¶
RETURN¶
¶
Frame:¶
  Test=MOUSE(0)¶
  x1=MOUSE(3) : y1=MOUSE(4)¶
  Pointer(0,0)=x1 : Pointer(0,1)=y1¶
  Pointer(1,0)=x1 : Pointer(2,1)=y1¶
  Value=4¶
  WHILE MOUSE(0)<>0¶
    Pointer(3,0)=MOUSE(5)¶
    Pointer(3,1)=MOUSE(6)¶
    Pointer(1,1)=Pointer(3,1)¶
    Pointer(2,0)=Pointer(3,0)¶
    GOSUB PlacePoint¶
  WEND¶
  LINE (x1,y1)-(Pointer(3,0),Pointer(3,1)),DrawColor,b¶
RETURN¶
¶
Box:¶
  Test=MOUSE(0)¶
  x1=MOUSE(3) : y1=MOUSE(4)¶
  Pointer(0,0)=x1 : Pointer(0,1)=y1¶
  Pointer(1,0)=x1 : Pointer(2,1)=y1¶
  Value=4¶
  WHILE MOUSE(0)<>0¶
    Pointer(3,0)=MOUSE(5)¶
    Pointer(3,1)=MOUSE(6)¶
    Pointer(1,1)=Pointer(3,1)¶
    Pointer(2,0)=Pointer(3,0)¶
    GOSUB PlacePoint¶
  WEND¶
  LINE (x1,y1)-(Pointer(3,0),Pointer(3,1)),DrawColor,bf¶
RETURN¶
¶
ConnectedLines:            ¶
  Test=MOUSE(0)¶
  x1=MOUSE(3) : y1=MOUSE(4)¶
  IF y1>186 THEN y1=186¶
  IF x1>311 THEN x1=311¶
  AREA (x1,y1)¶
  IF Adef=0 THEN Adef=1 : xa=x1 : ya=y1¶
  IF Adef<>1 AND x1=xa AND y1=ya THEN DoFill¶
  Adef=Adef+1 : IF Adef=20 THEN DoFill¶
  LINE (xa,ya)-(x1,y1),DrawColor¶
  xa=x1 : ya=y1¶
RETURN¶
¶
DoFill:¶
  Adef=0 : COLOR DrawColor,0 : AREAFILL ¶
RETURN¶
¶
Oval:¶
  Test=MOUSE(0)¶
  x1=MOUSE(3) : y1=MOUSE(4)¶
```

```
    Pointer(0,0)=x1 : Pointer(0,1)=y1¶
    Pointer(1,0)=x1 : Pointer(2,1)=y1¶
    Pointer(3,0)=x1 : Pointer(4,1)=y1¶
    Value=5¶
    WHILE MOUSE(0)<>0¶
      r1= ABS(x1-MOUSE(5))¶
      r2= ABS(y1-MOUSE(6))¶
      Pointer(1,1)=y1-r2 : Pointer(2,0)=x1+r1¶
      Pointer(3,1)=y1+r2 : Pointer(4,0)=x1-r1¶
      GOSUB PlacePoint¶
    WEND¶
    IF r1=0 THEN r1=.1¶
    IF r1<r2 THEN Factor=(r2/r1) : r1=r1*Factor :
r2=r2*Factor¶
    CIRCLE (x1,y1),r1,DrawColor,,,(r2/r1)¶
RETURN¶
¶
¶
Fill:¶
Test=MOUSE(0)¶
IF Click=0 THEN¶
    Click=1¶
    SOUND 440,6,200¶
    x=MOUSE(1) : y=MOUSE(2)¶
    RETURN¶
ELSE¶
    Click=0¶
    IF ABS(x-MOUSE(1))<11 AND ABS(y-MOUSE(2))<6 THEN¶
      PAINT (x,y),FillColor,DrawColor¶
    ELSE¶
      SOUND 440,6,200¶
    END IF¶
END IF¶
RETURN¶
¶
Eraser:¶
    Test=MOUSE(0)¶
    WHILE MOUSE(0)<>0¶
      x=MOUSE(1):y=MOUSE(2)¶
      PATTERN ,Solid%¶
      LINE (x,y)-(x+10,y+5),0,bf¶
      PATTERN ,FillPattern%¶
    WEND¶
RETURN¶
¶
Text:¶
    Test=MOUSE(0)¶
    x=MOUSE(1) : y=MOUSE(2)¶
    MENU OFF : MOUSE OFF¶
    MENU 1,0,0 : MENU 2,0,0¶
    WINDOW 5,"Enter Text:",(0,177)-(311,185),18,1¶
    CLS¶
    LINE INPUT Text$¶
    WINDOW CLOSE 5¶
    WINDOW 2¶
    MENU 1,0,1 : MENU 2,0,1¶
```

```
  MENU ON : MOUSE ON¶
  LOCATE INT(y/8.86)+1,INT(x/10)+1 : COLOR
DrawColor,FillColor¶
  PRINT Text$;¶
  COLOR DrawColor,0¶
RETURN¶
¶
PlacePoint:¶
  FOR x=0 TO Value-1¶
    xz=Pointer(x,0):yz=Pointer(x,1)¶
    IF xz<0 THEN xz=0 : Pointer(x,0)=0¶
    IF xz>311 THEN xz=311 : Pointer(x,0)=311¶
    IF yz<0 THEN yz=0 : Pointer(x,1)=0¶
    IF yz>186 THEN yz=186 : Pointer(x,1)=186¶
    AltColor(x)=POINT(xz,yz)¶
  NEXT x¶
  FOR x=0 TO Value-1¶
    PSET (Pointer(x,0),Pointer(x,1)),-(AltColor(x)=0)¶
  NEXT x¶
  FOR x=0 TO Value-1¶
    PSET (Pointer(x,0),Pointer(x,1)),AltColor(x)¶
  NEXT x¶
RETURN¶
¶
SelectColor:¶
  ColorChoice=0 : EndOK=0¶
  MOUSE OFF : MENU OFF¶
  WINDOW 3,"Color Palette",(4,20)-(245,160),18,1¶
  PATTERN ,Solid%¶
  FOR x= 1 TO (MaxColors+1)/8¶
    FOR y= 0 TO 7    ¶
      LINE (y*30,(x-1)*16)-((y+1)*30,x*16),(x-1)*8+y,bf¶
    NEXT y¶
  NEXT x¶
  LINE (10,72)-(50,95),DrawColor,b¶
  LINE (15,75)-(45,93),DrawColor,bf¶
  LOCATE 14,3 : COLOR 0,1 : PRINT "Draw";¶
  LINE (70,72)-(110,95),FillColor,b¶
  LINE (75,75)-(105,93),FillColor,bf¶
  LOCATE 14,10 : COLOR 1,0 : PRINT "Fill";¶
  LINE (135,72)-(235,95),1,b¶
  LOCATE 11,21: PRINT "Palette";¶
  LINE (190,109)-(230,132),1,b¶
  LOCATE 16,26 : PRINT "OK";¶
  PATTERN ,FillPattern%¶
  MOUSE ON : MENU ON¶
RETURN¶
¶
¶
ColorPalette:¶
  Test=MOUSE(0)¶
  x=MOUSE(3) : y=MOUSE(4)¶
¶
  GOSUB ChooseColor¶
¶
  PATTERN ,Solid%¶
```

```
        LINE (10,72)-(50,95),DrawColor,b¶
        LINE (15,75)-(45,93),DrawColor,bf¶
        LINE (70,72)-(110,95),FillColor,b¶
        LINE (75,75)-(105,93),FillColor,bf¶
        PATTERN ,FillPattern%¶
¶
        IF WINDOW(0)=3 AND 72<y AND y<95 THEN¶
          IF 70<x AND x<110 THEN ColorChoice=1¶
          IF 10<x AND x<50 THEN ColorChoice=0 ¶
          IF 135<x AND x<235 THEN¶
            PATTERN ,Solid%¶
            PAINT (137,74),3,1¶
            PATTERN ,FillPattern%¶
            GOSUB PaletteDef¶
            RETURN¶
          END IF¶
        END IF¶
        GOSUB OKCheck¶
¶
        IF ColorChoice=0 THEN¶
          LOCATE 14,3 : COLOR 0,1 : PRINT "Draw";¶
          LOCATE 14,10: COLOR 1,0 : PRINT "Fill";¶
        ELSE¶
          LOCATE 14,3 : COLOR 1,0 : PRINT "Draw";¶
          LOCATE 14,10 : COLOR 0,1 : PRINT "Fill";¶
        END IF¶
RETURN¶
¶
PaletteDef:¶
        IF ColorChoice=0 THEN NewColor=DrawColor ELSE
NewColor=FillColor¶
        PATTERN ,Solid%¶
        LINE (0,71)-(240,107),0,bf¶
        COLOR 1,0¶
        LOCATE 10,2 : PRINT "R";¶
        LOCATE 11,2 : PRINT "G";¶
        LOCATE 12,2 : PRINT "B";¶
        LOCATE 14,2 : PRINT STRING$(15," ")¶
        LINE (24,70)-(218,78),1,b¶
        LINE (24,80)-(218,88),1,b¶
        LINE (24,90)-(218,98),1,b¶
        LINE (222,70)-(238,98),NewColor,bf¶
        Mode=4¶
        PATTERN ,FillPattern%¶
RETURN ¶
¶
RGBDef:¶
        Test=MOUSE(0)¶
        x=MOUSE(3) : y=MOUSE(4)¶
        GOSUB ChooseColor¶
        IF ColorChoice=0 THEN NewColor=DrawColor ELSE
NewColor=FillColor¶
        GOSUB RGBRegulator¶
        GOSUB OKCheck : IF EndOK=1 THEN EndOK=3¶
        WHILE MOUSE(0)<>0¶
          x=MOUSE(1) : y=MOUSE(2)¶
```

```
      IF WINDOW(0)=3 AND x>26 AND x<218 AND y>70 AND y<98
THEN¶
      Colors%(NewColor,INT((y-71)/8.7))=INT((x-26)/12)¶
      GOSUB RGBRegulator¶
    END IF¶
  WEND¶
RETURN¶
¶
RGBRegulator:¶
  PATTERN ,Solid%¶
  LINE (25+r*12,71)-(37+r*12,77),0,bf¶
  LINE (25+g*12,81)-(37+g*12,87),0,bf¶
  LINE (25+b*12,91)-(37+b*12,97),0,bf¶
  r=Colors%(NewColor,0)¶
  g=Colors%(NewColor,1)¶
  b=Colors%(NewColor,2)    ¶
  LINE (25+r*12,71)-(37+r*12,77),1,bf¶
  LINE (25+g*12,81)-(37+g*12,87),1,bf¶
  LINE (25+b*12,91)-(37+b*12,97),1,bf¶
  PALETTE NewColor,r/16,g/16,b/16¶
  LINE (222,70)-(238,98),NewColor,bf¶
  PATTERN ,FillPattern%¶
RETURN¶
¶
ChooseColor:¶
  IF WINDOW(0)=3 AND x<240 AND y<(2^(Colors+1)) THEN¶
    fx=INT(x/30) : fy = INT(y/16)¶
    IF ColorChoice=0 THEN                           ¶
      DrawColor=fy*8+fx¶
    ELSE¶
      FillColor=fy*8+fx¶
    END IF¶
  END IF¶
RETURN¶
¶
OKCheck:¶
  IF x>190 AND x<230 AND y>109 AND y<132 THEN¶
    PATTERN ,Solid%¶
    PAINT (192,111),3,1 : EndOK=1¶
    PATTERN ,FillPattern%¶
  END IF¶
RETURN¶
¶
ColorDone:¶
  MENU 2,0,1 : Mode=1¶
  WINDOW CLOSE 3¶
  WINDOW OUTPUT 2¶
RETURN¶
¶
PatternEditor:¶
  MOUSE OFF : MENU OFF¶
  EndOK=0¶
  WINDOW 4,"Fill Patterns",(54,30)-(300,130),18,1¶
  LINE (0,0)-(132,66),3,b¶
¶
  FOR x=0 TO 2 ¶
```

```
      FOR y=0 TO 2 ¶
         FOR i=0 TO 7: FillPattern%(i)=AllPatterns%(y*3+x,i)
: NEXT i¶
         PATTERN ,FillPattern%¶
         LINE (144+x*34,y*25)-(175+x*34,23+y*25),1,bf¶
      NEXT y¶
   NEXT x¶
   GOSUB MarkPattern¶
¶
   LINE (5,68)-(65,82),1,b¶
   LOCATE 10,3 : PRINT "Clear";¶
   LINE (75,68)-(135,82),1,b¶
   LOCATE 10,12: PRINT "Inv.";¶
   LINE (5,85)-(65,100),1,b¶
   LOCATE 12,3 : PRINT "Load";¶
   LINE (75,85)-(135,100),1,b¶
   LOCATE 12,12: PRINT "Save";¶
   LINE (162,77)-(222,92),1,b¶
   LOCATE 11,24 : PRINT "OK";¶
¶
   FOR i=0 TO 7 :
FillPattern%(i)=AllPatterns%(PtrnNumber,i) : NEXT i¶
   GOSUB DrawPattern¶
¶
   MENU ON : MOUSE ON¶
RETURN¶
¶
DefinePattern:¶
   Test=MOUSE(0)¶
   x=MOUSE(3) : y=MOUSE(4)¶
   IF WINDOW(0)=4 AND x<132 AND y<66 THEN¶
     px=INT(x/8.25) : py=INT(y/8.25)¶
     Bit=FillPattern%(py) AND 2^(15-px)¶
     IF Bit=0 THEN¶
        FillPattern=FillPattern%(py) OR 2^(15-px)¶
     ELSE¶
        FillPattern=FillPattern%(py) AND (65535&-2^(15-
px))¶
     END IF¶
     IF FillPattern>32767 THEN FillPattern=FillPattern-
65536&¶
     FillPattern%(py)=FillPattern¶
     PATTERN ,Solid%¶
     LINE (px*8+4,py*8+2)-(px*8+9,py*8+8),-(Bit=0),bf¶
     PATTERN ,FillPattern%¶
     y1=INT(PtrnNumber/3) : x1=PtrnNumber-y1*3¶
     LINE (144+x1*34,y1*25)-(175+x1*34,23+y1*25),1,bf¶
     FOR i=0 TO 7 :
AllPatterns%(PtrnNumber,i)=FillPattern%(i) : NEXT i¶
     RETURN¶
   END IF ¶
   IF WINDOW(0)=4 AND x>142 AND x<244 AND y<75 THEN¶
     px=INT((x-143)/34) : py=INT(y/25)¶
     IF px+py*3=PtrnNumber THEN RETURN¶
     PtrnNumber=px+py*3¶
```

```
        FOR i=0 TO 7 :
FillPattern%(i)=AllPatterns%(PtrnNumber,i) : NEXT i¶
      GOSUB MarkPattern¶
      GOSUB DrawPattern¶
      PATTERN ,FillPattern%¶
      RETURN¶
    END IF ¶
¶
    IF WINDOW(0)=4 AND x<222 AND x>162 AND y<93 AND y>76
THEN¶
      PATTERN ,Solid%¶
      PAINT (164,78),2,1¶
      PATTERN ,FillPattern%¶
      EndOK=2 : RETURN¶
    END IF ¶
¶
    IF WINDOW(0)=4 AND x<135 AND y>68 AND y<100 THEN¶
      PATTERN ,Solid%¶
      IF x<66 AND x>4 AND y<82 THEN¶
        PAINT (6,69),2,1¶
        LINE (1,1)-(131,65),0,bf¶
        FOR i=0 TO 7 : AllPatterns%(PtrnNumber,i)=0 :
FillPattern%(i)=0 : NEXT¶
        PAINT (6,69),0,1¶
        PATTERN ,FillPattern%¶
        y1=INT(PtrnNumber/3) : x1=PtrnNumber-y1*3¶
        LINE (144+x1*34,y1*25)-(175+x1*34,23+y1*25),1,bf¶
      END IF ¶
      IF x<136 AND x>74 AND y<82 THEN¶
        PAINT (76,69),2,1¶
        FOR i=0 TO 7¶
          FillPattern%(i)=FillPattern%(i) XOR &HFFFF¶
          AllPatterns%(PtrnNumber,i)=FillPattern%(i)¶
        NEXT i¶
        GOSUB DrawPattern¶
        PAINT (76,69),0,1¶
        PATTERN ,FillPattern%¶
        y1=INT(PtrnNumber/3) : x1=PtrnNumber-y1*3¶
        LINE (144+x1*34,y1*25)-(175+x1*34,23+y1*25),1,bf¶
      END IF¶
      IF x<66 AND x>4 AND y>84 THEN GOSUB PtrnLoad¶
      IF x<135 AND x>75 AND y>84 THEN GOSUB PtrnSave¶
    END IF¶
RETURN¶
¶
MarkPattern:¶
  y1=INT(AltPattern/3) : x1=AltPattern-y1*3      ¶
  LINE (143+x1*34,y1*25-1)-(176+x1*34,24+y1*25),0,b¶
  y1=INT(PtrnNumber/3) : x1=PtrnNumber-y1*3¶
  LINE (143+x1*34,y1*25-1)-(176+x1*34,24+y1*25),3,b¶
  AltPattern=x1+y1*3¶
RETURN¶
¶
DrawPattern:¶
  MOUSE OFF : MENU OFF¶
  PATTERN ,Solid%¶
```

```
    LINE (1,1)-(131,65),0,bf ¶
    FOR y=0 TO 7¶
      FOR x=0 TO 15¶
        Bit=FillPattern%(y) AND 2^(15-x)¶
        IF Bit<>0 THEN LINE (x*8+4,y*8+2)-
(x*8+9,y*8+8),1,bf¶
      NEXT x¶
    NEXT y¶
    PATTERN ,FillPattern%¶
    MOUSE ON : MENU ON¶
RETURN¶
¶
PtrnLoad:¶
  MOUSE OFF : MENU OFF¶
  PAINT (6,86),2,1¶
  GOSUB EnterName¶
  IF Nam$="" THEN EndPtrnLoad¶
  OPEN Nam$ FOR INPUT AS 1¶
    FOR x=0 TO 8¶
      FOR y=0 TO 7¶
        AllPatterns%(x,y)=CVI(INPUT$(2,1))¶
      NEXT y¶
    NEXT x¶
  CLOSE 1¶
¶
EndPtrnLoad:¶
  WINDOW CLOSE 5 : WINDOW 4¶
  PAINT (6,86),0,1¶
  MOUSE ON : MENU ON¶
  FOR x=0 TO 8¶
    FOR y=0 TO 7¶
      FillPattern%(y)=AllPatterns%(x,y)¶
      PATTERN ,FillPattern%¶
      y1=INT(x/3) : x1=x-y1*3¶
      LINE (144+x1*34,y1*25)-(175+x1*34,23+y1*25),1,bf¶
    NEXT y¶
  NEXT x¶
  FOR i=0 TO 7 :
FillPattern%(i)=AllPatterns%(PtrnNumber,i) : NEXT¶
  GOSUB DrawPattern¶
RETURN¶
¶
PtrnSave:¶
  MOUSE OFF : MENU OFF¶
  PAINT (78,86),2,1¶
  GOSUB EnterName¶
  IF Nam$="" THEN EndPtrnLoad¶
  OPEN Nam$ FOR OUTPUT AS 1¶
    FOR x=0 TO 8¶
      FOR y=0 TO 7¶
        PRINT #1,MKI$(AllPatterns%(x,y));¶
      NEXT y¶
    NEXT x¶
  CLOSE 1¶
¶
EndPtrnSave:¶
```

```
      WINDOW CLOSE 5 : WINDOW 4¶
      PAINT (78,86),0,1¶
      MOUSE ON : MENU ON¶
RETURN¶
¶
PatternDone:¶
   MENU 2,0,1 : Mode=1¶
   WINDOW CLOSE 4¶
   WINDOW OUTPUT 2¶
   PATTERN ,FillPattern%¶
RETURN¶
¶
DrawLoad:¶
   MENU 2,0,0 : MENU 1,0,0¶
   MENU OFF : MOUSE OFF¶
   GOSUB EnterName¶
   WINDOW CLOSE 5¶
   WINDOW 2¶
   IF Nam$="" THEN EndLoad ¶
   OPEN Nam$ FOR INPUT AS 1¶
      Form$=INPUT$(4,1)¶
      Length=CVL(INPUT$(4,1))¶
      IF INPUT$(4,1)<>"ILBM" THEN BEEP : GOTO EndLoad¶
¶
ReadData:¶
      IF EOF(1) THEN EndLoad¶
      Chunk$=INPUT$(4,1)¶
      Length=CVL(INPUT$(4,1))¶
      IF INT(Length/2)<>(Length/2) THEN Length=Length+1¶
      IF Chunk$="BMHD" THEN BMHeader¶
      IF Chunk$="CMAP" THEN ColorMap¶
      IF Chunk$="BODY" THEN BodyMap¶
      Dummy$=INPUT$(Length,1)¶
   GOTO ReadData¶
¶
BMHeader:   ¶
      xd=CVI(INPUT$(2,1))¶
      IF xd>320 THEN EndLoad¶
      yd=CVI(INPUT$(2,1))¶
      IF yd>200 THEN EndLoad¶
      Dummy$=INPUT$(4,1)¶
      BitPlane=ASC(INPUT$(1,1))¶
      Dummy$=INPUT$(11,1)¶
      Addr=PEEKL(WINDOW(8)+4)+8¶
      FOR x=0 TO BitPlane-1¶
         PlaneAddr(x)=PEEKL(Addr+4*x)¶
      NEXT x¶
   GOTO ReadData¶
      ¶
ColorMap:¶
      FOR x=0 TO (Length/3)-1¶
         r=(ASC(INPUT$(1,1)) AND 240)/16¶
         g=(ASC(INPUT$(1,1)) AND 240)/16¶
         b=(ASC(INPUT$(1,1)) AND 240)/16¶
         PALETTE x,r/16,g/16,b/16¶
         Colors%(x,0)=r : Colors%(x,1)=g : Colors%(x,2)=b¶
```

501

```
            NEXT x¶
            IF INT(Length/3)<>(Length/3) THEN Dummy$=INPUT$(1,1)¶
         GOTO ReadData¶
            ¶
BodyMap:¶
            FOR y1=0 TO 199¶
              FOR b=0 TO BitPlane-1¶
                IF b<Colors THEN¶
                  FOR x1=0 TO 9¶
                    POKEL
PlaneAddr(b)+4*x1+40*y1,CVL(INPUT$(4,1))¶
                  NEXT x1¶
                ELSE¶
                    Dummy$=INPUT$(40,1)¶
                END IF¶
              NEXT b¶
            NEXT y1¶
         GOTO ReadData         ¶
¶
EndLoad:¶
         CLOSE 1¶
         MENU ON : MOUSE ON¶
         MENU 1,0,1 : MENU 2,0,1¶
RETURN¶
¶
DrawSave:¶
         MENU 2,0,0 : MENU 1,0,0¶
         MENU OFF : MOUSE OFF¶
         GOSUB EnterName¶
         WINDOW CLOSE 5¶
         WINDOW 2¶
         IF Nam$="" THEN EndSave¶
         OPEN Nam$ FOR OUTPUT AS 1 LEN=FRE(0)-500¶
            PRINT #1,"FORM";¶
            PRINT #1,MKL$(156+8000*Colors);¶
            PRINT #1,"ILBM";¶
            PRINT #1,"BMHD";MKL$(20);¶
            PRINT #1,MKI$(320);MKI$(200);¶
            PRINT #1,MKL$(0);¶
            PRINT #1,CHR$(Colors);¶
            PRINT #1,CHR$(0);MKI$(0);MKI$(0);¶
            PRINT #1,CHR$(10);CHR$(11);¶
            PRINT #1,MKI$(320);MKI$(200);¶
            ¶
            PRINT #1,"CMAP";MKL$(96); ¶
            FOR x=0 TO 31¶
              PRINT #1,CHR$(Colors%(x,0)*16);¶
              PRINT #1,CHR$(Colors%(x,1)*16);¶
              PRINT #1,CHR$(Colors%(x,2)*16);¶
            NEXT x¶
            ¶
            PRINT #1,"BODY";MKL$(8000*Colors);¶
            Addr=PEEKL(WINDOW(8)+4)+8¶
            FOR x=0 TO Colors-1¶
              PlaneAddr(x)=PEEKL(Addr+4*x)¶
            NEXT x¶
```

```
      FOR y1=0 TO 199¶
        FOR b=0 TO Colors-1¶
          FOR x1=0 TO 9 ¶
            PRINT#1,MKL$(PEEKL(PlaneAddr(b)+4*x1+40*y1));¶
          NEXT x1¶
        NEXT b¶
        PAddr=PlaneAddr(0)+40*y1¶
        POKE PAddr,PEEK(PAddr) AND 63¶
        POKE PAddr+39,PEEK(PAddr+39) AND 252¶
      NEXT y1¶
      ¶
      PRINT #1,"CAMG";MKL$(4);¶
      PRINT #1,MKL$(16384);¶
    CLOSE 1¶
      ¶
EndSave:¶
  MENU ON : MOUSE ON¶
  MENU 1,0,1 : MENU 2,0,1¶
RETURN¶
¶
EnterName:¶
  Altname$=Nam$¶
  WINDOW 5,"Enter Name:",(0,80)-(311,88),0,1¶
  CLS¶
  LINE INPUT Nam$¶
  IF Nam$= "=" OR Nam$="*" THEN Nam$=Altname$¶
RETURN¶
¶
Query:¶
  MENU 1,0,0 : MENU 2,0,0¶
  MENU OFF : MOUSE OFF¶
  WINDOW 5,"CAUTION!",(43,70)-(270,120),0,1¶
  COLOR 0,1 : CLS : LOCATE 2,2¶
  PRINT "Do you really want to"¶
  PRINT " lose your picture?"¶
  PATTERN ,Solid%¶
  LOCATE 5,12 : PRINT "Yes";¶
  LOCATE 5,21 : PRINT "No";¶
  LINE (77,31)-(127,46),0,b¶
  LINE (145,31)-(195,46),0,b¶
  SOUND 880,6,100¶
Pause:¶
  Test=MOUSE(0)¶
  WHILE MOUSE(0)=0¶
    x=MOUSE(1) : y=MOUSE(2)¶
  WEND¶
  IF (y<46 AND y>31) THEN¶
    IF (x<127 AND x>77) THEN PAINT (79,33),3,0 : OK=1 :
GOTO EndQuery ¶
    IF (x<195 AND x>145) THEN PAINT (147,33),3,0 : OK=0 :
GOTO EndQuery¶
  END IF¶
  GOTO Pause ¶
EndQuery:¶
  MENU ON : MOUSE ON : MENU 1,0,1 : MENU 2,0,1¶
  WINDOW CLOSE 5 : WINDOW 2¶
```

```
RETURN¶
¶
EndIt:¶
  MENU RESET¶
  SCREEN CLOSE 1¶
END¶
```

C.4 Statistical data manager

```
Setup:¶
  DIM Number$(58),Desc$(58),Value$(58)¶
  DIM Array$(50),Array(50)¶
  FOR x=1 TO 58¶
    IF x>4 AND x<55 THEN Number$(x)=STR$(x-4)¶
  NEXT x¶
  TopLine=1¶
¶
  Colors=3¶
  SCREEN 4,640,200,Colors,2¶
  WINDOW 99,"Graphics",,20,4¶
  PALETTE 7,.8,.2,.1¶
¶
  WINDOW 1,"Statistical-Data-Manager",(0,12)-
(631,111),22,-1¶
¶
  MENU 1,0,1,"Data   "  ¶
  MENU 1,1,1,"Load   "¶
  MENU 1,2,1,"Save   "¶
  MENU 1,3,1,"Print "¶
  MENU 1,4,1,"Delete"¶
  MENU 1,5,1,"Quit   "¶
  MENU 2,0,1,"Graphics"¶
  MENU 2,1,1,"Bar Graph"¶
  MENU 2,2,1,"Pie Chart"¶
  MENU 2,3,1,"Save Pic"¶
  MENU 3,0,0,""¶
  MENU 4,0,0,""¶
¶
  ON MENU GOSUB MenuControl¶
  MENU ON¶
¶
GOTO MainLoop¶
¶
MenuControl:¶
  Men=MENU(0)  : MenuPoint=MENU(1)¶
  IF Men=1 THEN¶
    IF MenuPoint=1 THEN GOSUB LoadData¶
    IF MenuPoint=2 THEN GOSUB SaveData¶
    IF MenuPoint=3 THEN GOSUB PrintData¶
    IF MenuPoint=4 THEN GOSUB ClearData¶
    IF MenuPoint=5 THEN Quit¶
  END IF¶
  IF Men=2 THEN¶
    IF MenuPoint=3 THEN¶
      MENU 1,0,0: MENU 2,0,0¶
      MENU OFF¶
        GOSUB EnterName¶
      WINDOW 99¶
```

```
      PicSave Nam$,99,0¶
    WINDOW 1¶
    MENU ON¶
    MENU 1,0,1 : MENU 2,0,1¶
  END IF¶
  IF MenuPoint=1 THEN Array$(0)="B"¶
  IF MenuPoint=2 THEN Array$(0)="P"¶
  Array(0)=TopLine¶
  IF Value$(Array(0)+4)="" THEN Array(0)=Array(0)-1¶
  FOR x=1 TO Array(0)¶
    Array$(x)=Desc$(x+4)¶
    Array(x)=VAL(Value$(x+4))¶
    IF Array(x)=0 THEN Array(x)=.01¶
  NEXT x¶
  MENU OFF¶
  MENU 1,0,0 : MENU 2,0,0¶
  WINDOW 99 : CLS¶
  ¶
  GOSUB Graphics¶
  ¶
  WINDOW 2,"Please press a key!",(350,0)-(631,0),20,4¶
  COLOR 0,1 : CLS¶
  WHILE INKEY$=""¶
  WEND¶
  WINDOW CLOSE 2¶
  WINDOW 1¶
  MENU ON¶
  MENU 1,0,1 : MENU 2,0,1          ¶
END IF¶
RETURN          ¶
¶
MainLoop:¶
  CLS¶
  IF TopLine>50 THEN TopLine=50¶
  IF LineOne>TopLine THEN LineOne=TopLine : BEEP¶
  IF LineOne<1 THEN LineOne=1 : BEEP¶
  PRINT "Number";TAB(10);"Description";TAB(45);"Value"¶
  FOR x=LineOne TO LineOne+8¶
    COLOR 1,0¶
    PRINT Number$(x);TAB(10);Desc$(x);TAB(45);Value$(x)¶
  NEXT x¶
  IF DescData=0 THEN StartSlice=10 : EndSlice=40¶
  IF DescData=1 THEN StartSlice=45 : EndSlice=55¶
  xp=StartSlice¶
¶
  GOSUB EnterText¶
  in$=""¶
¶
GOTO MainLoop¶
¶
¶
EnterText:¶
  IF xp<StartSlice THEN xp=StartSlice¶
  LOCATE 6,xp¶
  COLOR 0,3 : PRINT " "; : COLOR 1,0¶
  i$=INKEY$¶
```

```
      IF i$="" THEN EnterText¶
      IF i$=CHR$(2) THEN LineOne=1 : RETURN¶
      IF i$=CHR$(5) THEN LineOne=TopLine : RETURN¶
      IF i$=CHR$(4) THEN DeleteLine : RETURN¶
      IF i$=CHR$(14) THEN InsertLine : RETURN¶
      IF i$=CHR$(28) THEN GOSUB AcceptText : xp=StartSlice :
   LineOne=LineOne-1: RETURN¶
      IF i$=CHR$(29) THEN GOSUB AcceptText : xp=StartSlice :
   LineOne=LineOne+1: RETURN¶
        ¶
      TextPos=xp-StartSlice+1¶
      IF DescData=0 THEN Text$=Desc$(LineOne+4)¶
      IF DescData=1 THEN Text$=Value$(LineOne+4)¶
   ¶
      IF i$=CHR$(30) THEN¶
        IF TextPos<=LEN(Text$) THEN i$=MID$(Text$,TextPos,1)¶
      END IF ¶
   ¶
      IF i$=CHR$(13) OR i$=CHR$(9) THEN¶
        GOSUB AcceptText¶
        DescData=1-DescData¶
        IF DescData=0 THEN LineOne=LineOne+1¶
        xp=StartSlice¶
        IF TopLine<LineOne THEN TopLine=LineOne¶
        RETURN¶
      END IF¶
      IF i$=CHR$(8) OR i$=CHR$(31) THEN¶
        LOCATE 6,xp¶
        IF TextPos<=LEN(Text$) THEN¶
          PRINT RIGHT$(Text$,LEN(Text$)-TextPos+1);¶
        ELSE¶
          PRINT " ";¶
        END IF¶
        xp=xp-1 : IF xp<StartSlice THEN xp=StartSlice : BEEP
   : GOTO EnterText¶
        in$=LEFT$(in$,(LEN(in$)-1))¶
        GOTO EnterText¶
      END IF¶
      IF i$=CHR$(34) THEN i$=CHR$(39)¶
      IF i$ > CHR$(31) AND i$ < CHR$(127) THEN¶
        IF xp>=EndSlice THEN xp=EndSlice : BEEP : GOTO
   EnterText¶
        LOCATE 6,xp¶
        PRINT i$;¶
        in$=in$+i$¶
        xp=xp+1¶
      END IF¶
   GOTO EnterText¶
   ¶
   AcceptText:¶
      IF in$<>"" THEN¶
        IF DescData=0 THEN Desc$(LineOne+4)=in$¶
        IF DescData=1 THEN Value$(LineOne+4)=in$¶
        in$=""¶
        AltData=1¶
      END IF¶
```

```
RETURN¶
¶
DeleteLine:¶
  FOR x=LineOne+4 TO 54¶
    Desc$(x)=Desc$(x+1)¶
    Value$(x)=Value$(x+1)¶
  NEXT x¶
  TopLine=TopLine-1¶
  IF TopLine<1 THEN TopLine=1¶
RETURN¶
¶
InsertLine:¶
  IF TopLine>=50 THEN BEEP : RETURN¶
  FOR x=TopLine+4 TO LineOne+4 STEP -1¶
    Desc$(x+1)=Desc$(x)¶
    Value$(x+1)=Value$(x)¶
  NEXT x¶
  Desc$(LineOne+4)=""¶
  Value$(LineOne+4)=""¶
  TopLine=TopLine+1¶
RETURN¶
¶
SaveData:¶
  MENU 1,0,0 : MENU 2,0,0 ¶
  MENU OFF¶
  GOSUB EnterName¶
  WINDOW 1¶
  IF Nam$="" THEN EndSave¶
  OPEN Nam$ FOR OUTPUT AS 1¶
    PRINT #1,TopLine+4¶
    FOR x=1 TO TopLine+4¶
      WRITE #1,Desc$(x)¶
      WRITE #1,Value$(x)¶
    NEXT x¶
  CLOSE 1¶
  ¶
EndSave:¶
  MENU 1,0,1 : MENU 2,0,1¶
  MENU ON¶
  AltData=0¶
RETURN¶
¶
LoadData:¶
  IF AltData=1 THEN GOSUB Query¶
  MENU 1,0,0 : MENU 2,0,0¶
  MENU OFF¶
  GOSUB EnterName¶
  WINDOW 1¶
  IF Nam$="" THEN EndLoad¶
  FOR x=1 TO 58¶
    Desc$(x)=""¶
    Value$(x)=""¶
  NEXT x¶
  OPEN Nam$ FOR INPUT AS 1¶
    INPUT #1,NmbrData¶
    TopLine=NmbrData-4¶
```

```
      FOR x=1 TO NmbrData¶
        INPUT #1,Desc$(x)¶
        INPUT #1,Value$(x)¶
      NEXT x¶
      LineOne=TopLine¶
    CLOSE 1¶
    ¶
EndLoad:¶
  WINDOW 1¶
  COLOR 1,0¶
  CLS¶
  PRINT "Number";TAB(10);"Description";TAB(45);"Array"¶
  FOR x=LineOne TO LineOne+8¶
     PRINT Number$(x);TAB(10);Desc$(x);TAB(45);Value$(x)¶
  NEXT x¶
  MENU 1,0,1 : MENU 2,0,1¶
  MENU ON¶
  AltData=0¶
RETURN¶
        ¶
EnterName:¶
  Altname$=Nam$¶
  WINDOW 2,"Enter filename:",(50,80)-(580,88),0,-1¶
  CLS¶
  LINE INPUT Nam$¶
  IF Nam$= "=" OR Nam$="*" THEN Nam$=Altname$¶
  WINDOW CLOSE 2¶
RETURN¶
¶
PrintData:¶
  MENU 1,0,0 : MENU 2,0,0¶
  MENU OFF¶
  OPEN "PRT:" FOR OUTPUT AS 1¶
     PRINT #1,"File:";Altname$;CHR$(10)¶
     PRINT
#1,"Number";TAB(10);"Description";TAB(45);"Value"¶
     FOR x=4 TO TopLine+4¶
        PRINT #1,
Number$(x);TAB(10);Desc$(x);TAB(45);Value$(x)¶
     NEXT x¶
  CLOSE 1¶
  MENU 1,0,1 : MENU 2,0,1¶
  MENU ON¶
RETURN¶
¶
Query:¶
  WINDOW 2,"Attention!",(155,50)-(475,135),0,-1¶
  COLOR 0,1¶
  CLS¶
  LOCATE 2,3¶
  PRINT  "     Your data has not"¶
  PRINT  "        yet been saved."¶
  PRINT : PRINT  "        Save it now?"¶
  LOCATE 9,15 : PRINT "Yes"¶
  LOCATE 9,26 : PRINT "No"¶
  LINE (95,57)-(149,74),0,b¶
```

```
        LINE (183,57)-(236,74),0,b¶
        BEEP¶
WaitforMouse:¶
  Test=MOUSE(0)¶
  WHILE MOUSE(0)=0¶
  WEND¶
  x=MOUSE(1) : y=MOUSE(2)¶
  IF 95<x AND x<148 AND 57<y AND y<74 THEN¶
    PAINT (97,59),3,0¶
    GOSUB SaveData¶
    PAINT (97,59),1,0¶
    WINDOW CLOSE 2¶
    RETURN¶
  END IF¶
  IF 183<x AND x<236 AND 57<y AND y<74 THEN¶
    PAINT (185,59),3,0¶
    WINDOW CLOSE 2¶
    RETURN¶
  END IF¶
  GOTO WaitforMouse¶
¶
ClearData:¶
  IF AltData=1 THEN GOSUB Query¶
  RUN¶
  ¶
Quit:¶
  IF AltData=1 THEN GOSUB Query¶
  COLOR 1,0¶
  MENU RESET¶
  CLS¶
END¶
¶
Graphics:¶
  IF Array(0)=0 THEN RETURN ¶
  IF UCASE$(Array$(0))="B" THEN GOSUB BarGraph¶
  IF UCASE$(Array$(0))="P" THEN GOSUB PieChart¶
RETURN¶
¶
PieChart:¶
  Total=0¶
  FOR x=1 TO Array(0)¶
    Total=Total+Array(x)¶
  NEXT x¶
  Divi=Total/6.283 : Angle1=.0001 : BColor=1¶
  FOR x=1 TO Array(0)¶
    LColor=BColor¶
    IF LColor>(2^Colors)-1 THEN LColor=1¶
    BColor=LColor+1¶
    IF BColor>(2^Colors)-1 THEN BColor=1¶
    Angle2=Angle1+Array(x)/Divi¶
    CIRCLE (320,100),156,BColor ¶
    CIRCLE (320,100),150,BColor,-Angle2,-Angle1¶
    PAINT (320,32),LColor,BColor¶
    CIRCLE (320,100),150,BColor¶
    PAINT (320,32),0,BColor¶
    CIRCLE (320,100),150,BColor,-Angle1,-Angle2¶
```

```
      MidAngle=(Angle1+Angle2)/2¶
      px=320+165*COS(MidAngle)¶
      py=100-80*SIN(MidAngle)¶
      Distance=0¶
      IF MidAngle>1.57 AND MidAngle<4.72 THEN
Distance=LEN(Array$(x))¶
      IF Distance>15 THEN Distance=15¶
      COLOR LColor,0¶
      LOCATE (py/8.95)+1,(px/7.9)+1-Distance¶
      PRINT Array$(x);¶
      Angle1=Angle2¶
    NEXT x¶
¶
    CIRCLE (320,100),156,0¶
RETURN¶
  ¶
BarGraph:                              ¶
  Max=.0001 : LColor=0¶
  FOR x=1 TO Array(0)¶
    IF Array(x)>Max THEN Max=Array(x)¶
  NEXT x¶
  BarWidth=INT(600/(Array(0)))¶
  IF BarWidth>100 THEN BarWidth=100¶
  Factor=160/Max¶
  LOCATE 1,1 : PRINT Max;¶
  LOCATE 10,1 : PRINT Max/2;¶
  FOR x=0 TO 10¶
    LINE (1,170-x*16)-(5,170-x*16)¶
  NEXT x ¶
  FOR x=1 TO Array(0)¶
    LColor=LColor+1 : IF LColor>(2^Colors)-1 THEN
LColor=1¶
    LINE (30+(x-1)*BarWidth,170-Array(x)*Factor)-
(25+x*BarWidth,170),LColor,bf¶
    COLOR LColor,0¶
    LOCATE 23,(5+(x-1)*(BarWidth/7.9))¶
    PRINT Array$(x);¶
  NEXT x¶
RETURN¶
  ¶
SUB PicSave (Nam$,WindowNr%,ArrayYN%) STATIC¶
  IF ArrayYN%=1 THEN SHARED Colors%()¶
  IF ArrayYN%=0 THEN¶
    IF Colors%(0,0)<>2 THEN ERASE Colors% : DIM
Colors%(31,2)¶
    RESTORE ColorTable¶
    FOR x=0 TO 31¶
      READ Colors%(x,0),Colors%(x,1),Colors%(x,2)¶
    NEXT x¶
  ColorTable:  ¶
    DATA 2,3,10, 15,15,15, 0,0,0, 15,8,0¶
    DATA 0,0,15, 15,0,15, 0,15,15, 15,15,15¶
    DATA 6,1,1, 14,5,0, 8,15,0, 14,11,0¶
    DATA 5,5,15, 9,0,15, 0,15,9, 12,12,12¶
    DATA 0,0,0, 13,0,0, 0,0,0, 15,12,10¶
    DATA 1,1,1, 5,5,5, 6,6,6, 7,7,7¶
```

```
      DATA 8,8,8, 9,9,9, 10,10,10, 11,11,11¶
      DATA 12,12,12, 13,13,13, 14,14,14, 15,15,15¶
   END IF¶
   IF Nam$="" THEN EXIT SUB¶
   AltWindowNr=WINDOW(1)¶
   WINDOW WindowNr%¶
   Wide=WINDOW(2)¶
      IF Wide>320 THEN¶
         Wide=640¶
         Resolution=2¶
         Planes=16000¶
      ELSE¶
         Wide=320¶
         Resolution=1¶
         Planes=8000¶
      END IF¶
   Height=WINDOW(3)¶
      IF Height>200 THEN¶
         Height=400¶
         Planes=Planes*2¶
         Resolution=Resolution+2¶
      ELSE¶
         Height=200¶
      END IF¶
   Colors=LOG(WINDOW(6)+1)/LOG(2)¶
¶
   OPEN Nam$ FOR OUTPUT AS 1 LEN=FRE(0)-500¶
      PRINT #1,"FORM";¶
      PRINT #1,MKL$(156+Planes*Colors);¶
      PRINT #1,"ILBM";¶
      PRINT #1,"BMHD";MKL$(20);¶
      PRINT #1,MKI$(Wide);MKI$(Height);¶
      PRINT #1,MKL$(0);¶
      PRINT #1,CHR$(Colors);¶
      PRINT #1,CHR$(0);MKI$(0);MKI$(0);¶
      PRINT #1,CHR$(10);CHR$(11);¶
      PRINT #1,MKI$(Wide);MKI$(Height);¶
      ¶
      PRINT #1,"CMAP";MKL$(96); ¶
      FOR x=0 TO 31¶
         PRINT #1,CHR$(Colors%(x,0)*16);¶
         PRINT #1,CHR$(Colors%(x,1)*16);¶
         PRINT #1,CHR$(Colors%(x,2)*16);¶
      NEXT x¶
      ¶
      PRINT #1,"BODY";MKL$(Planes*Colors);¶
      Addr=PEEKL(WINDOW(8)+4)+8¶
      FOR x=0 TO Colors-1¶
         PlaneAddr(x)=PEEKL(Addr+4*x)¶
      NEXT x¶
      FOR y1=0 TO Height-1¶
         FOR b=0 TO Colors-1¶
            FOR x1=0 TO (Wide/32)-1 ¶

PRINT#1,MKL$(PEEKL(PlaneAddr(b)+4*x1+(Wide/8)*y1));¶
            NEXT x1¶
```

```
       NEXT b¶
       PAddr=PlaneAddr(0)+(Wide/8)*y1¶
       POKE PAddr,PEEK(PAddr) AND 63¶
       POKE PAddr+Wide/8-1,PEEK(PAddr+Wide/8-1) AND 252¶
     NEXT y1¶
     ¶
     PRINT #1,"CAMG";MKL$(4);¶
     PRINT #1,MKL$(16384);¶
   CLOSE 1¶
   WINDOW AltWindowNr   ¶
 END SUB¶
 ¶
```

C.5

Database program

```
Setup:¶
  PALETTE 0,0,.1,.4¶
  PALETTE 2,0,1,0¶
  ¶
Begin:¶
  CLS : LOCATE 1,1 : PRINT  "Select"¶
  LOCATE 1,32: COLOR 3,0 : PRINT "Filename:"; : COLOR
1,0¶
  IF Altname$<>"" THEN PRINT Altname$ ELSE PRINT "(no
file)"¶
  PRINT¶
  COLOR 0,3 : PRINT SPACE$(31)"AmigaBASIC
DataBase"SPACE$(31)¶
  LOCATE 5,32 : COLOR 3,0¶
  PRINT "Please Choose:"¶
  LOCATE 7,32¶
  COLOR 0,1 :PRINT " 1 "; : COLOR 1,0 : PRINT " Create
File"¶
  LOCATE 9,32¶
  COLOR 0,1 :PRINT " 2 "; : COLOR 1,0 : PRINT " Enter
data"¶
  LOCATE 11,32¶
  COLOR 0,1 :PRINT " 3 "; : COLOR 1,0 : PRINT " Read
file"¶
  LOCATE 13,32¶
  COLOR 0,1 :PRINT " 4 "; : COLOR 1,0 : PRINT " Search
file"¶
  LOCATE 15,32¶
  COLOR 0,1 :PRINT " 5 "; : COLOR 1,0 : PRINT " End"¶
Select:¶
  LOCATE 18,1 : PRINT SPACE$(80)¶
  LOCATE 18,32 :  COLOR 3,0 : PRINT  "Enter number:";¶
  COLOR 1,0 :  LINE INPUT number$¶
  number$=LEFT$(number$,1)¶
  IF number$<"1" OR number$>"5" THEN Select¶
  IF number$="1" THEN CreateFile¶
  IF number$="2" THEN EnterData¶
  IF number$="3" THEN DataSearch=0 : GOTO ReadData¶
  IF number$="4" THEN DataSearch=1 : GOTO ReadData¶
  PRINT  "Program ended."¶
END¶
¶
CreateFile:¶
  CLS : LOCATE 1,1 : COLOR 1,0 : PRINT  "Create File"¶
  LOCATE 1,32 : COLOR 3,0 : PRINT "Filename:";¶
  COLOR 1,0 : PRINT "(no file)" ¶
  COLOR 3,0 : LOCATE 3,1¶
  PRINT "Enter field name and field length."¶
  COLOR 1,0¶
```

```
  FOR x=0 TO 9¶
    Fieldname$="" : Length(x)=0¶
  NEXT x¶
  LOCATE 4,1 : PRINT "Name" : LOCATE 4,26 : PRINT "Length
(<40)"¶
  FOR x=0 TO 9¶
    NoOfFields=x¶
    LOCATE x+6,1 : LINE INPUT Fieldname$(x)¶
    IF Fieldname$(x)="" THEN x=10 :
NoOfFields=NoOfFields-1¶
    Fieldname$(x)=LEFT$(Fieldname$(x),25)¶
    LOCATE x+6,26 : PRINT SPACE$(40);¶
    LOCATE x+6,26 : LINE INPUT Length$¶
    IF Length$="" OR ABS(VAL(Length$))>40 THEN
Length$="40"¶
    Length(x)=INT(ABS(VAL(Length$)))¶
    IF Length(x)=0 THEN Length(x)=40¶
  NEXT x¶
¶
Corrections:¶
  GOSUB EntryOK¶
  IF Corr=0 THEN OpenFile¶
  IF Corr=1 THEN ErrorCorrection¶
GOTO Corrections¶
¶
ErrorCorrection:¶
  FOR x=0 TO NoOfFields¶
    LOCATE x+6,1 : PRINT SPACE$(80)¶
    LOCATE x+6,25 : PRINT  Length(x)¶
    LOCATE x+6,1 : PRINT  Fieldname$(x)¶
  NEXT x¶
  FOR x=0 TO NoOfFields¶
    LOCATE x+6,1 : LINE INPUT Fieldname$¶
    IF Fieldname$<>"" THEN
Fieldname$(x)=LEFT$(Fieldname$,25)¶
    LOCATE x+6,26 : LINE INPUT Length$¶
    IF ABS(VAL(Length$))>40 THEN Length$="40"¶
    IF Length$<>"" THEN Length(x)=INT(ABS(VAL(Length$)))¶
    IF Length(x)=0 THEN Length(x)=40¶
  NEXT x¶
  GOTO Corrections¶
¶
OpenFile:¶
  LOCATE 19,1 : PRINT  SPACE$(80);¶
  LOCATE 19,1 : COLOR 3,0 : PRINT  "Enter Filename:";¶
  COLOR 1,0 : LINE INPUT Nam$¶
  RecordLength=0¶
  FOR x=0 TO NoOfFields¶
    RecordLength=RecordLength+Length(x)¶
  NEXT x¶
  IF Nam$="" OR RecordLength=0 THEN BEEP : GOTO Begin¶
  OPEN "R",#1,Nam$,RecordLength¶
```

```
      FIELD #1,Length(0) AS Dat$(0),Length(1) AS
Dat$(1),Length(2) AS Dat$(2),Length(3) AS
Dat$(3),Length(4) AS Dat$(4),Length(5) AS
Dat$(5),Length(6) AS Dat$(6),Length(7) AS
Dat$(7),Length(8) AS Dat$(8),Length(9) AS Dat$(9)¶
    FOR x=1 TO NoOfFields¶
      LSET Dat$(x)=" " ¶
    NEXT x¶
  CLOSE 1¶
  OPEN Nam$+".Flds" FOR OUTPUT AS 2¶
    PRINT #2,NoOfFields¶
    PRINT #2,RecordLength¶
    PRINT #2,0¶
    FOR x=0 TO NoOfFields¶
      WRITE #2,Fieldname$(x)¶
      PRINT #2,Length(x)¶
    NEXT x¶
  CLOSE 2¶
  Altname$=Nam$¶
GOTO Begin¶
¶
EnterData:¶
  CLS : LOCATE 1,1 : PRINT "Enter data"¶
¶
  IF Nam$="" THEN¶
    LOCATE 3,1 : COLOR 3,0 : PRINT "Enter Filename:"¶
    COLOR 1,0 : LINE INPUT Nam$¶
    IF Nam$="=" OR Nam$="*" THEN Nam$=Altname$¶
    IF Nam$="" THEN Begin¶
    Altname$=Nam$¶
  END IF¶
  GOSUB FieldFileExistYN¶
  IF FileExist=0 THEN¶
    COLOR 3,0 : PRINT ¶
    PRINT "Press any key."¶
    WHILE INKEY$="" : WEND : COLOR 1,0¶
    GOTO Begin¶
  END IF¶
  GOSUB ReadFileField¶
  RecordNumber=NoOfRecords+1¶
  ¶
  OPEN "R",#1,Nam$,RecordLength  ¶
      FIELD #1,Length(0) AS Dat$(0),Length(1) AS
Dat$(1),Length(2) AS Dat$(2),Length(3) AS
Dat$(3),Length(4) AS Dat$(4),Length(5) AS
Dat$(5),Length(6) AS Dat$(6),Length(7) AS
Dat$(7),Length(8) AS Dat$(8),Length(9) AS Dat$(9)¶
  ¶
InputLoop:¶
      CLS : LOCATE 1,1 : COLOR 1,0 : PRINT "Enter new
data"¶
      LOCATE 1,32 : COLOR 3,0 : PRINT "File:";¶
      COLOR 1,0 : PRINT  Nam$¶
  ¶
      Inpt=0¶
      LOCATE 1,65 : PRINT "Record:";RecordNumber¶
```

```
        PRINT : COLOR 3,0¶
        PRINT  "Enter new data:" : COLOR 1,0¶
     FOR x=0 TO NoOfFields¶
        LOCATE 5+x,1 : COLOR 2,0 : PRINT Fieldname$(x)": "¶
     NEXT x : COLOR 1,0¶
     FOR x=0 TO NoOfFields¶
        LOCATE 5+x,LEN(Fieldname$(x))+3¶
        LINE INPUT Entry$¶
        IF Entry$<>"" THEN Inpt=1¶
        Entry$(x)=LEFT$(Entry$,Length(x))¶
        LSET Dat$(x) = Entry$(x)¶
     NEXT x¶
   Corrections2:¶
    GOSUB EntryOK¶
    IF Corr=0 THEN WriteRecord¶
    IF Corr=1 THEN EnterCorrection¶
   GOTO Corrections2¶
¶
  EnterCorrection:¶
     CLS : LOCATE 1,1 : COLOR 1,0 : ¶
PRINT  "Add Data"¶
     LOCATE 1,32 : COLOR 3,0 : PRINT "File:";¶
     COLOR 1,0 : PRINT  Nam$¶
¶
        LOCATE 1,65 : PRINT "Record:";RecordNumber¶
        PRINT : PRINT ¶
     FOR x=0 TO NoOfFields¶
        LOCATE 5+x,1 : COLOR 2,0 : PRINT Fieldname$(x)":
";¶
        COLOR 1,0 : PRINT Entry$(x)¶
   ¶
     NEXT x¶
     FOR x=0 TO NoOfFields¶
        LOCATE 5+x,LEN(Fieldname$(x))+2¶
        LINE INPUT Entry$¶
        IF Entry$<>"" THEN¶
          Inpt=1¶
          Entry$(x)=LEFT$(Entry$,Length(x))¶
          LSET Dat$(x) = Entry$(x)¶
        END IF¶
     NEXT x¶
     GOTO Corrections2¶
        ¶
WriteRecord:¶
  IF Inpt=1 THEN¶
    PUT #1,RecordNumber¶
    IF DataFlag=1 THEN DataFlag=0 : GOTO ReadLoop¶
    RecordNumber=RecordNumber+1¶
  END IF¶
  IF DataFlag=1 THEN DataFlag=0 : GOTO ReadLoop¶
NextYN:¶
  LOCATE 19,1 : PRINT SPACE$(80) : COLOR 3,0¶
  LOCATE 19,1 : PRINT "Next Record (Y/N)";¶
  COLOR 1,0 : LINE INPUT a$¶
  IF UCASE$(a$)="Y" OR a$="" THEN InputLoop¶
  IF UCASE$(a$)="N" THEN CloseFile¶
```

```
GOTO NextYN¶
¶
CloseFile:¶
  CLOSE 1¶
  OPEN Nam$+".Flds" FOR OUTPUT AS 2¶
    PRINT #2,NoOfFields¶
    PRINT #2,RecordLength¶
    PRINT #2,RecordNumber-1¶
    FOR x=0 TO NoOfFields¶
      WRITE #2,Fieldname$(x)¶
      PRINT #2,Length(x)¶
    NEXT x¶
  CLOSE 2¶
  Nam$=""¶
GOTO Begin¶
¶
ReadData:¶
    CLS : LOCATE 1,1 : PRINT "Read Data"¶
    IF DataSearch=1 THEN LOCATE 1,1 : PRINT "Search
Data"¶
    LOCATE 3,1 : COLOR 3,0 : PRINT "Enter filename:"¶
    COLOR 1,0 : LINE INPUT Nam$¶
    IF Nam$="=" OR Nam$="*" THEN Nam$=Altname$¶
    IF Nam$="" THEN Begin¶
    Altname$=Nam$¶
¶
    GOSUB FieldFileExistYN¶
    IF FileExist=0 THEN¶
      PRINT : COLOR 3,0¶
      PRINT "Press any key."¶
      COLOR 1,0¶
      WHILE INKEY$="" : WEND¶
      GOTO Begin¶
    END IF¶
    GOSUB ReadFileField¶
    IF NoOfRecords=0 THEN¶
      PRINT : BEEP¶
      COLOR 1,0¶
      PRINT "No records in file!"¶
      PRINT : COLOR 3,0¶
      PRINT "Press any key."¶
      COLOR 1,0¶
      WHILE INKEY$="" : WEND¶
      GOTO Begin¶
    END IF¶
  IF DataSearch=1 THEN GOSUB SearchData¶
  OPEN "R",#1,Nam$,RecordLength   ¶
      FIELD #1,Length(0) AS Dat$(0),Length(1) AS
Dat$(1),Length(2) AS Dat$(2),Length(3) AS
Dat$(3),Length(4) AS Dat$(4),Length(5) AS
Dat$(5),Length(6) AS Dat$(6),Length(7) AS
Dat$(7),Length(8) AS Dat$(8),Length(9) AS Dat$(9)¶
      RecordNumber=1¶
ReadLoop:¶
    CLS : LOCATE 1,1 : COLOR 1,0 : PRINT  "Read Data"¶
    LOCATE 1,32 : COLOR 3,0 : PRINT "File:";¶
```

```
    COLOR 1,0 : PRINT Nam$¶
    COLOR 3,0¶
    LOCATE 17,1 : PRINT  "[Cursor UP]   = Previous
Record"¶
    LOCATE 17,37 : PRINT "[F1]      = First Record"¶
    PRINT "[Cursor Down] = Next Record"¶
    LOCATE 18,37 : PRINT "[F2]      = Last Record"¶
    PRINT "[CTRL]-[P]    = Print Record"¶
    LOCATE 19,37 : PRINT "[HELP]    = Alter Record"¶
    PRINT "[F10]        = Main Menu";¶
  ReadRecord:¶
    COLOR 1,0¶
    IF RecordNumber>NoOfRecords THEN BEEP :
RecordNumber=NoOfRecords¶
    IF RecordNumber<1 THEN BEEP : RecordNumber=1¶
    LOCATE 1,65 : PRINT "Record:";RecordNumber¶
    GET #1,RecordNumber¶
    IF DataSearch=1 THEN LOCATE 1,1 : PRINT "Search Data"
: GOSUB ExamSearchData¶
    IF DataSearch=1 AND Found=0 THEN¶
       IF RecordNumber=NoOfRecords THEN Direction=-1¶
       IF RecordNumber=NoOfRecords AND FindRecord=0 THEN¶
          CLS¶
          LOCATE 5,10 : PRINT "No record found!"¶
          LOCATE 7,10 : COLOR 3,0¶
          PRINT  "Press any key."¶
          COLOR 1,0 : BEEP¶
          WHILE INKEY$="" : WEND : CLOSE 1 : GOTO Begin¶
       END IF¶
       IF RecordNumber=1 THEN Direction=1¶
       RecordNumber=RecordNumber+Direction¶
     GOTO ReadRecord¶
    END IF¶
    FindRecord=1¶
    FOR x=0 TO NoOfFields¶
       LOCATE 5+x,1 : COLOR 2,0 : PRINT Fieldname$(x)":
"¶
    NEXT x : COLOR 1,0¶
    FOR x=0 TO NoOfFields¶
       LOCATE 5+x,LEN(Fieldname$(x))+3¶
       PRINT  Dat$(x)¶
       Entry$(x)=Dat$(x)¶
    NEXT x¶
    Key$=""¶
    WHILE Key$="" : Key$=INKEY$ : WEND¶
    IF Key$=CHR$(28) THEN RecordNumber=RecordNumber-1 :
Direction=-1¶
    IF Key$=CHR$(29) THEN RecordNumber=RecordNumber+1 :
Direction=1¶
    IF Key$=CHR$(129) THEN RecordNumber=1¶
    IF Key$=CHR$(130) THEN RecordNumber=NoOfRecords¶
    IF Key$=CHR$(138) THEN EndLoad¶
    IF Key$=CHR$(16) THEN¶
       FOR x=0 TO NoOfFields¶
          LPRINT Fieldname$(x)":":Dat$(x)¶
       NEXT x¶
```

```
        LPRINT¶
      END IF¶
      IF Key$=CHR$(139) THEN DataFlag=1 : GOTO
EnterCorrection¶
GOTO ReadLoop¶
¶
EndLoad:¶
      CLOSE 1¶
      Nam$=""¶
GOTO Begin¶
¶
REM ************* Subprogram *******************¶
¶
SearchData:¶
  CLS : LOCATE 1,1 : COLOR 1,0 : PRINT "Search Data"¶
  LOCATE 1,32 : COLOR 3,0 : PRINT "File:";¶
  COLOR 1,0 : PRINT Nam$¶
  FOR x=0 TO NoOfFields¶
    LOCATE 5+x,1 : PRINT Fieldname$(x)":"¶
  NEXT x¶
  COLOR 3,0 : LOCATE 4,1  ¶
  PRINT  "Enter search string."¶
  COLOR 1,0¶
    FOR x=0 TO NoOfFields¶
      LOCATE 5+x,LEN(Fieldname$(x))+2¶
      LINE INPUT Entry$¶
      IF Entry$<>"" THEN¶
        Search$=LEFT$(Entry$,Length(x))¶
        SearchNo=x : x=10¶
      ELSE¶
        Search$=""¶
      END IF¶
    NEXT x¶
  Corrections3:¶
     GOSUB EntryOK¶
    IF Corr=0 THEN EndSearch¶
    IF Corr=1 THEN SearchCorr¶
  GOTO Corrections3¶
¶
  SearchCorr:¶
    LOCATE 5+SearchNo,1 : PRINT
Fieldname$(SearchNo)":"Search$¶
    LOCATE 5+SearchNo,LEN(Fieldname$(SearchNo))+2¶
    LINE INPUT Entry$¶
    IF Entry$<>"" THEN
Search$=LEFT$(Entry$,Length(SearchNo))¶
  GOTO Corrections3¶
   ¶
EndSearch:¶
  IF Search$="" THEN SearchNo=0 : DataSearch=0¶
  FindRecord=0¶
RETURN¶
¶
ExamSearchData:¶
    x=0¶
SearchLoop:¶
```

```
    x=x+1¶
    IF x>LEN(Dat$(SearchNo))-LEN(Search$) THEN Found=0 :
RETURN¶
    IF MID$(Dat$(SearchNo),x,LEN(Search$))=Search$ THEN
Found=1 : RETURN  ¶
GOTO SearchLoop  ¶
¶
EntryOK:¶
  LOCATE 19,1 : COLOR 3,0¶
  PRINT "Entry Okay? (Y/N)";¶
  COLOR 1,0 : INPUT "",a$¶
  IF UCASE$(a$)="Y" OR a$="" THEN Corr=0 : RETURN¶
  IF UCASE$(a$)="N" THEN Corr=1 : RETURN¶
GOTO EntryOK¶
¶
FieldFileExistYN:¶
  OPEN Nam$+".Flds" FOR APPEND AS 1¶
    IF LOF(1)<=0 THEN FileExist=0 ELSE FileExist=1¶
  CLOSE 1¶
  IF FileExist=0 THEN¶
    LOCATE 3,1 : PRINT  SPACE$(80) : BEEP¶
    LOCATE 3,1 : COLOR 1,0 : PRINT "File ";Nam$¶
    PRINT "not found!"¶
    KILL Nam$+".Flds"¶
    Nam$="" : COLOR 3,0¶
  END IF¶
RETURN¶
¶
ReadFileField:¶
  FOR x=1 TO 10¶
    Fieldname$(x)="" : Length(x)=0¶
  NEXT x¶
  OPEN Nam$+".Flds" FOR INPUT AS 2¶
    INPUT #2,NoOfFields¶
    INPUT #2,RecordLength¶
    INPUT #2,NoOfRecords¶
    FOR x=0 TO NoOfFields¶
      INPUT #2,Fieldname$(x)¶
      INPUT #2,Length(x)¶
    NEXT x¶
  CLOSE 2¶
RETURN¶
```

C.6

Speech utility

```
BuildScreen:¶
  CLS¶
  PALETTE 0,.1,.1,.4¶
  LOCATE 2,2 : PRINT "Text:"¶
  LINE (60,7)-(612,18),1,b¶
  LOCATE 22,6¶
  PRINT "Freq.    Speed    Tuning    Volume"¶
  LINE (40,30)-(65,160),1,b¶
  LINE (120,30)-(145,160),1,b¶
  LINE (205,30)-(230,160),1,b¶
  LINE (285,30)-(310,160),1,b¶
  LOCATE 6,56 : PRINT "Male        Female"¶
  LINE (420,30)-(495,48),1,b¶
  LINE (510,30)-(585,48),1,b¶
  LOCATE 9,56 : PRINT "Human      Comp."¶
  LINE (420,57)-(495,75),1,b¶
  LINE (510,57)-(585,75),1,b¶
  LOCATE 12,61 : PRINT "Speak"¶
  LINE (450,84)-(555,102),1,b¶
  LOCATE 17,61 : PRINT "Store"¶
  LINE (450,120)-(555,138),1,b¶
¶
StartingValue:¶
  FOR x=0 TO 8¶
    READ Speech%(x)¶
  NEXT x¶
  DATA 110,0,150,0,22200,64,10,0,0¶
  GOSUB ShowValue¶
¶
MainLoop:¶
  ON MOUSE GOSUB ReadMouse¶
  MOUSE ON¶
  WHILE 1 : WEND¶
¶
ReadMouse:¶
  Test=MOUSE(0)¶
  x=MOUSE(3) : y=MOUSE(4)¶
  IF x>39 AND x<311 AND y>29 AND y<161 THEN¶
    IF x<66 THEN¶
      Frequency:¶
      Speech%(0)=(255-(y-30)*(255/130))+65¶
      FreqValue=((320-Speech%(0))/255)*130¶
      LINE (41,31)-(64,31+FreqValue),0,bf¶
      LINE (41,32+FreqValue)-(64,159),3,bf¶
      y=MOUSE(6)¶
      IF y<31 THEN y=31¶
      IF y>159 THEN y=159¶
      IF MOUSE(0)<=-1 THEN Frequency¶
    END IF¶
```

```
IF x>119 AND x<146 THEN¶
  Speed:¶
  Speech%(2)=(360-(y-30)*(360/130))+40¶
  SpeedValue=((400-Speech%(2))/360)*130¶
  LINE (121,31)-(144,31+SpeedValue),0,bf¶
  LINE (121,32+SpeedValue)-(144,159),3,bf¶
  y=MOUSE(6)¶
  IF y<31 THEN y=31¶
  IF y>159 THEN y=159¶
  IF MOUSE(0)<=-1 THEN Speed¶
END IF¶
IF x>204 AND x<231 THEN¶
  Tuning:¶
  Speech%(4)=(23000-(y-30)*(23000/130))+5000¶
  TuningValue=((28000-Speech%(4))/23000)*130¶
  LINE (206,31)-(229,31+TuningValue),0,bf¶
  LINE (206,32+TuningValue)-(229,159),3,bf¶
  y=MOUSE(6)¶
  IF y<31 THEN y=31¶
  IF y>159 THEN y=159¶
  IF MOUSE(0)<=-1 THEN Tuning¶
END IF¶
IF x>284 AND x<311 THEN¶
  Volume:¶
  Speech%(5)=(64-(y-30)*(64/130))¶
  VolumeValue=((64-Speech%(5))/64)*130¶
  LINE (286,31)-(309,31+VolumeValue),0,bf¶
  LINE (286,32+VolumeValue)-(309,159),3,bf¶
  y=MOUSE(6)¶
  IF y<31 THEN y=31¶
  IF y>159 THEN y=159¶
  IF MOUSE(0)<=-1 THEN Volume¶
  END IF¶
END IF¶
IF x>419 AND x<496 AND y>29 AND y<49 THEN¶
  Speech%(3)=0¶
  PAINT (422,32),3,1 : PAINT (512,32),0,1¶
END IF¶
IF x>509 AND x<586 AND y>29 AND y<49 THEN¶
  Speech%(3)=1¶
  PAINT (422,32),0,1 : PAINT (512,32),3,1¶
END IF¶
IF x>419 AND x<496 AND y>56 AND y<76 THEN¶
  Speech%(1)=0¶
  PAINT (422,59),3,1 : PAINT (512,59),0,1¶
END IF¶
IF x>509 AND x<586 AND y>56 AND y<76 THEN¶
  Speech%(1)=1¶
  PAINT (422,59),0,1 : PAINT (512,59),3,1¶
END IF¶
IF x>59 AND x<613 AND y>6 AND y<19 THEN¶
  LOCATE 2,9 : PRINT  SPACE$(54)¶
  LOCATE 2,9 : LINE INPUT Text$¶
END IF¶
IF x>449 AND x<556 AND y>83 AND y<103 THEN¶
  PAINT (452,85),3,1¶
```

523

```
      SAY TRANSLATE$(Text$),Speech%¶
      PAINT (452,85),0,1¶
    END IF¶
    IF x>449 AND x<556 AND y>119 AND y<139 THEN¶
      PAINT (452,121),3,1¶
      LOCATE 2,9 : PRINT  SPACE$(54)¶
      LOCATE 2,9 : COLOR 0,3 : PRINT "Filename:";¶
      COLOR 1,0 : LINE INPUT Nam$¶
      IF Nam$<>"" THEN¶
        IF Nam$="=" OR Nam$="*" AND Altname$<>"" THEN
Nam$=Altname$¶
        OPEN Nam$ FOR OUTPUT AS 1¶
          PRINT #1, "REM DATAs made with AmigaBASIC-
Talker"¶
          PRINT #1, "DATA ";¶
          FOR x=0 TO 7¶
            PRINT #1,Speech%(x)",";¶
          NEXT x¶
          PRINT #1,Speech%(8)¶
        CLOSE 1¶
        Altname$=Nam$¶
      END IF¶
      LOCATE 2,9 : PRINT SPACE$(54)¶
      LOCATE 2,9 : COLOR 1,0 : PRINT  Text$¶
      PAINT (452,121),0,1¶
    END IF¶
¶
RETURN¶
¶
ShowValue:¶
  LOCATE 2,9 : PRINT  SPACE$(54)¶
  LOCATE 2,9 : PRINT  Text$¶
  IF Speech%(3)=0 THEN¶
    PAINT (422,32),3,1 : PAINT (512,32),0,1¶
  ELSE¶
    PAINT (422,32),0,1 : PAINT (512,32),3,1¶
  END IF¶
  IF Speech%(1)=0 THEN¶
    PAINT (422,59),3,1 : PAINT (512,59),0,1¶
  ELSE¶
    PAINT (422,59),0,1 : PAINT (512,59),3,1¶
  END IF¶
¶
  FreqValue=((320-Speech%(0))/255)*130¶
  LINE (35,31+FreqValue)-(70,31+FreqValue)¶
  LINE (41,31)-(64,31+FreqValue),0,bf¶
  LINE (41,32+FreqValue)-(64,159),3,bf¶
  ¶
  SpeedValue=((400-Speech%(2))/360)*130¶
  LINE (115,31+SpeedValue)-(150,31+SpeedValue)¶
  LINE (121,31)-(144,31+SpeedValue),0,bf¶
  LINE (121,32+SpeedValue)-(144,159),3,bf¶
  ¶
  TuningValue=((28000-Speech%(4))/23000)*130¶
  LINE (200,31+TuningValue)-(235,31+TuningValue)¶
  LINE (206,31)-(229,31+TuningValue),0,bf¶
```

```
     LINE (206,32+TuningValue)-(229,159),3,bf¶
     ¶
     VolumeValue=((64-Speech%(5))/64)*130¶
     LINE (280,31+VolumeValue)-(315,31+VolumeValue)¶
     LINE (286,31)-(309,31+VolumeValue),0,bf¶
     LINE (286,32+VolumeValue)-(309,159),3,bf¶
     ¶
RETURN¶
     ¶
  ¶
```

C.7

Synthesizer utility

```
Setup:¶
  DIM Waveform%(256)¶
  DEF FNYWaveform(a)=ABS(Waveform%(a)-128)¶
  ¶
  SCREEN 1,320,200,2,1¶
  WINDOW 2,"Waveform",(0,0)-(256,63),22,1¶
¶
  FOR x=0 TO 256¶
    Waveform%(x)=127*SIN(x/20)¶
  NEXT x¶
¶
¶
  WINDOW 3,"Function",(195,80)-(310,175),22,1¶
  WINDOW OUTPUT 3¶
  LINE (5,5)-(55,30),1,b¶
  PSET (5,17)¶
  FOR x=0 TO 48¶
    LINE -((x+5),17-10*SIN(x/3.8))¶
  NEXT x¶
  LINE (59,5)-(110,30),1,b¶
  LINE (59,18)-(67,7) : LINE -(83,27)¶
  LINE -(99,7) : LINE -(107,18)¶
  LINE (5,35)-(55,60),1,b¶
  LINE (7,47)-(7,37)¶
  LINE -(18,37) : LINE -(18,57)¶
  LINE -(30,57) : LINE -(30,37)¶
  LINE -(41,37) : LINE -(41,57)¶
  LINE -(53,57) : LINE -(53,47)¶
  LINE (59,35)-(110,60),1,b¶
  LOCATE 6,9 : PRINT  "Clear"¶
  LINE (5,65)-(55,90),1,b¶
  LOCATE 10,3 : PRINT "Save"¶
  LINE (59,65)-(110,90),1,b¶
  LOCATE 10,10 : PRINT "Load"¶
  ¶
  WINDOW OUTPUT 2¶
  GOSUB ShowWave¶
¶
¶
  ON MOUSE GOSUB MouseControl¶
  MOUSE ON¶
 ¶
  WINDOW 3¶
¶
KeyInput:¶
  a$=INKEY$¶
```

```
        F=0¶
        IF a$="" THEN F=0 : GOTO KeyInput¶
        IF a$=CHR$(9) THEN F=261.63¶
        IF a$="1" THEN F=277.18¶
        IF a$="q" THEN F=293.66¶
        IF a$="2" THEN F=311.13¶
        IF a$="w" THEN F=329.63¶
        IF a$="e" THEN F=349.23¶
        IF a$="4" THEN F=369.99¶
        IF a$="r" THEN F=392!¶
        IF a$="5" THEN F=415.3¶
        IF a$="t" THEN F=440!¶
        IF a$="6" THEN F=466.16¶
        IF a$="y" THEN F=493.88¶
        IF a$="u" THEN F=523.25¶
        IF a$="8" THEN F=554.37¶
        IF a$="i" THEN F=587.58¶
        IF a$="9" THEN F=622.25¶
        IF a$="o" THEN F=659.28¶
        IF a$="p" THEN F=698.48¶
        IF a$="-" THEN F=739.99¶
        IF a$="[" THEN F=784!¶
        IF a$="=" THEN F=830.61¶
        IF a$="]" THEN F=880¶
        IF a$=CHR$(93) THEN F=932.33¶
        IF a$=CHR$(13) THEN F=987.76¶
        IF a$=CHR$(139) THEN F=1046.52¶
        IF F=0 THEN KeyInput¶
¶
Play:¶
    Vol=127 : IF F=0 THEN l=0¶
    SOUND WAIT¶
    SOUND F,3,Vol,0¶
    SOUND F,3,Vol,1¶
    SOUND RESUME¶
GOTO KeyInput¶
¶
MouseControl:¶
    IF WINDOW(0)=2 THEN AlterWaveform¶
    IF WINDOW(0)=3 THEN AlterFunction¶
RETURN¶
¶
AlterWaveform:¶
    WINDOW 2¶
    WHILE MOUSE(0)<0¶
      x=MOUSE(5)¶
    IF x>256 THEN GOSUB ShowWave : RETURN¶
    IF x<1 THEN x=1¶
    y=MOUSE(6)¶
    IF y> 63 THEN GOSUB ShowWave :RETURN¶
    LINE (x-1,FNYWaveform(x-1)/4) - (x,FNYWaveform(x)/4),0¶
    LINE (x-1,FNYWaveform(x-1)/4)-(x,y),1¶
    Waveform%(x)=127-(y*4)¶
WEND¶
    GOSUB ShowWave¶
RETURN¶
```

```
¶
AlterFunction:¶
  Test=MOUSE(0)¶
  x=MOUSE(3)¶
  y=MOUSE(4)¶
  IF x>4 AND x<56 AND y>4 AND y<31 THEN¶
     WINDOW 3 : PAINT (7,6),3,1¶
     FOR x=0 TO 256¶
        Waveform%(x)=127*SIN(x/20)¶
     NEXT x¶
     GOSUB ShowWave¶
     WINDOW 3 : PAINT (6,6),0,1¶
  END IF¶
  IF x>58 AND x<111 AND y>4 AND y<31 THEN¶
     WINDOW 3 : PAINT (60,6),3,1¶
     FOR x=0 TO 256¶
        IF x<41 THEN Waveform%(x)=x*3 : a=x*3¶
        IF (x>=41 AND x<126) OR (x>=210) THEN a=a-2.57 :
Waveform%(x)=a¶
        IF x>=126 AND x<210 THEN a=a+2.57 : Waveform%(x)=a¶
     NEXT x¶
     GOSUB ShowWave¶
     WINDOW 3 : PAINT (60,6),0,1¶
  END IF¶
  IF x>4 AND x<61 AND y>34 AND y<61 THEN¶
     WINDOW 3 : PAINT (6,36),3,1¶
     FOR x=0 TO 256¶
        IF x<64 OR (x>=128 AND x<191) THEN
Waveform%(x)=127¶
        IF (x>=64 AND x<128) OR x>192 THEN Waveform%(x)=-
128¶
     NEXT x¶
     GOSUB ShowWave¶
     WINDOW 3 : PAINT (6,36),0,1  ¶
  END IF¶
  IF x>58 AND x<111 AND y>34 AND y<61 THEN¶
     WINDOW 3¶
     PAINT (60,36),3,1¶
     FOR x=0 TO 256¶
        Waveform%(x)=0¶
     NEXT x¶
     GOSUB ShowWave¶
     WINDOW 3 : PAINT (60,36),0,1¶
  END IF¶
  IF x>4 AND x<61 AND y>64 AND y<91 THEN¶
     WINDOW 3¶
     PAINT (6,66),3,1¶
     GOSUB EnterName¶
        IF Nam$="" THEN PAINT (6,66),0,1 : RETURN¶
        OPEN Nam$ FOR OUTPUT AS 1¶
          FOR x=0 TO 256¶
            PRINT #1,CHR$(127-Waveform%(x));¶
          NEXT x¶
        CLOSE 1¶
        WINDOW 3 : PAINT (6,66),0,1¶
  END IF¶
```

```
    IF x>58 AND x<111 AND y>64 AND y<91 THEN¶
      WINDOW 3¶
      PAINT (62,66),3,1¶
      GOSUB EnterName¶
      IF Nam$="" THEN PAINT (62,66),0,1 : RETURN¶
      OPEN Nam$ FOR INPUT AS 1¶
        FOR x=0 TO 256¶
          Waveform%(x)=127-ASC(INPUT$(1,1))¶
        NEXT x¶
      CLOSE 1¶
      WINDOW 3 : PAINT (62,66),0,1¶
      GOSUB ShowWave¶
    END IF¶
  RETURN¶
  ¶
  ShowWave:¶
    WINDOW 2 : CLS¶
      FOR x=1 TO 256¶
        LINE (x-1,FNYWaveform(x-1)/4)-
  (x,FNYWaveform(x)/4),1¶
      NEXT x¶
    WINDOW 3¶
    WAVE 0,Waveform%¶
    WAVE 1,Waveform%¶
  RETURN¶
  ¶
  EnterName:¶
    WINDOW 4,"Enter Filename:",(5,100)-(300,110),0,1¶
    CLS : LINE INPUT Nam$ ¶
    IF Nam$="=" OR Nam$="*" THEN Nam$=Altname$¶
    IF Nam$<>"" THEN Altname$=Nam$¶
    WINDOW CLOSE 4 : WINDOW 3¶
  RETURN¶
  ¶
```

D

Appendix D: Programs from the BASICDemos drawer

Commodore includes several demonstration programs along with AmigaBASIC on the Extras diskette. You'll find these programs in the BASICDemos drawer of the Extras diskette. The Amiga Workbench is an ever expanding and improving system. Programs are changed and added to the Workbench to upgrade and improve the Amiga operating system. Therefore the programs listed in this book may not appear in the drawers or diskettes listed. If a program does not appear in the drawer mentioned, try looking in other drawers on the Workbench and Extras diskettes for the program.

LIST-ME

LIST-ME tells you what the programs do and how they work. Just take a hint from its name and list it. The program is made up of REM lines (all of the lines begin with an apostrophe (')). You can read the text in the LIST window. The program is set up for 80 characters per line, so you can read the complete text in the LIST window. If you want, you can print this program on a printer, so that you'll have it available in hardcopy. We think that this Appendix should be enough information, though.

Music

AmigaBASIC makes music in this program. It's not bad. The people who wrote the program put a lot of effort into it. They converted a three-voice composition into DATA statements, and included line graphics to represent the whole thing.

The program section PlaySong: reads the DATA values and calculates frequencies. The DATA statements contain the notes written as letters (c, d, e, f, g, etc.) as well as information about the note lengths, octave changes, and rests.

They used a trick for computing the waveform. Instead of calculating the values of the desired sine wave directly, they put the calculated values in DATA statements, since reading is faster than calculating. A poor math student and AmigaBASIC have a lot in common. The formula for the values is in front of the DATA lines in the listing.

Event trapping is used to draw the graphics. Every two seconds ON TIMER calls the TimeSlice: subroutine. The graphic's size is automatically adjusted to the current window size.

Library

Here you can find out how to use LIBRARY functions to produce different type styles, for instance. The libraries graphics.map and dos.map are used for this. To find out the exact procedures, read about the functions DECLARE FUNCTION...LIBRARY and LIBRARY in Appendix B.

The subprogram DosLibDemo shows how to call AmigaDOS functions from AmigaBASIC. To use this section, you need to start AmigaBASIC from CLI, and not from the Workbench.

BitPlanes
ScreenPrint

There is a great deal possible in library programming that is normally impossible in AmigaBASIC. Both these programs are good examples of this. The Bitplanes listing should look familiar to you from reading Section 4.3. It is possible to read the starting addresses of screens and windows, or the current color layout.

ScreenPrint is a hardcopy routine that was extremely difficult to realize under AmigaBASIC library control. This program is designed specifically for whoever intends to do any intensive study into library programming. The BitPlanes program can be ended by a mouseclick; ScreenPrint stops as soon as you press the <Q> key.

Screen

Color rectangles are drawn with AREA on a 320*200 point screen using 32 colors (5 bitplanes). The program uses SIN and COS formulas to calculate the positions of the corners. The PATTERN command is used to include some simple fill patterns. If you enlarge or reduce the window size, the rectangle's size will change. Colors are chosen at random.

Demo

This program uses four windows and shows a little bit of multitasking in BASIC. The first window has two balls jumping around. The second window has lines that move around, similar to those that appear in the Music program. The third window contains the rectangles that were in Screen. The fourth window contains some brightly colored circles. You can enlarge the first window. As soon as the balls notice that the window is bigger, they use the new space. You can close the other three windows by clicking their close gadgets; the other programs will move quite a bit faster then. The window with the balls (the Animation window) turns out to be a reduced BASIC window. The subprograms NextLine, NextPoly, and NextCircle are called right after each other in a WHILE...WEND loop. They take care of the action in windows 2 to 4, while the object animation in window 1 is controlled by event trapping. The collision of balls with each other or the border is taken care of here. The Demo program reads how the balls should look from the file called ball.

Picture
Picture2

These are two copies of the same program. The *AmigaBASIC* manual from Commodore uses this program to help you get to know how AmigaBASIC works. Commodore uses mouse control and the screen GET and screen PUT commands. You can use the mouse to put a CIRCLE graphic on the screen. Since a chapter in the manual says to modify the program, there are two versions on the diskette.

ObjEdit

You know this one already—it's the object editor that you use to make graphic objects for animation. Section 1.11 describes how to use the program.

One piece of advice: if you've got 512K RAM and it doesn't bother you to have objects flicker, you can change the number of allowed colors in the listing of the object editor. At the beginning, the construction of an object file can be found after apostrophes. Then there's a DEF FN and a DIM command. In the following program section, you'll find commands at the end of lines that won't be executed because they are preceded by apostrophes ('). If you remove the apostrophes, you can assign the number of bitplanes to the variable Depth. You can choose 3 or 4 since the program only works on a 640*200-pixel screen. However, 16 colors is quite a bit. Remember that object files don't save colors. You need to have the program that reads them in set the colors.

Remember that each bitplane added increases the amount of flickering that shows up in bob animation in the current version of AmigaBASIC. To understand the ObjEdit program well, you need some experience with AmigaBASIC. If you have the time and the desire, you ought to examine the way the object editor is put together. The program uses event trapping just like our paint program.

Terminal

This program shows how to use a serial interface. If you're connected to something with a 9600 baud transfer rate, you can send and receive characters. For more information on OPENing a serial channel, see OPEN "COM1 :" in Appendix B.

ConvertFd

This is a utility program for people who work a lot with LIBRARY routines. LIBRARY files must be stored in a special format on diskette (.BMAP format) if AmigaBASIC is to use them. The BASICDemos drawer contains four libraries of this sort—exec.map, diskfont.map, dos.map and graphics.map; these programs are used by the Library program, lib2, and others. If you have other libraries that end with .FD, you can use ConvertFd to produce a .BMAP file. You'll find .FD files in the FD1.2 drawer of the Extras diskette. You should not use this program until you have some experience with libraries.

Speech

This program works a lot like our speech utility. First AmigaBASIC requests the Workbench. If you only have one disk drive, put the Workbench diskette in it. Then you can enter a line of text. It will be spoken after you hit the <RETURN> key.

There are six parameters that affect the voice. Pitch is the deepness of the voice, the frequency. Inflection has two settings and is in charge of inflection (the speech can have human inflection, or be in monotone). Rate affects the speed and Voice provides the gender of the voice (male or female). Tune regulates the sampling frequency which affects the voice pitch. Volume affects how loud the speech will be. The program is only intended for testing; it does not allow you to store values.

LoadACBM
LoadILBM-SaveACBM
SaveILBM

Commodore put these utilities into the Extras 1.2 diskette to compensate for the lack of IFF load and save commands in AmigaBASIC. These three programs mainly play the roles of libraries; they are unable to function on their own. First, let's discuss the meaning of ACBM. We have already discussed the ILBM, or interleaved bitmap, in Section 4.2 (Interchange File Format). This is the way that IFF pictures are saved—the graphic is saved line by line, with all the bitplanes of the first line saved, then the second line's bitplanes, and so on. This system has two advantages: First, You'll see the correct colors from the moment the picture is being loaded; second, the memory form is easily handled when switching different degrees of resolution. For this reason, all the IFF compatible programs known to us save in ILBM form.

There is a disadvantage to ILBM, however: Some computations must occur during loading which slow down the entire procedure, particularly in BASIC. You'll remember how slow our own IFF routines were.

With that, Commodore invented a new chunk type for its utilities which handle bitmap information: The ACBMs, or Amiga Contiguous BitMaps. This format saves individual bitplanes one after the other, and loads them into Amiga memory in the same way. The files are read very quickly, and no calculation time is involved. The speed factor is not without a price: ACBMs can only be saved from or loaded into memory in the degree of resolution in which they were created originally. See for yourself whether the advantages over ILBM outweigh the disadvantages of ACBM format.

There is yet another problem: What helps the speed factor when you don't want to read a "normal" IFF graphic? GraphiCraft and DPaint only save ILBMs. On to the three Commodore-generated programs:

LoadILBM-SaveACBM reads normal ILBMs, computes parameters, and saves the files as ACBMs. These ACBMs can then be read with the program LoadACBM. SaveILBM completes the trio; this program creates a movable line graphic, and saves it as an ILBM. An important advantage to these three routines: They are capable of handling color palette animation. The necessary data are found in a chunk within the IFF file in a section called CCRT.

NOTE:
If you want to merge these three routines in your own BASIC programs, you should be sure that an ILBM file comes at the end of the string. We want this to be compatible in the end.

E

A short
technical dictionary

The words printed in *italics* were used in the book without explaining them in great detail. You can find what they mean in this Appendix.

AmigaDOS

DOS is the abbreviation for Disk Operating System. This is the program that takes care of data transfer between the Amiga and its disk drives. It is also responsible for the organization of the data on the diskette. You can give AmigaDOS commands directly through CLI, the Command Line Interpreter contained in the Workbench.

ASCII

This is the abbreviation for American Standard Code for Information Interchange. This is a standard code which assigns a particular byte value to each character. You can find an ASCII table in Appendix B.5 (Calculations and BASIC functions) under the description of the CHR$ command.

BASIC

This is the abbreviation for Beginners All-purpose Symbolic Instruction Code. This is not a completely accurate description of BASIC; BASIC is neither a pure beginner language nor a particulary powerful symbol manipulator. However, BASIC was developed when most people were using complicated languages like assembly language, COBOL, and FORTRAN, which explains how it got this name.

Binary system

This is the number system also known as base two. Numbers have another digit for each power of two. 0 and 1 are used as the digits. The decimal numbers 1 to 11 look like this in binary:

decimal	binary	decimal	binary
0	0000	6	0110
1	0001	7	0111
2	0010	8	1000
3	0011	9	1001
4	0100	10	1010
5	0101	11	1011

Bit

This is an abbreviation for binary digit. A bit is the smallest unit of information. It can be either "on" or "off", "set" or "cleared", "true" or "false", 0 or 1. Eight bits taken together form one byte.

Bitplane

Each point on the screen corresponds to one bit when graphics are stored. To make it possible to use several colors, there are several more bits per screen point (pixel). Graphics are made up of several of these bitplanes. The bits which lie under each other determine the color of a screen point. See Figure 5 in Section 2.2 (Resolution) for an illustration of bitplanes.

Byte

Every memory location in the Amiga stores exactly one byte. A byte is 8 bits. This division comes from the time of 8-bit microprocessors. A byte can store a value between 0 (binary 00000000) and 255 (binary 11111111). Usually a byte is used to store a character or a letter.

Since each kilobyte (K) contains 2^{10} bytes, 1K contains not 1000 but 1024 bytes. 256K contains 262144 bytes; 512K contains 524288 bytes. You get a few more bytes than you thought.

Compatibility

If two devices are software compatible, they can use the same software. The Amiga 1000 can be made partially IBM-PC compatible through software or hardware (Sidecar™); the Amiga 2000 has ports into which an IBM-PC emulator can be connected. If two programs are data compatible, they can use the same data. This is frequently the case on the Amiga because of IFF.

Cursor

This is the marker that shows you where on the screen you are writing or working. There are several sorts of cursors on the Amiga. There is the pointer, the small arrow that moves when you move the mouse. There is the BASIC cursor that you see in the **LIST** and **BASIC** windows. Keyboard input is written at the cursor location. Other programs use other sorts of cursors.

D/A converter

This stands for Digital/Analog converter. It converts a digital signal (a list of numeric values) into an analog electrical current. The bigger the number, the stronger the voltage. This is used, for instance, to produce music on the Amiga. The chip that makes music, called Paula, has a built-in D/A converter.

To digitize music (convert it into numerical values), you need a program that does the reverse—an A/D converter.

Decimal numbers

These are the normal base 10 numbers. They contain the digits 0, 1, 2, 3, 4, 5, 6, 7, 8, and 9. This is sort of a number that humans find most natural; however, computers don't like them as much as humans do. See Intermission 3 for more information.

Directory

This refers to the directory of a diskette. It tells what files are available on that particular diskette.

Editor

An editor is a part of a program or operating system that is in charge of cursor control. It takes care of input, insertion, deletion, and correction of text on the screen. Look at the descriptions of *Screen editor* and *Line editor* as well. Simply stated, it allows you to make changes, whether it is a text editor, icon editor or object editor.

Hardcopy

The screen's contents are printed onto a sheet of paper. AmigaBASIC has difficulty making hardcopies; you need a utility program.

Hardware

Hardware consists of the devices and components of a computer (i.e., monitor, printer, keyboard). Hardware is the stuff you can touch (see *Software*).

Hexadecimal system

This is a very popular number system for computers. The hexadecimal system is also called base 16. It has the digits 0, 1, 2, ..., 8, 9, A, B, C, D, E, and F. To identify such numbers, we put a $ character to the left of the number. The first 36 hexadecimal numbers look like this:

Dec	Hex	Dec	Hex	Dec	Hex	Dec	Hex
0	$0	9	$9	18	$12	27	$1B
1	$1	10	$A	19	$13	28	$1C
2	$2	11	$B	20	$14	29	$1D
3	$3	12	$C	21	$15	30	$1E
4	$4	13	$D	22	$16	31	$1F
5	$5	14	$E	23	$17	32	$20
6	$6	15	$F	24	$18	33	$21
7	$7	16	$10	25	$19	34	$22
8	$8	17	$11	26	$1A	35	$23

IFF

This stands for Interchange File Format. This is a file format for Amiga data developed by Electronic Arts. Read Section 4.2 (Interchange File Format) for more information.

Interface

This is a connection that you can use to connect the Amiga to peripheral devices or data transfer connections. The Amiga has several interfaces; a parallel interface, a serial interface, an interface for extra disk drives, and various interfaces for video screens.

Interlace mode

This is in-between-line mode. By doubling the lines represented on the monitor, we can get a higher resolution. Read Section 2.2 (Resolution) for more information.

Interpreter

This is what AmigaBASIC is: The Amiga doesn't directly understand BASIC. That is expected, since the computer only thinks in terms of "current on, current off". The BASIC interpreter translates the BASIC commands into machine language commands the Amiga and its microprocessor can understand.

`Intuition`

This is a part of the Amiga operating system. `Intuition` is responsible for working with windows and taking care of similar tasks. Many `Intuition` routines can be used as subroutines in other programs.

Joystick

It is a device that registers direction (mostly used in games). You can hook two of these input devices to your Amiga.

Kernel

The kernel is part of the operating system on which all the other parts are based. It takes care of input, output and similar tasks. It is loaded from the Kickstart diskette (Amiga 1000) or the Kickstart ROM (Amiga 500 and Amiga 2000) and cannot be modified when it is in memory.

Line editor

This is an editor that only allows you to work on a single line at a time. You can't work on the whole screen like you can with a *screen editor*. The cursor can be moved left and right but not up and down. AmigaBASIC only has a line editor in the **BASIC** window.

Machine language

This is the language that the 68000 processor of the Amiga understands directly. It consists of just zeros and ones, but it can be made somewhat more understandable for people. Those who program in machine language use mnemonics like MOVEA, MOVEC, CMPI, and SBCD. Now you can see why machine language programmers think BASIC commands are so much easier.

Microprocessor

This is the brain of the computer; a chip that controls the most important functions of computing. A microprocessor can execute machine language commands very quickly. The Amiga has a 68000 microprocessor, which can execute almost 8 million of these commands per second. So that it can concentrate on the really important things, many routine tasks such as data exchange, putting things on the screen, and the like are handled by its co-processors Agnus, Denise, and Paula.

Multitasking

Multitasking means running several programs at the same time in a way that keeps each one independent from all the rest. While the user works with one program, others continue executing in the background. In this way, you can save time and output data from several sources at one time. Since the processor must divide its time amoung several tasks, each program will run slower than it would otherwise.

Near letter quality

Dot-matrix printers often produce output that is hard to read and looks bad. By using some tricks, they can be made to produce text that looks about as good as text printed on a typewriter or a daisywheel printer.

Operating system

The operating system is the program that always runs in the computer. It handles basic functions like keyboard input, screen displays, working with the interfaces, and doing other tasks. The Amiga operating system has several parts. Take a look at the descriptions of *Intuition*, *Kernel*, and *AmigaDOS*.

Peripheral devices

These are devices that can be hooked up to the Amiga. Examples are printers, plotters, second disk drives, hard drives, graphic tables, scanners, joysticks, etc. All peripherals are considered hardware.

Pixel

A pixel (picture element) is a single screen point. In the Amiga, bitplanes are used to represent a pixel with one to five bits in memory. A computer picture is built up using pixels. The more pixels that are used on the screen, the better the resolution will be, and hence the more realistic the picture. Colors are also very important here. You can find more information in Section 2.2 (Resolution).

Printer

A printer is a peripheral device used for printing data, text, and graphics on paper. You can use several types of printers with the Amiga; you set up the relationship between the two in the Preferences program on the Workbench diskette. Most printers are connected to the Amiga's parallel interface, but some use the serial interface (see Section 3.5 for more information). There are several kinds of printers: Dot-matrix (the most common); ink jet (the quietest); laser (the best and most expensive); and daisywheel (the nicest print next to laser printing) printers. The difference is the principle used to put characters on the paper. Daisywheel printers can't print graphics, since they are designed like typewriters. In near letter quality (NLQ) mode, dot-matrix printers can produce output that looks almost as good as daisywheel output.

RAM

This is an abbreviation for Random Access Memory. You can write values to this sort of memory and then read the values back later. The only problem is that its contents are erased when you turn off the computer. You need to save data that is stored in RAM on a diskette or hard disk.

ROM

This stands for Read Only Memory. In contrast to RAM, ROM isn't erased when the computer is turned off. You can't write your own data to ROM, and it's hard to get rid of what is there. This characteristic makes it good for the operatng system and similar things. The Amiga 500 and Amiga 2000 have most of the contents of the Extras diskette stored in ROM.

There is very little true ROM in the Amiga 1000. The ROMs only contain the loader program for the Kickstart diskette and the "hand holding disk" icons. The RAM section where the operating system is put can be locked up electronically so that it acts almost like ROM. However, it is still erased when the computer is turned off.

Screen

The picture that appears on the monitor is called the screen. You can find more on this in Section 2.3 (Screens).

Screen Editor or Full Screen Editor

An editor is responsible for controlling the cursor. A screen editor lets you move the cursor any place on the screen to input or correct things. The AmigaBASIC **LIST** window has a screen editor. This sort of editor is much more useful than a line editor.

Scrolling

Scrolling means that data disappears out one boundary of the screen so that you can see data that was previously hidden. In this way, you can see sections of the total picture on the screen. Think of an old biblical scroll—as you roll up the top, you unroll the bottom to read more of the scroll.

Software

This is the program and data in a computer's memory. You can't touch it, although you can touch the diskette it is written on. Hardware can only be used correctly when you have the right software.

Token

A token is a one-byte code for a BASIC command. AmigaBASIC uses tokens to save room on the diskette when programs are saved to diskette. Instead of storing the PRINT statement as the characters P, R, I, N and T, the token 172 is stored. When the program is read back in, AmigaBASIC replaces the token 172 with the PRINT statement.

Utility

This is a program that helps you perform a certain task. You can call any program that is useful a utility. This book contains a lot of useful programs, therefore, it contains a lot of utilities.

Index

Optional Diskette

For your convenience, the program listings contained in this book are available on an Amiga formatted floppy diskette. You should order the diskette if you want to use the programs, but don't want to type them in from the listings in the book.

All programs on the diskette have been fully tested. You can change the programs for your particular needs. The diskette is available for $14.95 plus $2.00 ($5.00 foreign) for postage and handling.

When ordering, please give your name and shipping address. Enclose a check, money order or credit card information. Mail your order to:

Abacus
5370 52nd Street SE
Grand Rapids, MI 49512

Or for fast service, call **616-698-0330**.
Credit Card orders only **1-800-451-4319**.

AmigaDOS: Inside & Out
Revised for 2.0
Vol.#8

AmigaDOS: Inside & Out covers the insides of AmigaDOS from the internal design up to practical applications. **AmigaDOS Inside & Out** will show you how to manage Amiga's multitasking capabilities more effectively. There is also a detailed reference section which helps you find information in a flash, both alphabetically and in command groups. Topics include: Getting the most from the AmigaDOS Shell (wildcards and command abbreviations) • Script (batch) files - what they are and how to write them.

More topics include:

- AmigaDOS - Tasks and handling
- Detailed explanations of CLI commands and their functions
- In-depth guide to ED and EDIT
- Amiga devices and how the AmigaDOS Shell uses them
- Customizing your own startup-sequence
- AmigaDOS and multitasking
- Writing your own AmigaDOS Shell commands in C
- Reference for 1.2, 1.3 and 2.0 commands

ISBN 1-55755-041-7. Suggested retail price: $19.95

Companion Diskette available: *Contains every program listed in the book- complete, error free and ready to run! Saves you hours of typing in program listings. Available only from Abacus.* **$14.95**

Amiga Disk Drives: Inside & Out
Vol.#9

Amiga Disk Drives: Inside & Out shows everything you need to know about Amiga disk drives. You'll find information about data security, disk drive speedup routines, disk copy protection, boot blocks, loading and saving programs, sequential and relative file organization and much more.

Topics include:

- Floppy disk operations from the Workbench and CLI
- DOS functions and operations
- Disk block types, boot blocks, checksums, file headers, hashmarks and protection methods
- Viruses and how to protect your boot block
- Trackdisk device: Commands and structures
- Trackdisk-task: Function and design
- MFM, GCR, track design, blockheader, datablocks, coding and decoding data, hardware registers, SYNC and interrupts

ISBN 1-55755-042-5. Suggested retail price: $29.95

Companion Diskette available: *Contains every program listed in the book- complete, error free and ready to run! Saves you hours of typing in program listings. Available only from Abacus.* **$14.95**

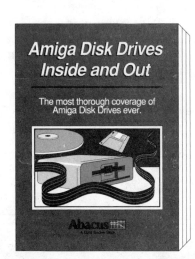

See your local dealer or order TOLL FREE 1-800-451-4319 in US & Canada

Amiga Graphics: Inside & Out   Vol.#13

Amiga Graphics: Inside & Out will show you the super graphic features and functions of the Amiga in detail. Learn the graphic features that can be accessed from AmigaBASIC or C. The advanced user will learn how to call the graphic routines from the Amiga's built-in graphic libraries. Learn graphic programming in C with examples of points, lines, rectangles, polygons, colors and more. Complete description of the Amiga graphic system- View, ViewPort, RastPort, bitmap mapping, screens, and windows.

Topics include:

- Accessing fonts and type styles in AmigaBASIC
- Loading and saving IFF graphics
- CAD on a 1024 x 1024 super bitmap, using graphic library routines
- Access libraries and chips from BASIC- 4096 colors at once, color patterns, screen and window dumps to printer
- Amiga animation explained including sprites, bobs and AnimObs, Copper and blitter programming

ISBN 1-55755-052-2. Suggested retail price: $34.95

Companion Diskette available: *Contains every program listed in the book- complete, error free and ready to run! Saves you hours of typing in program listings. Available only from Abacus.* **$14.95**

Amiga Desktop Video Guide   Vol.#14

Amiga desktop Video Guide is the most complete and useful guide to desktop video on the Amiga. **Amiga Desktop Video Guide** covers all the basics- defining video terms, selecting genlocks, digitizers, scanners, VCRs, camera and connecting them to the Amiga.

Just a few of the topics described in this excellent book:

- The basics of video
- Genlocks
- Digitizers and scanners
- Frame Grabbers/ Frame Buffers
- How to connect VCRs, VTRs, and cameras to the Amiga
- Animation
- Video Titling
- Music and videos
- Home videos
- Advanced techniques
- Using the Amiga to add or incorporate Special Effects to a video
- Paint, Ray Tracing, and 3D rendering in commercial applications

ISBN 1-55755-057-3. Suggested retail price: $19.95

Companion Diskette not available for this book.

Amiga Printers: Inside & Out   Vol.#15

Your printer is probably the most used peripheral on your Amiga system and probably the most confusing. Today's printers come equipped with many built-in features that are rarely used because of this confusion. This book shows you quickly and easily how to harness your printer's built-in functions and special features.

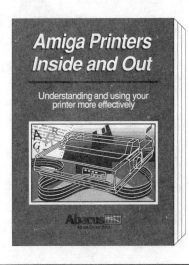

Topics include:

NEW

- How printers work, and why they do what they do
- Basic printer configuration using the DIP switches
- AmigaDOS commands for simple printer control
- Printing tricks and tips from the experts
- Recognizing and fixing errors
- WORKBENCH Printer drivers explained in detail
- Amiga fonts as printer fonts and much more!

ISBN 1-55755-087-5. Suggested retail price: $34.95

Companion Diskette Included at no additional cost: *Contains every program listed in the book- complete, error free and ready to run! Saves you hours of typing in program listings.*

Making Music on the Amiga   Vol.#16

The Amiga has an orchestrs deep within it, just waiting for you to give the downbeat. **Making Music on the Amiga** takes you through all the aspects of music development on this great computer. Whether you need the fundamentals of music notation, the elements of sound synthesis or special circuitry to interface your Amiga to external musical instruments, you'll find it in this book.

Topics include:
- Basics of sound generation
- Music programming in AmigaBASIC
- Hardware programming in GFA BASIC
- IFF formats (8SVX and SMUS)
- MIDI fundamentals: Concept, function, parameters, schematics and applications
- Digitization: Capture and edit sound, schematics, applications
- Applications: Using Perfect Sound, Aegis Sonix, Deluxe Music Construction Set, Deluxe Sound Digitizer, Audio Master and Dynamic Drums

NEW

ISBN 1-55755-094-8. Suggested retail price: $34.95

Companion Diskette Included at no additional cost: *Contains public domain sound sources in AmigaBASIC, C, GFA BASIC and assembly language.*

See your local dealer or order TOLL FREE 1-800-451-4319 in US & Canada

AmigaDOS Quick Reference

AmigaDOS Quick Reference is an easy-to-use reference tool for beginners and advanced programmers alike. You can quickly find commands for your Amiga by using the three handy indexes designed with the user in mind. All commands are in alphabetical order for easy reference. The most useful information you need fast can be found including:

- All AmigaDOS commands described with examples including Workbench 1.3
- Command syntax and arguments described with examples
- CLI shortcuts
- CTRL sequences
- ESCape sequences
- Amiga ASCII table
- Guru Meditation Codes
- Error messages with their corresponding numbers

Three indexes for instant information at your fingertips! The **AmigaDOS Quick Reference** is an indispensable tool you'll want to keep close to your Amiga.

ISBN 1-55755-049-2. Suggested retail price: $9.95
Companion Diskette not available for this book.